D0931436

Quantitative Models of Commodity Markets

Quantitative Models of Commodity Markets

Edited by Walter C. Labys

Ballinger Publishing Company ● Cambridge, Mass.
A Subsidiary of J.B. Lippincott Company

International Standard Book Number: 0-88410-254-8

Library of Congress Catalog Card Number: 74-13784

Printed in the United States of America

Library of Congress Cataloging in Publication Data

Labys, Walter C   1937–
   Quantitative models of commodity markets.

   1. Commercial products–Mathematical models. 2. Commodity exchanges.
I. Title.
HF1040.7.L34   332.6'44   74-13784
ISBN 0-88410-254-8

Contents

List of Figures

List of Tables

Foreword

This book is the first in a series of commodity studies which Ballinger plans to publish. Because of the vital importance of primary commodities in the present and future economic order, there is a need to make analytical economic research in this area more readily available for those who formulate policy and generally deal with commodity problems.

Each of the studies selected for the series will represent some form of econometric or quantitative modeling, although other analytical approaches are suitable. It is hoped that these books will contribute to the existing body of knowledge by: (1) examining theoretical problems encountered in applied research, (2) relating to the policy analysis needed to solve real-world problems, and (3) serving as a stimulus towards further research.

It is our desire that the availability of such studies will serve to improve our understanding of an extremely complex subject and will thereby facilitate the making of important policy decisions.

Walter C. Labys
Editor of the Series

Preface

This is a challenging time to present a quantitative study pertaining to the economic behavior of commodity markets. The past year has witnessed a host of commodity problems, sufficiently severe to disrupt national as well as international economic systems. Most noticeable has been the sharp fluctuations in commodity prices which can be attributed to a number of factors: Shifts in speculative activity from securities markets to commodity futures markets; use of the latter to hedge against fluctuations in exchange rates and monetary instability; closer cooperation among nations leading to the formation of producers' cartels; real and anticipated scarcities of food, fuel, and other strategic commodities; response of producers to years of declining relative prices; a shift in the technological-ecological availability of commodities; and a high rate of inflation further stimulated by the recent petroleum price increases. These problems are further magnified since fluctuations in commodity prices can lead to fluctuations in the overall macrosector. That the first General Assembly of the U.N. called to discuss economic problems was devoted to commodities is proof of this critical situation.

Thus, we find a real need to examine quantitative approaches to deciphering commodity problems. Quantitative models of commodity markets can help us to better understand the nature of these markets, to determine which policies might be optimal for solving related problems, and to forecast the future. The idea to compile a book containing commodity models arose while I was completing an earlier study: *Dynamic Commodity Models: Specification, Estimation and Simulation.* Whereas that book concentrates on the construction and application of the econometric form of market model, this study illustrates how that form has been developed to handle more complex market configurations. The basic modeling approach also has been extended to include programming and systems models as well as control theory.

Selecting the actual contents required examining many of the econometric and programming developments related to commodity modeling over the past decade. The most essential of these modeling approaches are briefly described in the first chapter which serves as an introduction: Econometric market models, industry process models, spatial equilibrium models, world trade models, industrial dynamics models, recursive programming models, and systems models. Examples of commodity models embodying the more important of these methodologies are presented in the next eleven chapters. In selecting the models for those chapters, I also considered two other criteria: the practicality of the work for further application and the critical importance of the commodity itself, i.e. petroleum, meat, marine resources, etc. The final chapter attempts to provide a perspective as to how recent advances could contribute to further modeling work.

Among those who might use this book, I would hope that *Commodity policy makers* in private, government, and international organizations might realize some of the benefits to be gained from adopting a modeling approach to policy analysis. *Commodity economists* might want to examine the analysis employed in the different studies to sharpen their perception of the market behavior of particular commodities. Since this book does survey current developments in commodity modeling, *commodity model builders* will be interested in applying some of these advances in their own work. Given the increasing number of *graduate students* and *research workers* interested in commodity modeling, this book will serve as a reference work to assist them in their efforts. Finally, *agricultural* and *resource economists, econometricians,* and *microtheorists* might find the book helpful as a "readings" text in a graduate-level course.

This book is the direct result of the cooperation of a number of economists to bring to light recent quantitative research on commodity models. Among those whom I would like to thank for their contributions are: Gerry Adams, James Griffin, Franklin Fisher, Paul Cootner, Martin Baily, Lester Myers, Joseph Havlicek Jr., Cliff Wymer, Max Langham, Han Kim, Louis Goreux, Dave Kendrick, Richard Haidacher, R.C. Kite, Jim Matthews, Frederick Bell, Richard Fullenbaum, Darrel Nash, Ernest Carlson, Frederick Waugh, Richard Kinoshita, and William Kost. Mary Lee Epps, Richard Raulerson, and Joseph Shaw were also particularly helpful in some of the comments and corrections they offered for the conclusions chapter. Also to be thanked are those economists who submitted papers, but which I regretfully could not include because of a lack of space. My thanks also to the publishers, whose permissions are acknowledged separately.

Help in preparing this manuscript was given by the secretarial staff of the Graduate Institute of International Studies. Mrs. Isabelle Dick is to be thanked in this regard. Finally, the models selected, as well as the views and opinions presented in Chapters 1, 8, and 13 are of my own doing, and for them I take full responsibility.

Walter C. Labys

Acknowledgments

Acknowledgments are due to the following journals for their kind permission to reprint the following articles: To the *Journal of the American Statistical Association* to use "An Economic-Linear Programming Model of the U.S. Petroleum Refining Industry," by F. Gerard Adams and James M. Griffin. To the *Bell Journal of Economics and Management* to use "An Econometric Model of the World Copper Industry," by F.M. Fisher and P.H. Cootner in association with M.N. Baily. And to the *American Journal of Agricultural Economics* to use "Evaluating Supply Control Policies for Frozen Concentrated Orange Juice with an Industrial Dynamics Model," by Richard C. Raulerson and Max R. Langham. In addition, the Wright-Allen Press, Inc. offered some excerpts and figures from *Dynamics of Commodity Production Cycles* by D.L. Meadows to help describe his Dynamic Commodity Cycle Model. Thanks are also due to Heath Lexington Books for permission to reproduce certain materials for "Dynamics of the International Lauric Oils Market" from W.C. Labys, *Dynamic Commodity Models: Specification, Estimation and Simulation.*

Chapter One

Introduction: A Taxonomy of Commodity Models and Their Policy Applications[1]

Why speak of a "taxonomy" of commodity models? This is necessary because the models can take a number of different analytical forms and their applications to commodity analysis differ considerably. There is also their rapid growth in numbers. Compare this situation with that of econometric and programming models of national economies: Where once these models were only reluctantly accepted by planners, they are now widely in use. Commodity model development is following the same pattern. One should refer to Adams [1] for his recent description of the increased applications of econometric and programming models to separate or multiple commodity markets, commodity industries, and commodity firms. The many models presented in the Appendix also confirm this phenomenon.

In this chapter, the basic purposes and methodologies of commodity modeling are introduced so that the different modeling developments appearing in the later chapters might be better evaluated. We start with a general definition of commodity modeling. It is then expanded by contrasting the different aspects of commodity behavior to be analyzed against the methodologies or modeling processes which can be employed. Finally, a brief description of each of the major methodologies is given.

COMMODITY MODELING DEFINED

Because commodity models are so diverse, we must begin with a fairly broad definition. A *commodity model* is a formal representation of a commodity market, industry or firm, where the behavioral relationships included reflect the underlying economic, political, and social institutions. To make this definition more meaningful, let us consider it from three points of view: Why build a commodity model? What information is needed? And what procedure do we follow?

1

Why build a commodity model? We do this to explain market behavior or market history, to analyze commodity policies, to make commodity decisions, or to forecast and predict important commodity variables.

What information is needed? Although this depends on the inherent structure of a model, knowledge of the following is usually required:

1. The actors involved in the market and their decision-making framework, e.g., the competitive versus noncompetitive nature of a market.
2. The surrounding economic political, social, and legal institutions.
3. Technical, social, and other forms of constraints which influence production processes, consumption patterns, etc.
4. Relevant principles of economic theory which can be applied to explain production, consumption, inventory holding, etc.
5. Methodologies which can be appropriately employed, including their relative advantages and disadvantages.
6. The availability and accuracy of market data.

What procedure do we follow? The above information is normally employed according to the following procedure:

1. Identification of the policy problems to be solved.
2. Adoption of a modeling approach to their solution based upon available methodologies or the design of new ones.
3. Specifications of the model incorporating the above institutions and constraints; selection of the most appropriate model based on statistical and judgmental observations.
4. Validation and refinement of the model so that it best reflects reality and best meets the requirements of the user.
5. Application of the model to the policy problems selected.

These steps are further described in Figure 1-1, using the example of a market equilibrium form of model. That the commodity models of interest can be validated is a most important part of the procedure. As compared to general systems or programming models for which validation is sometimes difficult, all of the models considered here are of a type whose effectiveness in explaining market behavior or forecasting can be determined. Otherwise, no way exists of distinguishing the quality of one model from another. An equally important feature of the procedure is that its steps are related in an iterative manner. That is, if the model does not explain well the behavior of a particular variable, or if the model does not provide the type of answers needed given the policy problems posed, then the model designer returns to an earlier stage either to improve the model specification or to suggest that other types of policy problems be examined.

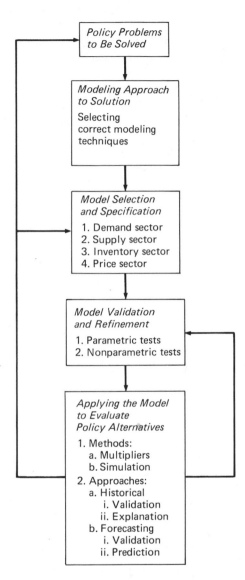

Figure 1-1. Procedure for Developing and Applying Commodity Models.

COMMODITY BEHAVIORAL ANALYSIS AND
THE MODELING PROCESS

Table 1-1 will help show how commodity models can be applied to a variety of problems or situations in its depicting of the interplay between behavioral analysis of interest and the modeling process to be adopted. Here, behaviorial analysis refers to that particular aspect of commodity behavior which we want to analyze. The modeling process is defined as answering a number of questions: What do the modeling techniques or methodologies describe? What is modeled? What aspects of commodity behavior are emphasized? And what forms of policy analysis are possible?

The different forms of commodity analysis possible have been ordered such that Table 1-1 delineates a number of steps in which a commodity decision maker or planner becomes progressively involved in a market environment of increased complexity. The behavioral analysis performed at the first or decision level would require explaining or predicting the activities of a single group of decision makers such as producers, consumers, or investors. This environment becomes only slightly more complex at the second or interaction level where the simultaneous interaction of a number of decision makers is analyzed.

Up to this point, we have considered the behavior of market participants whose activities are relatively independent of a broader set of economic influences at the national or international level. But what if we want to analyze this behavior as it relates to national and international economic activities? Here we arrive at forms of commodity analysis which have been of most interest in studies recently carried out or planned for the near future. Let us examine each of these more thoroughly.

1. Market stabilization analysis involves finding those control mechanisms or forms of market organization which lead to more stable prices or equilibrium positions.
2. Market planning analysis relates to the forecasting of long run outcomes, depending on the policy problems or market strategies of interest.
3. Agricultural process analysis explains the influence that farm level decisions, technology, aggregate demand and prices have on agricultural output.
4. Industrial process analysis describes the relationship that exists between national activities, technical transformation processes within industries, and commodity input demands.
5. Analysis of trade patterns requires the application of international trade theory at the commodity level so that impacts of tariffs, quotas, or pricing policies on commodity flows can be determined.
6. Economic growth analysis can solve problems of planning for growth where commodities represent the "engine" or primary sector of country growth.

Analyses such as the impact of investment or exchange rate changes on commodity development also fall into this category.
7. Analysis of interdependent systems implies consideration of commodity markets in relation to other important, related spheres of activity such as biological or social systems, or consideration of the future international distribution of commodity resources.

Other forms of commodity analysis could be added to this list, but the present selection covers the major work done thus far. The nonmarket environmental situation which is more complex has not yet been the subject of modeling analysis.

Let us now consider how one applies the modeling process to problems involving the market environment at national and international levels. Take, for example, the problem of analyzing commodity stabilization. Table 1-1 indicates that this problem requires use of modeling techniques that are capable of describing short run market and institutional behavior. One would thus make use of a market equilibrium model containing perhaps an inventory component to permit incorporation of buffer stock operation. To stabilize the market of interest, one might examine the impact of instigating futures activity or speculation and hedging operations, but if the welfare goals of interest call for a much lower price variance, then this approach would have to be abandoned. Policy analysis might thus be directed to learning how a buffer stock scheme could lower price variance to the desired level. Such stabilization analysis has in fact been carried out as reported in Chapter 9 by Kim, Goreux, and Kendrick using a buffer stock and by Labys in Chapter 8 also employing an export norm scheme.

COMMODITY MODELING AND THE
CHOICE OF METHODOLOGIES

The above attempt to interrelate commodity analysis and the modeling process can be extended to provide yet another perspective. In Table 1-2, the basic methodologies or model types employed in commodity model building are contrasted against the modeling process. Note that there are similarities between the forms of analysis previously selected and the methodologies to be employed. For example, econometric process models have been developed to analyze the industry process, and world trade models are intended to analyze commodity trade patterns, although at a highly aggregated level. Table 1-2 also represents a pivotal point in providing an explanation of the modeling process as related to each of the methodologies of interest. It should be referred to as we answer questions about that process: What do the methodologies describe? What is modeled? And what key variables are considered? While the following discussion contains references to specific commodity modeling studies, those listed in Table 1-2 can also be consulted.

Table 1-1.   Commodity Behavioral Analysis and the Modeling Process

Behavioral Analysis / *Modeling Process*	*What Do the Modeling Techniques Describe?*	*What Is Modeled?*
Market environment at decision level	Economic decision making	Actual decision making process
Market environment at interaction level	Simultaneous economic decision making	Interaction between decision makers within markets
1. Market stabilization	Short run economic and institutional behavior	Interaction between market behavior and stabilization goals
2. Market planning	Long run economic and institutional behavior	Interaction between market behavior and private and national goals
3. Agricultural process	Economic and agricultural behavior	Interaction between market behavior and agricultural activities
4. Industrial process	Economic and industrial behavior	Interaction between market behavior and manufacturing/ processing activities
5. Trade patterns	Economic behavior over space	Interaction between regional or national markets
6. Economic growth	Economic development and growth processes	Interaction between commodity production/ processing/ diversification and national growth
7. Interdependent systems	Economic, biological, social, and ecological behavior	Interaction between market behavior and supporting or constraining systems
Nonmarket environment	Social, political, and cultural processes	Processes such as those found in sociology, anthropology, international relations

Market Environment at National and International Levels (items 1–7)

What Aspects of Commodity Behavior Are Emphasized?	What Forms of Policy Analysis Are Possible?
Consumption, production, stock holding, investment	Impact of individual decisions on consumption, production
Market equilibrium and disequilibrium	Impact of decisions on market adjustments
Market stabilization and control, speculation and hedging	Impact of buffer stocks, production schemes, cartels on price behavior
Future consumption, production, prices	Impact of investment, technology, incomes on markets
Transformation between resource inputs and commodity outputs	Impact of technology, profits, weather, area, plantings on output
Sales, input requirements, transformation between outputs and inputs	Impact of national economic activities on industries and commodities
Imports, exports, prices, tariffs, quotas, transportation costs	Impact of tariffs, incomes, exchange rates on commodity transfers
Investment, resource allocation, changes in income and employment	Impact of commodity investment on national performance measures
Biological life cycles, pollution, energy demands, resource exhaustion	Interdependency of commodity and other systems, world interdependency
Cultural, social, geographical	Not known

Table 1-2.   Commodity Modeling and the Choice of Methodologies

Methodologies / Modeling Process	What Do the Methodologies Describe?	What Is Modeled?	What Key Variables Are Considered?	Examples of Commodity Applications*
Econometric market model	Demand and supply interacting to produce an equilibrium price	Behavior of decision makers in reaching market equilibrium	Demand, supply, imports, exports, inventories, prices	Copper (40) Tungsten (221) Cocoa (27, 28) Lauric oils (32) Rubber (179) Soybeans (192)
Econometric process model	Transformation of commodity inputs into finished products	Interaction between decision makers in industries, national economies, and markets	Demand, production, investment, inventories capacity utilization, materials inputs, prices	Petroleum (165) Steel (198)
Spatial equilibrium model	Assignment of spatial flows and equilibrium conditions	Behavior of decision makers in optimizing flows between regions	Demand, supply, imports, exports, tariffs, quotas, transportation costs, prices	Bananas (7) Sugar (204) Broilers (20) Livestock (110, 113) Palm oil (67) Groundnuts (162)
World trade model	Balances of commodity flows between regions	Behavior of decision makers in determining trade flows	Exports, imports, balance of payments, income, prices	No disaggregated models at present
Recursive programming model	Optimization of resource use including feedback	Behavior of decision makers in response to multiple feedback effects	Demand, production, purchases, investment, capital, labor, technology, prices	Coal (24) Iron and steel (201) Wheat, corn, soybeans (226)
Industrial dynamics model	Role of amplification and feedback delays on system equilibrium	Response of decision makers to actions influenced by previous responses, and so on	Consumption rate, production rate, inventory coverage, capacity utilization, prices	Aluminum (2) Copper (37) Hogs (100, 101) Orange juice (159) Broilers, cattle (22, 117)
Systems model	Imposition of decision rules on econometric or optimization models	Behavior of decision makers in reaching equilibrium or adjusting to various constraints	Varies depending on specific application	Beef (15) Rice (176) Livestock (106) Multicommodity (148) Petroleum (166) Fish (182)

*Number in parenthesis refers to citation in Appendix.

Market Models

The econometric market form of commodity model is considered first because it generally provides a basis from which the process, trade, and other methodologies follow.[2] Its particular characteristic is that it contains a set of relationships pertaining to the demand for a commodity, its supply and, in some cases, the inventories held. Each of these relationships is influenced by the level of commodity prices. When prices decline, demand normally would increase or, alternatively, the supply to the market would decrease. The effect of either of these adjustments, however, would be to force prices upward, causing the market to return to a condition of equilibrium.

Econometric market models basically consist of four equations, although in practice many more are present, e.g., see Labys [19] for a more thorough discussion of specifying and estimating models of this type.

$$D = f(D_{-1}, P, P^c, A, T)$$

$$Q = g(Q_{-1}, P_{-\theta}, N, Z)$$

$$P = h(P_{-1}, D, \Delta I)$$

$$I = I_{-1} + Q - D.$$

Definition of variables:

D = Commodity demand

Q = Commodity supply

P = Commodity prices

P^c = Prices of substitute commodities

$P_{-\theta}$ = Prices with lag distribution

I = Commodity inventories

A = Income or activity level

T = Technical factors

N = Natural factors

Z = Policy variable influencing supply.

Demand is explained as being dependent on prices, economic activity, prices of one or more substitute commodities, and possible technical influences such as the growth of synthetic substitutes. Other possible influencing factors and the customary stochastic disturbance term are omitted to simplify the example. Accordingly, supply would depend on prices as well as natural factors such as weather and yields, and a possible policy variable. A lagged price variable is included since for certain commodities there usually are long lags between changes in price and changes in supply; it takes years to put new acreage into production or to open new mines. Prices are explained by demand and inventories, although this equation is sometimes inverted to explain inventory demand. The model is closed using the market clearing identity which equates inventories with lagged inventories plus supply minus demand. Where the price equation is inverted to represent inventory demand, the identity can be recognized as the equivalent supply of inventories equation. Not closing the model would put it in a disequilibrium form, and conventional estimation techniques might have to be replaced by those advocated by Fair.[10]

The application of a market model requires that its variables be classified as endogenous variables or targets—$D, Q, I,$ and P; lagged endogenous variables—$D_{-1}, Q_{-1}, I_{-1},$ and P_{-1}; and exogenous variables—$P^c, A, T,$ and Z. Of the latter group Z is also known as an instrument or policy controllable variable. We normally refer to the above equation system in its matrix form

$$\Gamma Y + \beta_1 Y_{-1} + \beta_2 X = U$$

where $Y =$ a $G \times n$ matrix of current endogenous variables; $Y_{-1} =$ a $G \times n$ matrix of lagged endogenous variables; $X =$ a $M \times n$ matrix of exogenous and policy controllable variables; $U =$ a $G \times n$ matrix of current disturbance terms; Γ and $\beta_1 = G \times G$ matrices of coefficients on the current and lagged endogenous variables respectively; and $\beta_2 =$ a $G \times M$ matrix of coefficients on the exogenous and policy variables. Policy analysis is best discussed using the equivalent reduced form

$$Y = \pi_1 Y_{-1} + \pi_2 X + V$$

where $\pi_1 =$ a $G \times G$ matrix of reduced form coefficients on the lagged endogenous variables, and $\pi_2 =$ a $G \times M$ matrix of reduced form coefficients on the exogenous and policy variables X. The latter matrix is composed of coefficients called multipliers, which define the effects on the target variables of varying any of the instruments. By simulating the structural or reduced form of the model through suppressing or generating the stochastic terms, one can also assess these effects using policy simulation analysis. Note that the model containing lagged endogenous variables is a dynamic one and the resulting simulation would be evolutionary: the model can generate its own values for the endogenous variables with only the exogenous variables given. Validation can follow by investigating the model's stability as a set of first order difference equations or by verifying the cyclical response of the model through the use of stochastic simulation.

The market form of model has been applied to a large number of commodity studies. The markets of interest normally are assumed to be competitive, although in some cases forms of noncompetitive organization have been incorporated. Examples appearing in this book include the Fisher, Cootner, and Baily model of the copper industry, the Myers and Havlicek model of the U.S. beef, pork, and broiler markets, and the Labys model of the lauric oils market. Although the simple framework of market models is limited in its ability to capture commodity market realities, these models are a practical tool whose use is likely to increase with the growing interest in control theory and continuous time systems.

Process Models

Commodity models of the process type, although econometric models, differ from market models in several respects. Process models deal with supply and demand within an industry rather than across a market; they thus focus on the transformation of commodity inputs into finished products. Whereas market models balance supply and demand to produce an equilibrium price, prices in a process model are normally a function of production and material costs. The emphasis is also different: process models concentrate on the industrial production process, requirements for raw materials, and labor and plant capacity.

To see how a process model is formulated, one might review the model of the U.S. steel industry recently constructed by Higgins.[12] That model is designed to reflect lines of economic causality emanating from product demand and running recursively backwards towards production and demands for commodity inputs. The major relationships contained in the model pertain to domestic consumption, import demand, investment, domestic production, and commodity input demands. The industry process on which the model is based begins with the determination of product demand, the latter depending on general economic conditions. This demand can be said to induce finished product output, which requires a transformation to input requirements. These requirements are finally reflected in the demand for commodity inputs such as ore, coal, limestone, fuel, etc. Note that these demands are explained independently of prices, the latter being determined by cost considerations. Policy analysis using the model would rely on its explanation of key variables such as shipments of steel, value of finished goods' inventories, pig-iron consumption, etc.

To construct the simplest form of process model, one would begin with a structure containing three equations.[3]

$$D = f(P^p, A)$$

$$Q = g(L, C, K) = D$$

$$P^p = h\left(\frac{W \times L}{D}, \frac{P \times C}{D}\right)$$

Definition of variables:

Q = Product output

D = Demand for output

P^p = Product prices

A = Activity index

L = Labor inputs

K = Capital inputs

C = Commodity inputs

P = Commodity prices

W = Wage rates.

Whereas the demand equation is similar to that of the market model, the supply equation becomes an equation linking the output of a product to inputs of labor, raw materials or commodities, and capital stock. The identity shows that production is scheduled to equal demand requirements. The final equation explains product prices as a markup on costs of commodities and cost of labor per unit of output. Note that wage rates, product demand, and possibly other variables could be generated from a related macroeconometric model.

Policy analysis of this form of model takes place through simulating it, as for a market model. One can evaluate the effects on the target variables of varying the instruments or of varying those variables whose values are determined through alternative simulation runs of a macroeconometric model. It is also possible to introduce programming models to provide a more detailed description of the production process in transforming inputs into outputs. Appearing in Chapter 3, the Adams and Griffin model takes this approach in constructing a model of the petroleum industry.

Spatial Equilibrium Models

This form of model represents an outgrowth of econometric market models and linear programming spatial models. When formulated to represent a competitive market structure, it will normally embody the following components: (1) a system of equations describing the aggregate demand for one or more commodities of interest in each of the included markets as well as the aggregate supply of the commodities in each of the markets, (2) the distribution activities over space, and (3) the equilibrium conditions. While the demand and supply equations imply a structure similar to that of a market model, the equilibrium process is more adequately represented through the identification of the profits to be realized from the flow of commodities, i.e. the excess of a price differential between two points minus transportation costs. Profit maximization is assured through the use of linear programming which allows commodities to transfer until demand equals supply in every spatially separated market. So that policy decisions can be evaluated more realistically, the equilibrium conditions and other definitional equations are used to impose constraints on the model parameters.

Recent popularity of this method has stemmed largely from work by Takayama and Judge [30, 31], who formulated spatial equilibrium analysis as a quadratic programming problem; a "quasi-welfare function" is maximized subject to linear demand and supply functions for each of the included markets. Just how the model can be formulated can be seen using the example of a simultaneous, competitive market.[4] Demand and supply for each market or country are given first.

$$D_i = f(P_i, Z_i)$$

$$Q_i = g(P_i, Z_i).$$

The distribution activities over space or the interregional flow of commodities is obtained by decomposing demand and supply into shipments

$$D_j = \sum_i x_{ij} \qquad j = 1, 2, \ldots, n$$

$$Q_i = \sum_j x_{ij} \qquad i = 1, 2, \ldots, n$$

where x_{ij} denotes the quantities shipped from the ith region to the jth region. To this must be added the equilibrium conditions

$$r_{ij} x_{ij} = 0 \qquad \text{all } i, j$$

for which the per unit loss or gain from commodities sold is given by

$$r_{ij} = t_{ij} - (P_j - P_i) \qquad \text{all } i, j.$$

Definition of variables:

D_i = Commodity demand in region i

Q_i = Commodity supply in region i

r_{ij} = Net loss or gain in shipping a commodity from region i to region j

x_{ij} = Quantity shipped from region i to region j

t_{ij} = Transportation costs

P_i = Price in region i

Z_i = Exogenous or policy variables for region i.

Since in the same region the transportation cost is zero, r_{ii} must always be zero. To determine the $n(n - 1)$ interregional flows of commodities, only $n(n - 1)$ equations are thus needed.

This model works such that before equilibrium, commodity flows are possible as long as the price differential between any two regions exceeds the transportation costs. Here r_{ij} will be negative when P_j is greater than P_i by more than the amount of the transportation cost. When changes in an exogenous factor cause disequilibrium, the existence of a profit will result in commodity flows until equilibrium is restored, the latter situation usually a consequence of price adjustment. Competitive equilibrium would imply that both profits and shipments or flows must equal zero. A typical application would involve determining optimal levels of consumption and production of commodities in a region as well as the regional prices which would be consistent with the optimal set of flows. From a policy point of view, deficits or surpluses of commodities between regions can be detected, or effects of tariffs, quotas, or changes in exchange rates can be measured.

Examples of applications of spatial equilibrium analysis to commodity markets include the study of the U.S. broiler market by Lee and Seaver [17], the U.S. tomato market by Lee [18], and the U.S. beef market by Sohn [29]. The most recent extension of this method has been explaining international commodity flows, and the Kost EEC grain-livestock model given in Chapter 13 provides a good example. We should also mention the reactive programming version of spatial equilibrium formulated by King and Ho.[15] This algorithm has been recently applied to explaining commodity trade by Thiam [34] for palm oil, by Melo [22] for cocoa, and by Jellema [14] for groundnuts.

World Trade Models

World trade models are noted more as a means for explaining flows of commodity aggregates than flows of individual commodities. Where the latter have been of interest, spatial equilibrium models have been employed. World trade models, nonetheless, are worth considering because many commodity trade problems need to be analyzed in relation to capital flows and balance of payments, the most obvious case in point being petroleum. This type of model can also cope with problems of measuring the impact of changes in exchange rates.[5]

There are a number of different methodologies associated with world trade models, as have been described in the works of Rhomberg [25], Taplin [33], and Leamer and Stern [16]. These methodologies are normally classified as falling into one of two possible approaches using the following import-export matrix.

$$
\begin{array}{cccccc|c}
F_{11} & F_{12} & \cdots & F_{ij} & \cdots & F_{1n} & X_1 \\
F_{21} & F_{22} & \cdots & F_{2j} & \cdots & F_{2n} & X_2 \\
\cdots & \cdots & \cdots & \cdots & \cdots & \cdots & \cdots \\
F_{i1} & F_{i2} & \cdots & F_{ij} & \cdots & F_{in} & X_i \\
\cdots & \cdots & \cdots & \cdots & \cdots & \cdots & \cdots \\
F_{n1} & F_{n2} & \cdots & F_{nj} & \cdots & F_{nn} & X_n \\
\hline
M_1 & M_2 & \cdots & M_j & \cdots & M_n & T
\end{array}
$$

Let F_{ij} represent the commodity export flow between the ith country and the jth country. When the F_{ii} equal zero, then the ith row shows the exports of country i to all other countries. Similarly, the jth column describes the imports of country j from all other countries. The matrix when completed should give all flows in world trade.

$$\sum_j M_j = \sum_i X_i = \sum_i \sum_j F_{ij}.$$

Total world imports equal total world exports.

The two approaches can now be identified depending on the selection of flows to be studied and in the way the selected flows are introduced. The first, which has been termed the *transmissions* approach, can have separate equations to explain each of the M_j and X_i but does not necessarily attempt to compute the F_{ij}, the individual flows between countries. More particularly, it concentrates on tracing the short-run fluctuations in domestic activities between countries. The alternative or *structure of trade* approach tends to estimate individual F_{ij}'s directly, and then obtains M_j and X_i only as a summation of flows between countries. This approach would analyze the actual structure of trade based on income, population, geographical distances, and other related factors.

The transmissions approach has thus far proven to be the more practical, especially when operated within a consistency framework. Consider the following example which would add an income determination equation based on domestic conditions to the customary export and import functions.[6] The latter sets of equations would be formulated for as many countries as are included, in this case up to *n*.

$$M_i = f(Y_i) \qquad\qquad i = 1, 2, \ldots, n$$

$$X_i = g(a_{ij} M_j, RC_i).$$

The corresponding set of income equations explain aggregate demand as the sum of demand induced by the current level of economic activity, autonomous expenditures, and net trade.

$$Y_i = b_i Y_i + E_i + X_i - M_i.$$

Definition of variables:

M_i = Value of imports of country i

X_i = Value of exports of country i

Y_i = Income of country i

RC_i = Relative competitiveness of country i against other countries

a_{ij} = Country i's share of country j's imports

b_i = Coefficient reflecting demand induced by current Y_i

E_i = Autonomous expenditure.

By solving the system on the basis of given values for the independent variables, one obtains a forecast of trade flows (X_i and M_i) and income flows (Y_i). When the forecasts of total imports are inconsistent with respect to forecasts of total exports, an iterative procedure is used to provide a new set of forecasts based on a new set of assumptions regarding domestic conditions. The world totals are compared again and iteration continues until the forecasts of imports and exports are consistent. If consistency is obtained for each commodity group, then estimates of demand by importing countries and estimates of supply by exporting countries could be used to obtain a set of commodity prices. Applications of the transmissions approach have been only at the aggregative, country trade level as seen in the work of Adams and Meyer-zu-Schlochtern [2], and of Samuelson.[26]

The structure of trade approach has not lent itself as easily to quantitative analysis. Both import functions and a fixed coefficient trade share matrix have to be estimated. And exports must subsequently be based on the matrix transformation of the import estimates. The latter task is particularly difficult given wide differences in valuation bases (c.i.f. and f.o.b.). However, some progress in overcoming these difficulties has been reported by Armington [4] and by Taplin.[33]

Most recently, Taplin [32] has constructed a model of this form which disaggregates commodity imports and exports according to the four major SITC commodity groupings: (SITC 0–1) Food, beverages and tobacco; (2,4) raw materials except fuels; (3) fuels; and (5–9) manufactures and miscellaneous. Applying either approach to further commodity disaggregation would be extremely difficult.

Recursive Programming Models

One is reluctant to classify models of this type as commodity models since they presently concentrate on modeling production, investment and technological change, while tending to neglect the demand side of the market. However, recursive programming models can tell us something not only about the substitution between commodities during agricultural transition but also about the role of technological change in commodity extractive industries.

Of those who have contributed to the development of this approach, Day [8] is the most well known, especially for his efforts to incorporate the dynamics of supply response with problems of interdependence and technological change in agriculture. A recursive program can be described as consisting of a series of independent mathematical programming problems which are formulated and solved sequentially. The solution values of decision variables reached in one period are considered part of the environment in which decisions are made in subsequent periods. To formulate a model in this form, one must first estimate and solve the required behavioral and feedback relationships. The model is then operated by taking the initial period's conditions as given, solving the first period's linear programming problem, updating the endogenous and exogenous parameters, and solving the succeeding period's linear programming problem and so forth.

A good illustration of the formulation of a recursive programming model can be found in Day's [7] example of a generalized cobweb model. Two homogeneous agricultural commodities are produced using two factors, land and working capital. Their production levels as well as resource allocation are decided by maximizing gross short-run profits. This is accomplished using the following programming description of the production process.

$$\zeta(t) = \underset{Q_1, Q_2}{\text{MAX}} \; [V_1^* (t)Q_1 + V_2^* (t)Q_2]$$

subject to

$$Q_1 + Q_2 \leqslant L$$

$$C_1 Q_1 + C_2 Q_2 \leqslant K(t)$$

$$Q_1, Q_2 \geqslant 0.$$

Revenue values associated with the two factors are derived from the related dual

$$\phi(t) = \underset{R_1, R_2}{\text{MIN}} \; [R_1 L + R_2 K(t)]$$

subject to

$$R_1 + C_1 R_2 \geqslant V_1^*(t)$$

$$R_1 + C_2 R_2 \geqslant V_2^*(t)$$

$$R_1, R_2 \qquad \geqslant 0.$$

And recursivity is introduced through a feedback component consisting of three equations which describe anticipated unit profits per area, working capital and prices.

$$V_i^*(t) = P_i(t-1) - C_i \qquad\qquad i = 1, 2.$$

$$K(t) \;=\; \underset{i}{\Sigma}\, P_i(t-1)\, Q_i(t-1) - H$$

$$P_i(t) \;=\; \text{MAX}\; [0, a_i + b_i Q_i(t)] \qquad i = 1, 2.$$

Definition of variables:

$V_1^*(t), V_2^*(t)$ = Value of gross unit profits per unit area anticipated for each of the two commodities

$Q_1(t), Q_2(t)$ = Production in area units of each of the commodities

C_1, C_2 = Unit working capital requirements of the commodities

$L, K(t)$ = Amounts of land and working capital available for production at *beginning* of year t

R_1, R_2 = Expected marginal-net-revenue values of the two factors, L and $K(t)$

$P_1(t), P_2(t)$ = Price received for each commodity at the *end* of year t

H = Overhead, constant from year to year

a_i, b_i = Parameters associated with the linear demand function for each commodity.

That each farm unit has initial endowments of the available aggregate resource factors L and $K(t)$ in the same proportion is essential to solving the linear programming problem represented in the first three equations. That solution then yields the total supply of commodities $Q_1(t)$ and $Q_2(t)$. Representing the dual to this problem, the corresponding solution of the next three equations yields $R_1(t)$ and $R_2(t)$, the expected marginal-net-revenue values of L and $K(t)$.

Feedback effects are introduced into the solution process following the properties of the cobweb model. That is, current price can be expressed as a function of past prices, reflecting naive expectations; it can also be determined .concurrently with demand, when the market is in equilibrium. Thus, anticipated profits are computed from current expected prices $P_1(t)$ and $P_2(t)$, where these prices are determined in terms of their previous values $P_1(t - 1)$ and $P_2(t - 1)$. Total capital available for production at the beginning of a year $K(t)$ must also depend on last year's activities—the value of sales $P_i(t - 1) Q_i(t - 1)$ minus payments for overhead H. Finally prices $P_1(t)$ and $P_2(t)$ are determined, assuming a temporary equilibrium in markets where those commodities produced are also sold. As suggested above, this would require making $P_i(t)$ a linear function of the current demand for $Q_i(t)$. One can compare policy analysis undertaken using this model with that of the cobweb regarding stability of behavior, growth, and equilibrium.

So far, the commodity-related studies based on recursive programming have concentrated on analyzing processes of agricultural or industrial development. Singh and Day [28], for example, have constructed a simulation model which describes agricultural transition in the Punjab region of India; it projects likely future growth for the region with respect to several alternative development policies. More recently, Singh and Ahn [27] have used this approach in analyzing the impact on regional growth of wheat price support programs and accompanying credit policies in the Rio Grande do Sol region of Brazil. On the industrial side, Nelson [23] has evaluated the impact of production, investment, and technological change on geographical location in the U.S. steel industry. Finally, Day and Tab [9] have investigated the U.S. coal industry to determine how investment in new techniques has altered the industry's input-output structure, its supply of final products, and its derived demand for labor and other inputs over time.

Industrial Dynamics Models

This form of model, associated largely with the work of Forrester [11], studies the information characteristics of an industry or commodity activity to determine how the organizational structure, amplifications, and time delays within a system interact to influence its final performance. Meadows [21] is credited with extending this approach to commodity modeling; his generalized "Dynamic Commodity Cycle Model" incorporates a structure designed to simulate commodity price and production cycles. As shown in Figure 1-2, the essentials of that structure are two coupled negative feedback loops—

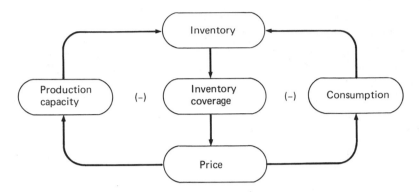

Figure 1-2.   Feedback Loop Structure of Production Cycles.
Source: D.L. Meadows. *Dynamics of Commodity Production Cycles.*
Cambridge, Mass.: Wright-Allen Press, Inc., 1970, p. 19. Reprinted
by permission of the publisher.

consumption and production—each acting to adjust inventory coverage to the
desired level.[7]

The feedback process can be explained using the example of a situation in which inventories are lower than desired, causing prices to increase. These increases affect changes in both the production and the consumption sectors, which act to return inventory to its desired level. The price increases lower per-capita consumption of the commodity. With less consumption drain, inventories will tend to rise. Production relationships act with the same effect. The increase in current price raises producer's price forecasts and thus the capacity they wish to utilize. After acquisition delays, additions in capacity result in increased production and higher inventory. Should inventory rise above its desired level, resulting price decreases would again be propagated around both the production and consumption loops to yield counteracting forces, decreased production, and increased consumption.

While such a structure might be assembled equation by equation, Meadows [21] has incorporated it into a generalized simulation model based on the DYNAMO [24] language. The structure of that model is described in the flow diagram of Figure 1-3. Its principal feature is that it shifts from a "period" or point change analysis to a "rate of change" form of analysis. This implies that all relationships are cast into differential equations. Effects of past or lagged values of variables are easily introduced through the form of delays in producing goods, in transferring productive capacity, in responding to price forecasts, in recognizing changes in retail prices, and in forecasting producer's price and consumption. For example, several periods of continuously low or high retail prices might be needed before producers sense this change and are able to adjust their rate of production. Finally, prices are determined as previously described using

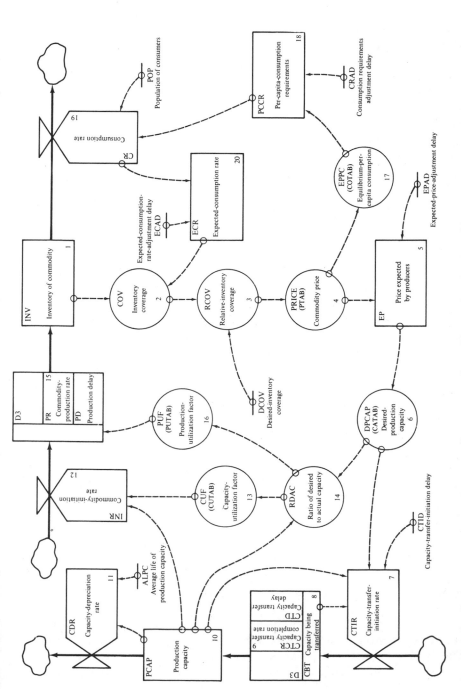

Figure 1-3. Flow Diagram of the Dynamic Commodity Cycle Model. Source: D.L. Meadows. *Dynamics of Commodity Production Cycles.* Cambridge, Mass.: Wright-Allen Press, Inc., 1970, p. 21. Reprinted by permission of the publisher.

Figure 1-2. As inventories rise above the desired level, those holding stocks will decrease price to discourage production and raise consumption. When inventories fall below the level desired by those holding them, prices will increase.

To apply either the industrial dynamics framework or the DCCM variant, the commodities of interest should feature a distinct cyclical pattern in production and prices. These cycles, furthermore, should result from certain amplifications and delays within the system. It is evident that this form of model can be applied only to a small range of commodities displaying a particular type of cyclical behavior. An example of a commodity study employing industrial dynamics is given in Chapter 7, which features the Raulerson and Langham model of the frozen concentrated orange juice industry. Meadows [21] himself has applied the DCCM to several commodity markets; among them are hogs, cattle, and broilers.

Systems Models

Formulating commodity models with a systems approach usually entails structuring the major objectives and variables to be considered as a complete system rather than constituting a single market or industry; it then incorporates one or more analytical or quantitative methods to produce a model emulating that system. Commodity systems models vary widely in character, depending principally on the choice of analytical methods. A typical systems model might begin with an econometric model and then include whatever decision rules are necessary to simulate the market of interest. Alternatively, it might combine an economic model with an engineering, biological, or linear programming model, depending on the range of total system characteristics to be taken into account. That systems models permit a tracing of the values of basic market variables over a large number of periods makes them useful for policy planning. One way of classifying the various approaches to systems models might be as follows:

Structural.   This systems approach, which involves no extensive econometric and mathematical modeling, has been suggested by Arthur. His ideal systems model [5] would be "a complex of numerous inter-related variables and dimensions relating to a definable set of objectives." It would include the formulation of system objectives, functions to be performed in fulfilling the objectives, the institutions and arrangements underlying the objectives, and a management control structure. The study of the world banana market by Arthur and his colleagues [5] is an illustration of this method.

Econometric and Programming.   This approach encompasses a class of models which can combine econometric or programming commodity models with decision rules describing market behavior and general computer simulation methods. See the Haidacher, Kite, and Matthews model in Chapter 10, which simulates the decision making process in surplus commodity removal programs, for a good example of a systems model. Another is the Crom [6] price-output model of the beef and pork markets in the U.S. A less decision-oriented systems model is the Alm, Duloy, and Gulbrandsen [3] model, which determines world market prices for agricultural commodities, utilizing alternative assumptions about national pricing policies. While the above examples are econometrically oriented, others incorporate programming or maximization models. The systems model devised by Holder, Shaw, and Snyder [13] for example, employs linear and nonlinear programming methods to determine optimal locations and quantity flows in the U.S. rice market. One difficulty with systems models is that their overconcern with "data fitting" can often result in a poor theoretical structure. Nonetheless, they are of use where several different "environments" influence a commodity market.

PLAN FOR THE BOOK

Up to now, I have described some of the commodity models included in this book from the point of view of the methodologies they embody. However, each of the studies in some way reflects recent contributions to the art of commodity model building. I would now like to focus on the nature of these contributions.

Let us begin with those studies involving the market form of model, which are the more plentiful. Chapter 3, featuring the Fisher, Cootner, and Baily model of the world copper market, estimates the system by a full-information maximum-likelihood method which takes into account serial correlation in equation disturbance terms. Simulation analysis is then performed using the recently developed TROLL simulation system. Chapter 4 presents the Epps model of the world coffee market which includes a noncompetitive market structure and incorporates as well an experimental design in the simulation analysis. In Chapter 5, the Myers and Havlicek multicommodity model of the beef, pork, and broiler markets concentrating on very short run behavior explains simultaneous interactions between commodities including cross elasticities at a multimarket level. Chapter 6, with the Wymer model of the world sugar market, not only shifts commodity analysis from discrete to continuous time, but also includes the estimation of the differential equation structure. The Labys model of the international lauric oils market in Chapter 7 shows how a market model may be formulated as a dynamic, stochastic system. Here dynamic supply equations explain production emanating from a perennial tree crop in tropical agriculture, and the influence of random changes in weather conditions on supply is introduced using stochastic simulation. In Chapter 8, Kim, Goreux, and Kendrick apply stochastic control theory to the world cocoa market so as to determine the usefulness of alternative decision rules for stabilization policy. Finally, Bell et al. in Chapter 9 present a market model of living marine resources which describes the main biological forces related to the maximum sustainable supply of fish and determines the impact of projected demand on future fish supply.

The remaining chapters relate to other forms of methodologies. The Adams and Griffin model of the U.S. petroleum refining industry given in Chapter 2 incorporates into a process model an engineering linear programming model describing industry inputs, outputs, and capacity utilization. Chapter 7 shows how industrial dynamics can be applied to an industry system; the model of Raulerson and Langham is used to appraise alternative supply control policies designed to reduce fluctuations in marketings of frozen concentrated orange juice and growers profits. The Haidacher, Kite and Matthews model in Chapter 10 simulates a planning decision framework, employing a systems model to test alternative policies related to multicommodity decisions. With Chapter 12, we have a model which represents a recent extension of the spatial equilibrium approach to multicommodity analysis in international trade, concentrating on the E.E.C. grain-livestock economy.

In the final chapter, we attempt to examine commodity modeling in perspective, suggesting possible areas for model improvement and further application. An Appendix listing some recent commodity models will facilitate further investigation and research.

NOTES

1. This represents a revised version of a paper originally prepared for the International Seminar on the Implications of Inflation in Industrial Countries and of Fluctuations in Exchange Rates for the Primary Exports of Developing Countries, Merton College, Oxford University, October 2–4, 1973.
2. Calling this an econometric market form of model seems more convenient than calling it an econometric equilibrium model as I have done previously in *Dynamic Commodity Models: Specification, Estimation and Simulation.*
3. A more complete description of this model structure appears in F.G. Adams, "From Econometric Models of the Nation to Models of Industries and Firms," *Wharton Quarterly Business Review* (Spring 1973).
4. The present description is developed more fully in T.C. Lee and S.K. Seaver, *A Positive Spatial Equilibrium Model of Broiler Markets: A Simultaneous Equation Approach,* Storrs Agricultural Experiment Station Bulletin No. 417, University of Connecticut, Storrs, 1972.
5. Applications of various forms of commodity models to determining the impact of inflation and changes in exchange rates has been discussed in the original version of this chapter, as referenced in Note 1.
6. This example is discussed more thoroughly in F.G. Adams, H. Eguchi, and F. Meyer-Zu-Schlochtern, *An Econometric Analysis of International Trade,* Organization for Economic Co-operation and Development, Paris, 1969.

7. Much of this description and the accompanying figures appear from D.L. Meadows, *Dynamics of Commodity Production Cycles,* Courtesy of the Wright-Allen Press, Cambridge, Mass.

REFERENCES

1. Adams, F.G. "From Econometric Models of the Nation to Models of Industries and Firms." *Wharton Quarterly Business Review* (Spring) 1973.
2. Adams, F.G., Eguchi, H., and Meyer-Zu-Schlochtern, F. *An Econometric Analysis of International Trade.* Organization for Economic Co-operation and Development, Paris, January 1969.
3. Alm, H., Duloy, J., and O. Gulbrandsen. "Agricultural Prices and the World Food Economy." Mimeographed. Institute for Economics and Statistics, University of Uppsala, 1969.
4. Armington, P.S. "A Theory of Demand for Products Distinguished by Place of Production." *IMF Staff Papers* 16 (1969): 159–78.
5. Arthur, H.B., Houck, J.P., and Beckford, G.L. *Tropical Agribusiness Structures and Adjustments: Bananas.* Boston: Harvard University Graduate School of Business Administration, 1968.
6. Crom, R., "A Dynamic Price-Output Model of the Beef and Pork Sectors." Technical Bulletin No. 1426, Economic Research Service of the U.S. Department of Agriculture, Washington, 1970.
7. Day, R.H. "Recursive Programming Models: A Brief Introduction," in G. Judge and T. Takayama (Eds.), *Studies in Economic Planning Over Space and Time.* Amsterdam, North Holland, 1974.
8. Day, R.H. *Recursive Programming and Production Response.* Amsterdam: North Holland Publishing Co., 1963.
9. Day, R.H. and W.K. Tabb. "A Dynamic Microeconomic Model of the U.S. Coal Mining Industry." SSRI Research Paper, University of Wisconsin, 1972.
10. Fair, R.C., and D.M. Jaffee. "Methods of Estimation for Markets in Disequilibrium." *Econometrica* 40 (1972): 497–514.
11. Forrester, J.W. *Industrial Dynamics.* Cambridge: The M.I.T. Press, 1965.
12. Higgins, C.I. "An Econometric Description of the U.S. Steel Industry." In *Essays in Industrial Economics*—Vol. II, L.R. Klein (Ed.). Philadelphia: Wharton School of Finance and Commerce, 1969.
13. Holder, Jr., S.H., Shaw, D.L. and Synder, J.C. "A Systems Model of the U.S. Rice Industry." Technical Bulletin No. 1453, Economic Research Service, U.S. Department of Agriculture, Washington, November 1971.
14. Jellema, B.M. "Analysis of the World Market for Groundnuts and Groundnut Products." Unpublished Ph.D. dissertation, North Carolina State University, Raleigh, 1973.
15. King, R.A. and Foo-Shiung Ho. "Reactive Programming: A Market Simulating Spatial Equilibrium Algorithm." Economics Special Report,

Department of Economics, North Carolina State University at Raleigh, 1965.

16. Leamer, E.E., and R.M. Stern. *Quantitative International Economics.* Boston: Allyn and Bacon, 1970.

17. Lee, T.C., and S.K. Seaver. *A Positive Spatial Equilibrium Model of Broiler Markets: A Simultaneous Equation Approach,* Storrs Agricultural Experiment Station Bulletin No. 417, University of Connecticut, Storrs, 1972.

18. Lee, W. Bong. "The Competitive Nonlinear Spatial Equilibrium Analysis: An Empirical Study of the U.S. Tomato Industry." Mimeographed. Bloomsburg State College, Bloomsburg, Pa., 1973.

19. Labys, W.C. *Dynamic Commodity Models: Specification, Estimation and Simulation.* Lexington, Mass.: Heath Lexington Books, 1973.

20. Labys, W.C. "A Taxonomy of Commodity Models and Their Policy Applications." Prepared for the International Seminar on the Implications of Inflation in Industrial Countries and of Fluctuations in the Exchange Rates of Major International Currencies for the Primary Exports of Developing Countries. Oxford University, October 2–4, 1973.

21. Meadows, D.L. *Dynamics of Commodity Production Cycles.* Cambridge: The Wright-Allen Press, 1970.

22. Melo, F.H. "An Analysis of the World Cocoa Economy in 1980." Unpublished Ph.D. dissertation, North Carolina State University, Raleigh, 1973.

23. Nelson, J.P. "An Interregional Recursive Programs Model of Production, Investment, and Technological Change." *Journal of Regional Science* 11 (1971): 33–47.

24. Pugh, A.L., *DYNAMO User's Manual.* Cambridge: The M.I.T. Press, 1963.

25. Rhomberg, R.R. "Possible Approaches to a Model of World Trade and Payments." *IMF Staff Papers* 14 (1967): 433–55.

26. Samuelson, Lee. "A New Model of World Trade." *OECD Economic Outlook* (December 1973): 3–22.

27. Singh, I.J., and C.Y. Ahn. *A Dynamic Model of Agricultural Development in Southern Brazil: Some Retrospective Policy Simulations (1960-70).* Occasional Paper No. 113. Department of Agricultural Economics and Rural Sociology, Ohio State University, Columbus, 1972.

28. Singh, I.J., and R. Day. "A Microeconometric Chronicle of the Green Revolution." Paper No. 7133, Social Systems Research Institute, University of Wisconsin, 1972.

29. Sohn, H.K. "A Spatial Equilibrium Model of the Beef Industry in the U.S." Unpublished Ph.D. dissertation, University of Hawaii, 1970.

30. Takayama, T., and G.G. Judge. "Equilibrium Among Spatially Separated Markets: A Reformulation." *Econometrica* 32 (1964): 510–24

31. Takayama, T., and G.G. Judge. *Spatial and Temporal Price and Allocation Models.* Amsterdam: North-Holland, 1971.

32. Taplin, G.B. "A Model of World Trade" in *The International Linkage of National Economic Models*. R.J. Ball, ed. Amsterdam: North-Holland, 1973.
33. Taplin, G.B. "Models of World Trade." *IMF Staff Papers* 14 (1967): 433–55.
34. Thiam, T.B. "Prices and Trade Prospects For Malaysian Palm Oil." Unpublished Ph.D. dissertation, North Carolina State University, Raleigh, 1973.

Chapter Two

An Economic–Linear Programming Model of the U.S. Petroleum Refining Industry

F. Gerard Adams
James M. Griffin

INTRODUCTION

The extension of econometric modeling to the level of the industry and the firm has opened wide horizons. Some of the most interesting possibilities for industrial models combine engineering information on technical coefficients and optimization with statistically estimated behavioral relationships. This article describes an econometric-linear programming model of the petroleum industry. This model is intended to provide a medium term perspective over the business cycle and to serve as a framework for long-term projections. It can also be used as a tool for simulation studies under alternative assumptions about economic conditions or policies.

      The structure of the model is described in simplified form in Figure 2-1. The Wharton Long Term Industry Model [9], on the left-hand side, determines the economic setting in which the petroleum model operates. Given the stocks of petroleum consuming equipment, economic activity determines product demands. A simple inventory adjustment to normal levels is assumed. Imports and exports are exogenous.

      Given product demands, inventory adjustments, and net imports, the requirements for the major petroleum products are determined, and they become endogenous constraints in the linear programming model (LP). Other inputs to the LP are the capacities of various types of refining equipment available and crude oil prices, both of which are treated as exogenous. Crude oil supplies are assumed to be adjusted to satisfy refining needs.[1] Constraints in the LP model include product quality specifications, process capacities, and product output requirements. The objective function is then set to minimize the cost of producing

F. Gerard Adams is professor, and James M. Griffin Associate professor, Department of Economics, University of Pennsylvania, Philadelphia, Penn. 19174.

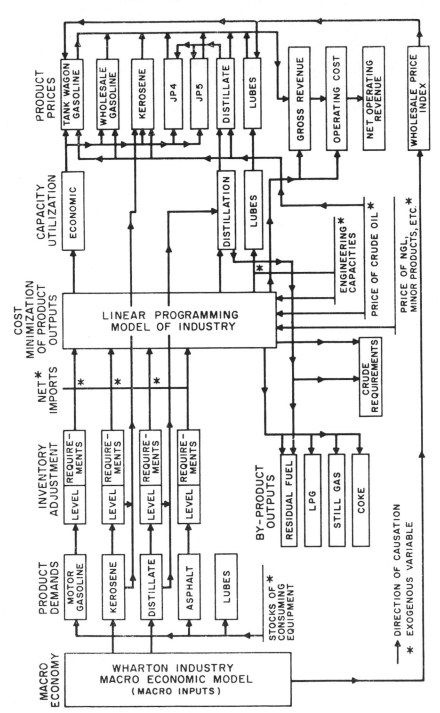

Figure 2-1.   Simplified Structure of Petroleum Industry Model.

these outputs. The LP solution determines the volume of crude oil inputs required, the capacity utilization measures, total operating costs, and the outputs of by-products, e.g., residual fuel oil. On the right-hand side of the diagram, product prices are then determined on the basis of a markup over crude cost, utilization of capacity, inventory levels, and a general inflation measure. By subtracting operating costs as calculated by the LP from a measure of gross revenue, an estimate of net operating revenue is obtained.

      The model, which is recursive in structure, consists of 14 equations estimated by econometric techniques, 7 identities, and an associated LP model of dimension 227 X 334. There are 44 exogenous variables (including only those variables from the LP model which are likely to vary) and 30 endogenous variables (including those calculated in the LP model).

SPECIFICATION OF THE PETROLEUM MODEL

In this section we consider the structural specifications of the parts of the model in the following order: domestic product demands, inventory adjustments, net imports, supply determination, and price determination. Due to the short-run insensitivity of product demands to price and due to the independence among product demands, the flow of causation is unidirectional. The product demand and price equations, which are highly overidentified, have been estimated by ordinary least squares, since problems of bias are not likely to be severe given the recursive structure of the model. A 5 percent *t* test criterion was used for inclusion of variables except in a few instances in which theoretical considerations were overriding. Cost minimization in the LP model based on engineering data determines the supply relationships explicitly.

Domestic Product Demand
      With the exception of certain power plants, it is generally not possible to substitute alternative fuels in engines or burners designed to run on a specific fuel. Consequently, the available stock of oil consuming equipment is a principal determinant of the demand for any given petroleum product. In the short run, economic factors determine the intensity with which equipment will be used, e.g., the number of miles the average truck is driven. Substitutions between fuels can take place only in the long run as new equipment is put in place. Consequently, one would expect that the short run price effects are not important.
[1]
      The demand for gasoline depends on the number, use, and efficiency of cars, trucks and buses. These factors make up the following technical identity:

$$DG = ECAR \cdot \frac{MD}{MPB}$$

where *DG* and *ECAR* are defined in Table 2-1, *MD* equals the miles driven per million equivalent cars, and *MPB* is the miles per 10^3 barrels. Since independent data on miles per barrel and number of miles driven are not available, considerable experimentation with proxy variables for efficiency and use (*MPB* and *MD*) was carried out. Consumption per vehicle was best explained by efficiency variables measuring the share of domestically produced cars on the road (imports use less gasoline per mile than American cars) and the share of non-air-conditioned cars (air-conditioning increases gasoline requirements). Equation (2-1) in Table 2-2 was estimated with the constraint of unitary elasticity of *DG* with respect to *ECAR*. Normalized on *DG*, this equation explains gasoline demand with a standard error of 52,000 barrels per day (*B/D*). Assuming no air-conditioning and imported cars, the constant term implies an annual demand of 17.2 barrels per car. This compares favorably with the 1958 average demand per car of 17.3 barrels per car.

The Wharton capacity utilization index for manufacturing and other cyclical variables were tried to catch fluctuations in automobile utilization related to business conditions, but such effects were not statistically significant. Also, the effect of cars owned by two-car families was insignificant. Finally, tests of the impact of gasoline price on consumption suggest, not surprisingly, that gasoline consumption is highly price inelastic, given the number and type of vehicles on the road.

Kerosene is used as a heating and industrial fuel as well as a fuel in commercial jet aircraft. Equation (2-2), the demand function for kerosene, takes into consideration the jet aircraft fleet, industrial activity, and a negative time trend to reflect the declining heating use over time. Lack of data on the number of kerosene heating burners necessitated the use of the time trend. Also included was the petroleum industry's heating degree days variable despite its low *t* value because of the sizeable sensitivity of heating uses to temperature. Price effects were here again not significant. The coefficient on JET suggests a daily consumption rate per jet aircraft of 226 barrels, and the mean elasticity with respect to *Xm* is 0.67.

Distillate[2] fuel demand for heating is closely related to the number of oil burners in use and to the weather. To a lesser extent, distillate is used for industrial purposes and for transportation (diesel fuel) which are closely related to manufacturing activity. Variables representing these factors are the basis for a good functional description of distillate consumption in Equation (2-3) of Table 2-2. According to Equation (2-3), the average oil burner annually consumes about 2,050 gallons of fuel oil, and the income elasticity, measured by *Xm*, is 0.37.

Approximately 40 percent of lubricating oil demand is for automotive consumption while most of the remainder is used directly by industry. In the demand function for lubricants, Equation (2-4), the stock of cars acts as a proxy

Table 2-1. Definitions of Variables

$BURN_{-1}$ = Stock of oil burners in 10^3 at beginning of year t (see American Petroleum Institute's *Petroleum Facts and Figures*).

CU = Capacity utilization based on capacity as minimum point of the industry's short run average cost function.

CUD = Crude oil distillation capacity utilization (crude oil runs to stills divided by crude oil distillation capacity).

CUL = Capacity utilization rate for lubricants (Capacity given in *Oil & Gas Journal,* "Annual Refining Issue").

DA = Demand for asphalt in thousands of barrels per day (written hereafter as B/D).

DD = Distillate demand in 10^3 B/D.

DDD = Heating degree days (0.7 New York + 0.3 Detroit) based on weighted consumption of PAD Districts I (East Coast) and II (Midwest).

DG = Demand for gasoline by trucks, buses, and cars in 10^3 B/D.

DK = Demand for kerosene in 10^3 B/D.

DL = Demand for lubricants in 10^3 B/D.

$ECAR$ = Stock of equivalent cars based on relative consumption in 1958 (1 truck = 2 cars; 1 bus = 4.7 cars) in millions of units.

$\dfrac{ID_{-1}}{DD}$ = Number of days inventory (inventory of distillate at beginning of year divided by distillate demand for the current year).

$\dfrac{IK_{-1}}{PPK}$ = Number of days inventory (inventory of kerosene at beginning of year divided by production of kerosene in current year).

JET = Commercial fleet of jet aircraft (*Aerospace Facts and Figures*).

MIL_{-1} = Total municipal and rural highway mileage[6] at beginning of year t. (See *Highway Statistics,* annual reports, Department of Transportation).

NAC = Ratio of non-air-conditioned cars to $ECAR$ (calculated by adding annual sales of new air-conditioned cars to nonfactory installations and assuming a car life of ten years).

NIM = Ratio of domestically produced cars to $ECAR$ (calculated by assuming a car life of ten years).

PC = U.S. average crude oil price ($/bbl). (All prices are from *Platt's Oil Price Handbook*).

PD = Average U.S. wholesale price of distillate.

PG = Average U.S. wholesale price of gasoline.

PGT = U.S. 55 city tankwagon gasoline price ($/bbl).

$PJP4$ = Average bid price on JP4 for 6 months government contracts (annual average = average of two 6 month bids).

$PJP5$ = Average bid price on JP5 for 6 months government contracts (annual average = average of two 6 month bids).

PK = Average U.S. wholesale price of kerosene.

PL = Price of lubes on Mid Continent (120 V at 210°, 0–10 pour point).

PW = U.S. wholesale price index (1957–59 = 100).

$TIME$ = Time trend (1948 = 1.0).

Xm = GNP originating in manufacturing and mining in billions of 1958 dollars.

Table 2-2. Behavioral Equations*

Estimated Equations	$\bar{R}^2$	SE	DW	Sample Period
Product demand equation				
(2-1) $\ln \dfrac{DG}{ECAR} = 3.855 + 2.3194 \ln NIM - 0.5827 \ln NAC$ $\quad (893.2)\ (4.02) \qquad\qquad (2.89)$	0.613	0.013	1.56	1948–69
(2-2) $DK = -10.1\ TIME + 0.0212\ DDD + 1.87\ Xm + 0.2261\ JET + 40.72$ $\quad (-4.76)\qquad (1.44)\qquad (4.05)\qquad (11.68)\qquad (0.40)$	0.991	14.6	1.83	1948–69
(2-3) $DD = 0.1337\ BURN_{-1} + 0.0929\ DDD + 3.054\ Xm - 365.4$ $\quad (23.84)\qquad\quad (3.57)\qquad (10.16)\quad (2.88)$	0.996	29.0	1.56	1948–68
(2-4) $\ln DL = 0.282 + 0.6008 \ln ECAR + 0.443 \ln Xm - 0.35\ TIME$ $\quad (0.23)\quad (2.07)\qquad\qquad (2.91)\qquad (2.40)$	0.828	0.040	2.29	1948–68
(2-5) $DA = 0.00016\ MIL_{-1} + 0.00023\ \Delta MIL + 263580.\dfrac{DG_t}{MIL_{-1}} - 580.7$ $\quad (4.06)\qquad\qquad (2.61)\qquad\quad (9.34)\qquad\qquad (5.36)$	0.994	5.9	2.40	1949–68
Technical adjustment equation				
(2-6) $\dfrac{\text{Actual crude oil inputs}}{\text{Calculated crude oil inputs}} = 1.347 - 0.372\ CUD$ $\qquad\qquad\qquad\qquad\quad (59.7)\quad (14.1)$	0.938	0.005	2.23	1955–68
(2-7) $\dfrac{\text{Actual residual output}}{\text{Calculated residual output}} = 4.011 - 3.557\ CUD$ $\qquad\qquad\qquad\qquad\quad (12.0)\quad (9.1)$	0.863	0.007	1.62	1955–68

Product price equation

$$(2\text{-}8)\ PGT = 1.5487 + 0.8621\ PC + 0.02002\ PW + 0.1804\ (CU - 0.881)^{0.5}$$
$$(3.26)\quad (3.90)\qquad (4.24)\qquad (1.09)$$
$$+\ 0.6971\ (CU_{-1} - 0.881)^{0.5} + 0.8393\ (CU_{-2} - 0.881)^{0.5}$$
$$(13.31)\qquad\qquad\qquad (8.90)$$
$$+\ 0.600\ (CU_{-3} - 0.881)^{0.5}$$
$$(7.02)$$

$\bar{R}^2 = 0.930 \qquad SE = 0.063 \qquad DW = 1.80 \qquad 1952\text{-}69$

$$(2\text{-}9)\ PG = 1.7364 + 0.7124\ PC + 1.133 \left(\frac{CU + CU_{-1}}{2} \right)$$
$$(2.17)\quad (4.34)\qquad (2.67)$$

$0.470 \qquad 0.091 \qquad 1.44 \qquad 1950\text{-}69$

$$(2\text{-}10)\ PK = 0.752 + 1.5396\ PC - 0.00668\ \frac{IK_{-1}}{PPK}$$
$$(1.67)\quad (10.10)\qquad (4.8)$$

$0.875 \qquad 0.098 \qquad 1.82 \qquad 1951\text{-}69$

$$(2\text{-}11)\ PD = 1.44 + 1.4174\ PC - 0.0095\ \frac{ID_{-1}}{DD} + 2.133 \left(\frac{CUD + CUD_{-1}}{2} \right)$$
$$(2.75)\quad (27.17)\qquad (4.38)\qquad\qquad (4.97)$$

$0.971 \qquad 0.056 \qquad 1.89 \qquad 1946\text{-}69$

$$(2\text{-}12)\ PJP5 = -6.256 + 1.4404\ PD + 4.993\ CU$$
$$(8.04)\qquad (8.54)\qquad (5.38)$$

$0.982 \qquad 0.054 \qquad 2.45 \qquad 1965\text{-}69$

$$(2\text{-}13)\ PJP4 = -3.6062 + 1.0655\ PD + 3.719\ CU$$
$$(6.93)\qquad (9.45)\qquad (5.99)$$

$0.953 \qquad 0.026 \qquad 2.70 \qquad 1965\text{-}69$

$$(2\text{-}14)\ \frac{PL}{PW} = 0.0253 + 0.0809\ CUL$$
$$(0.95)\quad (2.53)$$

$0.266 \qquad 0.066 \qquad 1.01 \qquad 1953\text{-}68$

*Given in parentheses below the coefficients are the t statistics. $\bar{R}^2$, the coefficient of determination, is corrected for degrees of freedom. SE is the standard error of the estimate and DW is the Durbin-Watson statistic. The notation "$-i$" implies that the variable is lagged i years.

for auto lubricating oil demand while a time trend reflects technological change leading to reduced lubricating oil requirements per car and *Xm* serves as a proxy for industrial uses. On *a priori* grounds, one would expect the elasticity with respect to *ECAR* to be a little higher relative to the elasticity with respect to *Xm* but the estimates are not unreasonable. The transformed standard error in terms of *DL* is a rather low 4,200 *B/D*.

Asphalt demand, which is related to the construction of highways and their maintenance, is given in Equation (2-5). Maintenance requirements can be approximated by highway mileage and by a measure of highway use, in this case gasoline consumption per mile of highway. The use of asphalt in new construction is measured by the change in highway mileage, only a part of which uses asphalt, however.

Inventory Adjustment

The model embodies a relatively simple inventory adjustment process. In the petroleum industry, stocks of refined finished products help to meet seasonal peak requirements in the summer for gasoline and in the winter for distillate heating oil. In many cases the same storage facilities serve alternatively for gasoline and for distillate and there is little opportunity for excess stocks to hang over from one year to the next. Accordingly, it is reasonable to assume that inventory adjustment occurs within one year and that refiners plan their inventory accumulation each year to bring their inventories from actual (IT_{-1}) to desired levels (IT^*). That is,

$$\Delta IT^* = IT^* - IT_{-1} \tag{2-15}$$

where ΔIT^* represents planned inventory change which enters the refiner's product output plan. Desired or "normal" inventories are estimated by a simple equation for the inventory to demand ratio as follows:

$$\frac{IT^*}{D} = \alpha \tag{2-16}$$

where D is product demand. Substituting estimated values of α from Equation (2-16) into (2-15) gives the standard inventory adjustment scheme

$$\Delta IT^* = \alpha D - IT_{-1} \tag{2-17}$$

which has been used for gasoline, kerosene, and distillate. In the cases of gasoline and distillate, the number of days' desired inventory estimated by this procedure is 44.7 and 75.9, respectively. For kerosene, heating and industrial uses were estimated to require 24.8 million barrels of inventories. Desired commercial jet fuel inventories were assumed to amount to 28.1 days' demand in accord with experience over the 1965–69 period.

Imports and Exports of Products

Imports and exports of petroleum products other than residual fuel oil are treated as exogenous variables. They have not been important for the U.S. petroleum industry since the early 1950s. Moreover, imports have been restricted to their pre-1959 levels under Oil Import Control regulations. Residual fuel oil, however, falls into a different category. Residual fuel oil is a by-product of petroleum refining activity in the United States, and its output is calculated by the LP model. The difference between U.S. demand for residual fuel and its output by domestic refineries is satisfied through imports.[3]

Supply Determination

For a technologically advanced process industry such as petroleum refining, a linear programming description of the production function has a number of advantages over the alternative approach of statistical production or supply functions, and is commonly used in the industry [8, 10]. In a joint product, multiprocess industry, moreover, statistical estimation is difficult in view of problems of simultaneous equations bias and multicollinearity.[4] Alternatively, the linear programming description of the production process is easily adaptable to joint production and multicapital processes. While statistical treatment of technological change is often limited to a time trend, the linear programming approach offers significant improvements because of its reliance on detailed engineering data concerning process and product quality characteristics. John Enos' [5] distinction of "within" and "between" process changes serves as a useful device to analyze the treatment of technological change in an *LP* model. "Between" process improvements occur when one process replaces another and are easily treated in the *LP* framework by adjusting the process capacity limits. "Within" process changes occur when improvements of a particular process are made. The treatment of technological change in this study is only partial, because it was not possible to include "within" process change by disaggregating processes by model type.

The linear programming model used to represent the aggregate U.S. petroleum refining industry is a modification of a typical Gulf Coast 200,000 barrel per day (*B/D*) refinery LP model by Bonner & Moore Associates.[3] The modified Bonner & Moore model represents, at best, a rough approximation to the aggregate industry production function, and serious aggregation problems may still remain. Unfortunately, an industry model consisting of approximately 170 individual refinery *LP* models was not practical. Considerable effort, however, was directed towards making the *LP* model more representative.[5]

To apply the *LP,* the required product outputs, which are established endogenously, are supplemented by exogenous information on quality specifications, and availability of raw material inputs, such as natural gasoline, iso and normal butanes, and process capacity constraints It is also necessary to specify the prices of by-products and the prices of factor inputs such as crude oil and natural gas liquids. Also treated as exogenous are the capacities of the twelve major refining processes, which had to be adjusted to a calendar day capacity basis to reflect average maintenance and breakdowns.[6] Given the prices of factor inputs, the capacity of the various process units, and the required outputs, the *LP*'s objective function is set to minimize the cost of meeting product requirements as follows:

$$\text{minimize } C'X$$
$$\text{(2-18)}$$
$$\text{subject to } AX \leqslant B$$

where C' is an $1 \times n$ vector of costs associated with the various processing activities. These costs include only variable costs for crude oil inputs, natural gas liquids, fuel, royalty, catalysts, etc. X is an $n \times 1$ vector of production activities available to the industry. A is an $m \times n$ matrix of technical coefficients based on engineering data and B is an $m \times 1$ vector of production constraints.

In the present application, nine outputs from the solution to Equation (2-18) are linked to the remainder of the model. These include the outputs of the four by-products, crude oil requirements, three measures of capacity utilization, and operating costs. In applying the model over an extended time period, minor adjustments were necessary to the calculated values for crude oil inputs and residual fuel output. The omission of "within process" technical change, coupled with the fact that utilization varies both over time and between refineries, implies that the "fixed" coefficients in the A matrix may not in reality be fixed. To reflect the phenomenon of a larger, more technically advanced refinery producing a proportionately greater share of output as crude oil distillation capacity utilization expands, a statistically estimated adjustment for crude oil inputs was necessary (see Equation 2-6 of Table 2-2). Since, for greater inputs of crude oil, the industry is more efficient than the model, there is a corresponding saving in that the industry produces fewer by-products than the model predicts. Equation (2-7) reflects this phenomenon.

Price Determination

Price determination in the petroleum refining industry is treated as a markup over production costs. The markup differs among products, depending on long run demand and supply elasticities, on capacity utilization, and also on the level of product inventories relative to anticipated normal demands. While in the aggregate over the entire year the industry faces a vertical product demand schedule and adjusts aggregate output accordingly, individual refiners facing elastic demand curves use marginal cost considerations to guide market participation. This is particularly relevant to the smaller, independent refiners. Thus, depending on the competitive structure in the various product markets, prices respond with varying lags. These notions have been built into the price determination process assumed.[7]

Crude oil costs constitute approximately 85 percent of variable cost inputs in petroleum refining. An increase in crude oil costs is reflected in average and marginal costs and is traditionally shifted along to the prices of petroleum products.[8] Product prices are also related to the degree of capacity utilization to reflect rising marginal costs[9] over the relevant output range. Capacity may be defined either by the minimum point of the industry's short run average cost curve[10] or by the industry's standard engineering measure, the capacity of the crude oil distillation process.[11] For either capacity utilization measure, product demands affect the numerator of the capacity utilization measure. Consequently, it could be argued that the coefficients are subject to simultaneous equation bias, but the short run insensitivity of product demands to price changes is likely to minimize this problem.

Inventory accumulation below or in excess of normal requirements also represents an influence on prices. Since the demand for petroleum products is perfectly inelastic, given the stock of petroleum consuming equipment, the entire industry adjustment must take place, as previously indicated, through an adjustment of output. This is implicit in the output determination mechanism which assumes that production will be sufficient to meet estimated demand plus the quantities required to adjust inventories to their normal level less net imports. Since this output determination mechanism does not function instantaneously, individual firms can dispose of inventories, in excess of their demand requirements, on the competitive market. Usually one thinks of this type of inventory effect as important in explaining weekly and monthly price variations, but likely to be mutually offsetting over the period of a year. For those products such as distillate and kerosene, which require large inventories relative to demand, the period for correcting inventory imbalances may require the full year, suggesting a systematic effect on annual price data.

Other cost factors or inflationary pressures are also important and may conveniently be summarized in terms of the wholesale price index. The complete formulation is as follows:

$$P_i = f\left(PC, PW, C, \frac{I_{i,-1}}{D_i}\right) \tag{2-19}$$

where

P = Price of product i

PC = Crude oil price

PW = U.S. wholesale price index

C = Some measure of capacity utilization e.g., either CU, CUD, CUL

$$\frac{I_{i,-1}}{D_i} = \text{Inventory to demand ratio for product } i.$$

Since gasoline is the primary product both in terms of volume and revenue, it is important to obtain an adequate description of its price. The tankwagon market is the primary benchmark for most sales, since the tankwagon price is the price charged by the major petroleum refiners to the service station. Branded sales to jobbers are traditionally based on a discount off the tankwagon price.

After considerable experimentation, Equation (2–8) was selected.[12] The impact of capacity utilization is nonlinear and lagged. In this equation the coefficient 0.881 represents a "floor" on capacity utilization which was reached in 1961. The square root term on capacity utilization coupled with the lag structure reflects the fact that, as capacity utilization remains near this floor for long periods, price wars spread rapidly and prices decline precipitously. One explanation for this is at very low levels of capacity utilization, marginal costs are low and relatively flat [7]. When refiners view this as a long run situation, excess supplies available to independent distributors result in severe price competition. Another implication of this equation is that the price of gasoline at the tankwagon level is marked up as crude oil prices rise, but only by .86 cents per barrel for every one cent per barrel increase in the price of crude oil.

The U.S. wholesale price index was introduced to reflect the inflationary trends in marketing costs, which are included in the tankwagon price. A five point increase in the wholesale price index would increase the tankwagon price ten cents per barrel.

For the approximate 25 percent of gasoline sold at the wholesale level, the price is explained by a similar relationship involving capacity utilization and crude oil price, Equation (2–9). PW was not significant, indicating that unlike marketing costs, gains in refining technology have offset long-run inflationary trends within the refinery gates. Again the coefficient on the price of crude oil is less than one. The lag structure on capacity utilization here is much shorter than for the tankwagon price. This may be attributable to the fact that the wholesale market is more competitive, i.e., either prices adjust more quickly since both independents and majors view the wholesale markets as an outlet for unwanted products, or wholesale prices are more representative of the prices in actual market transactions than are the tankwagon price quotations.

The price of kerosene is simply explained with a markup over crude oil cost and an inventory effect, Equation (2–10). Capacity utilization was not significant. The markup on crude oil price appeared high, suggesting that there may be some erosion over time. However, polynomial lags on crude oil price indicated no lagged effects of *PC.*

Introducing the same elements into the distillate price equation as for other fuels, Equation (2-11) reveals a high markup of fuel oil price on the price of crude oil. This is perhaps realistic as a short term response, and longer run forces must affect the expansion of oil burning heating equipment versus other ways of domestic heating. Inventories, relative to their normal level, affect the distillate fuel price. In the case of distillate fuel, the capacity utilization of the crude oil distillation process was appropriate as distillate is primarily a product of the distillation unit of the refinery and requires little, if any, downstream processing capacity.

In Equations (2-12) and (2-13), the prices of jet fuels (JP4 and JP5) were linked to the price of distillate (*PD*), since both fuels are essentially distillate base. Their lighter components, naphthas (JP4) and kerosene or commercial jet (JP5), become more valuable when downstream refining capacity utilization reflected in *CU,* is tight. Conversely, when capacity utilization is low, these lighter components can easily be manufactured with the spare refining capacity.

The price of lubricants is related to an engineering measure of lubricant capacity utilization, Equation (2-14). In this formulation, we deviate from the approach for the other products since crude oil costs represent only a small portion of production costs and inventories do not vary appreciably. The major costs are the processing costs represented by the U.S. wholesale price index.

Revenue and Cost Estimates

Highly approximate revenue and cost indexes for petroleum refining were calculated. Revenue was estimated on the basis of quantities of products produced and prices derived in the model for the major products, and operating costs are estimated by the *LP* model. Net operating revenue is then calculated as the difference between estimated gross revenues and operating costs.

SAMPLE PERIOD PERFORMANCE AND FORECASTS

Sample Period Performance

Sample period solutions are a way to evaluate the behavioral characteristics of the complete model and its ability to describe economic activity. The results over the period 1955-1968 are compared to actual values in Figure 2-2. These are dynamic, full system solutions, actual values having been used only for the exogenous variables and for lagged endogenous variables at the start of the simulation period. The calculated values trace movements over the sample period with substantial accuracy. As a predictor of petroleum product production and crude oil requirements, the model performs rather well (see Figure 2-2.1). Nevertheless, there are instances of persistent autocorrelated errors. For example, despite the small percent error in gasoline production, the

B. SAMPLE PERIOD SIMULATIONS (1955–68)

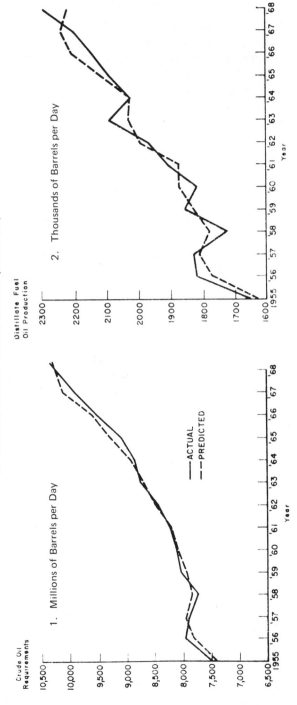

1. Millions of Barrels per Day

2. Thousands of Barrels per Day

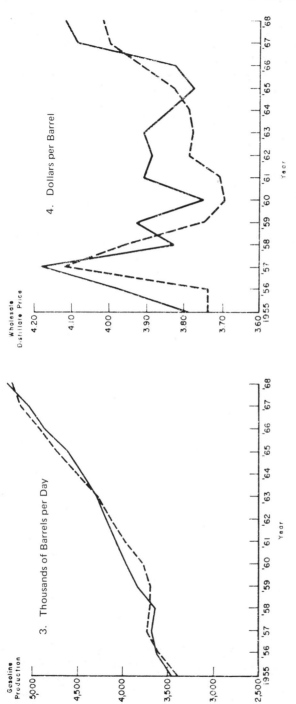

Figure 2-2. Sample Period Simulations (1955–1968).

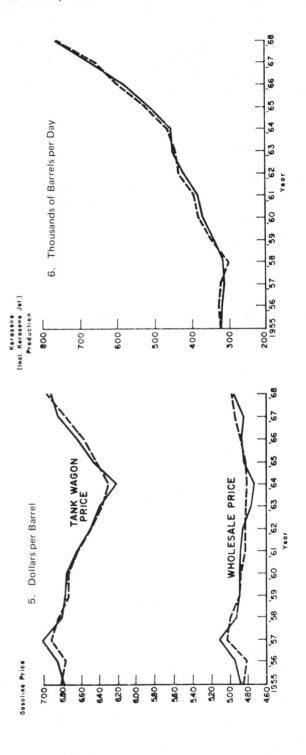

5. Dollars per Barrel

TANK WAGON PRICE

WHOLESALE PRICE

6. Thousands of Barrels per Day

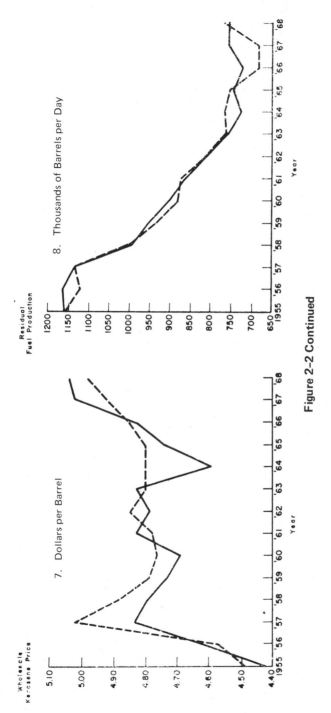

Residual Fuel Production

8. Thousands of Barrels per Day

Wholesale Kerosene Price

7. Dollars per Barrel

Figure 2-2 Continued

series is underestimated from 1959 to 1962 and overestimated for 1964 to 1967 resulting in similar errors in estimated crude oil requirements because of gasoline's importance to total crude oil requirements (see Figure 2-2.1 and 2-2.3). As an example of how the LP model determines by-product outputs, the actual and predicted output of residual fuel are shown in Figure 2-2.8.

For prices, errors are also relatively small and the pattern of price movements over the 1955 to 1968 period is fairly well represented, especially in gasoline prices (see Figure 2-2.4, 2-2.5, and 2-2.7). Mean absolute errors, which are summarized in Table 2-3 are modest, ranging little more than 2 percent in most cases.

Forecasts: 1970–1975

A basic forecast to 1975 and alternate forecasts embodying other assumptions concerning motor fuel lead requirements and the price of crude oil have been prepared with the model.

The view of overall economic conditions embodied into these forecasts is taken from the Wharton Long Term Industry Model [9] forecast of September 1970, in which the economy reached a normal full employment growth path from 1973 to 1975. Since the macro model does not directly project many of the principal inputs into the petroleum model, many variables relating to petroleum product demands, e.g., car population, number of oil burners, etc., have been linked to the model forecasts on an *ad hoc* basis, realizing that over such a five year period relative prices, technology, and pollution controls may affect the stock of petroleum consuming equipment. Estimates of available refinery processing unit capacities are, properly speaking, only realistic assumptions based on recent trends modified by future refinery require-

Table 2-3. Percent Mean Absolute Errors, 1955–1968 Dynamic Simulation

	Mean absolute error (%)
Crude oil requirement	*0.97*
Output:	
Gasoline	1.26
Kerosene + commercial jet fuel	2.01
Distillates	1.89
Residual fuel	2.36
Lubricating oils	1.60
Asphalt	2.05
Price:	
Gasoline (tankwagon)	0.65
Gasoline (wholesale)	1.01
Kerosene	2.10
Distillate	2.39
Lubricating oils	4.69

ments. Trend assumptions have also been made for other variables.[13] Clearly, with additional refinements many of these exogenous variables could be treated as endogenous. The assumptions for the basic forecast are summarized in Appendix Table 2A-1.

The basic forecast assumes that the strict HEW proposals of summer 1970 limiting the use of lead additives are enacted.[14] To meet these regulations, it is anticipated that refiners will produce a 91 octane regular gasoline with low lead additives and a 98 octane with higher lead for use in older cars (see Appendix Table 2A-1, Product Quality Specifications). In addition it has been assumed that, in expectation of these product changes, additional refining capacity primarily in the catalytic reforming units and to a lesser extent in the hydro and catalytic cracking units would be put in service. To allow for the fact that smaller refiners will be at a special disadvantage in the production of low lead fuels, a small upward adjustment in the gasoline price has also been introduced. The price of crude oil is assumed constant through 1975.[15]

The results of the forecast are summarized in Appendix Table 2A-2. Since most of the actual values for 1970 are available, the actual values for the endogenous variables are placed in parentheses below the forecast values in Appendix Table 2A-2. The assessment of the forecasts for 1970 is satisfactory. Crude oil requirements, kerosene demand, lubricant demand, asphalt demand, and gasoline prices appear well-represented. On the other hand, substantial forecast errors appear in the demands and outputs of gasoline and particularly distillate as well as the price of distillate. The unexpected surge in distillate demand is probably due to the increased heating demand resulting from the natural gas shortage and to industrial and utility uses requiring low sulphur fuels. This growth in distillate demand further served to reduce inventory levels, driving prices upward. Furthermore, the 25¢/bbl crude oil price increase in November 1970, at the onset of the heating oil season, explains at least 6¢/bbl[16] of the discrepancy between the actual and predicted distillate price.

The exogenous assumption on military jet demand was clearly in error, not reflecting the deescalation of military activity. The error on coke output, a by-product, is due to an artificially high yield on catalytic coke from the catalytic cracking process. These results for 1970 demonstrate the need to relate the assumptions and the results of econometric models to the real world as carefully and frequently as possible.

From 1970 to 1975, annual increases of product demand are projected at 3.4 percent for gasoline, 9.3 percent for kerosene and commercial jet fuel, and 2.7 percent for distillate fuel. This expansion of demand means an increase of requirements for crude oil from 10.8 million B/D in 1970 to 13.0 million B/D in 1975. The tankwagon price of gasoline is stable near $7.33/bbl for 1970 to 1973 and then rises to $7.74/bbl by 1975. It should be noted, however, that this increase is attributable to the adjustment, 42¢ per bbl in 1975, which has been introduced to allow for difficulties smaller refiners face in remaining competitive in the face of restrictions on the use of lead additives to maintain needed octane levels. Movements of other prices are small, except for a substantial increase in the price of lubricants.

Revenues increase more sharply, $14.3 million per day to 1975, than measured costs, $7.2 million per day. This is deceiving, however, since the calculation excludes capital costs. While the impact of the changeover to low lead on operating costs is small, because any increase in operating costs of the various processes can be offset by reductions in the cost of lead additives, capital costs will increase markedly both for new process capacity and for replacement of older units not able to meet new product specifications.

For the sake of brevity, alternative simulations are not presented, but it is interesting to summarize two such alternatives.[17] The first found that petroleum product prices would be generally stable over the period if new low-lead gasoline quality requirements were not imposed. This run assumed that the price of crude oil will not change and that less refining capacity will be built. On the other hand, a simulation which assumed increases in the price of crude oil resulted in estimated product price increases approximately sufficient to offset the increase in crude oil costs. Thus, the refiner's margin is unaffected. Such a result implies that crude oil costs do represent a real cost to the refiners despite the integrated nature of most petroleum companies. Also, it would suggest that policies to alter the price of crude oil would be fully reflected in final product prices. The simulation calculations illustrate the variety of simulation experiments for which an econometric-linear programming model of an industry might be used.

Table 2A-1.   Exogenous Assumptions for 1970–1975 Forecast

Variable	1970	1971	1972	1973	1974	1975
			Economic variables			
ECAR	123.4	129.2	133.7	138.3	143.0	147.8
NIM	0.933	0.913	0.902	0.892	0.883	0.874
NAC	0.773	0.742	0.714	0.689	0.664	0.641
DDD	5333	5333	5333	5333	5333	5333
Xm	242.8	250.8	267.7	281.4	298.4	311.7
JET	2729	3002	3462	3922	4382	4841
BURN	11422	11622	11822	12022	12222	12422
$MIL(10^3)$	3704	3724	3744	3764	3784	3804
			Net imports (10^3 B/D)			
Gasoline	65	70	75	80	85	90
Kerosene	130	150	170	190	210	230
Distillate	170	200	230	260	290	320
Lubricants	–50	–50	–50	–50	–50	–50
Asphalt	20	24	28	32	36	40
			Outputs of specialty products (10^3 B/D)			
JP5	350	350	350	350	350	350
Aviation Gas	80	80	80	80	80	80
Petrochemical feedstocks	275	300	325	350	375	400
			Exogenous prices ($/bbl)			
PC	3.10	3.10	3.10	3.10	3.10	3.10
PW	117.3	119.6	121.9	125.2	128.9	133.9
Asphalt	3.82	3.82	3.82	3.82	3.82	3.82
Residual Fuel	2.50	2.25	2.00	2.00	2.00	2.00
LPG	1.72	1.72	1.72	1.72	1.72	1.72
Still gas	1.32	1.32	1.32	1.32	1.32	1.32
Coke	1.00	1.00	1.00	1.00	1.00	1.00
			Process capacities (10^3 barrels per calendar day)			
Atmospheric distillation	12496	12961	13500	14143	14713	15313
Vacuum distillation	4423	4599	4783	5038	5276	5509
Catalytic cracking	5512	5582	5730	6175	6535	6898
Catalytic reforming	2722	2914	3045	3378	3582	3785
Hydro-cracking	687	819	922	1144	1244	1555
Alkylation	729	750	778	818	852	885
Isomeri-zation	280	280	280	280	280	280

(*continued*)

Table 2A–1 continued

Variable	1970	1971	1972	1973	1974	1975
Thermal cracking	315	275	215	135	42	–
Coking	755	790	806	837	873	914
Catalytic polymeri- zation	93	93	93	93	93	93
Raw material availabilities (10^3 B/D)						
Natural gasoline	597	612	620	627	627	627
Propane	5	5	5	5	5	5
Iso butane	85	85	85	85	85	85
Normal butane	50	50	50	50	50	50
Iso pentane	10	10	10	10	10	10
Product quality specifications						
Regular research octane*	93.5	92.5	91.0	91.0	91.0	91.0
Maximum lead (gms/gal)	4.0	1.5	0.5	0.5	0.5	0.0
Percent regular sales	41	35	20	30	40	50
Premium research octane*	100	99	98	98	98	98
Maximum lead (gms/gal)	4	4	4	4	3	3
Percent premium	59	65	80	70	60	50
Competitive adjustment						
Additional impact on gasoline price (c/gal)	–	0.105	0.210	0.210	0.315	0.420

*Similar adjustments were made for road and motor octane requirements.

Table 2A-2. Forecast Simulation Results 1970-1975

Variable	1970	1971	1972	1973	1974	1975
	Domestic demands (10^3 B/D)					
Gasoline	5768 (5870)	5917	6124	6341	6582	6820
Kerosene (incl. kero jet)	992 (979)	1059	1184	1304	1430	1548
Distillate	2399 (2543)	2450	2528	2596	2675	2743
Lubricants	131 (136)	132	135	137	139	140
Asphalt	427 (420)	439	454	470	488	505
	Refinery inputs & output (10^3 B/D)					
Crude oil input	10806 (10870)	11159	11564	11997	12485	13024
Gasoline	5738 (5836)	5860	6070	6285	6524	6754
Kerosene (incl. kero jet)	867 (859)	914	1024	1124	1230	1328
Distillate	2214 (2458)	2260	2314	2351	2401	2437
Lubricants	181 (181)	182	185	187	189	190
Asphalt	407 (402)	415	426	438	452	465
Petrochemical feedstocks	275 (275)	300	325	350	375	400
Aviation gasoline	80 (54)	80	80	80	80	80
Military jet fuel	350 (250)	350	350	350	350	350
	Byproduct outputs (10^3 B/D)					
Residual fuel	699 (706)	697	763	820	866	916
Still gas	375 (449)	422	385	385	395	438
Coke	418 (296)	430	444	446	460	479
LPG	274 (345)	323	289	276	273	319

(*continued*)

Table 2A–2 continued

Variable	1970	1971	1972	1973	1974	1975
			Prices ($/bbl)			
Tankwagon gasoline	7.33 (7.39)	7.36	7.34	7.33	7.51	7.74
Wholesale gasoline	5.01 (4.99)	5.08	5.18	5.19	5.29	5.40
Kerosene	5.19 (5.06)	5.22	5.24	5.24	5.25	5.25
Distillate	4.14 (4.30)	4.09	4.09	4.07	4.06	4.06
Lubricants	11.13 (–)	11.35	11.57	11.88	12.23	12.70
JP4	4.22 (–)	4.10	4.14	4.12	4.13	4.11
JP5 (commercial jet)	4.29 (–)	4.13	4.19	4.16	4.16	4.15
			Revenue and costs (10^3 $/D)			
Revenue	63149	65464	68441	70377	73765	77414
Costs	36201	37508	39058	40336	41739	43429

NOTES

1. The assumption of crude oil supplies adjusting to refinery needs and of an exogenous crude oil price is not inconsistent with reality. In the United States, regulatory controls imposed by conservation authorities on crude oil production and by the Oil Imports Administration on crude oil imports work to meet market requirements for crude oil at the prevailing price. Price changes at discrete intervals are triggered by costs or by the long run supply and demand balance.
2. The Bureau of Mines' definition for distillate is used, which includes No. 2–4 oils plus diesel fuels; see the U.S. Bureau of Mines' "Monthly Petroleum Statement," which is also the data source for all product volumes.
3. We have not considered here the question of meeting new regulations requiring low sulfur residual fuel, nor the impact of low sulphur regulations on residual fuel prices and its future by-product status. Rather residual fuel prices are treated as exogenous, being based on world prices.
4. For a discussion of this problem, see [11] and [4].
5. For a list of the modifications to the Bonner & Moore model [3], see [6, Appendix A]. For this study the yield of the average crude oil was changed to better explain the output of residual fuel. The U.S. aver-

age crude yields for the following distillation ranges were changed as follows:

	Old	*New*
680° – 875°	0.230	0.217
875° +	0.147	0.170

6. See "Annual Refining Issue," *Oil & Gas Journal,* March 15–April 1, annually. Process capacities are specified on a stream day basis for the following processes: atmospheric distillation, vacuum distillation, catalytic cracking, thermal cracking, hydrocracking, catalytic reforming, thermal reforming, alkylation, polymerization, isomerization, visbreaking, coking.

7. An alternative approach to price determination would be to make use directly of the shadow prices implicit in the cost minimization solution of the *LP*. In fact, while the shadow prices measure product opportunity costs, their use to explain actual prices proved to be not as effective as the somewhat less rigorous formulation which was used.

8. Crude costs are not merely internal transactions. In view of state conservation commission limitations on production and Oil Imports Administration restrictions on imports, crude oil can generally be sold at market prices. Its cost must be considered as real cost even in an integrated firm.

9. For a demonstration of the rising marginal cost phenomenon, see [7].

10. The industry's average cost curve measure of capacity was derived by using the modified Bonner & Moore model to minimize the cost of various output levels of a "full employment" product mix. Capacity is the output where the short run average cost function reaches a minimum. For a further discussion and comparison with the industry's standard capacity measure, crude oil distillation capacity, see [6].

11. In the lubricating oil price equation the *Oil & Gas Journal's* lubricating oil capacity series was used, as neither the minimum unit cost output or distillation measure of capacity are relevant to lubricant manufacturing (see *Oil & Gas Journal,* "Annual Refining Edition").

12. The values for CU_{-i} for $i = 0 \ldots 3$ were estimated using an Almon polynomial distributed lag estimation approach. The polynomial lag was of second degree and was constrained to zero at Cu_{t-4}. This approach results in the estimation of only two parameters as opposed to the four if ordinary least squares are applied to Cu_{-i} for $i = 0 \ldots 3$.

13. The following prices were treated as exogenous: residual fuel oil, asphalt, still gas, coke, and *LPG*. The price of aviation gasoline was based on a 3¢/gallon premium over the tankwagon price and petro-chemical feedstocks were assumed to sell on a parity with distillate fuel oil.

14. At the time of this research, this proposal had been made in the form of a letter to the various refiners to see if they could meet specified requirements. In effect, it proposed that all gasolines below 97 research octane be limited to 0.5 gms. lead per gallon by July 1971, with complete elimination of lead in regular grades by 1975. For premium grades, the lead levels will be reduced more slowly as indi-

cated in the product quality specifications in Appendix Table 2A–1. In the meantime, new rules have been put in effect.

15. The crude oil price increase which occurred late in 1970 has not been incorporated into this calculation.

16. Since the IPA A price series is weighted both by geographic area and by volume of sales, the effect of a crude price increase in November affects more than one-sixth of the year's sales of heating oils and thus the annual average price.

17. These results are available from the authors on request.

REFERENCES

1. Adams, F.G. and Griffin, J.M., "An Econometric Model of the U.S. Petroleum Refining Industry," L.R. Klein (ed.), *Studies in Industrial Econometrics,* Vol. 1, Philadelphia: Economic Research Unit, University of Pennsylvania, 1968.

2. Almon, Shirley, "The Distributed Lag Between Capital Appropriations and Expenditures," *Econometrica* 33 (January 1965), 178–96.

3. U.S. *Motor Gasoline Economics,* Vol. 1 and 2, Houston: Bonner & Moore Associates, Washington: American Petroleum Institute, pub. 4002, 4003, 1967.

4. Dhrymes, P.J. and Mitchell, B.M. "Estimation of Joint Production Functions," *Econometrica* 37 (October 1969), 732–6.

5. Enos, John, "A Measure of the Rate of Technological Progress in the Petroleum Refining Industry," *Journal of Industrial Economics* 6 (June 1958), 180–97.

6. Griffin, J.M., *Capacity Measurement in Petroleum Refining: A Process Analysis Approach to the Joint Product Case,* Lexington, Mass.: Heath Lexington Books, 1971.

7. Griffin, J.M., "The Process Analysis Alternative to Statistical Cost Functions: An Application to Petroleum Refining," *American Economic Review* 62 (March 1972), 46–56.

8. Manne, Alan, "A Linear Programming Model of the U.S. Petroleum Refining Industry," *Econometrica* 26 (January 1958), 67–106.

9. Preston, Ross, *The Wharton Long Term and Industry Model of the U.S. Economy,* Philadelphia: Economic Research Unit, University of Pennsylvania (forthcoming).

10. Symonds, G.H., *Linear Programming–The Solution of Refinery Problems,* New York: Esso Standard Oil Co., 1955.

11. Vinod, H.D., "Econometrics of Joint Production," *Econometrica* 36 (April 1968) 322–36.

Chapter Three

An Econometric Model of the World Copper Industry

Franklin M. Fisher
Paul H. Cootner
Martin Neil Baily

INTRODUCTION

In the conventional view, governmental regulation of economic activity arises
from imperfections in industrial organization, which lead to less-than-optimal
output and a socially undesirable distribution of income. In that model, the
role of regulation is to constrain the regulated industry to behave more like its
competitive counterparts—to increase output and reduce price below the levels
that would otherwise prevail. The classical economic literature of regulation is
oriented toward techniques for most efficiently achieving this goal or toward
measuring the degree to which actual regulatory efforts are successful.

    When we compare this regulatory model with practice, we find that
there is another large fraction of governmental activity based on a quite different
model. Even within the classical "regulated industries" sector much of the
regulatory effort is designed to require a level of output distinctly different from
the competitive standard, sometimes a higher level to subsidize certain consumers, or a restricted level to subsidize certain producers or promote certain social
goals. The requirement that railroads maintain unprofitable passenger service or
that there be a subsidy of local airline service by long-distance traffic is an
example of the former. In the latter case we can mention restrictions on competition between different modes of freight transport or on the interest rates paid
on deposits by financial institutions. In these cases, the implicit subsidies and
taxes are usually justified by the existence of external economies or disecono-
mies which render the competitive equilibrium inappropriate or wasteful,
although these putative imperfections are often asserted rather than demonstrated. This lack of empirical support leaves the regulatory process open to the

    Franklin M. Fisher, Professor of Economics, Massachusetts Institute of
Technology, and Paul H. Cootner, C.O.G. Miller Professor of Finance, Stanford University,
in association with Martin Neil Baily, Assistant Professor of Economics, Massachusetts
Institute of Technology.

charge that it is really a mechanism for redistributing income rather than for ameliorating market imperfections.

Once we accept the idea that governmental regulation of an industry is often undertaken with the goal of income redistribution in mind, we need not necessarily confine ourselves to the rather restricted arena of formal "regulated industries" to see the larger picture unfold. The rather clear theoretical case for regulation of natural gas pipelines broadens naturally to previously unregulated gas production companies and in particular to the redistribution of rents in the latter industry. In the case of restriction of farm output and control of agricultural prices the "monopsony" argument has largely fallen away to reveal the key income redistribution question, particularly since corporate farming has come to the fore. In the United States most of this latter type of "regulation" involves the redistribution of income among its citizens, but in other countries much governmental intervention is obviously keyed to an attempt to redistribute wealth from foreigners to local citizens by control of price and output. This process brings us full circle to the development of cartels (this time government sponsored) such as those which in many of our regulated industries served as the original motivation for intervention. We have seen attempts at such "cartels" in petroleum, cocoa, sugar, wheat, and copper, sometimes with, but often without, the cooperation of the consumer. The scope of action for such cartels is limited not only by the tightness of their controls, but also by the basic supply and demand characteristics of an industry in the absence of a cartel.

This chapter was motivated by the interest of the Chilean government in determining the behavior of the world copper market as a prerequisite to governmental planning. Since, in Chile, the industry accounts for a large share of total national output, employment, and exports, the Chileans have use for a model of the world copper economy for purposes of long-range planning. Furthermore, Chile potentially could exercise control over its segment of the copper industry to shift the world distribution of its income in its favor.

The study itself was undertaken with no political goal in mind. It was begun while the copper industry in Chile was still nominally in private hands, the hands of the U.S. producers, and was not completed until the seizure of control had been accomplished. But the model was formulated so that any one of the major producing countries could estimate the impact of various national economic policies upon its share of copper income.

What the model does not include is the secondary impact of one country's efforts to control its national output upon the national policies of other producing countries. Obviously, these secondary impacts will depend in part upon the primary result of the policies and the character of any agreements among the producing countries.

THE GENERAL FORM OF THE MODEL

This study presents an econometric model of the world copper industry, relatively disaggregated to incorporate different supply equations for each of the major producing countries and different demand equations for each of the principal consuming areas. Largely for reasons of data, the model is an annual one and there is no breakdown into types of copper use. Attention in the constructon and use of the model centers on the geographic differences in the industry and on the two-price system generally prevailing, wherein much of the copper in the United States moves at the U.S. producer price and most other copper moves at the London Metal Exchange (LME) price (which, in recent years, has often been well above the U.S. producer price). A general simplified outline of the structure of the model is as follows.

We begin with the U.S. market. the U.S. producers set the U.S. producer price to reflect what they believe to be a sustainable (and profitable) long-run level of copper prices, taking into account their own resulting supply decisions. Believing it in their interest to have a relatively stable price, they then take that price as given for the time being and decide on the amount of copper they will supply at that price. Other countries selling at the U.S. producer price do the same. This determines the supply of primary copper in the United States (except for imports).

Consumers of copper, on the other hand, take price as given. Some of those consumers will be able to buy at the U.S. producer price; some of them will not. The latter consumers can import copper at the LME price or can purchase scrap. Total demand for copper is also strongly influenced by indicators of general industrial activity and by the free market price of aluminum, the principal substitute.

The supply of secondary copper in the United States depends in the model on the total amount of primary copper produced in the past, on the ease with which that copper can be gathered as scrap, and on the scrap price, which is very highly correlated with the LME price, as one would expect.[1] The ease of collection is assumed to be measured by the relative amount of previously produced copper collected in the previous year, being low when that was high and when a great deal of the readily available copper has already been collected.

The difference between U.S. total copper consumption and U.S. available supplies (primary, secondary, and imports) is the change in U.S. inventories. If inventories tend to increase for some period of time and the LME price is below the U.S. producer's price, then producers gradually conclude that they set too high a price and the proper *long-run* price is below the U.S. producer price. On the other hand, if inventories are being depleted over some period of time and the LME price is well above the U.S. producer price, then the producers gradually conclude that the proper *long-run* price is above the U.S. producer price. They then readjust the U.S. producer price in the indicated direction and the process begins again.

The model for the rest of the world operates in a similar fashion except that the LME price to which it responds is a free market price most of the time. Given expectations about the LME price, producers selling at that price make output decisions and consumers buying at that price make consumption decisions (which are, of course, influenced by other variables as well). Scrap supply depends on factors similar to those operating in the United States. Given the total supply of primary from producing countries, total supply of secondary, and net exports to the U.S., the total supply of copper available for consumption outside the U.S. is determined. The difference between this and total copper actually consumed gives the additions to inventories. The LME price responds to the size of inventories relative to total use of copper.

The two markets are linked in three ways. First, as already stated, the U.S. scrap price is highly correlated with the LME price, as both markets are generally free. Second, there is some flow of copper between the United States and the rest of the world. Finally, producers consider a large difference between the LME and the U.S. producer price as a signal that the U.S. market is probably out of long-run equilibrium and that the U.S. producer price should be adjusted.

HOW AND WHY DOES THE TWO-MARKET SYSTEM WORK?

The two-market system described above obviously requires further discussion. In particular, when the U.S. producer price is substantially below the LME price, as has often been the case in recent years, what keeps arbitrage from reducing the LME price and depleting U.S. stocks?[2] Further, why do the U.S. producers consider it in their interest to maintain such a situation?

Part of the answer to the first question is that there do exist forces tending to bring the two prices closer together, although these forces are neither fast acting nor strong. When the LME price is above the U.S. price for an extended period because demand is high, U.S. stocks do get drawn down and the producer price, adjusted upward. Nevertheless, a high degree of arbitrage does not take place, presumably because in such a situation, when U.S. producers ration their sales, favored customers are unwilling to jeopardize their long-run relations with the producers for the sake of the short-run gains from arbitrage. Presumably, producers can fairly readily discover if a large customer is reselling on the LME.

The question remains, however, as to why it is in the interests of the producers to act in this way rather than to adjust the price upward immediately to the market-clearing level and to reap the short-run returns from selling to more customers at higher prices. The basic answer seems to lie in the lag structure of behavior on both sides of the copper market. It will be a repeated theme of this study and is well borne out in the results below that speeds of adjustment in the copper industry are very low. On the supply side this comes from the length of time necessary to bring new mines into production and the high investment in the working of existing mines. On the demand side it occurs, at least in part, because of the length of time required to readapt some copper-using equipment to aluminum. Such long lags mean that the price elasticities of demand and supply are both substantially higher in the long than in the short run, and, as we shall see, supply elasticity, in particular, is quite small in the short run and rather substantial in the long run. This leads to a fairly unstable situation in the short run where a small increase in the exogenous factors affecting demand can easily raise short-run market-clearing prices very considerably, even though the price which equilibrates long-run supply and long-run demand may not be much affected.

In this situation, the major U.S. producers may hesitate to raise price to reap short-run rewards for fear of doing two things. First, a large rise might encourage customers who can use aluminum to invest in aluminum-using machinery. Both the experience gained with that machinery and the time required to change back to copper would mean that, when prices fell, such customers would not switch back again for a long time. Indeed, it is not hard to see that, given the fact that the changeover is costly, copper producers may gain more by keeping prices to such customers just below the point at which the changeover to aluminum becomes profitable than they would by going above that point and later trying to regain those customers as price fell toward its long-run equilibrium: the regaining of those customers would require a fall in price not merely to its original level but to a level low enough to compensate for the cost of switching back to copper. Since an inability to obtain copper would also provide an incentive to switch to aluminum, this argument suggests that the producers operate by rationing only those customers who cannot switch or for whom the cost of switching is low. This further suggests that manufacturers of wire are generally able to purchase at the U.S. producer price, but it is difficult to obtain direct evidence on this point.[3]

A second reason for not raising the U.S. producer price to the short-run market-clearing level may be that such a rise would be taken by other, possibly new, producers as a signal that the long-run price was rising. This would begin to bring new mines into production and, given that the lags are so long, the resulting effects on supply would not disappear when the circumstances substantially raising the short-run market-clearing price ceased to operate. In this situation, the producers may prefer to forego the possible short-run profits rather than encourage new production which will appear on the market when the situation has changed.

Obviously, this second argument assumes that the short-run nature of the given situation is seen differently by the U.S. producers and the operators of potential new mines. However, once having established a system whereby the U.S. producer price is an index of what the U.S. producers believe to be a sustainable long-run price, those producers may hesitate to change it because a new, higher U.S. producer price may be taken to signal a high long-run price and may be acted on as such.

These considerations are difficult to support with hard evidence, although the producers are explicitly disturbed about irreversible substitution effects. They at least make plausible a situation whose existence must be recognized in any adequate model of the copper industry.

DISTRIBUTED LAGS AND ESTIMATION METHODS

Since, as stated, many of the crucial reactions in the copper industry take a good deal of time, we have formulated the corresponding equations of the model in terms of distributed lags, with the dependent variable being influenced by past as well as present independent variables. The simplest and best-known formulation of distributed lags, and the one we have employed, is the Koyck or geometric lag,[4] which can also be formulated as a stock adjustment model along the following lines.

We take as an example the supply curve of mine-produced copper in some country. Denote the amount of copper supplied in year t by S_t and the price received by the producers in question by P_t. Given the price, the producers would like to supply an amount S_t^*, which depends on P_t according to the long-run supply equation

$$S_t^* = \alpha + \beta P_t,\tag{3-1}$$

for example. However, since it takes time to adjust supply, the producers do not immediately move to a new value for S_t^* in response to a new value for price, but only begin to move in that direction. If we assume that it is only possible to move some fixed fraction, μ, of the desired distance in any year, then

$$S_t - S_{t-1} = \mu(S_t^* - S_{t-1}), \quad 0 < \mu < 1.\tag{3-2}$$

Substituting (3-1) into (3-2) and rearranging terms:

$$S_t = \mu\alpha + \mu\beta P_t + (1 - \mu)S_{t-1}.\tag{3-3}$$

Lag (3-3) and obtain an expression for S_{t-1}, then lag it again and obtain one for S_{t-2}, and so forth. Repeated substitution of the lagged versions into (3-3) yields

$$S_t = \alpha + \mu\beta \sum_{\theta=0}^{\infty} \lambda^\theta P_{t-\theta}, \quad \lambda = 1 - \mu,\tag{3-4}$$

so that supply in year t depends on present and past prices with the weights given to lagged prices declining geometrically with the length of the lag. In this model, the short-run effect of price on supply is given by $\mu\beta$, but the long-run effect is given by β itself. If μ is relatively small, so that adjustments take place fairly slowly, then the long-run effect can be much larger than the short-run effect. We would expect this in the case of copper supply.

There is another model which leads to the form (3-4) and its equivalent (3-3) (other than postulating (3-4) directly). This is to suppose that adjustment can in fact be completely made but that supply depends upon *expected* price, with expectations being formed in an adaptive way, as follows. Suppose that the supply curve is given by

$$S_t = \alpha + \beta P_t^*, \tag{3-5}$$

where P_t^* denotes expected long-run price. Suppose further that price expectations are formed by revising earlier expectations in the direction of actual prices, according to the relation

$$P_t^* - P_{t-1}^* = \mu(P_t - P_{t-1}^*), \quad 0 < \mu < 1. \tag{3-6}$$

Here μ is no longer the speed of adjustment of supply, but rather the speed of adjustment of price expectations. Equation (3-6) is equivalent to

$$P_t^* = \mu P_t + (1 - \mu)P_{t-1}^*, \tag{3-7}$$

so that expected price this year is a weighted average of expected price last year and actual price. Repeated lagging of (3-7) and substitution of lagged values of P_t^* yields

$$P_t^* = \mu \sum_{\theta=0}^{\infty} \lambda^\theta P_{t-\theta}, \quad \lambda = 1 - \mu, \tag{3-8}$$

so that expected price is also a weighted sum of present and lagged prices, with the weights declining geometrically with the length of the lag. Substitution of (3-8) into (3-5) now yields (3-4).

Despite the fact that the two models are equivalent as regards the final supply equation, the stock-adjustment version makes much more sense than the adaptive expectations version for relations in the copper industry. It is perfectly clear that adjustments do take a considerable time; moreover, price expectations are not likely to be formed in the way described by (3-6) to (3-8), since, especially in the U.S. market, participants are likely to take current price as a much better index of relatively long-run price than a weighted average of past prices, with λ much different from zero. Our interpretation will run in terms of the stock-adjustment model, therefore, and we have made no attempt to incorporate simultaneously the adaptive expectations feature.

Estimation of the stock-adjustment model requires some care. The easiest form in which to estimate it is (3-3), but merely estimating this by ordinary least squares (aside from the fact that P_t is an endogenous variable) will lead to inconsistency if the error term is autocorrelated. Such autocorrelation is quite likely in such models. It is not possible to treat satisfactorily a very general model of autocorrelation, and we have settled for a model in which the error term in question is first-order autocorrelated, an assumption which probably comes as close to the truth as any which the data will support. Thus, denoting the error term in (3-3) by u_t, and assuming it enters additively, we assume

$$u_t = \rho u_{t-1} + e_t, \tag{3-9}$$

where e_t is assumed to have expectation zero and variance-covariance matrix $\sigma^2 I$, thus not itself being autocorrelated. For cases (not the supply equations) in which the right-hand side variables of such equations are predetermined (being either exogenous to the model or lagged endogenous variables), we proceed by choosing estimates of ρ and the other parameters to minimize the sum of squares e_t. This is a consistent estimator and, if e_t is normally distributed, it is also maximum likelihood. On the normality assumption, asymptotic standard errors can be computed.[5]

When (as in the supply equations) one or more of the righthand side variables are endogenous, an adaptation of the same technique, due to Fair, is used.[6] This is an instrumental variables technique which takes care of simultaneous equations bias as well as autocorrelation of the sort (3-9). It requires that among the instruments be the current and once lagged values of all predetermined variables in the equation and the lagged values of all endogenous variables in the equation. In the results below, we indicate the instrumental variables used in estimating each equation.

Before closing this section, we may remark that the autocorrelation assumption (3-9) is restrictive, not merely because it is first-order, but also because it is assumed that, given u_{t-1}, u_t is not correlated with the *past* values of disturbances from other equations in the model. This is far better than assuming it is uncorrelated with the *current* values of such disturbances, but it is still a strong assumption. More general assumptions are very difficult to handle, however.

Estimation of the supply equations for scrap copper presents certain special difficulties, since those equations, as will be seen below, are nonlinear in the parameters. We shall discuss the methods used in the section on the scrap supply equations.

SUPPLY OF PRIMARY COPPER

In this section, we report the results for estimation of supply curves for primary copper (mine production). Separate supply curves were estimated for the United States, Chile, Zambia, Canada, and the Rest-of-World. The relative importance of the various suppliers can be seen from the figures for 1963, Table 3-1.[7]

The principal suppliers for which separate supply curves were not estimated are Peru, Republic of Congo, and Japan. Data problems prevented such

Table 3-1. Mine Production of Copper, 1963 (Thousands of Metric Tons)

United States	1100.6
Chile	601.1
Zambia	588.1
Canada	410.6
Rest-of-world*	1174.4
Total*	3874.8

*Excludes Eastern-bloc countries.

estimation for the Congo; Japanese production did not seem large enough to warrant a separate effort; and an attempt to estimate a separate equation for Peru failed.

A supply curve for Chile was estimated. Since part of the purpose of the model is to examine the likely effects of alternative Chilean policies, that supply curve is used only for purposes of comparison. Forecasts will be made which examine the effects of departures from the supply relationship which has obtained in the past.

For the United States, the price of copper used in the supply equation was the *Engineering and Mining Journal* (EMJ)[8] price deflated by the U.S. wholesale price index. The EMJ price is a weighted average of the U.S. producer price and the LME price, with the U.S. producer price getting more than 97.5 percent of the weight (this equation is reported in the section on prices). It apparently reflects the prices at which copper is actually traded in the United States a bit more accurately than does the U.S. producer price. Nevertheless, according to the description of the model given in the opening section, it ought to be the U.S. producer price itself which enters the supply relation. Experimentation shows that the results obtained using the EMJ price are uniformly better and more reasonable than those obtained using the U.S. producer price directly, and we have proceeded on that basis. This phenomenon can be rationalized by observing that when the EMJ and U.S. producer prices get substantially out of line, the chances are good that the latter price will be revised so that the EMJ price may capture long-run expectations a bit better than does its principal component.

Denoting U.S. mine production (thousands of metric tons) by USMP and the EMJ price (cents per pound) divided by the U.S. wholesale price index (1957 - 1959 = 1.00) by USP_{EMJ}, the estimated U.S. supply equation is[9]

$$USMP_t = -160.04 + 14.27 \ USP_{EMJt} + 0.7261 \ USMP_{t-1}$$

$$(4.769) \qquad (0.2043)$$
$$(2.996) \qquad (3.554) \qquad\qquad (3\text{-}10)$$

$\rho = 0.5$ Years: 1949–1958, 1962–1966.

In this, as in all later equations (except where noted), the figures in the first line of parentheses are the asymptotic standard errors of the corresponding estimated coefficients; the figures in the second line of parentheses are the ratios of the estimated coefficients to their asymptotic standard errors. Small sample significance tests are not known for such estimates, but a good rule of thumb is that a coefficient at least twice its asymptotic standard error indicates a statistically significant relationship.

The figure denoted as ρ is the estimated first-order autocorrelation coefficient of the disturbance in the equation; see Equation (3–9), above. The final estimates are obtained by searching over alternate values of ρ ranging from –1.0 to +1.0 by steps of 0.1 and choosing those results (for all parameters) for which the sum of squares being minimized is least.

As indicated, the years 1959–1961 and 1967–1968 have been omitted (our data run through 1968 in other equations). This has been done to eliminate the effect of major copper strikes in the U.S. in 1959 and 1967–1968.[10]

The slow speed of adjustment in U.S. copper supply is indicated by the coefficient of lagged mine production. Only a little more than a quarter (1.00–0.73) of the gap between desired production and actual production is closed each year. This is naturally reflected in a fairly large difference between short- and long-run supply elasticities. At the point of means for the period, the short-run price elasticity of supply is approximately 0.453, while the long-run elasticity is approximately 1.67. U.S. adjustment speed, however, while slow, appears faster than the adjustment speed of some of the other producing countries. We now turn to the results for those other countries.

There is some difficulty in deciding on the appropriate price variable to use in the Chilean supply curve because of the effect of the special exchange rates which have been used to tax the copper producers and because of the Chilean inflation. Fortunately, Mamalakis and Reynolds[11] calculate a series for the price received by the producers and, while this only goes through 1959, it has been brought up-to-date by Vittorio Corbo Lioi, who kindly made it available to us. We denote that price (the money price is taken as 1.00 in 1965 and deflated by the Chilean wholesale price index, which is 1.00 in 1958) by ChP. Denoting Chilean mine production (thousands of metric tons) by ChMP, the results are as follows:

$$\text{ChMP}_t = 91.37 + 415.4 \ \text{ChP}_t + 0.7206 \ \text{ChMP}_{t-1}$$
$$\qquad\qquad (164.9) \qquad (0.1309)$$
$$\qquad\qquad (2.520) \qquad (5.505) \qquad\qquad\qquad\qquad (3\text{–}11)$$

$\rho = -0.1$ Years: 1948–1968.

The speed of adjustment is just about the same as in the United States. At the point of means for the period, the short-run elasticity of supply is approximately 0.112, rather less than for the United States. Long-run elasticity, moreover, is approximately 0.402, considerably less than the comparable U.S. figure. Chilean mine production does not appear to have been very price sensitive.[12]

For Canada, we used the EMJ price converted to Canadian dollars and deflated by the Canadian wholesale price index (1958 = 1.00) as the price variable.[13] Denoting this by $CanP_{EMJ}$ and denoting Canadian mine production (thousands of metric tons) by CanMP, the results are:

$$CanMP = -43.73 + 2.129\ CanP_{EMJt} + 0.9873\ CanMP_{t-1}$$
$$(0.8738)\phantom{CanP_{EMJt} +}(0.03932)$$
$$(2.437)\phantom{CanP_{EMJt} + }(25.11)\phantom{+ 0.9873\ CanMP_{t-1}xxx}(3\text{-}12)$$

$\rho = -0.4$ Years: 1948–1967.

Clearly, the speed of adjustment is extremely low, far lower than for the United States or Chile. Less than 2 percent of desired adjustments take place in any one year. At the point of means for the period, the short-run elasticity of Canadian supply is approximately 0.188 and the long-run elasticity is far greater, being estimated at 14.84, although the exact figure is not very reliable.

The situation is similar for the estimated supply curve for Zambia. Here we used the LME price (pounds sterling per long ton) deflated by an index of the cost of living for Europeans in Zambia (1958 = 1.00).[14] Denoting this price by ZP_{LME} and Zambian mine production (thousands of metric tons) by ZMP, the results are:

$$ZMP_t = -69.19 + 0.1269\ ZP_{LMEt} + 1.103\ ZMP_{t-1}$$
$$(0.4446)\phantom{ZP_{LMEt} + }(0.3138)$$
$$(0.2832)\phantom{ZP_{LMEt} + }(3.547)\phantom{+ 1.103\ ZMP_{t-1}xxx}(3\text{-}13)$$

$\rho = -0.3$ Years: 1955–1957, 1961–1965.

The poorer quality of these results compared to the others doubtless reflects the poor data and the number of observations that had to be dropped because of strikes and political troubles. At the point of means, the short-run price elasticity of Zambian supply is approximately 0.0684, while the long-run elasticity is *far* greater. Indeed, as estimated, the effects of past prices never die out, although the coefficient of lagged mine production is not significantly above unity;[15] but the speed of adjustment is obviously extremely slow, although *ultimately* the Zambian supply curve is nearly flat. The very high long-run elasticities ought to be expected where new mines are developing and old ones far from exhausted.

The remaining supply curve estimated was for the Rest-of-World. The price variable used was the LME price expressed in dollars per long ton deflated

by the U.S. wholesale price index (1957 - 1959 = 1.00).[16] Denoting this by
USP_{LME} and Rest-of-World mine production (thousands of metric tons) by
RWMP, the results are

$$RWMP_t = -28.44 + 0.2222 \, USP_{LMEt} + 0.8832 \, RWMP_{t-1}$$
$$ (0.09561) \qquad (0.09601)$$
$$ (2.324) \qquad\quad (9.199) \hspace{4cm} (3\text{-}14)$$

$\rho = 0.5$ Years: 1948–1968.

The speed of adjustment here is still low, but it is higher than in Zambian and
Canadian results. At the point of means for the period, the short-run elasticity of
Rest-of-World supply is approximately 0.1963 and the long-run elasticity is
approximately 1.680.

This completes the results for primary supply. In the estimation of
the equations in this section, the instrumental variables used in addition to those
required for the Fair method (see the preceding section) were as follows: the
lagged ratio of non-U.S. stocks of copper to non-U.S. total use of copper (this
appears in the price equations below); the lagged value of whichever of the LME
and EMJ price did not appear in the particular equation being estimated; the
lagged value of separately accounted for Western Hemisphere total mine production, taken as moving primarily at the EMJ price (United States, Chile, and
Canada); and the lagged value of the remaining mine production, taken as
moving primarily at the LME price (Zambia and Rest-of-World).[17] In the case of
Chile, both the lagged LME and the lagged EMJ price were used as were the two
ratios of the Chilean price (ChP) to the other two prices, since those ratios presumably reflect exogenous governmental actions in Chile.[18]

SECONDARY SUPPLY

We now consider the supply of copper from scrap. Here we divide the world
into the United States and the Rest-of-World. The breakdown available in the
data is somewhat different for the two regions. Some idea of the order of magnitudes involved may be gained from Table 3–2, which reports figures for 1963.

**Table 3–2.   Secondary Supply of Copper, 1963 (Thousands of
Metric Tons)**

U.S. old scrap collection	382.7
U.S. new scrap	629.3
Rest-of-world total scrap*	1328.9
Total*	2340.9

*Excludes Eastern-bloc countries.

Old scrap is scrap created by the destruction of old fabricated products; new scrap, on the other hand, is scrap created in the fabricating process itself. It is either returned to the refiner or used again by the fabricator. While it is clear that both types of scrap are part of secondary supply, it is not quite so clear whether new scrap should also be included in the variable representing the demand for copper or whether it should be subtracted. While it is possible to argue on both sides of that question, the results for the demand equations (reported in the next section) are far better when direct use of scrap is included in demand, so *all consumption figures in this study include such scrap.*[19]

Obviously, the two different ways in which scrap is generated suggest two different models, and for the United States, the data permit their construction. We begin with the more complex case of old scrap.

The prime determinants of old scrap collections in our model are (1) the amount of copper available for collection in the broadest sense, (2) the ease with which that copper can be collected, and (3) the price paid for it.

In the broadest sense, the amount of copper available for old scrap collection in the United States is the total amount of copper embodied in already produced copper products. The change in the available scrap supply during year t is given by the identity:

Change in available scrap supply = primary production
+ net imports of refined copper
+ net imports of fabricated copper
- increases in stocks of copper. (3-15)

If we knew the amount of copper available for collection in any given base year, then the amount available in any other year could be calculated from (3-15). We do not have such a benchmark figure, however, and, as a result, we have estimated that figure as a parameter in our old scrap equation. Thus letting K_t be the copper available at the beginning of year t, we write

$$K_t \equiv K_{1948} + K_t^*, \qquad (3-16)$$

where K_t^* is obtained by cumulating (3-15) from the beginning of 1948 and K_{1948} is to be treated as a parameter (all figures below are in thousands of metric tons).[20]

It is only in the broadest sense, of course, that all copper in the United States is available for collection. In part, we account for this in our model by explaining what fraction of K_t is in fact collected. It must be recognized, however, that K_{1948} does not represent the cumulation of (3-15) from time immemorial, but rather represents the amount of copper in a narrower sense available for scrap collection at the beginning of 1948. This narrower sense applies, of course, to copper produced or imported since 1948, so that K_t^* also is broader than is strictly appropriate. Fortunately, it is easy to see that the fact that not all produced or imported copper is really available for collection matters very little to our model or results.

Denote United States old scrap collections (thousands of metric tons) in year t by $USOS_t$.[21] The dependent variable in our equation below (its lagged value will also appear) will be $\log(USOS_t/K_t)$. Now suppose that instead of K_t being available, some constant fraction of K_t, say δ, is available. Then the true dependent variable should be $\log(USOS_t/\delta K_t) = \log(USOS_t/K_t) - \log \delta$. Hence the only effect of the difference between using K_t and δK_t is to place a term in $\log \delta$ in the constant term of our results.

Obviously, this argument makes it convenient to use a logarithmic model here; moreover, it is natural to do so, since it is natural to think in terms of explaining the fraction of available scrap which is actually collected.

As a proxy for a measure of the difficulty of collection, we use the fraction of available scrap that was collected as such in the preceding year. This is not a very direct measure of difficulty, but it makes sense if we think of available copper as in forms and locations of differing ease of collection. One expects the copper easiest to collect to be collected first; hence if a relatively large amount of the available copper was collected last year, copper is likely to be relatively hard to collect this year. Accordingly (and quite unusually) we should expect the coefficient of the lagged dependent variable to be *negative.*

There is a separate scrap price in the United States, but it is very highly correlated with the LME price, as one would expect, since both are free market prices.[22] We found that it made little difference to the results which price was used, and, accordingly, we simplified the model slightly by using the LME price expressed in dollars per long ton and deflated by the U.S. wholesale price index (1957 – 1959 = 1.00). We denote that price by USP_{LME}.

Unfortunately, the estimation of the old scrap supply equation runs into a minor but rather annoying difficulty. The equation is not linear in K_{1948}. Accordingly, we proceeded by choosing alternate values for K_{1948} and then estimating the resulting equation, intending to choose the version in which the final sum of squares was minimized.[23] As it turns out, however, the results are quite insensitive to the value of K_{1948} chosen, suggesting that any estimate thereof will have a very large asymptotic standard error. (The asymptotic standard errors reported below are all conditional on the values of K_{1948} chosen.) This would not be surprising—although it does not occur in the results for the Rest-of-World, reported below—since it indicates that scrap collections are not very dependent on copper produced before 1948; however, the sum of squares to be minimized continues to decline slowly as a function of K_{1948} until that parameter is well beyond any reasonable value.

Fortunately, this makes essentially no difference to our estimate of the price sensitivity of old scrap supply, our estimate of the effect of former collections, or our implied forecast of old scrap collections. We therefore present results for high and for low values of K_{1948} as well as for a value chosen to bear roughly the same relation to U.S. consumption as the similarly estimated figure for the Rest-of-World (below) bears to Rest-of-World consumption. That value of K_{1948} is 60,000 thousand metric tons. When it is used, we obtain

$$\log \left(\frac{USOS_t}{60,000 + K_t^*} \right) = -9.878 - 0.3731 \log \left(\frac{USOS_{t-1}}{60,000 + K_{t-1}^*} \right) \qquad (3\text{-}17)$$
$$(0.1261)$$
$$(-2.960)$$

$$+ 0.4222 \log USP_{LMEt}$$
$$(0.1064)$$
$$(3.968)$$

$\rho = 0.9$ Years: 1950–1968
Sum of Squared Residuals = 0.08338.

By way of comparison, if we use alternate estimates of K_{1948} of 20,000 and 140,000 metric tons, we obtain, respectively,[24]

$$\log \left(\frac{USOS_t}{20,000 + K_t^*} \right) = -9.093 - 0.3761 \log \left(\frac{USOS_{t-1}}{20,000 + K_{t-1}^*} \right) \qquad (3\text{-}18)$$

$$+ 0.4371 \log USP_{LMEt}$$

$\rho = 0.9$ Sum of Squared Residuals = 0.08755

and

$$\log \left(\frac{USOS_t}{140,000 + K_t^*} \right) = -10.88 - 0.3822 \log \left(\frac{USOS_{t-1}}{140,000 + K_{t-1}^*} \right)$$
$$+ 0.4417 \log USP_{LMEt} \qquad (3\text{-}19)$$

$\rho = 0.7$ Sum of Squared Residuals = 0.07208.

In all these equations, the short-run elasticity of old scrap supply with respect to the LME sprice is about +0.42 to +0.44. The implied long-run elasticity is lower because high scrap collections in one period mean lower ones in the next period (other things equal), being about +0.31 to +0.32. The different choices for K_{1948} affect only the second decimal place, and that only in a very minor way.

Our model for new scrap is much simpler; we estimated it as a linear function of total consumption. Denoting U.S. new scrap collections by USNS[25] and total consumption (total use) by USC (both in thousands of metric tons), the estimated equation is[26]

$$\text{USNS}_t = -275.2 + 0.3961 \text{ USC}_t$$
$$(0.0524)$$
$$(7.555) \tag{3-20}$$

$\rho = 0.2$ Years: 1947–1968.

We could find no evidence of a significant price effect here. The elasticity with respect to USC is 1.48 at the point of means.

Outside the United States, the data do not permit a breakdown into old and new scrap and we estimated a single equation for total scrap supply. This was necessarily a hybrid of the two types estimated for the United States. Denoting Rest-of-World secondary supply by RWS and Rest-of-World total consumption by RWC* (both in thousands of metric tons), the results are as follows:[27]

$$\log\left(\frac{\text{RWS}_t}{53,000 + K_t^*}\right) = -5.241 - 0.6278 \log\left(\frac{\text{RWS}_{t-1}}{53,000 + K_{t-1}^*}\right)$$
$$(0.4729)$$
$$(-1.328)$$

$$+ 0.2546 \log \text{USP}_{\text{LME}t} + 0.9534 \log\left(\frac{\text{RWC}_t^*}{53,000 + K_t^*}\right) \tag{3-21}$$
$$(0.09879) \qquad\qquad (0.3204)$$
$$(2.557) \qquad\qquad (2.978)$$

$\rho = 0.2$ Years: 1952–1968.

Short-run price elasticity is about +0.25 and short-run elasticity with respect to total copper consumption about +0.95. The corresponding long-run figures are about +0.16 and +0.52. In comparing these to the U.S. figures (recalling the hybrid nature of the equation), it is clear that they are not very different.

DEMAND

We come now to the estimation of demand equations for copper.[28] Separate demand equations were estimated for the United States, Europe, Japan, and the Rest-of-World. Attempts to estimate separate equations for individual European countries resulted in unsatisfactory demand equations, although the results for Europe as a whole were reasonably satisfactory. Why this should be true is hard to say. Aside from purely statistical reasons, such as the possibility that the disturbances in the demand equations in two neighboring countries may be negatively correlated, a partial explanation may lie in either of two facts. First, individual European countries may differ in the skill with which they manage to buy on the LME. If the success of their buying agents varies over time, the use of an annual LME figure may be better for Europe as a whole than for individual countries. Second, we have treated industrial production as a single aggregate. If intra-European exports have a different copper-using component than European industrial production generally, then an aggregate relation in which such exports are netted out may do better than individual ones. Neither of these explanations seems wholly adequate, however.[29]

The relative importance of the various areas in copper consumption is shown by the figures for 1963 in Table 3-3. We begin with the United States, for which data are best. It is clear that the principal elements of a copper demand equation must be the price of copper, the price of substitutes, and measures of industrial activity. For the first, we used USP_{EMJ}, the EMJ price deflated by the U.S. wholesale price index. The remaining variables require some discussion, however.

The principal substitute for copper is, of course, aluminum. The obvious choice for a price to use is the deflated U.S. price of aluminum (deflation takes care of more general substitutes for copper). When this was attempted, the attempt failed, but it failed in an informative way. Without the inclusion of any aluminum price, a reasonably satisfactory looking demand equation was obtained. When the U.S. aluminum price was included, however, not only did its coefficient fail to be positive (as should be the case for a substitute), but it was significantly negative and the whole equation changed radically. One cannot properly conclude from this merely that aluminum substitution fails to show up in the U.S. demand equation for copper; it does show up in a way which makes no economic sense but which cannot be ignored.

Fortunately, the reason for this is fairly easy to find. The U.S. producer price of aluminum is an administered price which, like the producer price of copper, is changed only infrequently. Unlike the copper price, however, the aluminum price is often an unrealistic quotation which is either widely discounted or produces severe rationing on other occasions.[30] A reasonably satisfactory way

Table 3-3. Total Use of Copper, 1963 (Thousands of Metric Tons)

United States	2320.4
Europe	2631.8
Japan	592.1
Rest-of-world*	526.0
Total*	6070.3

*Excludes Eastern-bloc countries.

to take account of this artificial, administered price is to use a free market aluminum price as an index of the real cost of obtaining aluminum. Since the London price was also controlled for part of the period, the most readily available price is the German price of aluminum in deutsche mark per metric ton and we used this converted to dollars and deflated by the U.S. wholesale price index (1957 - 1959 = 1.00). It is denoted by USA1P, but the initials represent the deflator and not the source of the money price.[31]

Since even a short-run adjustment to prices is likely to be delayed, we used both copper and aluminum prices lagged by one year, so that demand depends on last year's (and previous years') prices.

There is more than one possible choice for an index of copper-using industrial activity. The two most obvious are the Federal Reserve Board index of industrial production and index of construction materials.[32] Ideally, one would want to use both, but they are so correlated that no sensible result is obtained when both are included. We present results below using each. The index of industrial production (1963 = 100) is denoted by USIP and the index of construction materials (1957 - 1959 = 100) by USCM.

One more matter needs to be discussed before proceeding to the results. A demand equation should not include changes in inventories of copper. Changes in inventories of copper *held as such* are not included in the consumption data; they are treated separately below. There is another way in which copper inventories can be held, however; that is in the form of fabricated products. Unfortunately, there are no data on the inventories of copper fabricated products. There are data, however, on inventories of durable goods. If we assume that the change in the copper content of such inventories is reasonably linearly related to the total change in the inventories themselves, then that total change should be included in the demand equation. We denote it as ΔUSID. (It is measured in billions of dollars deflated by U.S. wholesale price index, 1957 - 1959 = 1.00.)

This argument has an important further and testable consequence. We are using a Koyck distributed lag in copper demand, as described above, and already used for supply. The logic of the adjustment model leading to that lag suggests that the appropriate lagged variable to use is not lagged copper consumption as measured, but lagged copper consumption corrected for the (lagged) change in durable inventories. This, however, leads to the following.

The basic assumption on which we include the change in inventories in the equation is that the change in copper inventories held as finished goods is linearly related to the total change in inventories; that is, that the change in such copper inventories in year t is well approximated by a term $(\alpha + \beta\Delta USID_t)$. Denoting U.S. copper consumption in year t as measured (thousands of metric tons) by USC_t,[33] the stock adjustment model implies that instead of having USC_t on the left and λUSC_t on the right (where $\mu = 1 - \lambda$ is the speed of adjustment, we should have $(USC_t - \alpha - \beta\Delta USID_t)$ on the left and $\lambda(USC_{t-1} - \alpha$

$- \beta \Delta USID_{t-1}$) on the right; so that (letting γX_t stand symbolically for all the other variables already discussed) the full demand equation reads

$$USC_t - \alpha - \beta \Delta USID_t = \delta + \gamma X_t + \lambda(USC_{t-1} - \alpha - \beta \Delta USID_{t-1}), \qquad (3\text{-}22)$$

where δ is a parameter. Rearranging this, we obtain

$$USC_t = (\delta + \alpha - \lambda\alpha) + \gamma X_t + \beta \Delta USID_t - \lambda\beta \Delta USID_{t-1} + \lambda USC_{t-1}, \qquad (3\text{-}23)$$

so that not only should $\Delta USID_{t-1}$ be included, but its coefficient should turn out to be minus the product of the coefficients of $\Delta USID_t$ and USC_{t-1}. It would, of course, be possible (although slightly cumbersome) to impose this constraint in estimating the equation, but it is far preferable not to impose it and see whether it is approximately satisfied in the results. If it is, we have gained a check on a joint implication of the adjustment model assumed and on the argument as to inventories of copper held in finished form. In this event, the constraint is indeed approximately satisfied, thus reinforcing our faith in the assumptions made.

We are now ready for the results. When the index of construction materials is used, the estimated demand equation is[34]

$$USC_t = -194.7 - 15.26\ USP_{EMJt-1} + 9.721\ USA1P_{t-1}$$
$$ (1.903) \qquad\quad (4.794)$$
$$ (-8.020) \qquad\quad (2.028)$$

$$+\ 7.029\ USCM_t + 54.11\ \Delta USID_t$$
$$\quad (1.265) \qquad\quad (5.904)$$
$$\quad (5.557) \qquad\quad (9.166)$$

$$-\ 39.97\ \Delta USID_{t-1} + 0.7363\ USC_{t-1}$$
$$\quad (7.667) \qquad\qquad (0.1218)$$
$$\quad (-5.213) \qquad\qquad (6.046) \qquad\qquad\qquad (3\text{-}24)$$

$R^2 = 0.991 \quad \rho = -0.8 \quad$ Years: 1950-58, 1962-1966.

When the index of industrial production is used, the results are similar:

$$USC_t = -14.75 - 12.37\ USP_{EMJt-1} + 8.290\ USA1P_{t-1}$$
$$ (1.752) \qquad\quad (4.642)$$
$$ (-7.060) \qquad\quad (1.786)$$

$$+ 5.078 \text{ USIP}_t + 60.49 \ \Delta\text{USID}_t$$

$$\begin{array}{cc} (0.9134) & (6.413) \\ (5.559) & (9.431) \end{array}$$

$$- 44.40 \ \Delta\text{USID}_{t-1} + 0.7910 \text{ USC}_{t-1}$$

$$\begin{array}{cc} (7.102) & (0.1126) \\ (-6.251) & (7.024) \end{array} \tag{3-25}$$

$R^2 = 0.991$ $\rho = -0.8$ Years: 1950–1958, 1962–1966.

In either case, the results are spectacularly good. Most of the estimated coefficients are several times their asymptotic standard errors, the only exception being the coefficient of aluminum price in (3-25). It is particularly noteworthy that this is true of the coefficient of copper price, an unusual feature for econometric estimates of demand equations. More important, every coefficient has the expected sign and the constraint on the coefficient of ΔUSID_{t-1} is very closely satisfied. In (3-24), that coefficient is -39.97, whereas the product of the coefficients of ΔUSID_t and USC_{t-1} is 39.84; in (3-25), the coefficient is -44.40, whereas the corresponding product is 47.84.

In terms of elasticities, the two equations are very close. From (3-24), at the point of means for the period, the elasticity of copper consumption[35] with respect to copper price is -0.2131 in the short run and -0.9002 in the long run. From (3-25), the corresponding figures are -0.1727 and -0.8168, respectively. The elasticity with respect to the price of aluminum implied by (3-24) is +0.2392 in the short run and +1.010 in the long run; the corresponding figures from (3-25) are +0.2040 and +0.9759, respectively. Finally, the elasticity with respect to the index of construction materials is 0.3318 in the short run and 1.402 in the long run, from (3-24). The comparable elasticities from (3-25) with respect to the index of industrial production are 0.1529 and 0.7317, respectively. Note that the last set of elasticities measures roughly the same thing in both equations, since in either equation the variable in question is serving as a proxy for economic activity in general.[36]

When we turn to consuming areas outside the United States, the results are less striking. In large part, this is probably due to the better quality of U.S. data. In particular, much better data on changes in stocks of copper exists for the United States than for most other countries; moreover, only for the United States was it possible to utilize data on stocks of durable goods in general to perform the correction for copper held in the form of finished goods which proved so spectacularly successful in (3-24) and (3-25).

The demand equation for Europe is similar to that for the United States, in that it includes copper price, aluminum price, lagged copper consumption, and an index of industrial activity. The copper money price used was, of course, the LME price (pounds sterling per long ton), and the aluminum money price used was again the German aluminum price (deutsche mark per 100 kilograms). Both of these were then converted to dollars. Construction of an appropriate deflator requires some discussion, however.

For each European country, we formed a dollar-equivalent whole-sale price index, by taking the country's own wholesale price index (1958 = 1.00) and dividing it by an index of the country's exchange rate vis-à-vis the dollar. The latter was an index of local currency per dollar, scaled to be 1.00 in 1958. These individual country indexes, now in a common unit, were combined in a weighted average, the weights being proportional to 1963 industrial produc-tion.[37] The weights are shown in Table 3–4. Three different indexes of produc-tion were tried, all with very similar results. They were the OECD Europe industrial production index,[38] the United Nations index of manufacturing, and the United Nations index of industrial production. The United Nations indexes[39] have somewhat wider coverage than the OECD index. We report the result using the former index of industrial production.

The dependent variable was total use of copper (thousands of metric tons) for all noncommunist Europe. We denote it by EURC. The two prices are denoted by $EURP_{LME}$ and $EURA1P$, respectively, and the index of industrial production (1958 = 100) by EURIP.

The estimated European demand equation is

$$EURC_t = -1220 - 0.2693\ EURP_{LMEt-1} + 28.52\ EURA1P_{t-1}$$
$$(0.1961) \qquad\qquad (24.92)$$
$$(-1.373) \qquad\qquad (1.144)$$

$$+\ 9.045\ EURIP_t + 0.5426\ EURC_{t-1}$$
$$(5.795) \qquad (0.3395)$$
$$(1.561) \qquad (1.598) \qquad\qquad\qquad\qquad\qquad (3-26)$$

Table 3–4. Weights of Individual Countries in European Price Index (Percent)

Germany	26.6
United Kingdom	21.3
France	19.6
Italy	10.0
Belgium and Luxembourg	3.5
Sweden	3.5
Switzerland	3.5
Netherlands	3.3
Spain	3.3
Austria	2.0
Finland	1.3
Portugal	0.8
Greece	0.5
Ireland	0.5
Total	100.0*

*Individual weights as given do not sum to 100.0 because of rounding.

$R^2 = 0.934$ $\rho = -0.1$ Years: 1952–1968.

The elasticities at the point of means are as follows: with respect to copper price, -0.0878 in the short run and -0.1920 in the long run; with respect to aluminum price, $+0.6133$ in the short run and 1.341 in the long run; and with respect to industrial production, $+0.4534$ in the short run and $+0.9913$ in the long run.

The results indicate a somewhat slower speed of adjustment than was found for the United States. Elasticities with respect to copper price are lower and with respect to aluminum price higher than for the United States. Elasticities with respect to industrial production are roughly the same. It must be remembered, however, that the results for Europe are not nearly so reliable as those for the United States. Moreover, it is not possible to make all the same adjustments for changes in copper stocks for both the United States and Europe, so that, in particular, the effect of changes in the stocks of copper held as finished goods is included rather than separately accounted for. Given this, it is nontrivial to have obtained a demand equation with all coefficients being of the expected sign and reasonable magnitude and bigger than their respective asymptotic standard errors.

The results for Japanese demand are rather different. Only here in the model could we find no evidence of a lagged adjustment process. This may be due to the very rapid growth of the Japanese economy, since a situation in which a significant fraction of industrial capacity is new each year is also likely to be one in which a significant part of copper demand does not depend on the relative adjustment of old capacity to new price situations. Nevertheless, it seems doubtful that adjustment is so rapid as to be complete in a single year (although it must be remembered the price entered in the model is last year's price). Also related to the rapid growth of Japan is the fact that we would expect the variables with large effect on Japanese copper demand to be those which are related to industrial production. Despite this, we did find a negative effect of copper price; aluminum price did not appear to play any role.

We present two equations which differ only in the measure of copper-using activity. (The two measures are too collinear to use in the same equation.) The first equation is an index of total industrial production (1955 = 100) denoted by JIP. The second is an index of the production of construction materials (1955 = 100) denoted by JCM.[40] The price variable used was the LME price expressed in yen per long ton, deflated by the Japanese wholesale price index (1958 = 1.00); it is denoted by JP_{LME}. Japanese consumption of copper (thousands of metric tons) is denoted by JC.

The two equations are as follows:

$$JC_t = 124.2 - \underset{\substack{(0.0001312) \\ (-1.780)}}{0.0002334\ JP_{LMEt-1}} + \underset{\substack{(0.0716) \\ (24.06)}}{1.723\ JIP_t} \qquad (3\text{-}27)$$

$R^2 = 0.982$ $\rho = 0.0$ Years: 1951–1968

and

$$\text{JC}_t = 66.96 - 0.0002316 \, \text{JP}_{\text{LME}t-1} + 2.433 \, \text{JCM}_t$$
$$\quad\quad\quad\quad (0.0001570) \quad\quad\quad\quad (0.1413)$$
$$\quad\quad\quad\quad (-1.475) \quad\quad\quad\quad\quad (17.22) \quad\quad\quad\quad\quad\quad\quad\quad (3\text{-}28)$$

$R^2 = 0.975$ $\rho = 0.1$ Years: 1954–1968.

The results using the index of industrial production seem somewhat more reliable than those using the index of construction materials, although this may merely reflect the fact that they are based on three more years of data. In any case, the implications of both equations are quite similar. There is no difference between short- and long-run elasticities. From (3–27), the elasticity of Japanese consumption with respect to price is –0.09428 at the point of means for the period; from (3–28), that elasticity is –0.1184. From (3–27), at the point of means, the elasticity with respect to the index of industrial production is 0.6014; from (3–28), the comparable elasticity with respect to the index of construction materials is 0.9921.

Finally, a demand equation was estimated for the Rest-of-World. Here the prices were the LME price and the German aluminum price, both expressed in dollars and both deflated by the U.S. wholesale price index (1957 – 1959 = 1.00).[41] The former price is denoted as before, by USP_{LME} and the latter, as before, by USA1P. For a production index, we used that compiled by the United Nations.[42] The production index is denoted by RWIP (1963 = 100). The dependent variable is Rest-of-World total use of copper (thousands of metric tons) and is denoted by RWC. The results are as follows:

$$\text{RWC}_t = -11.82 - 0.1212 \, \text{USP}_{\text{LME}t-1} + 0.8828 \, \text{USA1P}_{t-1}$$
$$\quad\quad\quad\quad\quad (0.03746) \quad\quad\quad\quad (3.014)$$
$$\quad\quad\quad\quad\quad (-3.237) \quad\quad\quad\quad (0.2929)$$

$$\quad\quad + 1.971 \, \text{RWIP}_t + 0.7646 \, \text{RWC}_{t-1}$$
$$\quad\quad\quad (0.8127) \quad\quad\quad (0.1613)$$
$$\quad\quad\quad (2.426) \quad\quad\quad\quad (4.740) \quad\quad\quad\quad\quad\quad\quad\quad (3\text{-}29)$$

$R^2 = 0.939$ $\rho = -0.3$ Years: 1951–1968.

The result as to the effects of aluminum price is unreliable; the remaining coefficients are considerably larger than their asymptotic standard errors. At the point of means, the estimated elasticities are as follows: with respect to copper price, –0.2177 in the short run and –0.9248 in the long run; with respect to aluminum price, +0.1074 in the short run and +0.4561 in the long run; and with respect to industrial production, +0.4087 in the short run and +1.736 in the long run. The price elasticities are fairly similar to those found for the United States.

In general, the demand results show copper demand to be rather inelastic with respect to copper price, even in the long run. The most important determinants of copper demand, as one would expect, are the levels of industrial activity in the consuming countries.

PRICES

So far, there are two prices directly used in the model, the LME price and the EMJ price. As already mentioned, however, the latter is a constructed price which is very closely associated with the U.S. producer price. Indeed, expressing all three in common units, and denoting the three prices by P_{EMJ}, P_{LME}, and P_{Prod}, least squares regression (with no constant term) reveals

$$P_{EMJt} = 0.9762\,P_{Prodt} + 0.01538\,P_{LMEt}$$
$$\qquad\quad (0.00842) \qquad (0.007045)$$
$$\qquad\quad (115.9) \qquad\quad (2.183) \qquad\qquad\qquad\qquad (3\text{-}30)$$

$R^2 = 0.999$ Years: 1946–1968;

the sum of the coefficients is not very far from unity.[43] We have already outlined the way in which the model describes the setting of the U.S. producer price. Essentially, that price is set as an intended maintainable price, being adjusted relatively slowly. Adjustments in it are made in response to indications that the U.S. market is drifting out of equilibrium. One such indication is clearly the accumulation of private stocks of copper in the United States; another is a large difference between the U.S. producer price and the LME price. We find that both of these have a definite effect.

Denoting the change in U.S. private stocks of copper during year t by ΔUSS_t and measuring it in thousands of metric tons, we divide it by U.S. consumption in year t to obtain a measure of the relative size of stocks. Assuming that decisions are taken for this year with an eye to last year's variables, we enter the resulting ratio lagged as well as the lagged difference between the LME and the U.S. producer price. Denoting deflation by the U.S. wholesale price index (1957 – 1959 = 1.00) by the prefix US, as before, the estimated equation (where all prices are in deflated dollars per long ton) is as follows:[44]

$$USP_{Prodt} = 320.8 - 1856\,\frac{\Delta USS_{t-1}}{USC_{t-1}}$$
$$\qquad\qquad\quad (825.4)$$
$$\qquad\qquad\quad (-2.248)$$

$$+ 0.2689 \ (USP_{LMEt-1} - USP_{Prodt-1}) + 0.5980 \ USP_{Prodt-1}$$

(0.1461)   (0.2452)

(1.840)   (2.438)   (3-31)

$R^2 = 0.556$ $\rho = 0.2$ Years: 1952-1966.

  Note that while the speed of adjustment is well below unity, it is high relative to that found for supply adjustments and for U.S. demand adjustment. About 40 percent of the gap between desired and actual price is covered in a year. The other two coefficients have the expected sign.[45]

  We turn now to the equation explaining the LME price. Here we also expect the size of copper stocks to play the chief role (although, of course, these will be stocks outside the United States); however, the rationale behind this is a bit different from that in the case of the U.S. producer price. Whereas that price is an administered price and the equation just reported describes the behavior of those administering it, the LME price is basically a free price. Hence the equation describing LME price determination is describing the behavior of a market. In effect, one can think of the LME price as adjusting until holders of stocks are satisfied to hold them.[46] In this view, it should be the size of stocks (relative to consumption) rather than the change in stocks that counts for the LME price; however, as one might expect the relationship to be long run, it is sensible to use a distributed lag and also to investigate the effect of lagged stocks as well as current ones.

  When this is done, however, a striking result emerges. In every version of the equation tried,[47] what appears to matter is the change in the stocks-consumption ratio and not its level. Indeed, when the change and the level of the ratio are both used in the equation (which is equivalent to using both the current and the lagged values of the ratio), not only is the coefficient of the level very close to zero (and small relative to its asymptotic standard error) but also it is slightly positive, which does not make economic sense.

  Denoting the level of Rest-of-World stocks at the end of year t by $RWST_t$, the two best equations are as follows:[48]

$$USP_{LMEt} = 285.6 - 3620 \left(\frac{RWST_t}{RWC_t} - \frac{RWST_{t-1}}{RWC_{t-1}} \right)$$

(1565)

(-2.312)

$$+ 0.7957 \ USP_{LMEt-1}$$

(0.4886)

(1.628)   (3-32)

$\rho = -0.3$ Years: 1952-1968

and

$$\text{USP}_{\text{LME}t} = 415.2 - \underset{\substack{(738.8) \\ (-2.626)}}{1939.7} \left(\frac{\text{RWST}_{t-1}}{\text{RWC}_{t-1}} - \frac{\text{RWST}_{t-2}}{\text{RWC}_{t-2}} \right)$$

$$+ \underset{\substack{(0.1769) \\ (3.369)}}{0.5960} \text{USP}_{\text{LME}t-1} \tag{3-33}$$

$\rho = -0.1$ Years: 1953–1968.

Now, the difficulty in accepting equations such as these is their long-run implications under certain circumstances. In them, the LME price goes down when stocks go up relative to consumption, a perfectly reasonable result. The possibly surprising thing, however, is that if one considers what would eventually happen to price if the stocks-consumption ratio were to remain unchanged indefinitely, the implication is that the LME price would approach an equilibrium level *independent of the level at which the stocks-consumption ratio remained constant.* What the stocks-consumption ratio had been doing before entering the constant phase would matter for the short and middle run, but in the long run, a constant stocks-consumption ratio would lead to the *same* price, whatever the constant level. This is not a result which is instantaneously acceptable, although its importance for short-run or even middle-run forecasting is extremely limited. We can, however, go a long way toward rationalizing it along the following lines.

The LME price not only adjusts according to the desire to hold copper stocks, but, much more fundamentally, it serves as the long-run equilibrator of supply and demand. If, over a very long period, there is no change in the stocks which people desire to hold, then, asymptotically, stocks will not affect the price, which then, asymptotically, approaches the level at which long-run supply and long-run demand are in balance; so that stocks will not in fact change. We have already seen, however, that the supply of copper is extremely elastic in the long run, so that such an asymptotic price, as far as we can predict, is a constant (in real terms) approximating the almost horizontal level of the long-run supply curve.[49] Indeed, if we recall that the change in stocks is *defined* as the difference between total supply and total demand, it becomes apparent that the price adjustment equations merely state that price adjusts in the direction of excess demand and does not move (in the long run) if supply and demand are in long-run balance. It must be emphasized that such arguments and implications are only asymptotic and that speeds of adjustment are slow enough in the copper industry that the long run is very long and not very relevant. Short-run movements in demand (and supply) and consequent short-run changes in stocks will have much more to do with the price over any reasonable horizon than will whatever asymptotic level would be approached were everything forever in equilibrium.

For what it is worth, however, the asymptotic equilibrium level of the LME price is $1,506 per long ton from (3-32) and $1,164 per long ton from (3-33) (in 1969 dollars). This compares to an average price of $1,490 (current dollars) in 1969.[50] It must be strongly emphasized that this statement in no way constitutes a prediction that the LME price will approach this level over the next several years.

CLOSING THE MODEL

Only three more relationships remain to close the model. These are the two identities accounting for changes in stocks and the equation describing net exports of copper from the rest of the world into the United States.

The first two relationships are easy to describe. Let $\Delta USGS_t$ be the change in U.S. government stocks during year t (thousands of metric tons) and let RWX_t denote net exports from the rest of the world to the United States (thousands of metric tons).[51] Then the change in U.S. private stocks is given by the identity

$$\Delta USS_t \equiv USMP_t + USOS_t + USNS_t + RWX_t - USC_t - \Delta USGS_t, \qquad (3\text{-}34)$$

which is to say that the change in U.S. private stocks is the total supply (mine production, old scrap, new scrap, and imports) less consumption and the amount going into U.S. government stocks. Note that new scrap is included in our consumption figures and is netted out of the change in stocks, as it should be, since what matters is copper put through the refining process once during the year less the disappearance of copper into true consumption and government stocks.

A similar identity gives the change in stocks in Rest-of-World. As already remarked,[52] there are no benchmark figures for the size of stocks outside the United States, so we have cumulated the change in stocks from the end of 1949. Therefore, aside from our inability to account for governmental stocks outside the United States,[53] our Rest-of-World stock figures differ from correct ones by an unknown constant. This matters only to the LME price equation, and, as discussed in the preceding section, it matters very little since only changes appear to be important in that equation.

The identity giving the change in Rest-of-World stocks is

$$\Delta RWS_t \equiv ChMP_t + CanMP_t + ZMP_t + RWMP_t$$

$$+ RWS_t - EURC_t - JC_t - RWC_t - RWX_t, \qquad (3\text{-}35)$$

which says that the change in Rest-of-World stocks is given by the sum of mine production outside the U.S. (Chile, Canada, Zambia, and Rest-of-World) plus Rest-of-World scrap supply less consumption of copper outside the U.S. (Europe, Japan, and Rest-of-World) less net exports to the United States.

The estimation of the equation explaining net exports to the United States (RWX) is not a simple matter. One naturally expects a prime factor in that equation to be the difference between the producer price and the LME price, but simple attempts to explain net exports by this difference do not get very far. The reason is not hard to find. When the producer price is well below the LME price, there is often rationing of primary copper in the United States and copper may flow into, rather than out of, that country.

This suggests trying several devices. One of these is to divide the difference between producer price and LME price into two variables, depending on whether that difference is positive or negative. When this was done, the results were often suggestive; but when the other variables about to be discussed were added to the equation, the coefficients on the two price-difference variables became almost equal, lending powerful support to the view that the other variables had adequately accounted for the rationing problem.

Those other variables are as follows. The first is the excess of U.S. consumption over U.S. mine production, an indication of the shortfall which must be filled by secondary copper, stock changes, and imports. The second, denoted XD, is a dummy variable representing the presence or absence of export controls in the United States (recall that RWX is *net* exports). This variable was given the value of unity for 1949–1952, 1955–1956, and 1966–1968. For 1953, it was set at 0.75, for 1954 at 0.25, and for 1957 at 0.5 (fractional values occurring when controls were imposed or taken off in the middle of a year). For all other years, the variable was set equal to zero.

The resulting equation was as follows (note that the prices are in deflated dollars per long ton):

$$RWX_t = -795.5 + 1.397 \, (USP_{\text{Prod}\,t} - USP_{\text{LME}\,t})$$
$$(0.6310)$$
$$(2.214)$$

$$+ \, 0.9340 \, (USC_t - USMP_t) + 145.8 \, XD_t$$
$$(0.4238) \qquad\qquad\qquad (55.22)$$
$$(2.204) \qquad\qquad\qquad (2.640) \qquad\qquad\qquad (3\text{--}36)$$

$\rho = -0.1$ Years: 1952–1968.

The results are strikingly good, particularly since, as mentioned, attempts to explain net exports without the two final variables lead to very poor results. Elasticity calculations do not mean much when the variables lie close to zero, so we do not give them. An increase in the U.S. producer price of one cent per pound, with the LME price constant, increases net exports to the U.S. by about 31 thousand metric tons, other things being equal. (By way of comparison, net exports were about 201 thousand metric tons in 1963, so there is substantial price sensitivity.) An increase in the gap between U.S. consumption and mine production is filled, other things being equal, about 93 percent by imports into the United States. This figure seems a little high, but (aside from the fact that a more plausible figure would lie within one asymptotic standard error of the point estimate) it must be remembered that this is *not* the same statement as the assertion that 93 percent of the entire gap is filled by imports. Even if the two prices were identical and export controls not present, the large negative constant term would mean that much less of the gap is filled by imports on the average than at the margin.[54]

GENERAL CONCLUSIONS

We have outlined the general way in which the model works. The remainder of this study will discuss specific forecasts. Between these general and specific discussions are the conclusions to be drawn from the model as estimated and reported in the preceding sections. This section briefly treats some of the more significant conclusions.

The overriding fact about the copper market is the very high elasticity of supply coupled with a low adjustment speed and relatively low short-run elasticities. Thus while long-run equilibrium price—that price which would make long-run supply equal long-run demand for current levels of the various exogenous variables—may be well below current price, there is no marked tendency for price to approach such a long-run equilibrium. Steady growth in the activity variables influencing demand, even at a relatively low rate, leads to prices forever above long-run equilibrium because of the inelasticity of short-run supply. In essence, the demand curve is continually shifting outward and new supply coming slowly into production.[55]

On the other hand, this very fact means that prices are sensitive to a reduction in the rate of growth of the exogenous activity variables, especially to a decrease therein. If those variables slacken their growth rate or stop growing altogether, the new supply induced by previously high prices will come on-stream and prices will drop. Since demand is relatively price inelastic, such a drop can be quite substantial. Indeed, it is clear that whereas the high long-run elasticity of supply makes for a stable, if largely irrelevant, long-run price, the low short-run elasticities of supply and demand make for a relatively unstable short-run price which is very sensitive to changes in general economic conditions. This is more true of the LME price than it is of the U.S. producer price, whose fluctuations are deliberately reduced by the price-setters.

Such instability enters the model, of course, through stock accumulation. A fall in demand, given the low short-run and high long-run elasticity of supply, leads to a sharp increase in copper stocks. This in turn depresses the price, which will remain depressed as long as stock accumulation continues. An upturn in general economic conditions, on the other hand, will lead to an outward shift in demand and a decumulation of stocks, providing an upward push on price. Because of the long time required to make adjustments, however, the actual timepath of prices is not a simple one. The remainder of this study discusses forecasts of that path (and of the timepath of the other variables as well) under various assumptions as to Chilean supply.

USING THE MODEL: FORECASTS AND PREDICTIONS

In this section, we discuss the behavior of the model when it is used to generate predictions of the endogenous variables under various specific numerical assumptions about the exogenous variables. In order to do so, we must both describe those assumptions and discuss the form in which the model was simulated.[56]

Clearly, the forecasts of any econometric model depend heavily on the forecasts of the exogenous variables used therein. Since the latter forecasts are not certain, the forecasts given here for the copper market can only be taken as indicative, even apart from the question of the validity and adequacy of the present model. Further, the reliability of all forecasts decreases as projections move farther into the future. On the other hand, the *differences* in forecasts which result when specific assumptions are changed can be very revealing about the true state of affairs regardless of whether the future values of exogenous variables used throughout are inaccurate and whether the forecasts themselves are in error. This will be important when we discuss the elasticity of demand facing Chile and the effect of new sources of copper supply.

It is obviously important, however, to use *sensible* forecasts of exogenous variables. In our case, with the period used for estimation ending in 1968, we generated forecasts for 1969-1975. We were able to use actual values of almost all of the exogenous variables for 1969 and 1970. Reasonable forecasts were typically available for 1971 and 1972. For 1973-1975, we made essentially arbitrary assumptions, usually as to constant percentage changes. The details will be found in Appendix 3B. Before proceeding, we had to decide exactly what version of the model to use. This involved two minor and two major decisions.

The first decision concerns the fact that there are two alternate versions of the United States demand equation, (3-24) and (3-25), and two of the Japanese demand equation, (3-27) and (3-28). In both cases, the two equations are distinguished by whether they use an industrial production index or a construction materials index. Collinearity did not permit using both. In the case of Japan, the equation using an index of industrial production seems slightly superior to the one using an index of construction materials: in both cases, it is easier to construct forecasts of the index of industrial production than of the index of construction materials; and letting industrial production be the primary force seems more satisfactory than assigning that role to construction materials (although collinearity suggests that this does not matter very much). Accordingly, in both cases we used the demand equation involving the index of industrial production.

The second problem concerns the Zambian supply equation (3-13) which (for obvious reasons) is not terribly satisfactory. Since that equation is not very different from a time trend, we replaced it for simulation purposes with such a trend, regressing Zambian mine production on time to obtain

$$ZMP_t = 334.4 + 28.08t$$
$$(2.497)$$
$$(11.25) \tag{3-37}$$

$R^2 = 0.9405$ Years: 1954-1957, 1960-1965.

However, perhaps due to political disturbances, Zambian mine production was well below trend in 1969, the first year of our simulation period and the last for which full data were available. Therefore, for 1969, we used actual Zambian mine production, returning to the trend for 1970-1975.

All other endogenous variables were forecast after 1968, actual values for 1968 being used for the lagged terms. A full set of values for the endogenous variables was not available for 1969.

The first major decision concerns the two alternative equations for the LME price, (3-32) and (3-33). These equations differ as regards the timing of the stock change affecting the price: in (3-32) the change is over the same year as the price observation; in (3-33) it is over the preceding year. These are mild grounds for believing that the former is appropriate—if the latter were, the LME price would be easy to predict and the resulting speculation would destroy the predictive value of the equation—but the argument is not a strong one. Accordingly, we began by experimenting with both versions, which we shall call the "simultaneous" and "lagged" models in order to see which version gave more sensible results.

As it turned out, those experiments were decisively in favor of the simultaneous version. While neither version did a very good job in predicting the LME price over the 1969-1971 period (a matter to which we shall return), the lagged version generated erratic behavior for the U.S. producer price and for imports into the United States. The former variable, in particular, fluctuated while the LME price rose steadily. The reason for this is easy to find. Imports in the model depend on the gap between U.S. demand and U.S. primary supply and on the difference between the two prices [see Equation (3-36)]. In the lagged version, the flow of imports into the United States affects no current price; so that it does not really serve as a method of arbitrage between the two markets. Exports from the United States do not depress and imports into the United States do not increase the current LME price; any such effect follows in the succeeding year as do effects on the U.S. producer price. This is contrary to the relatively free-market nature of the LME and leads to the fluctuating predictions mentioned above. Those fluctuations disappear when the simultaneous version of the model is used and the LME price allowed to adjust currently to diminish the intermarket flow. Accordingly, in what follows, we use the simultaneous version of the model throughout.

Similar experimentation was employed to decide the second major question of whether the estimated autocorrelation structure of the disturbances should be used in simulation and forecasting. The argument in favor of retaining that structure is that it contains important and useful information; not to use it is to ignore important historical regularities. On the other hand, it might be argued that those regularities are merely historical; disturbances are the part of the model we know essentially nothing about, and reliance on the continuance of the same autocorrelation structure is reliance on continued systematic behavior of the unknown. As it turns out, the forecasts are not very different using the two methods and the complete set of results given below are those retaining the estimated autocorrelation structure.

We now turn to the results of the simulation experiments. The first such experiment, the "base" experiment, is simply a set of forecasts using the model as given and assuming that all producers continue to be on their estimated supply curves. The results are given in Table 3–5.

The first thing to notice about these forecasts is that they are undoubtedly better as one-year projections than as forecasts over several years. This is particularly evident as regards the forecasts of the LME price [frame (d)]. The forecasted LME price (in pounds sterling per long ton) is 619.8 for 1969; the actual average 1969 price was 625. As this represents a rise of 100 over 1968, the forecast is remarkably good (remember that we began forecasting with 1969). The forecasts for 1970 and 1971 are not good, however. The LME price fell to an average of 597 for 1970 and fell very drastically in 1971, being 528 at the end of the first quarter and 429 at midyear. Our forecast, however, shows a rise in 1970 (to 678.1) and, while we do forecast a fall in 1971, it is nowhere near the correct magnitude. On the other hand, it may be remarked that predictions of the U.S. producer price are quite satisfactory for the same period (but are low for 1969).

What accounts for this? There are several possibilities. In the first place, one naturally expects the model to do better in short-run forecasting. Since the model is dynamic, predictions several years into the future use predictions one or two years into the future as inputs. Thus errors tend to lead to further errors and the model tends to wander. Put more simply, in forecasting 1969, we were able to use actual values of the endogenous variables for 1968 for

Table 3-5. Base Forecast

(a) Primary supply (thousands of metric tons)

Year	United States	Chile	Zambia	Canada	Rest-of-world
1969	1137.7	679.5	719.4	526.1	1516.2
1970	1281.7	700.0	783.7	577.1	1622.3
1971	1376.6	712.4	811.8	603.8	1708.1
1972	1463.8	724.0	839.8	644.3	1789.7
1973	1515.4	736.3	867.9	680.7	1871.7
1974	1568.8	749.2	896.0	722.5	1954.3
1975	1616.5	764.4	924.1	766.4	2042.3

(b) Scrap (thousands of metric tons)

Year	United States new scrap	United States old scrap	Rest-of-world scrap
1969	909.0	486.4	1949.5
1970	838.0	494.3	1988.0
1971	860.0	500.5	2104.6
1972	882.9	516.3	2216.2
1973	934.2	531.0	2334.6
1974	947.5	546.8	2462.2
1975	995.7	565.5	2606.2

(c) Demand (thousands of metric tons)

Year	United States	Japan	Europe	Rest-of-world
1969	2971.5	1238.6	3167.5	665.7
1970	2806.9	1417.0	3361.3	692.7
1971	2865.1	1568.2	3483.9	713.0
1972	2923.7	1755.6	3617.6	745.9
1973	3053.3	1928.1	3748.4	780.3
1974	3086.9	2115.4	3887.3	815.0
1975	3208.5	2321.6	4033.5	850.1

(d) Prices

Year	LME price ($£/long ton$)	United States producer price ($¢/lb$)	EMJ price ($¢/lb$)
1969	619.8	37.3	37.4
1970	678.1	49.1	49.0
1971	638.9	51.3	51.2
1972	679.3	55.4	55.3
1973	736.6	57.2	57.1
1974	798.9	61.7	61.7
1975	877.4	65.7	65.7

(e) Exports (thousands of metric tons)

Year	Rest-of-world to United States
1969	252
1970	114
1971	9
1972	−12
1973	−24
1974	−72
1975	−78

the lagged endogenous variables in the equations; in forecasting 1970 and later years, on the other hand, we could only so use the forecasted values of those variables for 1969 and later years.

Second, for 1969 (and in nearly all cases for 1970), actual values of the exogenous variables were used in the forecasts. For 1971 and thereafter, only values which were themselves forecasts could be used. As events catch up with such forecasts of the exogenous values, their effect on our own forecasts for the copper market becomes increasingly severe. This was obviously very important in 1971, but even for 1970 we had to use a forecast of the appropriate aluminum price, which may have had a substantial effect.

Third, large new discoveries and the expectation of further ones may have depressed the price in a way not captured by the model. Our supply equations do include new discoveries, but only in a general and systematic way. Sudden success, particularly in new areas, will not be captured in our short-run forecasts. (We examine the effects of the appearance of a large new supplier below.)

Fourth, it is possible that the model correctly predicts underlying tendencies but misses short-run deviations. If one believes this, then one must also believe that the fall in the LME price in 1970–1971 was in some sense an aberration, which is far from clear. Certainly, the model suggests that the general trend is up (recall that the forecasts are in current pounds sterling).

Finally, the model may simply be in error, although its success in fitting the sample period and in predicting 1969 makes one hopeful. In any case, the forecasts of the LME price for 1970–1971 are not good and the model may be at fault. Clearly our Equation (3–30) for predicting EMJ price of copper is unfortunate and should be modified, since it yields the quite unreasonable implication that this "average" of the LME price and the producer price falls slightly below both. It is not possible, however, to say if this error plays any important role in the results, although this seems unlikely. Only time and further experimentation will tell.

If the model has any validity, even if individual forecasts are in error, comparisons between forecasts using different assumptions may be very revealing. This is easiest to see where the source of the error is in the values of the exogenous variables used; but it is true in other cases as well. Differences between forecasts may be more accurate as reflections of differences between supposedly corresponding actual situations than forecast levels are as reflections of actual levels.

Before exploring such differences, however, a few points are in order regarding the base forecasts of Table 3–5, taking them at face value. The first of these has already been mentioned. According to those forecasts, the outlook over the next few years is for copper shortage with rising prices, particularly for 1972. Second, the gap between the LME price and the U.S. producer price is predicted to narrow (due to the removal of export controls) but not to disappear.

Third, and most interesting of all, despite the rising prices, Chilean output is projected as growing at a very slow rate compared with that of any other producer. It seems clear that if the incorrectly high LME price for 1970–1971 were replaced by the much lower actual price, the forecasted behavior of Chilean output would be a decline. *Note that the model forecasts this behavior as part of normal Chilean supply response, independent of unusual political or labor difficulty.* This has clear implications as to the reasons for the actual sluggishness of Chilean output over the last two years and the pressure on the copper companies by the Chilean government.

The next simulation experiment was designed to see the effects of such sluggish Chilean production on prices and on Chilean revenue. In this experiment, we altered the model by assuming that Chilean mine production would be greater than that forecast by the model by 10 percent in every year of 1969–1975. Since the model does not forecast great changes in Chilean output, this is roughly the same as assuming an increase in each year's output of 10 percent of 1969 production. The same set of experiments also serves to show the effect of an increase of the same magnitude by another producing country. The results are presented in Table 3–6.

The principal feature of these results when compared with the base forecast is seen at once: the assumed increase in Chilean supply does not have much effect on prices. In particular, the behavior of the LME price is not much different from the case of the base forecast. The larger differences, as we should expect, come in the earlier years before the market adjustment. The increase in Chilean supply (over the base forecast) is largely absorbed by decreases in other supplying countries and offset (to a lesser degree) by demand increases.

In other words, Chile is a sufficiently small part of the world market for the demand curve facing her to be quite elastic. This is borne out if we compare the forecasts of Chilean copper revenue generated by the two sets of forecasts. See Table 3–7. For comparison, we also show forecasted Chilean revenue, on the assumption that the extra output in the alternative forecasts is sold at the LME price by a country other than Chile.

A very rough estimate of the elasticity of the demand facing Chile is about 5½ in the short run and about 8½ in the long run when offsetting reactions in other countries have had time to take place. It is clearly to Chile's advantage to increase her output if she can do so without creating *unusual* offsetting activities in other producing countries.

Our final simulation covers the case of an "unusual" event, the discovery of a large new source of supply. In this experiment, we assumed that a new supplier began producing (or old ones increased production) suddenly in 1973 at a rate equal to that which the model forecasts for Chile. In other words, this experiment supposed that a new supplier with the Chilean supply curve began producing in 1973. Comparing these results to those of the base forecast should give at least a rough idea of the likely effect of a large new source of

Table 3–6. Alternate Forecast 1: Chilean Supply Up 10 Percent in Every Year

(a) Primary supply (thousands of metric tons)

Year	United States	Chile as forecast by model	Extra Chile	Zambia	Canada	Rest-of-world
1969	1137.5	677.9	67.8	719.4	526.1	1511.9
1970	1268.8	696.5	69.7	783.7	575.3	1612.7
1971	1359.0	708.4	70.8	811.8	600.9	1695.6
1972	1442.5	720.0	72.0	839.8	640.2	1776.0
1973	1495.0	732.7	73.3	867.9	675.9	1857.6
1974	1548.9	746.0	74.6	896.0	717.0	1940.1
1975	1597.7	761.4	76.1	924.1	760.3	2028.1

(b) Scrap (thousands of metric tons)

Year	United States new scrap	United States old scrap	Rest-of-world scrap
1969	909.0	483.4	1942.2
1970	838.1	491.5	1986.2
1971	864.4	498.8	2104.6
1972	889.3	515.2	2217.5
1973	942.1	530.3	2336.4
1974	955.5	546.1	2463.1
1975	1003.8	565.0	2607.4

(c) Demand (thousands of metric tons)

Year	United States	Japan	Europe	Rest-of-world
1969	2971.5	1238.6	3167.5	665.7
1970	2807.1	1418.6	3366.5	695.0
1971	2876.3	1570.4	3493.6	718.0
1972	2939.7	1757.0	3627.5	751.9
1973	3073.3	1929.0	3757.0	786.4
1974	3107.0	2116.0	3894.1	820.7
1975	3228.9	2322.1	4039.1	855.4

(d) Prices

Year	LME price (£/long ton)	United States producer price (¢/lb)	EMJ price (¢/lb)
1969	610.7	37.3	37.4
1970	665.2	48.1	48.0
1971	630.5	50.6	50.5
1972	673.1	54.6	54.5
1973	732.3	56.7	56.7
1974	794.8	61.2	61.2
1975	873.2	65.3	65.3

Table 3-6 continued

(e) Exports (thousands of metric tons)

Year	Rest-of-world to United States
1969	279
1970	135
1971	42
1972	22
1973	14
1974	-35
1975	-41

Table 3-7. Alternative Forecasts of Chilean Revenue (Millions of 1957-1959 Dollars)

Year	Base Forecast	Alternative Forecast 1 (Chilean Production)	Alternative Forecast 1 (Other Production)
1969	880.7	952.2	865.6
1970	955.7	1026.4	933.1
1971	952.9	1028.4	934.9
1972	990.1	1073.7	976.1
1973	1040.3	1132.1	1029.2
1974	1093.4	1191.4	1083.1
1975	1166.8	1272.4	1156.7

supply such as Australia. The results are presented in Table 3-8, which includes forecasts of Chilean revenue under the supposed circumstances.

As opposed to the results of the first alternative forecast, Table 3-6, it is clear that these figures differ markedly from those of the base forecast. The appearance of the new supplier causes a fall rather than a large rise in the LME price in 1973 and delays any large recovery and rise until 1975. Even in the latter years, prices are more than 10 percent lower than in the base forecasts (100 pounds sterling per long ton).

More remarkable, however, is the fact that prices still rise substantially in 1975 as other suppliers reduce their outputs, making room for the new ones, and demand responds to past lower prices. This may be taken as another indication that the outlook for the mid-1970s is for reasonably high copper prices. It must be remembered, however, that (1) all these forecasts are predicated on reasonably high rates of growth in the major consuming countries; (2) such predictions are shakiest for 1975; and (3) we make no attempt to forecast past that date, by which time the full effects of the hypothesized new supplier may not have been felt.

Table 3-8. Alternate Forecast 2: Appearance of New Supplier Equal to Chile in 1973-1975

Year	United States	Chile	New Supplier	Zambia	Canada	Rest-of-world
1969	1137.7	679.5	0	719.4	526.1	1516.2
1970	1281.7	700.0	0	783.7	577.1	1622.3
1971	1376.6	712.4	0	811.8	603.8	1708.1
1972	1463.8	724.0	0	839.8	644.3	1789.7
1973	1513.6	720.6	720.6	867.9	680.5	1831.0
1974	1449.0	716.3	716.3	896.0	704.5	1862.6
1975	1451.2	724.7	724.7	924.1	736.7	1920.0

(b) Scrap (thousands of metric tons)

Year	United States new scrap	United States old scrap	Rest-of-world scrap
1969	909.0	486.4	1949.5
1970	838.0	494.3	1988.0
1971	860.0	500.5	2104.6
1972	882.9	516.3	2216.2
1973	934.2	501.2	2254.8
1974	948.1	516.8	2428.3
1975	1036.9	547.7	2598.7

(c) Demand (thousands of metric tons)

Year	United States	Japan	Europe	Rest-of-world
1969	2971.5	1238.6	3167.5	665.7
1970	2806.9	1417.0	3361.3	692.7
1971	2865.1	1568.2	3483.9	713.0
1972	2923.7	1755.6	3617.6	745.9
1973	3053.2	1928.1	3748.4	780.3
1974	3088.5	2128.8	3934.1	837.2
1975	3312.5	2340.0	4122.8	897.5

(d) Prices

Year	LME price (£/long ton)	United States producer price (¢/lb)	EMJ price (¢/lb)
1969	619.8	37.3	37.4
1970	678.1	49.1	49.0
1971	638.9	51.3	51.2
1972	679.3	55.4	55.3
1973	642.5	57.2	57.0
1974	663.7	50.0	50.0
1975	772.4	57.6	57.6

Table 3–8 continued

(e) Exports (thousands of metric tons)

Year	Rest-of-world to United States
1969	252
1970	114
1971	9
1972	−12
1973	233
1974	131
1975	261

(f) Chilean revenue (millions of 1957–1959 dollars)

Year	Chilean revenue
1969	880.7
1970	955.7
1971	952.9
1972	990.1
1973	888.0
1974	868.5
1975	973.9

APPENDIX 3A

Data Used in the Model

Almost all data on copper were obtained from the annual publication *Metal Statistics*.[57] This journal seems the most reliable, consistent source of data covering the world industry; although more detailed data for the United States alone are available from the Bureau of Mines and the Copper Development Association. The data in *Metal Statistics* are revised frequently and so the most recent figures available were used.[58]

Prices. The EMJ and LME prices were taken from the average figure in *Metal Statistics*[59] and the producer price from *Metal Statistics: The Purchasing Guide of the Metal Industries*. The figure was the average producer price of electrolytic copper.[60] Wholesale price indexes were taken from the *United Nations Statistical Yearbook*[61] and exchange rates from *International Financial Statistics*.[62]

Primary Supply. Mine production data for the United States, Chile, Canada, and Zambia were taken from *Metal Statistics*.[63] The Rest-of-World figure was the Free World Figure[64] less the countries above. Mine production rather than smelter production was used because some secondary copper is introduced at the smelting stage. Since we estimate secondary production separately, using smelter production would involve double counting.

Secondary Supply. Total scrap supply for the United States was taken as the sum of production of secondary refined copper plus direct use of scrap.[65] Direct use of scrap includes new and old scrap in good condition which does not require re-refining. For the United States there is a figure for old scrap[66] which we used to estimate the old scrap model. The difference between total scrap supply and old scrap was then used in the new scrap model. Sample figures for 1963 are given in Table 3A-1.

The figure for item (5) does not correspond to the new scrap figure given in *Metal Statistics*,[67] since the latter excludes direct use of new scrap. For the Rest-of-World (see Table 3A-2) the total scrap supply was defined in the same way as direct use plus secondary refined.[68] There is no breakdown into old scrap for countries other than the United States.

In computing the figure for K_t (the stock of copper lying around) we used primary production and net imports of refined;[69] and change in stocks was the computed figure explained below. The net imports of fabricated items were from *Metal Statistics* with each item weighted approximately by copper content.[70] The weights were based on McMahon's figures.[71] See Table 3A-3.

Net imports for the Rest-of-World are the negative of the U.S. figure.

Table 3A–1.   United States Scrap, 1963 (Thousands of Metric Tons)

(1)	Production of secondary refined copper	274.0
(2)	Direct use of scrap	738.0
(3)	Total scrap supply (1) plus (2)	1012.0
(4)	Old scrap	382.7
(5)	New scrap (3) minus (4)	629.3

Table 3A–2.   Rest-of-World Scrap, 1963 (Thousands of Metric Tons)

(1)	Production of secondary refined	388.0
(2)	Direct use	940.9
(3)	Total scrap supply (1) plus (2)	1328.9

Table 3A–3.   Weights Used in Calculating Net Imports of Copper Fabrications

Copper (scrap, alloy scrap (copper content) rods, tubes, wire, plate, other)	1.00
Brass (rods, tubes, wire)	0.65
Muntz metal	0.60
Zinc (wire, rods, powder)	0.70

Demand.   The total use of copper figure for each country's demand equation was consumption of refined copper plus direct (or actual) use of scrap.[72]

The exogenous variables used in the demand equations were obtained as follows:[73]

1. Indexes of industrial production for all countries and groups of countries from the United Nations *Statistical Yearbook.*
2. German price of aluminum from *Metal Statistics.*
3. United States index of construction materials from *The Bulletin of the Federal Reserve Board.*
4. United States inventories of durables from *The Economic Report of the President.*
5. Japanese index of construction materials from *Monthly Statistics of Japan.*

Stocks of copper.   Stocks of copper were computed as a residual and the best explanation is provided by the sample figures given in Table 3A–4.

The figures are all from *Metal Statistics* except: (1) government stocks, which came from McMahon and Copper Development Association and (2) imports of copper ores which were from the latter, up to 1953.[74]

Table 3A–4.   Sample Figures for the United States, 1963
(Thousands of Metric Tons)

(1)	Mine production	1100.600
(2)	Net imports of refined, unrefined, and ores	201.958
(3)	Old scrap	382.700
(4)	New scrap	629.300
(5)	Total supply (1) plus (2) plus (3) plus (4)	2314.558
(6)	Total use of copper	2320.400
(7)	Decrease in stocks (6) minus (5)	5.842
(8)	Decrease in government stocks	10.310
(9)	Increase in private stocks (8) minus (7)	4.468

A similar computation was made for the Rest-of-World except that figures for government stocks (held by the United Kingdom government for a short period) were not available. Net imports of the Rest-of-World are the negative of the U.S. figure.

The figures for changes in stocks do not provide a benchmark. For the United States the benchmark for private stocks was 614.162 thousand metric tons at the end of 1949. This figure was stocks of copper at primary smelting plants plus refined copper held by fabricators reported in McMahon.[75] For the Rest-of-World, the benchmark was zero at the end of 1949.

APPENDIX 3B

Forecasts Used in Simulation

The exogenous variables in our model are essentially composed of three groups of figures: price indexes and exchange rates; indexes of production; and variables specifically related to the copper industry. We now discuss the forecasts used of each of these.

Price Indexes and Exchange Rates.

Actual exchange rates were available through 1971. For 1972–1975, exchange rates were assumed constant at end-of-1971 values, assuming that these adequately reflected the effects of the international monetary crisis.

The situation as regards the price indexes for the various countries is more complicated. Here, again, actual figures were available for 1969 and 1970. For 1971 for the United States, Canada, Japan, and Europe and for 1972 for all of these except Europe, we constructed price indexes from the implicit deflators forecast by various econometric models.[76] For the remaining years to 1975—and for the Chilean price index for 1971–1975—we assumed constant inflation rates more or less consistent with past experience: 5 percent for the United States,

Japan, and Europe; 3 percent for Canada, and 36 percent for Chile. Note that we were unable to take account of the anti-inflation program in the United States.

Production Indexes. Here again actual figures were available through 1970. For the United States and Japan, forecasts for 1971 and 1972 were constructed from the GNP forecasts of the models listed above[77] by assuming a ratio of production index to GNP constant at the 1970 level. For the remaining years and countries, constant growth rates were assumed: 10 percent for Japan; and 4 percent for the United States, Europe, and the Rest-of-World.

Figures on inventories of durable goods in the United States, available through 1970, were constructed from the Wharton EFA forecasts for 1971 and 1972 and taken as constant in real terms thereafter. Basically, both the production indexes and the price indexes show steady growth except for the U.S. recession in 1970.

Other Variables. Four other exogenous variables remain. Figures on the first of these, the change in U.S. government stocks of copper, are available through 1970. We assumed zero change thereafter. Figures for the German aluminum price were not readily available after 1968. We assumed a constant real dollar price of aluminum. Similarly, we assumed that Chilean policies as to prices received for copper would remain constant from 1968; here, again, events have overtaken the assumption. Finally, export quotas were removed in the United States in September, 1970. We set the dummy variable corresponding to such quotas equal to unity in 1969, 0.75 in 1970, and zero thereafter. Since the relaxation of controls was undoubtedly anticipated, 0.75 may be too high for 1970.[78] The precise values used for all of these variables are shown in Table 3B-1.

NOTES

1. Despite the fact that the two prices are very highly correlated, they do not seem to be equal after allowances for transportation and conversion costs. A simple explanation of this is not readily available.
2. Export quotas are part of the answer and enter our model below. But they are not the whole story.
3. This implication was first drawn by McNicol.[10]
4. See Koyck [8] and Nerlove.[13]
5. See Cooper [2] for details.
6. See [4]. Fair observes that the asymptotic standard errors for his estimator are difficult to calculate; but this is not the case, since instead of replacing sample values by probability limits, one can calculate the sample version of the asymptotic standard errors, relying on the fact that the formulas are only asymptotic in any case.
7. "Rest-of-World" in any section of this study denotes the countries not explicitly studied in that section.

Table 3B-1. Values of Exogenous Series Used for Forecasting and Simulation

(a) Price indexes

Year	United States (1957-1959 = 100)	Canada (1958 = 100)	Chile (1958 = 100)	Japan (1958 = 100)	Europe (1958 = 100)
1969	113.0	122.4	10024.5	109.8	112.8
1970	117.1	124.3	13714.5	113.6	120.7
1971	122.4	127.8	18701.4	120.0	128.0
1972	127.2	131.3	25515.5	126.6	134.4
1973	133.6	135.2	34701.1	132.9	141.1
1974	140.3	139.3	47193.5	139.5	148.2
1975	147.3	143.4	64183.1	146.5	155.6

(b) Production indexes

Year	United States (1963 = 100)	Europe (1958 = 100)	Japan (1955 = 100)	Rest-of-world (1963 = 100)	U.S. durable inventories (billions of dollars)
1969	138.8	186.3	702.2	147.6	63.6
1970	134.7	195.6	814.7	155.8	65.9
1971	138.5	203.5	905.0	162.1	67.1
1972	145.0	211.6	1005.6	167.0	70.2
1973	150.8	220.1	1106.2	173.7	73.7
1974	156.8	228.9	1216.8	180.7	77.4
1975	163.1	238.0	1338.5	187.9	81.3

(c) Other variables

Year	Export quota dummy	Change in U.S. govt. stocks (thousands of metric tons)	German aluminum price DM/metric ton
1969	1.00	53.6	226.3
1970	0.75	-6.4	216.5
1971	0.00	0.0	190.3
1972	0.00	0.0	197.7
1973	0.00	0.0	207.6
1974	0.00	0.0	218.0
1975	0.00	0.0	228.9

8. Data sources are listed and discussed in Appendix 3A.
9. As with all the equations, the "Years" figures indicate the observations on the dependent variable directly used in the final regression. Two earlier years of data are used in the estimation method.
10. The data began before 1949, but the lags involved in the equation and the estimation method used mean the loss of two years at the start of the time period. Similarly, eliminating 1959 means eliminating 1960 and 1961 from direct use as observations.
11. See [11].
12. For comparison, a similar equation using the EMJ price and the U.S. whole-sale price index was estimated. It differed from (3–11) in having a *very* slow speed of adjustment and hence a high long-run (but not short-run) price elasticity. The price term was smaller relative to its asymptotic standard error than in (3–11), however, and we accept (3–11) as the superior equation. The alternative results were:

$$\text{ChMP}_t = -54.43 + 2.740 \text{ USP}_{\text{EMJ}t} + 0.9517 \text{ ChMP}_{t-1}$$
$$(1.566) \qquad\qquad (0.0736)$$
$$(1.750) \qquad\qquad (12.92) \qquad\qquad\qquad (3\text{–}11a)$$

$$\rho = -0.2 \quad \text{Years: } 1948\text{–}1968.$$

13. Some fraction of Canadian supply is sold at the LME price. Preliminary attempts were made to include the LME price in the equation, but they were unsuccessful.
14. There is not much choice in terms of available data. There is also an incomplete series on the cost of living of Africans in Zambia.
15. In forecasting with the model, this equation is replaced with a trend. See p. 85.
16. This is not a very satisfactory deflator, but it is difficult to see how to improve it much.
17. In the case of the Zambian supply curve (3–13), where there were relatively few observations, only the sum of the last two variables was used.
18. In a few cases in which data on instrumental variables were missing for a year or so at the beginning of the period, we extrapolated backwards to construct them. Note that this was not done for the variables actually appearing in the equation being estimated.
19. This follows usage in the data sources which call such a variable "total use." Note that "consumption" in the sources does not include direct use of scrap as do our "consumption" variables. (This is not the same issue as that discussed in the text.) See Appendix 3A for the way in which new scrap figures were calculated and for further discussion.
20. 1948 is used as a benchmark because changes in copper stocks are unknown before that date. The estimated equation begins with 1950 because K_{t-2} is required by the estimation method. A similar statement holds for the Rest-of-World, p. 70, where K_{1950} is taken as a benchmark and estimation starts with 1952.

21. The figure actually used was collection of old scrap. This includes a small amount of *imported* scrap which does not precisely fit the model being discussed.

22. As already mentioned, it does not appear to be the case that the two prices are equal after allowance for transportation and conversion costs. We are unable to explain this.

23. The actual estimation procedure used was fairly complicated. First, USP_{LME} was regressed on its own lagged value; the lagged value of the EMJ price; the lagged change in the ratio of stocks outside the United States to total consumption outside the United States; the lagged sum of mine production in the U.S., Chile, and Canada; and the similar lagged sum for all other countries. This yielded a predicted value of USP_{LME}, which we shall call $\widehat{USP}_{LME}$. Then, for each choice of K_{1948}, Fair's method [4] was used to estimate the final equation, with the instrumental variables being those required by the method plus the logarithm of $\widehat{USP}_{LME}$. Note that different Fair method instruments arise for different choices of K_{1948} and that each such estimation requires a search of values of ρ.

24. Asymptotic standard errors are not presented in (3–18) and (3–19) since they are for comparative purposes only and the extra computation does not seem warranted. They would be much the same as in (3–17).

25. Our new scrap figures, for reasons of consistency, were taken as direct use of scrap plus secondary refined less old scrap. See Appendix 3A, Table 3A–1.

26. Estimation was by Fair's method with additional instrumental variables, lagged EMJ and LME prices, lagged U.S. mine production, and U.S. industrial production.

27. The estimation method was similar to that described above for U.S. old scrap, except that we formed not only $\widehat{USP}_{LME}$ and used its logarithm as an instrumental variable, but also RWC* and used *its* logarithm as an instrumental variable. In this first stage of the procedure, the same regression was used as before to form USP_{LME}. In the formation of $\widehat{RWC}^*$, the regressors were the lagged EMJ and LME prices, lagged $\widehat{RWC}^*$, and the two lagged sums of mine productions.

28. As used in this study, "demand" means "total use." See note 19 above.

29. It is true that our estimates ignore the two episodes of attempted in‌terference with the LME in the middle 1950s and middle 1960s. This may have affected the results (although it is hard to see just how) but has little to do with the aggregation question discussed in the text.

30. In the fall of 1971, for example, one producer lowered the price from $0.29 to $0.23, stating that the reduction merely reflected "ridiculous" discounting.

31. We have treated the aluminum price as exogenous to the copper market (in the short run) which is somewhat questionable but not too poor an approximation.

32. See Federal Reserve System.[5]
33. This includes copper that will become new scrap.
34. In equations estimated by the Hildreth-Lu technique, $1 - R^2$ is the sum of squares of errors in the original equation to be estimated divided by the centered sum of squares of the dependent variable in that equation.
35. These are elasticities of USC_t with respect to the several variables, not of copper consumption after the implicit correction for the change in durable goods inventories. The latter cannot be computed without some assumption about the constant term, α, which appears in (3–22).
36. The linear form used for the demand equation must be considered only an approximation, especially where such activity variables are concerned, so these last elasticities have perhaps less meaning than do the elasticities with respect to copper and aluminum prices.
37. These are the weights given by the Organization for Economic Cooperation and Development to its European members in its industrial production index. See Organization for Economic Cooperation and Development, *General Statistics* (Paris: OECD, 1970).
38. *Ibid.*
39. See [15].
40. *Monthly Statistics of Japan.*
41. This is not a very satisfactory deflator, but it is difficult to see how to improve it significantly.
42. Excluding the United States, Europe, and Japan. See [15].
43. While this is true, some minor anomalies that could be produced because the sum is not unity were not recognized until we formulated the forecasts. We could (and did) get LME prices far in excess of the producer price and we still had an EMJ price slightly below the producer price, particularly because the weight on the LME price is so small; i.e., about the same size as the discrepancy between the sum of the coefficients and one. These anomalies have only minor effects, however. It should be noted that casual discussions of the weights in the trade suggest a 10-percent weight on LME price.
44. 1967 and 1968 were omitted because of the copper strike. Figures on the change in government stocks of copper required to calculate the change in private stocks are not available before 1949.
45. Elasticity calculations do not make much sense for this equation, since both of the operative variables can (and do) change sign over the period.
46. There is a vast literature on this subject. See, for example, Telser.[14]
47. There were a number of these. They included versions with and without lagged price and with current and lagged stocks-consumption ratios being for year t and $t - 1$ or for year $t - 1$ and $t - 2$. In addition, since stocks figures do not exist for the total non-U.S. region, they had to be constructed by cumulating figures for changes in stocks from the estimates given in the next section. This is a satisfactory procedure, given a benchmark estimate of stock level in a particular year, but no

such estimate exists except for the United States, where only the change in stocks enters the model in any case. For the rest of the world, stocks were arbitrarily assumed zero at the end of 1949. The only effect of this is in the equation under discussion, where stock levels are divided by consumption. This suggests adding a correction to the equation in the form of the current and lagged reciprocals of consumption. When this was done, the corrections mattered little, but the phenomenon under discussion in the text persisted. Note that the stocks-consumption ratio is very close to the change in stocks divided by consumption, so that the correction should not matter if only changes are important; this slightly reinforces that finding.

48. The only instrumental variables used in estimating (3–33) were those required by Fair's method.

49. This is consistent with the argument in Herfindahl [7], pp. 230–35, that long-run marginal costs in copper supply are nearly constant.

50. It may be worthwhile noting that these equilibrium prices are somewhat above that price which would in a long-run steady state make the U.S. Producer Price and the LME Price the same, using Equation (3–31). Thus our model has a very long-run implication for equilibrium of a producer price below the LME price. This is, of course, not a material issue in terms of the short- or middle-run forecasting ability of the model. We are indebted to Zvi Griliches for commenting on this point.

51. Excluding scrap already counted in old scrap collections.

52. See note 47 above.

53. Figures on governmental stocks do not exist. The only non-U.S. government stocks whose existence are known to us were held in small amounts by the United Kingdom during the Korean War.

54. In the estimation of (3–36), the following instrumental variables were used in addition to those required by the Fair method: lagged mine production (including the United States) and lagged stocks/use outside the United States. Note that XD was taken as exogenous (indeed it is the only exogenous variable in (3–36)). It is true, of course, that the imposition of export controls is a function of the situation in the U.S. copper market. We assume that it depends on lagged rather than current variables, however.

55. This basic result was also found in a preliminary study done some years ago by one of the authors. See Fisher.[6]

56. The computations described in this section were carried out by Nancy Greene using the TROLL system of the National Bureau of Economic Research Computer Research Center.

57. See [12].

58. There is one exception to this. The figures given for U.S. direct use of scrap were, through an oversight, not always used in revised form in calculating other variables. The difference is small, however, and experimentation showed the effects to be negligible. In order that the reader may check the definition of the variables used in the

model we give, below, page number references to *Metal Statistics, Ibid.,* Vol. 56, 1969.

59. *Ibid.,* p. 284.
60. See [1], 1970 ed., p. 131.
61. See [15].
62. The International Monetary Fund. Year-end rates were used, creating a minor inaccuracy.
63. [12], pp. 190, 196, 198, and 188, respectively.
64. *Ibid.,* p. 19.
65. *Ibid.,* p. 190.
66. *Ibid.*
67. *Ibid.*
68. *Ibid.,* p. 25.
69. *Ibid.,* pp. 190 and 192–93, respectively.
70. *Ibid.,* p. 194.
71. See [9].
72. Figures are given in [12], pp. 24 and 25.
73. See [15]; [12], p. 277 (average); [5]; *The Economic Report of the President;* and *Monthly Statistics of Japan,* respectively.
74. See [9], p. 252, and [3], respectively.
75. See [9], p. 250.
76. The forecasts were kindly made available to us by L.R. Klein. The models were: (1) United States: Wharton EFA Mark III Quarterly Model (GNP deflator); (2) Canada: TRACE econometric model of University of Toronto (implicit deflator for consumer expenditure); and (3) Europe: German model of Institut fur Gesellschafts und Wirtschaftswissenschaften of the University of Bonn (implicit GNP deflator) and Belgian model of Free University of Brussels (implicit GNP deflator). In all cases we took the ratio of the desired price index to the available one to be constant from 1970. In the case of Europe, Belgium and Germany were combined with their usual relative weights and the rest of Europe assumed to move proportionally.
77. See note 76.
78. We are indebted to Dave McNicol for assistance here.

REFERENCES

1. The American Metal Market Company. *Metal Statistics: The Purchasing Guide of the Metal Industries.* New York: The American Metal Market Co., annual.
2. Cooper, J.P. "Asymptotic Covariance Matrix of Procedures for Linear Regression in the Presence of First-Order Serially Correlated Disturbances." *Econometrica,* forthcoming.
3. Copper Development Association. *Copper Supply & Consumption 1948–1967.* New York: Copper Development Association, 1968.

4. Fair, R.C. "The Estimation of Simultaneous Equation Models with Lagged Endogenous Variables and First Order Serially Correlated Errors." *Econometrica,* Vol. 38, No. 3 (May 1970), pp. 507–16.

5. Federal Reserve System, Board of Governors. *Federal Reserve Bulletin.* Washington, D.C.: Federal Reserve Board, monthly.

6. Fisher, F.M. "The Price of Copper and the Level of Chilean Copper Exports in the Next Decade." Unpublished manuscript, 1962.

7. Herfindahl, O.C. *Copper Costs and Prices: 1870–1957.* Baltimore, Md.: Johns Hopkins Press, 1959.

8. Koyck, L.M. *Distributed Lags and Investment Analysis.* Amsterdam: North-Holland Publishing Co., 1954.

9. McMahon, A.D. *Copper: A Materials Survey.* Washington, D.C.: U.S. Department of the Interior, Bureau of Mines, 1964.

10. McNicol, D. "An Econometric Model of the Copper Industry." Unpublished Ph.D. dissertation in progress. Massachusetts Institute of Technology.

11. Mamalakis, M. and Reynolds, C.W. *Essays on the Chilean Economy.* Homewood, Ill.: Richard D. Irwin, Inc., 1965.

12. Metallgesellschaft Aktiengesellschaft. *Metal Statistics.* Frankfurt am Main: Metallgesellschaft Aktiengesellschaft, annual.

13. Nerlove, M. *The Dynamics of Supply: Estimation of Farmers' Response to Price.* Baltimore, Md.: Johns Hopkins Press, 1958.

14. Telser, L.G. "Futures Trading and the Storage of Cotton and Wheat." *Journal of Political Economy,* Vol. 66, No. 3 (June 1958), pp. 233–55.

15. United Nations. *Statistical Yearbook.* New York, annual.

Chapter Four

A Simulation of the World Coffee Economy

Mary Lee Epps[1]

Economists have built numerous econometric models of commodity markets in recent years. However, in very few of these models has an oligopolistic structure been assumed to underlie the market being studied and almost none have been used to conduct computer simulation experiments. Indeed, the technique of simulation analysis, although frequently used to study problems of both the individual firm and the general economy, has been largely overlooked by commodity analysts. In addition, few simulation studies of any kind include more than the most perfunctory efforts either to validate the model being used or to apply systematic techniques of analysis to simulation experiment outcomes.

In this chapter I describe a computer simulation of the international coffee market, placing particular stress on the methodology followed. The research involved four principal steps. First, a theoretical model was developed, emphasizing the role of Brazil as a dominant, price-fixing oligopolist. Based upon this theoretical framework, an empirical model was derived utilizing quarterly data for the period 1955 through 1965. This empirical model was then subjected to intensive validation analysis, using the inequality coefficients developed by Henri Theil [8] to compare actual values of the endogenous variables with those predicted by deterministic simulations over the data period. Finally, four policy simulation experiments were conducted to evaluate the impact on revenues of various levels of Brazilian minimum export price and of three International Coffee Organization policy instruments including export quotas, indicator prices, and production goals. Tukey's analysis of variance method of setting up simultaneous confidence intervals for multiple comparisons was used to determine the statistical significance of the results of these experiments. [6]

THE WORLD COFFEE MARKET: AN OLIGOPOLY

There are two economically important species of coffee: arabicas, which are grown in most Latin American countries; and robustas, which account for

eighty percent of African production. The arabica species includes both un-
washed arabicas, also known as Brazils, grown in Brazil, Ethiopia, and Bolivia
and washed arabicas, or milds, grown in the rest of Latin America and in Kenya,
Tanzania, and a few other countries of Africa and Asia.

The three varieties differ substantially in quality. Washed arabicas
are particularly prized for their mild flavor and command a premium price.
Brazils, which occupy an intermediate position, are technically good substitutes
for both milds and robustas. Finally, robustas have a rather strong flavor and are
typically priced below the other two varieties. Robustas, whose output has
mushroomed since World War II, are particularly well-suited to the production
of soluble (i.e., instant) coffee.

Coffee accounts for a major share of total value in world agricultural
trade and is an important source of foreign exchange for a number of developing
countries. Table 4-1 illustrates the dependence of several Latin American and
African countries on coffee export earnings during the 1960s.

Countries such as Colombia and Ethiopia, that derive well over fifty
percent of their total foreign exchange from coffee, are particularly vulnerable
to the wide swings in price that have traditionally characterized the international
coffee trade. These price fluctuations are largely due to two factors. First, coffee
is a tree crop with typically a two to five year lag between planting and the first
economically significant harvest. As a result, although plantings may increase
markedly, production in the short run is unable to respond quickly to high

**Table 4-1. Coffee Earnings as a Percentage of Total Foreign
Exchange: Annual Averages and Range, 1960-1966**

Country	Average	High	Low
Latin America			
Colombia	69.6	75.6	62.4
El Salvador	54.3	67.3	46.2
Guatemala	53.9	67.7	46.0
Brazil	50.7	56.2	44.3
Costa Rica	47.5	53.3	41.1
Haiti	46.9	55.6	38.9
Africa			
Urundi[a]	78.4	93.9	70.6
Rwanda[a]	75.2	80.0	65.6
Ethiopia	59.3	87.5	45.5
Uganda	48.8	56.0	35.7
Ivory Coast	43.2	50.0	36.6
Angola[b]	42.5	50.7	35.4

[a]1964-1966 only.

[b]Based on six years (1964 not available).

Source: Pan American Coffee Bureau, *Annual Coffee Statistics* (1966), Table REV 6,
pp. A-78, A-79.

prices. Only after a lag of several years, when the new trees begin to bear fruit, will there be a sudden and frequently excessive spurt in supply.

A second factor which has helped exaggerate these price fluctuations is the high susceptibility of Brazilian output to frost and drought, particularly since the 1950s when coffee production became established in the frost-prone regions of Paraná province. Until recently, Brazil maintained large stockpiles of coffee which could be used in years of poor harvests. Nevertheless, speculation and importers' preference for new-crop coffee have invariably led to at least temporary price spurts when news of serious frosts reached the market.

Historically, Brazil has played a central role in the world coffee economy. Although contributing very substantially to fluctuations in production, Brazil has also borne most of the burden of stabilizing world market prices, alternately building up and drawing down stocks in order to maintain a stable flow of exports. Since the 1950s Brazil has regulated this export flow by manipulating a minimum export price.

In Colombia, the semigovernmental Colombian Federation of Coffee buys coffee at controlled prices and stockpiles surpluses. In addition, some of the smaller countries have occasionally attempted to limit exports, but, in general, these producers have had little impact on world market prices.

Interest in international cooperation among coffee producers revived in the mid-1950s with the sharp drop in world market prices. Beginning with a gentleman's agreement among a few Central American nations, Colombia, and Brazil, and progressing through a series of one-year arrangements which gradually expanded to include more and more producers, the efforts culminated in the signing of a long-term (five-year) agreement which went into effect October 1, 1963 and was renewed in 1968. (Although the agreement was recently extended for an additional two-year period, all the economic provisions including the export quota and indicator price systems described below have been deleted, effective September 30, 1973.[9] However, recent reports have indicated that producers have agreed among themselves to retain some supplies during the 1973–1974 coffee year.[5])

The 1962 Agreement included most of the important world producers of coffee plus a number of major consuming countries. Among its goals were the objectives of achieving "a reasonable balance between supply and demand . . . at equitable prices . . . ." and of alleviating "the serious hardship caused by burdensome surpluses and excessive fluctuations in the prices of coffee. . . ."[2]

The most important instrument available to the International Coffee Organization (ICO) in achieving these objectives was the annual export quota. At the beginning of each coffee year, the Organization set an over-all quota on the basis of estimated world imports for the coming year[2] and probable nonmember exports. This over-all quota was then distributed among the members in proportion to their share of the basic export quota as recorded in Annex A of the Agreement.

Exporting members for several years were unable to agree on common criteria for allocating production goals, a second instrument envisioned by the 1962 Agreement. Finally, in 1969 the Executive Board announced output goals for the 1972-1973 coffee year, based on demand estimates for that year. At the same time agreement was reached to limit total exporting members' stocks to fifty percent of over-all demand for coffee in 1972-1973, and a formula for allocating these stocks among participating producers was established.[3]

The world coffee industry is composed of a limited number of national suppliers. Brazil alone accounts for one-third to one-half of world exports and is a dominant force in the world market. With the exception of Colombia, no other producing nation wields much market power.

In a 1940 article surveying oligopoly theory, Stigler describes an oligopoly composed of one large producer and many small producers which very closely resembles the preagreement structure of the international coffee industry.[7] Stigler's analysis is based on two assumptions. The first assumption is that one firm sells such a large proportion of the commodity that the other (small) firms individually ignore any effect they may have on prices. The second assumption is that the dominant firm behaves passively; i.e., that it sets the price and then satisfies residual demand after the minor firms have sold all they wish to sell at the prevailing price.

The first assumption closely describes actual coffee production today with Brazil as the dominant producer. The second assumption also approximates reality. Numerous students of coffee have noted the tendency for Brazil to set price and then to act as a residual supplier, making up the difference between Latin American and African supply and world demand. Production and export data support this view. Latin America and Africa tend to export a high and fairly constant percentage of production. On the other hand, Brazilian exports tend to be fairly stable although production and stockpiling activities fluctuate widely.

The most important difference between today's coffee industry and Stigler's hypothetical oligopoly is differentiation of product. Brazilian, mild arabica, and robusta varieties differ substantially in quality. Historically, their prices have differed correspondingly, reflecting the normal valuation of these quality differences. Although these normal price differentials are occasionally disturbed, market forces tend to restore them to equilibrium.

Because of this differentiation of product, Stigler's model must be adapted slightly in order to apply it to coffee. In particular, for the industry as a whole there are now three supply curves and three interrelated demand curves, one for each variety of coffee. Taking exportable production as given, the mild and robusta export supply curves are horizontal at a very low price until exports approach exportable production. The curves then rise steeply, and since most of the smaller Latin American and African suppliers did not stockpile coffee in the years before the Agreement, the supply curves become vertical as exports approach exportable production.

Milds and robustas are poor substitutes for each other but good substitutes for Brazils. Therefore, the demand curve for each of the two varieties is a function of its own price and the price of Brazils. In order to determine the world market price for Brazils and thus fix the mild and robusta demand curves, we will assume the following. Brazil's chief policy instrument is the minimum export price. Market information is sketchy. Brazil's policy makers have some rather vague notions of a demand curve which is highly inelastic to price declines and which shifts gently outward by two or three percent per year with population and income growth. In addition, they know last year's price and export levels and have access to the United States' Foreign Agricultural Service estimates of mild and robusta exportable production.

Brazil's policy makers must choose a price support policy on the basis of this limited information. In a normal production year, the safest assumption is that the current market situation will be similar to the situation prevailing in the previous period. With so little information the best Brazil can hope for is to keep price at the same level as last period. Therefore, the policy makers will set minimum export price in period t equal to the world market price in period $(t - 1)$, less an allowance for transportation. At this price, Brazil expects to sell at least as much as in the previous period and therefore to maintain export revenues. Since demand is inelastic to price declines, a lower price would be associated with a decline in revenues. A higher price which was not justified by supply conditions would be likely to meet considerable consumer resistance, resulting in declining exports and revenues.

Occasionally, Brazilian production will be abnormally low, as, for example, when the crop is affected by a severe frost. At such times the Brazilian authorities may set minimum price somewhat above the level they would choose in a normal year. The government will draw down stockpiles during these periods in order to supplement exportable production.

Since the establishment of the International Coffee Agreement, Brazil has continued to actively restrict exports in bumper crop years by manipulating minimum export price. Therefore, the basic model will continue to hold during a period of international cooperation with the exception that ICO quotas now act as an effective ceiling to exports. If the first solution yields mild or robusta exports greater than export quotas, then the model is reestimated with exports equal to the export quota. The system is then solved for optimum Brazilian exports. If equilibrium Brazilian exports are greater than the ICO Brazilian quota level, we solve the system again with Brazilian exports equal to the export quota.

THE EMPIRICAL MODELS

Quarterly data spanning an eleven-year period from the second quarter of 1955 through the fourth quarter of 1965 was used to fit two alternative empirical models: Model A, designed to represent the coffee industry during a period without international cooperation and Model B for periods with an active ICO enforcing export quotas. Figure 4-1 compares the structure of the two models.

Consider first Model A, the model designed for periods with no effective international organization. In most important respects this empirical version closely follows the oligopoly model summarized above. Brazil is the dominant oligopolist, controlling world market price by manipulating minimum export price. Mild and robusta exports depend largely on exportable production with seasonal factors causing some variations within the coffee year. (For robusta exports, own-price is an additional explanatory variable.) The world demand curve for each variety has been broken down into two regional demand functions (for the United States and for a group of Western European nations plus Canada[3]) with rest-of-world imports a residual. In addition, for the United States a planned-additions-to-inventories equation has been added to improve the fit of the model. However, neither of these changes fundamentally affects the basic model structure. Mild and robusta demand curves for the United States and for the group of European nations plus Canada are functions of own-price and of the price of Brazils, the chief substitute. The demand equation for Brazils is a function of all three prices. Finally, in keeping with the assumption that Brazil is a dominant oligopolist fixing price and then satisfying residual world demand, exports of Brazils are defined as the sum of world imports.

Let us turn now to Model B, designed for periods in which an effective International Coffee Organization actively limits national exports to export quota levels. The most important difference between this model and Model A lies in the Brazils sector. The minimum export price remains the key Brazilian policy instrument. However, whereas in Model A the export supply function for Brazils was assumed to be horizontal at the level of Brazilian minimum export price plus transport costs, in Model B the supply function becomes vertical at the point where exports equal export quotas. In this case we can no longer assume that exports play a purely passive role, with minimum price determining world market price and exports expanding to satisfy world demand at that price. Instead, although the Brazilian authorities continue to depend on the minimum export price to control supply and, indeed, usually set this price high enough to hold exports well below quota levels, we must allow for the possibility that occasionally, the minimum price level is set too low, and exports press against the quota ceiling. Therefore, in Model B, instead of allowing exports of Brazils to passively adjust to world demand, we introduce two alternative export equations. Either exports of Brazils are a function of exportable production and minimum export price, or exports equal the export quota for Brazils, whichever estimate is smaller.

Model A
(without an effective ICO)

Model B
(with an effective ICO)

$$BMIN = f(PB_{t-1}, \overline{STOCK}^*, \ldots)$$

$$EXB = f(\overline{EPB}, BMIN, \ldots)$$

$$PB = f(BMIN, \ldots) \qquad PB = f(EXB, \ldots)$$

$$INV1^* = f(\Delta PB_{t-1}, \Delta INV1_{t-1}, \ldots)$$

$$\boxed{\begin{array}{l} EXR = f(PR, \overline{EPR}) \\ PR = f(EXR, PB) \end{array}}$$

$$\boxed{\begin{array}{l} EXR = f(PR, \overline{EPR}) \\[4pt] \dfrac{M1R}{POP1} = f(PR, PB, \Delta INV1^*, \ldots) \\[4pt] \dfrac{M2R}{POP2} = f(PR, PB, \ldots) \\[4pt] EXR \equiv M1R + M2R + \overline{M3R} \end{array}}$$

$$\frac{M1R}{POP1} = f(PR, PB, \Delta INV1^*, \ldots)$$

$$\frac{M2R}{POP2} = f(PR, PB, \ldots)$$

$$M3R \equiv EXR - M1R - M2R$$

$$EXM = f(\overline{EPM}, \ldots)$$

$$PM = f(EXM, PB)$$

$$\frac{M1M}{POP1} = f(PM, PB, \Delta INV1^*, \ldots)$$

$$\frac{M2M}{POP2} = f(PM, PB, \ldots)$$

$$M3M \equiv EXM - M1M - M2M$$

$$\frac{M1B}{POP1} = f(PB, PM, PR, \Delta INV1^*, \ldots)$$

$$\frac{M2B}{POP2} = f(PB, PM, PR, \ldots)$$

$$EXB \equiv M1B + M2B + \overline{M3B} \qquad M3B \equiv EXB - M1B - M2B$$

Figure 4-1. A Comparison of the Two Basic Models.*

*See pages 114–115 for a key to the variable name abbreviations. Boxes around sets of equations indicate simultaneous blocks. A bar above a variable name indicates that the variable is exogenous.

Table 4-2. Abbreviations

$BMIN_t$	= Brazilian minimum export price (in current United States cents per pound).
$CPI1_t$	= The United States consumer price index of food.
$CPI2_t$	= The consumer price index (all consumer goods) for the group of European nations plus Canada.
EPB_y	= Exportable production of Brazils in year y (in thousands of bags).
EPR_y	= Exportable production of robustas in year y (in thousands of bags).
EPM_y	= Exportable production of milds in year y (in thousands of bags).
EXB_t	= Total exports of Brazils in quarter t (in thousands of bags).
EXM_t	= Total exports of milds in quarter t (in thousands of bags).
EXR_t	= Total exports of robustas in quarter t (in thousands of bags).
$INV1_t$	= Actual United States inventories at the end of the quarter (in thousands of bags).
$INV1^*_t$	= Planned United States inventories at the beginning of the quarter (identically equal to actual inventories at the end of the quarter).
$\dfrac{M1B}{POP1}_t$	= Per capita imports of Brazils to the United States in quarter t (in bags per thousand persons).
$\dfrac{M1M}{POP1}_t$	= Per capita imports of milds to the United States (in bags per thousand persons).
$\dfrac{M1R}{POP1}_t$	= Per capita imports of robustas to the United States (in bags per thousand persons).
$\dfrac{M2B}{POP2}_t$	= Per capita imports of Brazils to Canada plus a group of European nations including Belgium-Luxembourg, the Netherlands, Germany, France, Italy, the United Kingdom, Norway, Sweden, Denmark, Austria, and Portugal (in bags per thousand persons).
$\dfrac{M2M}{POP2}_t$	= Per capita imports of milds to the same group of European countries plus Canada (in bags per thousand persons).
$\dfrac{M2R}{POP2}_t$	= Per capita imports of robustas to the same group of European countries plus Canada (in bags per thousand persons).
$M3B_t$	= Imports of Brazils by the rest of the world (computed as total Brazilian exports minus imports to the United States minus imports to the group of European nations plus Canada) (in thousands of bags).
$M3M_t$	= Imports of milds to the rest of the world (computed as total mild exports minus imports to the United States minus imports to the European group) (in thousands of bags).
$M3R_t$	= Imports of robustas to the rest of the world (computed as total robusta exports minus imports to the United States minus imports to the European group) (in thousands of bags).
PB_t	= World market price of Brazils (in current United States cents per pound).
PM_t	= World market price of milds (in current United States cents per pound).
PR_t	= World market price of robustas (in current United States cents per pound).
$Q1$	= A dummy variable equal to one in the first quarter of the calendar year.

Table 4–2 continued

$Q2$ = A dummy variable equal to one in the second quarter of the calendar year.

$Q3$ = A dummy variable equal to one in the third quarter of the calendar year.

$REVB_t$ = Revenues earned by Brazils in period t (computed as the product of the world market price of Brazils times total exports of Brazils) (in millions of United States dollars).

$REVM_t$ = Revenues earned by milds in period t (computed in the same way as revenues earned by Brazils) (in millions of dollars).

$REVR_t$ = Revenues earned by robustas in period t (computed in the same way as revenues earned by Brazils) (in millions of dollars).

$STOCK*_t$ = Expected end-of-year net change in Brazilian stocks at the beginning of quarter t of coffee year y. (Equal to exportable production in year y less actual exports in quarters 1 through $(t - 1)$ of year y less expected exports in quarters t through 4 assuming no change in minimum price. Expected exports in the final quarters of the year with minimum price unchanged were assumed equal to actual exports in period $(t - 1)$.)

T = Time trend.

W_t = A dummy variable equaling one for severe frost or drought in Brazil during quarter t.

$Y1_t$ = United States income per capita deflated by the consumer price index (seasonally adjusted) (in thousands of United States dollars).

$Y2$ = OECD index of industrial production for the group of European countries plus Canada (weighted by each country's share in total green coffee imports in 1962).

Excluding the quota ceilings, which in Model B limit exports of all varieties, the only other difference between Models A and B occurs in the robusta sector. In our empirical work, the robusta sector was consistently troublesome. We had a great deal of difficulty obtaining a United States import function for robustas in which the coefficient for robusta price had the proper negative sign. This identification problem manifested itself again when, in fitting the robusta price equation, we obtained a positive coefficient for world exports, suggesting that demand factors largely determine price. In a period of effective ICO quotas, it is completely unacceptable to have such a robusta price equation in which the positive export coefficient implies that reductions in export quota levels depress world market prices. Therefore, in Model B we have dropped the robusta price equation. Instead, supply and demand form a mutually simultaneous system with robusta price determined as the market clearing price at which world demand equals world supply. (See Appendix 4A for the fitted equations for Model A and for the Brazil and robusta sectors of Model B.)

Although we have retained the robusta price equation in Model A, there are conceptual problems here also, since the positive export coefficient is inconsistent with the causal chain implied by the block recursive structure of the model. In Model A price is taken as predetermined in estimating both the United

States and European demand functions. However, the positive export coefficient in the robusta price equation implies that price varies directly with export demand (i.e., that demand factors largely determine exports and therefore the price and import demand functions should properly form a mutually simultaneous system.)

Partly because of this problem with Model A, we experimented with two other formulations of the model which avoid this structural inconsistency. In Figure 4-2 we compare Model A with alternative versions A1 and A2 which are also suitable for a period in which there is no effective international collaboration. In both these versions the entire robusta sector forms a single simultaneous system of equations, thus avoiding the inconsistency in the block-recursive structure of Model A.

As illustrated in Figure 4-2, there are three interrelated ways in which the mild and robusta sectors of Models A, A1, and A2 differ from each other. (For all three models, the Brazils sector is identical.) These differences include:

1. The formulation of the mild and robusta sectors. For each of the two sectors, Model A contains four equations and one identity with prices, exports, United States imports, European imports, and rest-of-world imports all determined endogenously. Models A1 and A2, on the other hand, contain just three behavioral equations and one identity per sector. In both these model variants, rest-of-world imports are exogenous.

2. The determination of mild and robusta exports and price. In Model A2, for both varieties, exports are an explicit function of exportable production while price is determined implicitly as the market clearing level at which world import demand equals world export supply. Model A1, on the other hand, includes an explicit price equation while exports are determined as identically equal to world imports. In Model A, both exports and prices are determined by behavioral equations.

3. The third difference among the models relates to variations in their block recursive structures as illustrated in Figure 4-2, where boxes enclose simultaneous groups of equations. Thus, Model A is almost completely recursive with only the robusta price and export equations mutually simultaneous. On the other hand, in Models A1 and A2 the entire robusta and mild sectors (excluding the mild export equation in A2) form independent simultaneous blocks. Because all simultaneous systems of equations were estimated by two-stage least squares, the coefficient estimates for equations contained in the mild and robusta sectors differ among the three models. In Appendix 4A we present the fitted equations for Model A. In all cases the structure of the behavioral equations included in Models A1 and A2 are identical to those of Model A presented here. However, for the mild and robusta sector equations, coefficient estimates will differ among the three models with the technique of estimation (and, where two-stage least squares is used, with the set of predetermined variables.)

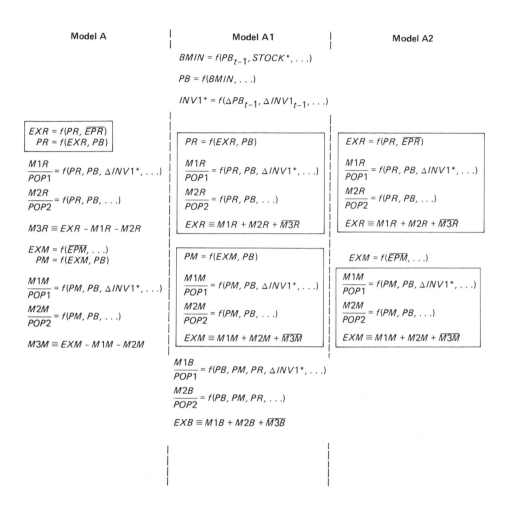

Figure 4-2. Three Alternative Model Formulations in a Period with No Effective International Coffee Agreement.*

*See pages 114–115 for a key to the variable name abbreviations. Boxes around sets of equations indicate simultaneous blocks. A bar above a variable name indicates that the variable is exogenous.

MODEL VALIDATION

Having proposed several alternative versions of an empirical quarterly model of the international coffee industry, the next step is to compare the relative success of the alternative versions in making predictions and, on this basis, to choose that version (or those versions) to be used in conducting four stochastic policy simulations. The four policy experiments, designed to determine the impact of various policy instruments on producer revenues, include: Experiment I, investigating the production goals instrument assuming no constraints on exports and spanning the production years 1957–1958 through 1967–1968; Experiment II, investigating the effectiveness of Brazil's minimum export pricing policies under the assumption of no effective export quota constraints and spanning the period 1958–1967; Experiment III, determining the effectiveness of various export quota levels assuming an active International Coffee Organization and covering the years 1964–1967; and, finally, Experiment IV, examining the indicator price system, again assuming an active International Coffee Organization and spanning the period 1964–1967.

Since for different policy experiments we will make significantly different assumptions about market conditions, we did not restrict ourselves to selecting a single model to be used in all four policy simulations. Instead, for each experiment, we first eliminated any of the models whose form was inconsistent with the particular set of conditions assumed and then used the remaining models to conduct a series of deterministic validation simulations. We thus obtained simulated quarterly series of prices, exports, and imports corresponding to each model. By using various validation techniques to compare these predictions with actual data for the period, we were able to choose that model variant which, while consistent with the assumptions of the experiment, yielded the best predictions. (At the same time we were able to obtain an idea of how good the predictions of the "best" model variant might be.)

We have already determined that Model B is the only empirical version suitable for simulations involving export quota constraints. Therefore, we selected that version for policy Experiments III and IV in which we assume that an active International Coffee Organization is enforcing export quotas. In this case we conducted two deterministic validation simulations—the first spanning the period 1960–65, those years of the original data period in which export controls were effective, and the second covering 1966–67, using newly available figures.

For Experiments I and II we assume that no export quotas are operative. Therefore, in selecting a model version for these two policy experiments, we considered Models A, A1, and A2, using each model variant to conduct a deterministic validation simulation spanning the years 1956–59, a period in which no important export constraints were operative.

We used both graphical and statistical techniques to analyze the output of our validation simulations. For the graphical analysis, we plotted actual and predicted values of each endogenous variable against time.[4] For the statistical analysis we compiled the inequality coefficients and related statistics developed by Henri Theil.[8]

Theil's measure of forecasting error is the root mean square log prediction error. In terms of predicting relative changes in the endogenous variable, the statistic is as follows:

$$\sqrt{\frac{1}{n}\sum_{i=1}^{n}\left[\log\left(1+\frac{p_i-a_{i-1}^*}{a_{i-1}^*}\right)-\log\left(1+\frac{a_i-a_{i-1}}{a_{i-1}}\right)\right]^2}$$

where p_i is the predicted level of the endogenous variable in period i; a_{i-1}^* is the level of the endogenous variable in period $(i-1)$ as well as it is known at the time of the forecast (in a simulation run spanning several periods, a_{i-1}^* would be the value of the endogenous variable generated by the simulation in period $(i-1)$); and a_i is the actual observed value of the endogenous variable in period i. Letting

$$P_i = \log\left(1+\frac{p_i-a_{i-1}^*}{a_{i-1}^*}\right) \tag{4-1}$$

and

$$A_i = \log\left(1+\frac{a_i-a_{i-1}}{a_{i-1}}\right) \tag{4-2}$$

this statistic can be expressed more simply as

$$\sqrt{\frac{1}{n}\sum_{i=1}^{n}(P_i-A_i)^2}$$

Based on this statistic of prediction error, Theil has developed an inequality coefficient which compares the root mean square log prediction error of forecasts using the model to be validated with the log prediction error of forecasts of no change. (In a validation run spanning several periods, a forecast of no change is the forecast obtained by predicting the value of the endogenous variable in period t to be equal to the value generated by the model in period $(t-1)$.) This inequality coefficient, U, is given by Equation 4-3.

$$U = \sqrt{\sum_{i=1}^{n} (P_i - A_i)^2 \Big/ \sum_{i=1}^{n} A_i^2} \tag{4-3}$$

The statistic U has a range from zero in the case of a perfect forecast to one if the predictions are only as good as the naive hypothesis of no change, to infinity as the researcher's predictions become progressively worse when compared to the hypothesis of no change.

The mean square error, the square root of which is the numerator of Theil's inequality coefficient, provides some additional information concerning the seriousness of different types of prediction error affecting the forecasts. Theil breaks down the mean square error as follows:

$$\frac{1}{n} \sum_{i=1}^{n} (P_i - A_i)^2 = (\bar{P} - \bar{A})^2 + (s_p - s_a)^2 + 2(1 - R)s_p s_a, \tag{4-4}$$

where P_i and A_i are defined as in Equations 4-1 and 4-2; $\bar{P}$ and $\bar{A}$, s_p^2 and s_a^2, are the means and variances of the P_i and A_i over the n periods of the simulation; and R, defined as

$$\frac{1}{n} \left[\sum_{i=1}^{n} (P_i - \bar{P}) (A_i - \bar{A}) \Big/ s_p s_a \right],$$

is the correlation coefficient of the P_i and A_i.

If $(\bar{P} - \bar{A})^2$ is greater than zero, then the predicted values are biased. The researcher can usually correct this form of error. If $(s_p - s_a)^2$ is greater than zero, then the predicted and realized values have unequal variances. This suggests that certain important variables have been omitted from the predicting equation, causing a large stochastic error component. If $2(1 - R)s_p s_a$ is greater than zero, then R is less than one. Little can be done to reduce this type of error.

Dividing each of these terms by their sum, the mean square prediction error, we obtain the inequality proportions:

$$U_m = \frac{(\bar{P} - \bar{A})^2}{\dfrac{1}{n} \sum_{i=1}^{n} (P_i - A_i)^2},$$

the bias proportion;

$$U_s = \frac{(s_p - s_a)^2}{\frac{1}{n} \sum_{i=1}^{n} (P_i - A_i)^2} ,$$

the variance proportion; and

$$U_c = \frac{2(1 - R)s_p s_a}{\frac{1}{n} \sum_{i=1}^{n} (P_i - A_i)^2} ,$$

the covariance proportion.

Earlier, we stated that in order to select a model variant for policy Experiments I and II in which export quotas are inoperative, we conducted three deterministic validation simulations using Models A, A1, and A2 and spanning the 1956-59 period. In Table 4-3 we present Theil's inequality coefficient, *U,* comparing actual with predicted values for each of the three models. Based on an analysis of these and related validation statistics, we quickly concluded that Model A2 yielded the least satisfactory predictions of the three models and could be eliminated. For the other two models, the inequality coefficients revealed few important differences in forecasting ability.

In Table 4-3 we also present the inequality proportions and correlation coefficients for the two models. Although the correlation coefficients are roughly similar for both models, there are noticeable differences in the inequality proportions between models. These proportions suggest that, on the whole, Model A1 is better formulated than Model A with, for Model A1, no variance proportion greater than twenty percent. On the other hand, in Model A the high variance proportions for both robusta exports and revenues suggest that one or more important variables have been omitted from the robusta export equation.

In addition to permitting us to compare the forecasting success of Model A with that of Model A1, the various validation statistics presented in Table 4-3 give us useful information on the ability of both models to predict specific endogenous variables. In particular, both models are quite unsuccessful at predicting prices. This is confirmed both by negative coefficients of correlation between actual and predicted values and by large inequality coefficients. Forecasts of United States inventories and per capita United States demand for both robustas and Brazils were also disappointing. Here again inequality coefficients for both models were greater than 1, while the correlation coefficients were undesirably low.

Table 4-3. Theil's Inequality Coefficients for Models A, A1; and A2 and Inequality Proportions and Correlation Coefficients for Models A and A1 (1956-1959)

Variable[a]	Model A				Model A1				Model A2
	U^b	R^c	Ineq. Props.[d] Var.	Cov.	U^b	R^c	Ineq. Props.[d] Var.	Cov.	U^b
PR	1.10	-0.17	0.29	0.70	1.29	-0.42	0.11	0.88	5.08
M1R[e]	1.47	-0.02	0.00	1.00	1.65	-0.09	0.02	0.98	1.85
M2R[e]	0.61	0.79	0.09	0.91	0.61	0.79	0.12	0.88	0.77
EXR	0.87	0.75	0.88	0.12	0.54	0.84	0.08	0.92	0.69
REVR	0.90	0.46	0.61	0.39	0.79	0.75	0.05	0.95	1.48
PM	1.16	-0.26	0.08	0.92	1.12	0.03	0.03	0.97	2.51
M1M[e]	0.65	0.76	0.18	0.81	0.78	0.67	0.02	0.97	0.69
M2M[e]	0.98	0.45	0.00	1.00	1.04	0.43	0.00	1.00	1.37
EXM	0.53	0.86	0.21	0.78	0.51	0.90	0.10	0.90	0.53
REVM	0.44	0.91	0.30	0.69	0.55	0.87	0.06	0.93	0.41
PB	1.19	-0.35	0.08	0.91	1.19	-0.35	0.08	0.92	1.18
M1B[e]	1.12	0.14	0.08	0.92	1.08	0.19	0.11	0.89	1.33
M2B[e]	0.55	0.83	0.04	0.96	0.61	0.79	0.03	0.97	0.89
EXB	0.90	0.46	0.16	0.84	0.87	0.51	0.19	0.81	1.12
REVB	1.01	0.33	0.08	0.92	0.97	0.38	0.10	0.90	1.24
INV1	1.36	0.00	0.00	1.00	1.36	0.00	0.00	1.00	1.36

[a]For a key to the variable abbreviations, see pp. 114 and 115.

[b]U, the inequality proportion, $= \sqrt{\sum_{i=1}^{n}(P_i - A_i)^2 / \sum_{i=1}^{n} A_i^2}$, where $P_i = \log[1 + p_i - p_{i-1})/p_{i-1}]$ and $A_i = \log[1 + (q_i - q_{i-1})/q_{i-1}]$. ($p_i$ is the predicted level of the variable in period i and q_i is the actual level of the variable in period i.)

[c]R, the correlation coefficient, $= \frac{1}{n}[\sum_{i=1}^{n}(P_i - \bar{P})(A_i - \bar{A})/s_p s_a]$, where s_p and s_a are the standard deviations of P and A, respectively.

[d]The variance proportion, $U_s = (s_p - s_a)^2 / \frac{1}{n}\sum_{i=1}^{n}(P_i - A_i)^2$ and the covariance proportion, $U_c = 2(1-R)s_p s_a / \frac{1}{n}\sum_{i=1}^{n}(P_i - A_i)^2$. (The bias proportion, U_m, can be derived using the formula: $U_m = 1 - U_s - U_c$. In no case was the bias proportion greater than 0.01.)

[e]Based on per capita regression equations.

In spite of these problems with price and United States demand forecasts, the overall performance of both models was quite satisfactory. In particular, revenue forecasts, which will play a key role in our analysis of the policy simulation experiment outcomes, were reasonably good.

The historical validation analysis has indicated that Models A and A1 yield more or less equally successful forecasts. However, as noted earlier, Model A also suffers from a structural inconsistency in the robusta sector where price varies directly with world export demand, yet is assumed to be predetermined in the regional demand equations. Therefore, Model A1 was chosen for Experiment II, the Brazilian minimum price policy simulation experiment, in which we will examine the impact of alternative minimum price levels on revenues of all three varieties of coffee.

Despite the advantages of Model A1, this model could not be used for Experiment I, the production-goals simulation in which it is also assumed that no export quotas are in effect. This policy simulation experiment investigated the impact of different production mean levels on producers' revenues. Since mild and robusta exportable production appear explicitly as explanatory variables only in the export supply equations and Model A1 omits these equations, it would not be a suitable formulation for the production goals experiment. Instead, we used Model A for this experiment.

The remaining two policy simulations, Experiments III and IV, deal with export quota levels and indicator prices, two policy instruments established by the ICO. For these experiments Model B, summarized in Figure 4-1, was used. In Table 4-4 we present Theil's inequality coefficients and related statistics for two deterministic simulation runs using this model. The first of these runs spans the years 1960-1965, that part of the estimation period in which export quotas were operative. The second validation run covers the years 1966-1967 and gives information on the forecasting power of Model B outside the original estimation period.

For both periods, the forecasts generated by Model B were disappointing with inequality coefficients greater than one for nine of the seventeen endogenous variables. As in the validation runs for 1956-1959, the price predictions were particularly unsatisfactory, with price forecasts for all three varieties consistently larger than actual values. Fortunately, projections of revenue changes and levels, at least for milds and Brazils, were more successful. For these two varieties, only the inequality coefficient associated with Brazilian revenues for the 1966-1967 period was greater than one and, although predicted revenue levels were consistently larger than actual values, the size of the discrepancies was not unreasonable.

THE POLICY SIMULATION EXPERIMENTS

In recent years researchers, by using computer simulation analysis, have for the first time been able to conduct controlled experiments in the social sciences. If

Table 4-4. Theil's Inequality Coefficients, Inequality Proportions, and Correlation Coefficients for Model B (1960–1965 and 1966–1967)

	1960–65		Inequality Props.[d]			1966–67		Inequality Props.[d]		
Variable[a]	U[b]	R[c]	*Bias*	*Var.*	*Cov.*	U[b]	R[c]	*Bias*	*Var.*	*Cov.*
PR[e]	8.72	−0.18	0.01	0.73	0.26	5.81	−0.37	0.00	0.56	0.44
M1R[e]	2.27	0.36	0.00	0.41	0.59	4.59	0.32	0.00	0.71	0.29
M2R[e]	0.78	0.69	0.00	0.00	1.00	0.99	0.53	0.02	0.00	0.98
EXR	0.70	0.78	0.00	0.56	0.44	1.32	−0.21	0.01	0.05	0.94
REVR	3.32	0.68	0.01	0.76	0.22	2.11	0.54	0.00	0.50	0.50
PM	1.98	0.15	0.00	0.19	0.81	2.47	−0.12	0.02	0.26	0.73
M1M[e]	1.12	0.07	0.00	0.14	0.86	0.63	0.78	0.06	0.03	0.92
M2M[e]	0.77	0.64	0.00	0.37	0.63	0.88	0.48	0.00	0.25	0.75
EXM	0.82	0.59	0.00	0.40	0.60	0.75	0.66	0.00	0.28	0.72
REVM	0.76	0.66	0.00	0.28	0.72	0.54	0.84	0.03	0.12	0.85
PB	1.33	0.57	0.01	0.22	0.77	3.89	−0.04	0.01	0.59	0.40
M1B[e]	2.32	−0.48	0.00	0.08	0.92	3.58	−0.05	0.15	0.34	0.51
M2B[e]	0.97	0.51	0.00	0.00	1.00	2.40	−0.25	0.00	0.17	0.83
EXB	0.71	0.73	0.00	0.01	0.99	0.99	0.37	0.02	0.08	0.89
REVB	0.81	0.61	0.01	0.08	0.91	1.17	0.06	0.03	0.07	0.90
INV1	1.77	−0.17	0.00	0.03	0.97	1.51	0.34	0.04	0.17	0.79
BMIN	3.77	0.11	0.02	0.51	0.47	6.86	−0.08	0.05	0.73	0.23

[a]For a key to the variable abbreviations, see pp. 114 and 115.

[b]U, the inequality proportion, $= \sqrt{\sum_{i=1}^{n}(P_i - A_i)^2 / \sum_{i=1}^{n} A_i^2}$, where $P_i = \log[1 + (p_i - p_{i-1})/p_{i-1}]$ and $A_i = \log[1 + (a_i - a_{i-1})/a_{i-1}]$. ($p_i$ is the predicted level of the variable in period i and a_i is the actual level of the variable in period i.)

[c]R, the correlation coefficient, $= \frac{1}{n}[\sum_{i=1}^{n}(P_i - \bar{P})(A_i - \bar{A})/s_p s_a]$, where s_p and s_a are the standard deviations of P and A, respectively.

[d]U_m, the bias proportion, $= (\bar{P} - \bar{A})^2 / \frac{1}{n}\sum_{i=1}^{n}(P_i - A_i)^2$; U_s, the variance proportion, $= (s_p - s_a)^2 / \frac{1}{n}\sum_{i=1}^{n}(P_i - A_i)^2$; and U_c, the covariance proportion, $= 2(1-R)s_p s_a / \frac{1}{n}\sum_{i=1}^{n}(P_i - A_i)^2$.

[e]Based on per capita regression equations.

the investigator wishes to avoid the complication of introducing random shocks to the model, he may choose to conduct a simple deterministic simulation, permitting him at minimal cost in terms of computer time to isolate the impact of changes in particular policy instruments while holding all other factors constant. On the other hand, simulations involving a series of stochastic replications, while more costly, can provide information on the range of results that may be expected—information which can be invaluable if fluctuations outside particular limits entail exceptional costs. In addition, if the instrument can not be perfectly controlled by the policy maker as in our production goals experiment, then a meaningful deterministic simulation may not be possible.

If for these or other reasons the researcher opts for a stochastic simulation involving a series of replications, each spanning multiple observation intervals, then the task of data analysis becomes formidable. In such cases analysis of variance can be a useful technique for summarizing results while at the same time permitting the investigator to make probabilistic statements comparing alternative instrument levels.

With the exception of the production goals experiment where no deterministic simulation was possible, we conducted both deterministic and stochastic simulations in our policy experiments.[5] Since little information on costs was available, it was not possible to analyze the impact of various policy measures on profit levels. However, for nations producing coffee, variable short term supply costs tend to be low and stable over a wide range of exports. In addition, for national producers maintenance of foreign exchange export earnings is frequently a more crucial target than maintenance of profits and these foreign exchange receipts depend directly on revenues. Therefore, in analyzing the outcomes of the simulation experiments we decided to concentrate on revenue projections for each of the three varieties of coffee.

Analysis of variance was used to analyze the results of the stochastic simulations. In a stochastic experiment comparing the impact of several alternative levels of a particular policy instrument, one-way analysis of variance will be a suitable technique of analysis if the set of J observations associated with factor level i, $\{y_{ij}\}$, $j = 1, \ldots, J$, are independently and normally distributed. In the stochastic experiments presented here, twenty replications were made of the basic n quarter experiment. For each replication associated with factor level i, the mean over n quarters of Brazil, mild, and robusta revenues was obtained. For a particular variety of coffee, mean revenues associated with different stochastic replications will be independent and, by the Central Limit Theorem, they will be approximately normally distributed. Therefore, analysis of variance is a suitable test of the hypothesis that there are no significant differences in mean revenues associated with different factor levels.

In order to replicate a particular experiment, random error terms were introduced into the model equations. For recursive equation i we simply generated normally distributed random error terms with zero mean and variance

σ_i^2, equal to that part of the observed variance of the dependent variable not explained by the empirical equation. For simultaneous blocks of equations in which the error terms are interdependent, we used a multivariate normal, random number generator.[6]

In applying analysis of variance to the results of our stochastic simulations, we began by using Fisher's F statistic to test the hypothesis for each variety of coffee that the mean revenues associated with the various factor levels do not differ significantly from the over-all mean. If at the 0.05 level we rejected this hypothesis for a particular variety, we then applied Tukey's t method of multiple comparison to determine which factor levels had the largest impact on the variety's mean revenues.[6]

Because of space limitations, we will present here a detailed discussion of only the first policy experiment, that of examining production goals. However, at the end of this section we will briefly summarize the results of the other three simulations.

The objective of the production goals experiment is, in the context of a period of generally conceded overproduction (the mid-1960s), to investigate the impact of reductions in the mean production levels of the three coffee varieties on revenues and on the availability of fresh coffee supplies to consumers. For this experiment a deterministic simulation would serve no purpose since, although we will assume fixed production means, output levels must be expected to fluctuate around these means. In addition, a stochastic simulation involving several iterations per factor level will permit us to determine the probability that supplies of fresh coffee will fall below "adequate" levels from a consumer standpoint.

For this experiment we will assume that, for each coffee variety, production has stabilized and, therefore, is not influenced by a time trend but rather is simply normally distributed about the mean level. The variance and current mean production values used to stochastically generate these normally distributed production figures were estimated from production data for each variety, after making certain adjustments to eliminate the time trend from mild and robusta output figures.[7]

For the simulation experiment we will consider three alternative mean output levels: (1) the "current" mean production level, (2) eighty-five percent of the current level, and (3) seventy percent of the current level. We will assume that for each variety, variance remains constant as the mean output level changes. Because the experiment is stochastic we will use analysis of variance to determine the effect of different production means for each variety on average revenues of that type of coffee and of the other two varieties. One objective of the experiment will be to investigate the impact of different combinations of mean production levels on average revenues. Therefore, we will use a three-way analysis of variance design with the mean for each of our three coffee varieties as a separate factor. With three mean production levels being examined, this implies three cubed, or twenty-seven simulation runs to obtain a complete three-way analysis of variance table.

In analyzing the results of these simulation runs, we first obtained a set of F ratios for each of the three varieties of coffee. These preliminary F tests indicated that changes in own mean production and changes in mean output of the primary substitute[8] caused significant variations in revenues for all three varieties at the five percent level. Therefore, we examined, by variety, a subset of the contrasts associated with each of these two factors. In all cases we used the present mean production level as the control variable and we set up confidence intervals for simple differences between the main effect associated with the current production mean and the other main effects. In Table 4-5 we present, by variety and for both the significant factors of own and primary-substitute mean output, the revenue main effects linked with each factor level, the contrasts in these main effects, and their associated confidence intervals.

Since Brazils are the chief substitute for both milds and robustas, variations in average output of Brazils had a significant impact on revenues of all three varieties. This is reflected in Table 4-5 where main effects resulting from changes in the mean output of Brazils are presented in the "Factor O" columns for Brazil revenues and in the "Factor $S1$" columns for mild and robusta revenues. As the table indicates, mean revenues for all three varieties of coffee varied inversely with output of Brazils with, in all three cases, a reduction of Brazilian mean production to seventy percent of current levels resulting in a significant increase in revenues at the 0.05 level.

Changes in mean production of milds yielded significant F statistics for both revenues of Brazils, for which milds are the chief substitute, and earnings of milds themselves. For mild revenues, the main effects, contrasts, and related confidence intervals presented in the "Factor O" columns of Table 4-5 indicate that mild revenues varied directly with own production such that a mild production cut to either eighty-five percent or seventy percent of current levels resulted in a significant drop in earnings at the five percent level. On the other hand, although Brazilian revenues tended to vary inversely with mild production, none of the contrasts were significant at the ten percent level.

Finally, variations in robusta output had a significant impact only on own revenues. In this case robusta revenues varied directly with output, with average revenues significantly decreased at the 0.05 level by a cut in robusta output to seventy percent of current levels.

In conducting this simulation experiment we assumed that, in addition to Brazil, mild and robusta producers maintained some stocks; therefore we did not constrain annual exports to be less than or equal to exportable production for any variety. However, because of the strong preference of most consuming nations for new-crop coffee, we also investigated the possibility that reductions in production could result in inadequate supplies of fresh coffee. In Table 4-6 we present the probabilities that adequate supplies of fresh milds,

Table 4-5. Experiment I: The Production Goals Experiment. Main Effects with Selected Contrasts and Associated Confidence Intervals for Revenues Earned by the Three Varieties of Coffee (in millions of dollars)

Mean Production Level[a]	Θ	Variety	Factor 0: Own Mean Production — Main Effects[b] (Θ_i)	Contrasts ($C_i = \Theta_i - \Theta_1$)	5% Confidence Intervals	Factor S1: Mean Production of Primary Substitute — Main Effects[b] (Θ_i)	Contrasts ($C_i = \Theta_i - \Theta_1$)	5% Confidence Intervals	Primary Substitute
$1.00\,\overline{X}$	Θ_1	Brazils	-23.9	—	—	-5.3	—	—	Milds
$0.85\,\overline{X}$	Θ_2	Brazils	1.1	25.0	$-7.7 \leqslant C_2 \leqslant 57.7$	-1.0	4.3	$-28.4 \leqslant C_2 \leqslant 37.0$	Milds
$0.70\,\overline{X}$	Θ_3	Brazils	22.9	46.8	$14.1 \leqslant C_3 \leqslant 79.5$	6.3	11.6	$-21.1 \leqslant C_3 \leqslant 44.3$	Milds
$1.00\,\overline{X}$	Θ_1	Robustas	15.5	—	—	-11.1	—	—	Brazils
$0.85\,\overline{X}$	Θ_2	Robustas	0.6	-15.0	$-31.5 \leqslant C_2 \leqslant 1.6^{c}$	-0.4	10.8	$-5.8 \leqslant C_2 \leqslant 27.3^{c}$	Brazils
$0.70\,\overline{X}$	Θ_3	Robustas	-16.1	-31.6	$-48.2 \leqslant C_3 \leqslant -15.1$	11.5	22.6	$6.1 \leqslant C_3 \leqslant 39.2$	Brazils
$1.00\,\overline{X}$	Θ_1	Milds	37.0	—	—	-24.4	—	—	Brazils
$0.85\,\overline{X}$	Θ_2	Milds	0.8	-36.3	$-70.8 \leqslant C_2 \leqslant -1.7$	0.8	25.2	$-9.4 \leqslant C_2 \leqslant 59.8$	Brazils
$0.70\,\overline{X}$	Θ_3	Milds	-37.8	-74.8	$-109.4 \leqslant C_3 \leqslant -40.2$	23.6	48.1	$13.5 \leqslant C_3 \leqslant 82.6$	Brazils

[a] $\overline{X}$ represents the present mean production level.

[b] The main effect, Θ_i, is defined as the mean for level i minus the over-all mean.

[c] Significant at the 0.10 level.

Table 4-6.   The Probability That There Will Not Be Adequate Supplies[a] of Fresh Coffee[b] (in percent)

Mean Production Level[c]	*Milds*	*Robustas*	*Brazils*
$1.00\bar{X}_b$	05	00	16
$0.85\bar{X}_b$	04	00	30
$0.70\bar{X}_b$	04	00	48
$1.00\bar{X}_m$	00	00	29
$0.85\bar{X}_m$	02	00	31
$0.70\bar{X}_m$	11	00	34
$1.00\bar{X}_r$	04	00	28
$0.85\bar{X}_r$	04	00	34
$0.70\bar{X}_r$	04	00	33

[a]For the purposes of this table, "supplies of fresh coffee" are defined as production in year *t* plus the change in stocks over the two preceding years.

[b]Probabilities are based on the number of years in relevant simulation runs for which world demand exceeded the supply of fresh coffee as defined in note a. (e.g., runs associated with $1.00\bar{X}_b$ are those in which mean production of Brazils was held constant at 100 percent of present levels.

[c]$\bar{X}$ is the current mean production level.

robustas, and Brazils would not be available for each of the nine mean output levels. (Adequate supplies of fresh coffee of variety *i* were assumed available for those years in which production in year *t* plus changes in stocks over the two preceding years exceeded demand in year *t*.)

As Table 4-6 indicates, the probability that reasonable supplies of fresh Brazils will not be on hand to satisfy demand increased substantially as the Brazil production mean declined. On the other hand, although there was about a ten percent chance that mild supplies would be inadequate at very low production levels (i.e., at seventy percent of current levels), for higher levels of mild production the probability of a supply shortfall was minimal. Finally, for robustas the probability of inadequate supplies was near zero at all production levels.

Summarizing our findings, robusta producers would clearly lose revenue if production is reduced. Since such a cut in output would not significantly help other producers or consumers, we can objectively conclude that robusta output should not be reduced.

From the producer's viewpoint it is equally clear that a cut in mean production of Brazils to seventy percent of current levels would result in increased earnings for all three varieties of coffee. However, in this case such a reduction would be highly undesirable from a consumer viewpoint. Therefore, any policy recommendation must involve a value judgment, weighing the well-being of consumers against that of producers. A possible compromise solution might be a production goal for Brazils of eighty-five or ninety percent of the present level.

The situation with respect to mild output is even more complex. In this case mild revenues varied directly with mild production with highly significant contrasts in the main effects. On the other hand, Brazilian revenues demonstrated a weak inverse relation with mild production. Thus we are faced with the dilemma of weighing the virtual certainty that any cut in production will result in lost mild revenues against the probability that such a cut in mild output would increase Brazilian revenues. In this case a possible compromise solution might be a mild production goal slightly below (for example, ninety-five percent of) current levels.

In Tables 4-7 and 4-8 we summarize the most significant results of two additional simulation experiments. The first of these, Experiment II, examined the effects of Brazilian minimum export price on export revenues earned by each of the three varieties of coffee. As Table 4-7 indicates, there was a strong direct relation between Brazilian minimum export price and revenues earned by all three varieties.

Experiment III investigated the impact of alternative ICO export quota levels on earnings. The results of this experiment were more complex. Since the F ratio associated with average revenues of Brazils was not significant at the 0.10 level, we concluded that variations in quota levels had no important effect on Brazil's export earnings. On the other hand, our investigation revealed a statistically significant nonlinear relation between mild revenues and quota levels with revenues increasing as protection was relaxed, but falling when quotas were removed completely. Finally, robusta revenues rose significantly when quotas were cut by ten percent and declined when quotas were lifted altogether. However, there was little difference between revenues earned at current quota levels and those associated with a ten percent increase in export limits.

Experiment IV investigating the indicator price system yielded no statistically significant F ratios, and therefore we concluded that the presence or absence of indicator prices had minimal impact on coffee revenues.

CONCLUSIONS

Our simulation experiments have indicated that among the policy instruments tested, only indicator prices failed to have a significant impact on coffee revenues. However, any policy decisions based on the positive results of the minimum export price, production goals, and export quota experiments must be tempered by an awareness of certain model weaknesses highlighted by our earlier validation analysis. In particular, the model used in Experiment III, the export quota experiment, yielded very poor predictions when subjected to validation tests. (In spite of this qualification, the results of the experiment and particularly the unresponsiveness of Brazilian revenues to quota changes seem quite consistent

Table 4-7. Experiment II: The Brazilian Minimum Export Price Experiment. Main Effects with Selected Contrasts and Associated Confidence Intervals for Revenues Earned by the Three Varieties of Coffee (in millions of dollars)

BMIN Level	Variety	Θ	Main Effects* (Θ_{ji})	Contrasts with Θ_6 as Control $(C_{ji} = \Theta_{ji} - \Theta_{j6})$	5% Confidence Intervals
15¢	Brazils	Θ_{b1}	-208	-405	$-415 \leqslant C_{b1} \leqslant -394$
30¢	Brazils	Θ_{b2}	-116	-313	$-323 \leqslant C_{b2} \leqslant -302$
45¢	Brazils	Θ_{b3}	-30	-227	$-237 \leqslant C_{b3} \leqslant -216$
60¢	Brazils	Θ_{b4}	49	-147	$-158 \leqslant C_{b4} \leqslant -137$
75¢	Brazils	Θ_{b5}	123	-73	$-84 \leqslant C_{b5} \leqslant -63$
90¢	Brazils	Θ_{b6}	197	—	—
BMIN endog.	Brazils	Θ_{b7}	-14	-211	$-221 \leqslant C_{b7} \leqslant -200$
15¢	Robustas	Θ_{r1}	-91	-191	$-197 \leqslant C_{r1} \leqslant -185$
30¢	Robustas	Θ_{r2}	-56	-157	$-163 \leqslant C_{r2} \leqslant -150$
45¢	Robustas	Θ_{r3}	-20	-120	$-126 \leqslant C_{r3} \leqslant -114$
60¢	Robustas	Θ_{r4}	19	-81	$-87 \leqslant C_{r4} \leqslant -75$
75¢	Robustas	Θ_{r5}	57	-43	$-49 \leqslant C_{r5} \leqslant -37$
90¢	Robustas	Θ_{r6}	100	—	—
BMIN endog.	Robustas	Θ_{r7}	-10	-111	$-117 \leqslant C_{r7} \leqslant -105$
15¢	Milds	Θ_{m1}	-168	-253	$-261 \leqslant C_{m1} \leqslant -244$
30¢	Milds	Θ_{m2}	-70	-154	$-163 \leqslant C_{m2} \leqslant -145$
45¢	Milds	Θ_{m3}	6	-79	$-88 \leqslant C_{m3} \leqslant -70$
60¢	Milds	Θ_{m4}	54	-30	$-39 \leqslant C_{m4} \leqslant -22$
75¢	Milds	Θ_{m5}	81	-4	$-13 \leqslant C_{m5} \leqslant 5$
90¢	Milds	Θ_{m6}	84	—	—
BMIN endog.	Milds	Θ_{m7}	14	-71	$-79 \leqslant C_{m7} \leqslant -62$

*For revenues earned by variety j, the main effect, Θ_{ji} is defined as the mean of factor level i minus the over-all mean.

Table 4-8. Experiment III: ICO Quota Levels Experiment. Robusta and Mild Revenue Main Effects with Selected Contrasts and Associated Confidence Intervals (in millions of dollars)

Quota Levels[a]	Variety	Θ	Main Effects[b] (Θ_{ji})	C	Contrasts (C_{ji})	5% Confidence Intervals
0.9Q	Robustas	Θ_{r1}	14.5	$\Theta_{r1} - \Theta_{r4}$	30.7	$18.3 < C_{r1} < 43.1$
1.0Q	Robustas	Θ_{r2}	2.3	$\Theta_{r2} - \Theta_{r4}$	18.5	$6.1 < C_{r2} < 31.0$
1.1Q	Robustas	Θ_{r3}	-0.6	$\Theta_{r3} - \Theta_{r4}$	15.6	$3.2 < C_{r3} < 28.0$
0.0Q	Robustas	Θ_{r4}	-16.2	—	—	—
0.9Q	Milds	Θ_{m1}	-10.8	$\Theta_{m1} - \Theta_{m3}$	-24.5	$-43.2 < C_{m1} < -5.7$
1.0Q	Milds	Θ_{m2}	-2.3	$\Theta_{m2} - \Theta_{m3}$	-15.9	$-34.6 < C_{m2} < 2.8$
1.1Q	Milds	Θ_{m3}	13.6	—	—	—
0.0Q	Milds	Θ_{m4}	-0.5	$\Theta_{m4} - \Theta_{m3}$	-14.1	$-32.8 < C_{m4} < 4.6$

[a]Q represents actual ICO quota levels after adjusting for exports to Annex B countries. See [1], pp. 140–141.

[b]For revenues earned by variety j, the main effect, Θ_{ji}, is defined as the mean of factor level i minus the over-all mean.

with observation.) Similarly, the results of Experiment II, the minimum price experiment, although based on a more reliable model, seem almost too good to be true. In this case, the structural assumption that minimum export price almost completely determines world market price, while yielding successful predictions for the data period tested, may be too strong when combined with a completely rigid minimum export price such as that envisioned by the experiment.

In this chapter we have concentrated on describing Experiment I, the production goals experiment partly because we feel the results of this experiment are particularly reliable. Our validation work indicated that the model used for the experiment yielded quite successful predictions, and, in addition, the nature of the experiment suggests that any structural weaknesses remaining in the model should not seriously impair the results. Finally, our prediction that any reduction in Brazilian production might seriously reduce supplies of fresh coffee available to consumers seems to be coming to pass in the current market situation, characterized by high coffee prices and Brazilian production shortfalls.

APPENDIX 4A

The Fitted Equations[9]

Model A

$$BMIN^{[10]} = \underset{(17.49)}{0.81744} \, PB_{t-1} - \underset{(-1.84)}{0.000134} \, STOCK^* - \underset{(-2.70)}{7.3796} \, W_{t-4} + \underset{(2.43)}{5.8188}, \, R^2 = 0.92$$
$$DW = 2.70$$

$$PB \quad = \underset{(68.79)}{1.0713} \, BMIN + \underset{(6.26)}{17.9216} \, W_{t-2}, \, R^2 = 0.93$$
$$DW = 1.75$$

$$INV1^* = \underset{(2.22)}{52.90} \, (PB_{t-1} - PB_{t-2}) + \underset{(5.48)}{48.23} \, POP1_t + \underset{(2.56)}{0.40} \, (INV1_{t-1} - INV1_{t-2})$$

$$+ \underset{(2.21)}{652.44} \, W_{t-4} - \underset{(-3.58)}{5726.08}, \, R^2 = 0.56$$
$$DW = 1.84$$

$$PR^{[11]} \quad = \underset{(1.96)}{0.001581} \, EXR + \underset{(12.98)}{0.5790} \, PB, \, R^2 = 0.54$$
$$DW = 0.52$$

$$EXR^{[11]} = \underset{(2.08)}{11.6284} \, PR + \underset{(12.97)}{0.1860} \, EPR, \, R^2 = 0.66$$
$$DW = 2.76$$

$$\frac{M1R}{POP1} = \underset{(0.87)}{-0.02429} \, PR + \underset{(0.83)}{0.02259} \, PB + \underset{(2.78)}{0.1958} \, CPI1 + \underset{(2.85)}{0.005631} \, Y1$$

$$+ \underset{(4.62)}{0.001246} \, (INV1_t - INV1_{t-1}) - \underset{(1.51)}{0.4461} \, Q2 - \underset{(4.07)}{1.1881} \, Q3 - \underset{(5.40)}{26.3869}$$

$$R^2 = 0.80$$
$$DW = 1.16$$

$$\frac{M2R^{[12]}}{POP2} = \underset{(1.36)}{0.01092} \, PB - \underset{(-1.25)}{0.01303} \, PR + \underset{(4.30)}{0.01692} \, Y2 + \underset{(1.82)}{0.01204} \, CPI2$$

$$+ \underset{(2.71)}{0.3499} \, Q1 + \underset{(3.68)}{0.4657} \, Q2, \, R^2 = 0.82$$
$$DW = 1.73$$

$$M3R \quad \equiv EXR - M1R - M2R$$

$$EXM \quad = \underset{(44.35)}{0.2187} \, EPM + \underset{(5.30)}{900.7278} \, Q1, \, R^2 = 0.58$$
$$DW = 2.36^{[13]}$$

$$PM = -0.002196\ EXM + 1.0647\ PB + 12.6732, R^2 = 0.89$$
$$(-2.54) \qquad\quad (15.94) \qquad\quad (2.44) \quad DW = 0.73$$

$$\frac{M1M}{POP1} = -0.1525\ PM + 0.06227\ PB - 0.2241\ T + 0.001782\ (INV1_t - INV1_{t-1})$$
$$(-2.23) \qquad\quad (0.88) \qquad\quad (-5.85) \qquad\quad (3.68)$$

$$+ 0.01234\ Y1 + 1.2057\ Q1 - 1.4480\ Q2 - 1.6143\ Q3, R^2 = 0.54$$
$$(9.73) \qquad\quad (1.97) \qquad\quad (-2.46) \qquad\quad (-2.77) \quad DW = 1.91$$

$$\frac{M2M}{POP2} = -0.03127\ PM + 0.01574\ PB + 0.01682\ Y2 + 0.0203\ CPI2$$
$$(2.18) \qquad\quad (0.95) \qquad\quad (3.75) \qquad\quad (2.70)$$

$$+ 0.2301\ Q2, R^2 = 0.88$$
$$(1.92) \qquad DW = 2.19$$

$$M3M \equiv EXM - M1M - M2M$$

$$\frac{M1B}{POP1} = -0.2279\ PB + 0.1898\ PM + 0.02654\ PR + 0.006388\ Y1$$
$$(-2.56) \qquad\quad (2.94) \qquad\quad (0.57) \qquad\quad (-3.59)$$

$$+ 0.004469\ (INV1_t - INV1_{t-1}) + 1.3528\ Q1 - 1.3397\ Q3 + 24.3761$$
$$(9.83) \qquad\qquad\qquad (2.74) \qquad\quad (-2.72) \qquad\quad (6.35)$$

$$R^2 = 0.82$$
$$DW = 1.73$$

$$\frac{M2B}{POP2} = -0.07849\ PB + 0.02145\ PR + 0.02964\ PM - 0.09118\ T + 0.04939\ Y2$$
$$(-2.78) \qquad\quad (1.33) \qquad\quad (1.44) \qquad\quad (-4.63) \qquad\quad (9.24)$$

$$-0.5894\ Q2, R^2 = 0.66$$
$$(-3.53) \qquad DW = 1.16^{13}$$

$$EXB \equiv M1B + M2B + \overline{\overline{M3B}}$$

Selected Equations: Model B

$$EXB = 0.02526\ EPB - 31.894\ BMIN + 1083.86\ W_{t-2} - 826.61\ Q1$$
$$(1.76) \qquad\quad (-2.79) \qquad\quad (1.91) \qquad\quad (2.39)$$

$$- 918.4\ Q2 + 5217.5, R^2 = 0.53$$
$$(-3.12) \qquad (7.29) \quad DW = 2.48$$

$$PB^{12} = \underset{(-4.55)}{-0.0080\,EXB} + \underset{(2.27)}{13.26\,W_{t-2}} + \underset{(11.07)}{79.775}, \begin{array}{l} R^2 = 0.28 \\ DW = 0.63 \end{array}$$

$$EXR^{11} = \underset{(2.22)}{11.9473\,PR} + \underset{(13.38)}{0.1852\,EPR}, \begin{array}{l} R^2 = 0.66 \\ DW = 2.76^{13} \end{array}$$

$$\frac{M1R^{11}}{POP1} = \underset{(-2.09)}{-0.1054\,PR} + \underset{(1.97)}{0.0845\,PB} + \underset{(3.14)}{0.2728\,CPI1} + \underset{(2.04)}{0.004597\,Y1}$$

$$+ \underset{(4.54)}{0.001415}\,(INV1_t - INV1_{t-1}) - \underset{(-1.61)}{0.5341\,Q2} - \underset{(-3.66)}{1.1880\,Q3} - \underset{(-5.24)}{32.5612}$$

$$R^2 = 0.75$$
$$DW = 1.15$$

$$\frac{M2R^{11,12}}{POP2} = \underset{(-1.28)}{-0.01891\,PR} + \underset{(1.41)}{0.01463\,PB} + \underset{(3.95)}{0.01626\,Y2} + \underset{(1.90)}{0.01306\,CPI2}$$

$$+ \underset{(2.69)}{0.3485\,Q1} + \underset{(3.64)}{0.4633\,Q2}, \begin{array}{l} R^2 = 0.81 \\ DW = 1.76^{13} \end{array}$$

$$EXR \equiv M1R + M2R + \overline{M3R}$$

PR is that price which equilibrates demand and supply.

NOTES

1. This paper is based on the author's unpublished Ph.D. dissertation.[1]
2. Imports by the new markets listed in Annex B of the Agreement were not subject to the quota.[2]
3. The European countries included are Belgium-Luxembourg, the Netherlands, Germany, France, Italy, the United Kingdom, Norway, Sweden, Denmark, Austria, and Portugal.
4. The results of the graphical analysis are described in detail in [1].
5. We felt that stochastic simulations were justified in the first three experiments because of the presence of production and export constraints. However, in retrospect it might be argued that the additional information gained by conducting these stochastic simulations did not justify their high cost.
6. We used Nagar's method to estimate the covariance matrix of disturbance terms for each simultaneous equation block.[4]
7. The methods used to estimate the mean and variance for production of each variety are described in detail in [1]. For robustas, the current production mean level was 14.7 million bags with a variance of 823

thousand bags. For milds, the present mean was 19.2 million bags with a variance of 701 thousand bags. For Brazils, the current mean level was 21.6 million bags with a variance of 8.8 million bags.

8. For milds and robustas, the primary substitute was Brazils. For Brazils, the main substitute was milds.

9. Unless otherwise indicated, all equations were estimated from a sample of 43 quarterly observations beginning with the second quarter of 1955 and extending through the fourth quarter of 1965. See [1], Appendix D, for data sources. Figures in parentheses are *t* statistics.

10. Estimated from a sample of thirty-two quarterly observations for the periods: the fourth quarter of 1952 through the second quarter of 1955; the second quarter of 1959 through the fourth quarter of 1962; and the fourth quarter of 1963 through the fourth quarter of 1965.

11. Computed by two-stage least squares.

12. Estimated from a sample of fifty-five quarterly observations spanning the years 1952 through 1965.

13. The Durbin-Watson statistic was computed for the regression with a constant term.

REFERENCES

1. Epps, Mary Lee. "A Computer Simulation of the World Coffee Economy." Unpublished Ph.D. dissertation, Duke University, 1970.

2. *International Coffee Agreement, 1962*. Appendix B in U.S. Senate, Committee on Finance, *Coffee,* Report No. 53, 89th Cong., 1st Sess., 1965.

3. International Coffee Organization, International Coffee Council. "Production Goals and Stock Policy," Resolution No. 206 (ICC–14–Res.206) (March 28, 1969).

4. Nagar, A.L. "Stochastic Simulation of the Brookings Econometric Model," *The Brookings Model: Some Further Results.* Edited by J.S. Duesenberry, G. Fromm, L.R. Klein, and E. Kuh. Chicago: Rand McNally, 1969, pp. 423–57.

5. *New York Times.* August 31, 1973.

6. Scheffé, Henry. *The Analysis of Variance.* New York: John Wiley & Sons, Inc., 1959.

7. Stigler, George. "Notes on the Theory of Duopoly," *Journal of Political Economy* 48 (August 1940), pp. 521–41.

8. Theil, Henri. *Applied Economic Forecasting.* Chicago: Rand McNally, 1966.

9. U.S. Department of Agriculture, Foreign Agricultural Service. *FCOF,* "Foreign Agricultural Circular," No. 3–73, (July 1973).

Chapter Five

Monthly Price Structure of the U.S. Beef, Pork, and Broiler Markets

Lester H. Myers
Joseph Havlicek, Jr.

Recent history has demonstrated the importance of the livestock-meat sector of the U.S. economy. For the first time in over twenty years consumers were faced with meat shortages, uncontrolled price spirals, and government intervention. Likewise, meat producers were subjected to highly inflated feed costs, an apparent unsatiable demand, government controls, and spotty consumer boycotts of beef products. This period of time has very visibly demonstrated several key characteristics about the livestock-meat sector. First, it illustrated the interrelated nature of the three basic meats (beef, pork, and broilers) in the minds of consumers. Beef shortages quickly led to the substitution of other meats by consumers with the subsequent short-run demand pressures forcing pork and chicken prices to record levels. Second, it illustrated the interrelationship between the feedgrain sector and the livestock-meat sector. High feedgrain prices forced decreases in pork and broiler production which further enhanced the spiral of consumer prices. Finally, it demonstrated the basic difference between a long-run supply function concept and a short-run market supply response for a storable commodity. Live animals (hogs and cattle) can be "stored" on the farm for brief periods of time and during the 'price freeze' of beef prices producers actually withheld supplies in anticipation of higher prices after the freeze was lifted. Thus, even with historically high prices for live cattle, short-run marketings declined. This is contrary to the usual concept of supply response.

The model represents an attempt at formalizing the underlying structural relationships of the U.S. livestock meat economy and quantifying the structural parameters of this system. Emphasis in the model is on the hog-

Associate Professor, Food and Resource Economics Department, University of Florida (Myers) and Professor, Department of Agricultural Economics, Virginia Polytechnic Institute and State University (Havlicek).

pork subsector, however, the interrelated nature of the livestock-meat sector prohibits the economic examination of one subsector without simultaneous consideration of the other primary meat products.

Previous studies have either (1) focused on the measurement of substitution relationships between meats at the retail level, (2) evaluated live cattle and hog price relationships, or (3) looked at the relationships for one commodity (e.g. hogs) across market levels. This study broadens the scope of the previous work in the sense that a system is developed which permits simultaneous interaction between meats at the retail level and between market channels.

Specifically, this study is concerned with identifying and measuring the underlying monthly structural relationships of the livestock-meat economy in the United States. The objectives are: (1) to determine possible seasonal patterns in the supply and demand of livestock and meat products; (2) to determine the interrelationships between pork, beef, and broilers at the retail level; (3) to delineate the interrelationship between the consumer and farm levels of the market system for pork and beef; and (4) to evaluate the impacts at the farm level of changes in certain variables at the retail level.

ECONOMIC MODEL

The economic model used to represent the monthly structure of the livestock-meat economy is based on the assumptions that hog and beef producers and meat packers maximize profits, produce essentially a homogenous product and individually do not influence product or input prices. On the consumer side, it is assumed that all consumers face an equivalent price, that the average quantity response to income changes among consumers is a valid approximation of individual responses to income changes, that each consumer's preferences are independent of preferences of other consumers, and that each consumer maximizes his satisfactions subject to his income or budget constraint.

The model consists of a set of eight behavioral equations:

1. The farm market supply of live slaughter hogs.
2. The farm market supply of live slaughter cattle.
3. The retail to farm margin for pork.
4. The retail to farm margin for beef.
5. The supply of pork to the retail sector.
6. The retail demand for pork.
7. The retail demand for beef.
8. The retail demand for broilers.

The development of each of these relationships is considered separately.

Farm Supply of Slaughter Hogs

The number of slaughter hogs on farms in any given month comes from two sources: (1) the inventories of slaughter hogs at the beginning of the month and (2) those hogs which reach some minimum slaughter weight during the month. Within the planning period of a month the producer can do very little to alter the size of this stock of slaughter hogs. For the purposes of this study, the number of slaughter hogs is considered fixed within the month. There are three alternative uses for hogs of slaughter weight: (1) all or part of them may be sold to meat packers for pork production, (2) at least a portion of them may be held over in the form of live hog inventories on farms and sold next month, and (3) some may be retained for breeding purposes. Neglecting breeding stock, the total number of hogs of slaughter weight is allocated between the first two alternatives.

The allocation between slaughter and inventory is determined by: (1) the current market demand for slaughter hogs, (2) the anticipated demand for slaughter hogs in the near future, and (3) the desires of producers to sell hogs for slaughter during the current month. Because total available quantity is fixed for the current time period, knowledge of any two of the above three relationships is sufficient to derive the third.

In developing the short-term supply model for live slaughter hogs, the following assumptions are made: (1) the number of the hogs (NH_{jk}), excluding breeding stock, reaching a minimum slaughter weight during a given month is predetermined, but the number (n_{1jk}) and the average weight (w_{1jk}) of hogs slaughtered during the month are not predetermined; (2) hogs not sold in the current month ($NH_{jk} - n_{1jk} = n_{2jk}$) must be sold during the next month; (3) producers incur additional costs by carrying slaughter hogs beyond a minimum slaughter weight, and (4) anticipated returns from inventory carryover depend upon expected future prices and nonpecuniary yields which may accrue to producers for certain inventory levels.

The variable quantities for the jth month are n_{1jk}, n_{2jk}, w_{1jk} and w_{2jk}; where w_{2jk} is the average weight of n_{2jk} when sold for slaughter. It is assumed that $n_{2,j-1,k}$ must be sold during the jth month and that the value of w'_{2jk} is the average weight of $n_{2,j-1,k}$ when sold for slaughter.

The total liveweight supplied for slaughter during the jth month of the kth year is:

$$QH_{jk} = n_{1jk}\, w_{1jk} + n_{2,j-1,k}\, w'_{2jk}. \tag{5-1}$$

QH_{jk} may be determined by solving for the factors that affect n_{1jk} and w_{1jk} since $n_{2,j-1,k}$ and w'_{2jk} were determined in the $(j-1)^{\text{th}}$ month.

In maximizing anticipated net revenue from NH_{jk}, hog producers are subject to the constraint:

$$NH_{jk} = n_{1jk} + n_{2jk}.$$ (5-2)

The constrained anticipated net revenue function for the jth month of the kth year is:

$$VH_{jk} = PH_{jk}\, n_{1jk}\, w_{1jk} + a\, EPH_{jk}\, n_{2jk}\, w_{2jk}$$

$$- c\,(n_{1jk}, n_{2jk}, w_{1jk}, w_{2jk}) + \lambda\,(NH_{jk} - n_{1jk} - n_{2jk})$$ (5-3)

where:

VH_{jk} is the constrained anticipated net revenue for hogs attaining a minimum slaughter weight in the jth month of the kth year;

PH_{jk} is the price of slaughter hogs in the jth month of the kth year;

$a = \left(\dfrac{1}{1 + r_{jk}}\right)$ is the discount factor for equating future prices to current prices, (where r_{jk} is the interest rate for the jth month of the kth year);

EPH_{jk} is the expected price of slaughter hogs in the next month following the jth month of the kth year;[1]

$c(n_{1jk}, n_{2jk}, w_{1jk}, w_{2jk})$ is the cost function, including cost of carrying slaughter hogs for an additional time period, which is assumed to be twice differentiable and nondecreasing; and

λ is an undetermined Langrangian multiplier not equal to zero.

Solving the equations representing the necessary conditions for maximum anticipated net revenue from NH_{jk}, for $n_{1jk}, n_{2jk}, w_{1jk}, w_{2jk}$ and λ subject to the constraint specified in (5-2) yields both n_{1jk} and w_{1jk} as functions of $PH_{jk}, EPH_{jk}, r_{jk}$ and NH_{jk}. Combining n_{1jk} and w_{1jk} and expressing the relationship in linear form provides the following expression.

$$n_{1jk}\, w_{1jk} = \beta_{0j} + \beta_{1j}\, PH_{jk} + \beta_{2j}\, EPH_{jk} + \beta_{3j} r_{jk} + \beta_{4j}\, NH_{jk}$$ (5-4)

where the β_{ij}'s are parameters. Based on the second-order conditions of a constrained maximum, the following a priori information about the β_{ij}'s in (5-4) is known:

$$\beta_{1j} > 0; \quad \beta_{2j} < 0; \quad \text{and } \beta_{3j} > 0.$$

The sign of β_{4j} is mathematically indeterminate from the first and second order conditions, but it has to be positive for equilibrium to be maintained between two successive months or time periods.[2]

Expected Prices. An "expectation" model that will explain future prices in terms of actual known variables is needed to estimate the parameters of the model. Unfortunately, theory is not explicit when it comes to the formulation of an expectation model. However, a few studies have attempted to uncover the factor producers consider when formulating an "expected" price. Schultz and Brownlee [15] concluded that Iowa hog farmers seemed to simply project current prices as their future price expectations. This conclusion is the basis for the application of the cobweb theorem to the hog-pork economy.

Although current prices no doubt play a large role in the formulation of future prices, it probably is an oversimplification to assume that expected prices are simply an extension of current prices. Deviations from current prices may occur because of changing production and demand patterns which result from seasonal and cyclical factors. The expectation model used in this study is specified as follows:

$$EPH_{jk} = PH_{jk} + \theta CH_{jk} + \delta SH_{jk} \tag{5-5}$$

where:

EPH_{jk} is the expected price of slaughter hogs in the next month following the jth month of the kth year.

PH_{jk} is the actual price of live hogs in the jth month and the kth year.

CH_{jk} is a measure of the relative position on the hog production cycle.

θ is the coefficient which reflects the effects that cyclical production patterns have on price expectations.

SH_{jk} is a measure of seasonal factors which affect slaughter hog production.

δ is the coefficient which reflects the effects that seasonal production patterns have on price expectations.

In estimation the seasonal influences are accounted for by using zero-one variables to allow the levels of supply response to fluctuate from month to month.

Supply Response for Slaughter Hogs. The specific live hog supply response relationship to be estimated is:

$$\beta_{11} QH\nabla + \beta_{12} PH\nabla + \alpha_{11} NH + \alpha_{12}R + \alpha_{13} PCR + \alpha_{14} CH + \alpha_{15} T = \mu_1 \tag{5-6}$$

The variables are defined as follows:[3]

$QH\nabla$ is the total liveweight of hogs commercially slaughtered in the U.S. (million pounds).

$PH\nabla$ is a weighted average price per hundred pounds of barrows and gilts sold (dollars/cwt.).

NH is the total number of live hogs on farms 6 months and older, other than breeding stock, during the month. It includes beginning inventories and the pig crop reaching 6 months of age during the month (thousand head).

R is the discount on prime 90-day bankers' acceptances at N.Y.C. and is included to account for short-term interest rates used in discounting expected prices back to current prices.

PCR is the average price per bushel of No. 3 yellow corn at Chicago (dollars/bushel).

CH is the measure of cyclical production patterns in hogs and is a ratio of the total liveweight of hogs slaughtered during the months "j –12" through "j – 1" to the total liveweight slaughtered during the months "j – 24" through "j – 13."

T is time as measured by numbering months consecutively with January 1949 = 1.

μ_1 is a random error term with the usual assumptions that:

(a) $E(\mu_{1jk}) = 0$ for all j and k

(b) $E(\mu_{1jk}, \mu_{1st}) = 0$ for $j \neq s$ and/or $k \neq t$

σ_1^2 for $j = s$ and $k = t$.

In Equation (5–6) and all subsequent equations, endogenous variables are denoted with ∇ attached to the variable name ($QH\nabla$ and $PH\nabla$) and are preceded by "β" coefficients. Variables not denoted with a ∇ and preceded by "α" coefficients are predetermined variables in that their values are assumed to be determined by factors outside the livestock-meat sector of the economy or prior to the current time period. The α's and β's refer to parameters whose values will be estimated by statistical procedures.

The quantity of hogs commercially slaughtered is assumed to depend upon the current hog price and on the expected hog price for the next month. The relationship between quantity and the current hog price is hypothesized to be positive and the relationship between quantity and the expected hog price for the next month is hypothesized to be negative. However, the expected hog price as specified in (5–5) is a function of the current hog price. The nature of the price expectation model results in the coefficient of current hog price in Equation (5–6) being the sum of two structural parameters. These two parameters have opposite signs based upon a priori knowledge. Since it is impossible to isolate the values of each individual parameter, it is not possible to specify the sign of the coefficient of current price prior to estimation. [12, p. 1400].

Time is included in the hog supply, and all other supply and margin equations, to reflect the aggregate effects of "left-out" economic variables which tend to exhibit steady influences over time. In particular, it is assumed to reflect the effects of technological changes occurring over the period of study. Technological changes affecting the hog supply level include the change from one litter to multilitter systems, the gradual change to meat type hogs, and the gradual introduction of improved housing and management practices.

Farm Supply of Slaughter Cattle

Beef competes for the consumer's meat dollar at the retail level. Because of this interrelationship, the beef sector is considered in the analysis of the hog-pork sector. The National Commission on Food Marketing [13, p. 93] reported that a major proportion of the changes in retail beef prices is reflected back to farm prices within a 3-week period. This being the case, it is also necessary to include the market supply relationships for slaughter cattle at the farm level as an integral part of the hog-pork model.

The supply of cattle for slaughter during a given month may be derived in a manner similar to that used for the supply of slaughter hogs. The assumption that live animals may be retained on farms as inventory carryovers from month to month is even stronger with cattle than with hogs. With hogs it is assumed that inventories of marketable hogs may be sold in the $(j + 1)^{th}$ month. The situation is somewhat different with cattle because the range of weight at which slaughter cattle are marketed extends over several hundred pounds. The length of time that slaughter animals are within this weight range is longer than a month and slaughter cattle may be retained on farms as live inventories more than a month. Cattle that are not sold for slaughter during the current month do not have to be sold for slaughter during the following month. In formulating the behavioral relationship for the farm supply of slaughter cattle it is assumed that a new "expected" price is formulated each month for the next month and the decision to sell or continue holding is based on the new "expected" price.

Assuming that cattle producers maximize net returns from a given stock of cattle which reaches a minimum market weight during a given month, the monthly supply response for live slaughter cattle is:

$$\beta_{21} \, QC\nabla + \beta_{22} \, PC\nabla + \alpha_{21} \, R + \alpha_{22} \, PCR + \alpha_{23} \, T + \alpha_{24} \, NC + \alpha_{25} \, CC = \mu_2. \quad (5\text{-}7)$$

Variables appearing in Equation (5-7) which haven't been defined previously are:

$QC\nabla$ is the total liveweight of cattle commercially slaughtered in the U.S. (million pounds).

$PC\nabla$ is the average cost per 100 pounds for all cattle slaughtered under federal inspection (dollars/cwt.).

NC   is the number of cattle and calves on feed in 26 states at the beginning of the month (thousand head).

CC   is a measure of cyclical production patterns in cattle and is a ratio of the total liveweight of cattle slaughtered during months "$j - 12$" through "$j - 1$" to the total liveweight slaughtered during months "$j - 24$" through "$j - 13$."

As with the supply of live hogs for slaughter, the estimated supply response of live cattle for slaughter to current price changes could be positive or negative because current prices influence expected prices as well as current slaughter.

Farm-Retail Marketing Margins

The connecting link between farm prices and retail prices is the marketing margin. For pork, the marketing margin is defined as the difference between the retail price for a pound of pork and the farm price for an equivalent amount of hog on a liveweight basis. Although marketing margins are, in general, a much talked about but little researched area of economic activity, some attempt has been made to group margins into several classifications and types.[4] Margins which appear to have an underlying structure are called "systematic" as opposed to "nonsystematic" margins which stem from oligopolistic forms of competition.[4] In this study, it is assumed that the marketing margins for beef and pork are of a "systematic" nature.

"Systematic" margins include: the absolute (or cents per pound) margin and the percentage margin. The percentage margin may be a percent of either the farm, wholesale, or retail price. Both types may be further classified according to whether they are constant or variable. Constant margins are inelastic to changes in price or quantity while variable margins respond to changes in prices or quantities or both.

Margins for pork and beef have been studied by several researchers; however, no general conclusion has been reached regarding their exact nature. Based mainly upon graphical analysis, Breimyer [2] argued that, during periods of short supplies of livestock, packers bid up the live prices. Thus, short supplies lead to smaller margins while larger quantities result in higher margins. Although this conclusion is widely held to be true, attempts to empirically measure the effects of supplies on margins for meat have, in general, yielded insignificant results. A 1960 study of the farm to retail margins of a number of foods by Buse and Brandow [3] was inconclusive regarding the effects of quantities consumed on the farm to retail price spreads for beef and pork. When annual data for the period 1921–1957 were used, they found negative elasticities between consumption and the marketing margins for both meats. These elasticities were not statistically significant at the 0.05 level. When quarterly data were used for the period 1946–1957, positive elasticities resulted with the elasticity for pork being significant at the 0.05 level. Maki [10, p. 629] also found that production explained an insignificant (at the 0.05 level) amount of the variation in the farm prices of beef and pork when wholesale prices were included as an explanatory variable.

Retail to Farm Margin for Pork. It is assumed that the retail to farm margin for pork is not constant in the short-term but is influenced by cost factors, quantities of hogs marketed, and by the particular price levels themselves. The procedure used in this study to attain a measure of margins, for both pork and beef, is to first estimate a farm price equation and then to derive the margin function from the estimated results. The equation for the farm level price of hogs from which the retail to farm margin for pork is obtained is:

$$\beta_{31} \, PH\nabla + \beta_{32} \, QH\nabla + \beta_{33} \, PP\nabla + \alpha_{31} \, T + \alpha_{32} \, W = \mu_3 \tag{5-8}$$

Variables not defined previously are:

$PP\nabla$ is the average retail price per pound for retail pork cuts and sausage in U.S. urban areas (cents/pound).

W is an index of hourly wages paid to production workers in the meat packing industry (1957–59 = 100).

The marketing margin is obtained from Equation (5-8) by: (1) adjusting the coefficient of retail pork prices by the net yield of the retail cuts per pound to put live prices and retail prices on a comparable basis; (2) solving the estimated equation for retail pork prices; and (3) subtracting farm prices from both sides of the equation so that the resulting function pertains to the difference between the retail price for pork and the farm level price for hogs, both based on comparable units. This procedure is explained in more detail in the results section.

Retail to Farm Margin for Beef. The margin function for beef is specified under the same assumptions as the margin function for pork. The equation for the farm level price of cattle is:

$$\beta_{41} \, PC\nabla + \beta_{42} \, QC\nabla + \beta_{43} \, PB\nabla + \alpha_{41} \, T + \alpha_{42} \, W = \mu_4 \tag{5-9}$$

where:

$PB\nabla$ is the average retail price per pound of choice grade carcass cuts of beef in U.S. urban areas (cents/pound).

The margin function for beef is derived from Equation (5-9) in a manner identical to the derivation of the pork margin function.

Retail Level

Retail Pork Supply.   Total supplies of pork available for consumption during a given month are derived from two sources: (1) the stocks of cold storage holdings at the beginning of the month and (2) the slaughter of live hogs during the month. The amount of pork produced during the month is simply a function of the total liveweight of hogs slaughtered. Not all pork available for consumption during a given month must be consumed during the month. Some may be put in cold storage for later sale to consumers. The behavioral equation for the amount of pork supplied to the retailer sector for consumption is specified in this section. The amount going into storage is the beginning of the month cold storage stocks plus the pork produced during the month minus the pork supplied for current consumption.

The economic model used to explain the current supply of pork for consumption purposes is quite similar to the live hog supply model. The essential characteristics and assumptions are the same.

The major holders of cold storage stocks are assumed to be the meat packers, and they hold cold storage stocks in hopes of increasing their net revenues. Similar to live hogs, the decision to hold stocks for sale later depends upon relevant costs and returns. The costs of storing pork are regarded as being an increasing function of the size of holdings.

Cold storage stocks may be safely held for periods of time longer than one month. Again it is assumed that a new "expected" price is formulated by meat packers each month and that the decision to sell or continue holding stocks is based upon this new "expected" price.

Assuming that meat packers attempt to maximize anticipated net revenues, the monthly supply response of pork for consumption is:

$$\beta_{51} \ QPS\nabla + \beta_{52} \ QH\nabla + \beta_{53} \ PP\nabla + \alpha_{51} \ R + \alpha_{52} \ CH + \alpha_{53} \ T$$

$$+ \ \alpha_{54} \ QSP = \mu_5 \tag{5-10}$$

where:

$QPS\nabla$ is the total consumption, both civilian and military, of commercially produced pork (million pounds).

QSP is total pork in cold storage at the beginning of the month (million pounds).

Retail Demand for Pork. The remaining behavioral relationship needed to determine the allocation of available supplies of pork is the consumer demand function for pork. The theory of consumer demand has been well developed and can be appropriately applied to the specification of the monthly demand for pork at the retail level. Theory suggests that the quantity demanded of a good depends upon the price of the good, the prices of all other related goods, and consumer incomes. In the case of retail demand for pork, it is not feasible to consider all food items as related, even though in reality there may be a relationship between pork and many other individual food items. For the purpose of this study, only selected other meats will be considered explicitly as being related food items.

Beef, pork, and broilers constitute the three major meats in terms of consumption in the United States, hence beef and broilers are considered substitutes for pork at the retail level. The retail demand function for pork expressed in linear form is as follows:

$$\beta_{61} \, QPD\nabla + \beta_{62} \, PP\nabla + \beta_{63} \, PB\nabla + \beta_{64} \, PCH\nabla + \alpha_{61} \, I + \alpha_{62} \, POP = \mu_6 \qquad (5\text{-}11)$$

where:

$QPD\nabla$ is the total consumption, both civilian and military, of commercially produced pork (million pounds).

$PCH\nabla$ is the average price of frying chicken in retail stores in urban areas in the U.S. (cents/pound).

I is average disposable per capita income in U.S. (dollars/person/month).

POP is the total United States population including armed forces (million people).[5]

Retail Demand for Beef. Given that pork, beef and broilers compete for the consumer's meat dollar, it is assumed that the direction of causality among the quantities and prices of the three meats is multidirectional and that quantities and prices are jointly determined. Therefore, retail demand relations for beef and broilers are also specified.

Consumer demand for beef depends upon the same factors as the demand for pork. The explicit relationship may be written as:

$$\beta_{71} \, QBD\nabla + \beta_{72} \, PP\nabla + \beta_{77} \, PB\nabla + \beta_{74} \, PCH\nabla + \alpha_{71} \, I + \alpha_{72} \, POP = \mu_7 \qquad (5\text{-}12)$$

where:

$QBD\nabla$ is the total production of domestically produced beef (million pounds).

The use of total beef production as a measure of beef consumption neglects the effects of storage changes. Although the monthly cold storage holdings of beef have recently averaged over 300 million pounds, the month-to-month difference in cold storage holdings is relatively small. This suggests that the monthly consumption of domestically produced beef is very close to monthly production. During 1949, the most that monthly production differed from monthly consumption was 4.0 percent of production, while in 1972 the largest difference was 9.3 percent of production.[23, 24] Virtually all of this discrepancy can be accounted for by net imports. While net beef imports represent about 5-10 percent of domestic production, the main effect is in the nonfed beef sector.[8] To keep the model manageable, the statistical analysis does not include beef imports and, as such, pertains only to domestically produced beef.

For the purposes of this study, it is assumed that monthly consumption is essentially dressing percentage times monthly slaughter; hence, a retail supply relationship for beef is not included in the model. The market clearing identity for beef at the retail level is:

$$QBD\nabla = KC \cdot QC\nabla \tag{5-13}$$

where:

KC is dressing yield for converting live cattle to carcass weight.

Retail Demand for Broilers. Broilers exhibit somewhat different supply characteristics at the farm level than do hogs or cattle. Once broilers reach market weight, they cannot be held on the farm to take advantage of future price increases. The number of broilers marketed during a given month is the result of decisions that were made 2 to 3 months previously. Therefore, the number of broilers marketed and the amount of broiler meat produced during a given month are predetermined in an economic sense.

The retail demand function for broilers is specified with the assumption that the quantity of broilers is a predetermined variable and that the retail price of broilers is affected by the quantities of pork, beef, and broilers consumed, as well as personal disposable income. The broiler demand relation is:

$$\beta_{81} \; PCH\nabla + \beta_{82} \; QPD\nabla + \beta_{83} \; QBD\nabla + \alpha_{81} \; I + \alpha_{82} \; QCHD$$

$$+ \; \alpha_{83} \; POP = \mu_8 \tag{5-14}$$

where:

$QCHD$ is the total consumption of broilers (million pounds).

Variations in month to month cold storage holding of broilers are quite small in relation to production.[26, 27] [6] Also, exports represent only around 1 percent of production.[26, 27] Thus, monthly broiler production is essentially identical to monthly consumption. Since the quantity produced is predetermined, the quantity consumed is also considered to be predetermined and no retail supply function for broilers is included in the model.

Supply-Demand Identity for Pork.   To have market equilibrium, the quantity of pork supplied must equal the quantity of pork demanded for each observation period. The identity specified in 5-15 expresses this equilibrium.

$$QPD\nabla = QPS\nabla. \tag{5-15}$$

Equations (5-6) through (5-15) complete the description of the monthly livestock-meat sector of the economy. Eight of these equations are stochastic and must be estimated. Relationships (5-13) and (5-15) are identities needed to complete the model.

DATA

Subperiod Selection
The empirical analysis in this study focuses on the time period of one month. There are several reasons for selecting the month as the period of study. First, a model is desired which will delineate and explain the short-term price and quantity fluctuations which occur but which may or may not be explained by factors contributing to longer-run trends in prices and supplies. Second, the time period represented by a single observation should be short enough so that important seasonal differences in the structural parameters are not covered up in terms of an average, but at the same time not so short as to preclude economic fluctuations. Finally, economic data are available in the form of monthly observations. Empirical estimates are based on data from February 1949 through December 1970.

Empirical Variables
Selection of the empirical variables to be used in estimating the parameters of the behavioral equations was made on the basis of approximating, as closely as possible, the variables specified in the theoretical economic model. Data availability, statistical limitations, and the necessity for aggregation all serve to cause deviations from theoretical specifications. Despite these obstacles, an attempt was made to use secondary data as summarized by the United States Department of Agriculture and various other government agencies as much as possible. When not directly available, variables were con-

structed from existing data in a manner to conform as closely as possible to the type of variable needed in the empirical model. The derivation of variables not published directly is given in this section.

Arriving at a "representative price" associated with aggregate quantities supplied or demanded for the United States is improbable, if not impossible. Price series used in the analysis can only be considered "representative," in the sense that all other price series for the same commodity move in the same directions, since the series used apply directly to only a limited number of markets. Cattle prices are represented by the estimated average cost of all cattle per hundredweight of slaughter for packers under federal inspection. Live hog prices for eight markets: Chicago, Indianapolis, Kansas City, Omaha, St. Louis National Stock Yards, Sioux City, So. St. Joseph and So. St. Paul, were weighted, averaged and reported as a single monthly price by the United States Department of Agriculture [23, 24] from 1949 through 1969. After 1969, only seven markets were included in the average due to the closing of the Chicago market.

Numbers of hogs on farms available for slaughter (NH) in any given month are not available in published form. Essentially this variable, as used in Equation (5-6), consists of two variables: (a) the number of hogs available for sale on farms at the beginning of the jth month and (b) the number of hogs reaching a marketable age during the month. The derivation of each component is discussed separately.

Beginning of the month farm inventories of marketable hogs are derived from published data series in the following manner. Inventories for January 1 for the years 1949 through 1963 are reported by the United States Department of Agriculture [23, 24] as hogs on farm 6 months old and older other than sows and gilts. Beginning in 1963 this series was revised to report hog inventories on farms December 1 by weight classes. To make this series comparable to the previous series, December 1 inventories for the years 1963 through 1967 include all 180-pound and above hogs plus 25 percent of those in the 120-179 pound weight class reported as "other" hogs on farms. Using the above months as benchmarks, inventories for the remaining months are computed in the following manner. Beginning inventory for the jth month is obtained from the beginning inventory for the $(j - 1)^{th}$ month by adding the pig crop reaching a marketable slaughter weight during the $(j - 1)^{th}$ month and the adjustments for changes in the size of the breeding stock and subtracting farm slaughter in the $(j - 1)^{th}$ month, total commercial slaughter in $(j - 1)^{th}$ month and the death loss for the $(j - 1)^{th}$ month. Farm slaughter and breeding stock adjustments are only reported on a yearly basis. They are proportioned out on a monthly basis according to the percentage of total annual commercial slaughter. Death loss includes all unaccounted for hogs, using the yearly balance, and is expressed as a percentage of the total pig crop.[7]

Numbers of hogs reaching a marketable slaughter weight during the

j^{th} month are derived by multiplying the number of cows farrowing during the $(j - 6)^{th}$ month by the average litter size and adjusting for death losses. The time it takes for a hog to reach a minimum marketable slaughter weight is arbitrarily set at six months.[8]

Short-term interest rates are included in the model to reflect the discounting of expected future prices. The interest rate on bankers' acceptances, prime 90 days at New York City, is used as a "representative" rate. Some reasons for its use in the empirical model are: (1) it is applicable to short periods of time (90 days), (2) it fluctuates considerably depending upon short-run economic conditions, and (3) it is readily available on a monthly basis through the Board of Governors of the Federal Reserve System.

Numbers of cattle on farms available for slaughter are not compiled and reported. As an indicator of this variable, the number of cattle and calves on feed in 26 states is used in the empirical analysis. These numbers are reported for January 1 for all years used in the study and for April 1, July 1 and October 1 for 1960 through 1968. The quarterly figures for years prior to 1960 were derived from the average percentage that the quarterly numbers were of the January 1 numbers for 1960 through 1966. Specifically, numbers on feed April 1 were taken to be 93.4 percent of January 1 numbers. July 1 numbers were computed as 84.6 percent of April 1 numbers, and October 1 numbers as 96.8 percent of July 1 numbers. Monthly inventories for in-between months for all years were derived by simply smoothing out the quarterly difference over three months. Since 1968, only 23 states have been reported in this series on a quarterly basis. However, January 1 figures are still reported for the three deleted states (Wyoming, Utah, and Nevada). Thus it was possible to adjust the series since 1968 to a 26 state basis by using a procedure similar to that used for the period prior to 1960.

Average hourly wages paid to production workers in the meat packing industry are reported monthly by the United States Department of Labor.[30] Since wages represent only some of the costs associated with marketing services, they were indexed on the basis of 1957–59 = 100 to form a "marketing cost" variable.

Personal income is reported by months by the United States Department of Commerce [29] but disposable income is not. Both personal and disposable income are reported by quarters. Monthly figures for disposable income were derived by weighting monthly personal income figures by the ratio of quarterly disposable income to quarterly personal income. Since the monthly observations were on a yearly rate basis, they were divided by 12.

Broiler consumption was not reported on a monthly basis prior to 1969. Because of the relatively short growing period for broilers, consumption can be derived fairly accurately from broiler chick placement data. Numbers of live broilers produced were derived from lagged weekly placements for 22 reporting states. The placements were adjusted by a mortality factor which was gradually reduced from 5 percent of placements in 1949 to 3 percent in 1957 and later years. Length of the lag was decreased from 12 weeks in 1949 to 9 weeks in 1958 through 1968, to account for changing technology. Placements prior to 1954 were also adjusted upward because less than 22 states reported before that year.[9] Monthly data were derived by adjusting weekly data to a daily basis and then readjusting to a monthly basis according to the number of days in the month.

Total consumption is then derived by the following formula:

$$
\text{Consumption} = \frac{\text{total broilers}}{\text{marketed}} \times \frac{\text{average weight}}{\text{per bird}} \times \frac{\text{average dressing}}{\text{yield}}
$$

$$
+ \frac{\text{beginning cold}}{\text{storage stocks}} - \frac{\text{ending cold}}{\text{storage stocks}} - \text{exports.}
$$

Average dressing yield has gradually increased from 69.12 percent in 1949 to 72.0 percent for 1958 through 1968. Exports are accounted for only since 1961 because prior to then broiler exports were negligible. Since 1968, broiler production is reported directly by the U.S.D.A. [26] and consumption may be derived by adjusting production for net changes in cold storage holdings and for exports.

General price levels influence certain endogenous variables in the economic model. To account for secular changes in the general price level, all farm prices and wages paid in the meat packing industry are deflated using the Wholesale Price Index (1957–59 = 100). All retail prices and disposable incomes are deflated using the Consumer Price Index (1957–59 = 100).

STATISTICAL PROCEDURES AND RESULTS

Economic theory provides limited information regarding the exact form of the behavioral relationships to be estimated. In this analysis, relationships that are linear in actual variates are used. The hypothesized model of the monthly livestock-meat economy includes ten jointly determined (endogenous) variables. Unique parameter estimates can be attained only if the system of equations is just identified or overidentified. The order condition for identifiability requires that the number of predetermined variables excluded from the relationship must be at least as great as one less than the number of endogenous variables included in the equation. Using this criterion, all equations to be estimated in the hog-pork model are overidentified. Two-stage least-squares methods were used to estimate the parameters of the model.

Several methods available for describing structural differences among subperiods are: (1) separate equations for each subperiod, (2) analysis of covariance using zero-one variables, and (3) the introduction of season, or month, as an explicit variable.[10] The procedure employed in this study is a variation of the analysis of covariance model.[11] Zero-one variables are used to allow for month-to-month differences in intercept values. Thus, it is assumed that seasonal influences affect the levels of the monthly behavioral relationships but do not affect the slope coefficients.

Monthly Differences in Intercept Values

Zero-one variables were used to allow for differences in the levels of the surfaces among months for all the behavioral equations except the pork and beef margin relationships. January was considered the base month in each case and 11 dummy variables were used to measure the monthly deviations from the base month. Seasonal indices for each of the supply equations and for the three retail demand relationships are presented in Figure 5-1. In each graph the average level of the respective relationships over all months is indicated by a seasonal index of 100.

Figure 5-1 is basically self-explanatory. However, several points should be emphasized. First, there is a marked lack of seasonality in the demand for beef and broilers. Pork demand, on the other hand, is quite seasonal in nature with a peak 51 percent above the average in October and a trough 41 percent below the average in February. Pork supply also exhibits a well defined seasonal pattern. The pork supply pattern is more extreme than the demand pattern. Hog and cattle supply are both subject to seasonal patterns, but cattle supply peaks in October while hog supply peaks in December. Cattle supplies are stronger during the summer than hog supplies.

Estimated Slope Coefficients

The estimated behavioral equations of the monthly livestock-meat economy are presented below.[12] Except for the margin equations constant terms are omitted since they were permitted to vary from month to month and have been presented graphically in Figure 5-1.[13] Figures in parentheses are ratios of estimated coefficients over their respective standard errors.

Slaughter hog supply:

$$QH\nabla = -24.66\ PH\nabla + 0.009\ NH + 29.640\ R + 274.845\ PCR$$
$$(5.85)(3.67)(3.49)(6.08)$$

$$+\ 240.660\ HC + 1.424\ T$$
$$(1.86)(5.29)$$

$$R^2 = 0.85^{14}$$

$$(5\text{-}16)$$

Slaughter cattle supply:

$$QC\nabla = -41.584\ PC\nabla + 0.094\ NC + 32.541\ R + 221.024\ PCR$$
$$(6.20)(5.38)(3.00)(2.97)$$

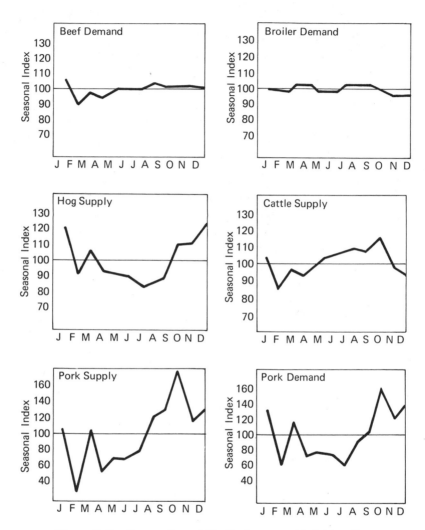

Figure 5-1. Seasonality of Six Endogenous Variables. Source: Table 5A-1.

$$- \underset{(0.28)}{64.148} CC + \underset{(6.25)}{3.472} T$$

$$R^2 = 0.96. \tag{5-17}$$

Pork Margin:

$$PH\nabla = \underset{(0.76)}{-2.908} - \underset{(3.56)}{0.0020} QH\nabla + \underset{(20.81)}{0.573} PP\nabla - \underset{(4.47)}{0.162} W + \underset{(5.53)}{0.059} T$$

$$R^2 = 0.85. \tag{5-18}$$

Beef Margin:

$$PC\nabla = \underset{(0.95)}{4.337} - \underset{(2.75)}{0.0019} QC\nabla + \underset{(17.46)}{0.419} PB\nabla - \underset{(5.48)}{2.16} W + \underset{(6.65)}{0.092} T$$

$$R^2 = 0.83. \tag{5-19}$$

Retail pork supply:

$$QPS\nabla = \underset{(9.83)}{0.314} QH\nabla + \underset{(1.36)}{1.099} PP\nabla + \underset{(0.11)}{0.254} R + \underset{(7.75)}{0.160} QSP$$

$$+ \underset{(5.15)}{186.033} HC + \underset{(14.37)}{1.107} T$$

$$R^2 = 0.96. \tag{5-20}$$

Retail pork demand:

$$QPD\nabla = \underset{(15.17)}{-11.890} PP\nabla + \underset{(3.96)}{2.406} PP\nabla + \underset{(3.70)}{5.786} PCH\nabla$$

$$+ \underset{(3.93)}{2.776} I + \underset{(2.68)}{5.103} POP$$

$$R^2 = 0.90 \tag{5-21}$$

Retail beef demand:

$$QBD\nabla = \underset{(3.06)}{2.926} PP\nabla - \underset{(12.47)}{9.229} PB\nabla + \underset{(1.59)}{3.025} PCH\nabla$$

$$+ \underset{(7.96)}{6.852} I + \underset{(4.30)}{9.962} POP$$

$$R^2 = 0.98. \tag{5-22}$$

Retail broiler demand:

$$PCH\nabla = -0.0044\ QPD\nabla - 0.0070\ PBD\nabla - 0.0189\ QCHD \qquad (5\text{-}23)$$
$$\quad\ \ (0.93) \qquad\qquad (1.56) \qquad\qquad (2.53)$$

$$+\ 0.479\ I - 1.050\ POP$$
$$\quad (8.97)\quad\ \ (13.08)$$

$$R^2 = 0.96.$$

With two exceptions, the estimated coefficients for Equations (5-16) through (5-23) are consistent with a priori expectations. The coefficient for cattle cycle (*CC*) in the cattle supply equation (5-17) was expected to be positive. The negative sign for the estimated coefficient is inconsistent, in a theoretical sense, with the logic of the variable as discussed previously. However, the ratio of the estimate to its standard error is less than one suggesting that the position on the cattle cycle does not significantly affect expected prices and subsequent cattle supplies. The second unexpected negative sign is associated with the coefficient for population in the broiler demand equation. Broiler prices have trended downward during the period of analysis due to major supply increases and some of this time trend may be picked up in the population coefficient. Even though the sign is wrong, the ratio of the estimated coefficient to its respective standard error is quite large.

The price variables in the live hog and cattle supply functions have negative signs. This is contrary to our normal concept of the price-quantity slope for a supply relationship. In the context of this model it is rational if one accepts the price expectation model as formulated and the associated inference that producers' response to expected price outweighs their response to current price when making short-term marketing decisions.[15] The pork supply equation has a positive price-quantity slope, suggesting that processors react differently to current and expected prices than do cattle and hog producers.

Since live hog prices (*PH*∇) are on a liveweight basis and retail pork prices (*PP*∇) on a retail-cut basis, the derivation of retail to farm price spreads for pork involves an adjustment of the coefficients of Equation (5-18). The coefficient for *PP*∇ was multiplied by the reciprocal of the net yield of the major retail cuts per pound; i.e., 2.13.[16] The margin equation is then obtained by solving Equation (5-18) for *PP*∇ and subtracting *PH*∇ from both sides. The margin function is:

$$MP = (PP' - PH\nabla) - 2.383 + 0.0016\ QH\nabla$$

$$-\ 0.181\ PH\nabla + 0.133\ W - 0.048\ T \qquad (5\text{-}24)$$

where:

PP'   is the price of a quantity of retail pork equivalent to one pound of liveweight of slaughter hogs.

Equations (5-18) and (5-24) indicate that slaughter quantities ($QH\nabla$) have a positive effect on retail to farm pork price spreads. An increase (decrease) of 10 million pounds of hogs slaughtered is associated with an increase (decrease) in the marketing margin of about 1.6 cents per hundredweight. This result tends to support Breimyer's argument that during periods of relatively smaller supplies, packers tend to bid up farm prices and thus decrease margins. [2, p. 692]

It is apparent that the use of monthly data leads to a set of conclusions regarding the nature of pork margins quite different from those based on annual data. Using annual data and expressing retail pork prices, adjusted to be equivalent to farm prices, as a function of farm prices and time, Harlow [7, pp. 44-45] concluded that: (1) the retail to farm margin is not affected by farm price levels, and (2) margins have been increasing steadily over time. These conclusions are clearly in contrast to those indicated by Equation (5-24). Not only are hog prices important to short-term margins, but after the effects of packers wages (*W*) are accounted for, there appears to be a time trend of decreasing margins. This suggests that the costs of marketing services, as measured by packer wages, have caused margins to increase over time, but that other factors, for example, technological advancements in the processing and retailing of pork and pork products, have tended to decrease margins over time.

As with the pork margin equation, the coefficient of the $PB\nabla$ in (5-19) must be adjusted to put live cattle prices and beef prices on a comparable basis. The coefficient of $PB\nabla$ was multiplied by the reciprocal of the net yield of retail beef per pound; i.e., 2.12.[17] The margin equation is:

$$MB = (PB' - PC\nabla) = -4.883 + 0.0021 \, QC \, \nabla$$

$$+ \, 0.126 \, PC\nabla + 0.243 \, W - 0.104 \, T \qquad\qquad (5\text{-}25)$$

where:

PB'   is the price of a quantity of retail beef equivalent to one pound of liveweight of slaughter cattle.

The margin relationships for beef and pork differ in that cattle prices are positively related to beef margins whereas hog prices are negatively related to pork margins.

The three retail demand relationships are consistent with a priori expectations. The estimated coefficients tend to support the argument that pork, beef, and broilers compete for the consumer's meat dollar. They also indicate that each of the three meats has a positive income elasticity of demand.

ELASTICITIES, CROSS ELASTICITIES AND FLEXIBILITIES

Average Elasticity and Flexibility Estimates[18]

Estimates of elasticities and cross elasticities for beef, pork, and broilers, evaluated at the means of the data for all 263 observations used in the analysis are presented in Table 5-1. Since the broiler demand Equation (5-23) was estimated with broiler prices as a function of pork, beef, and broiler consumption, elasticity estimates for broilers could be computed only after the three retail demand equations were solved simultaneously for demand quantities in terms of prices and disposable income. The retail-farm margin equations for pork and beef are used to estimate the relative responsiveness of demand quantities of pork and beef at the retail level to relative changes in farm prices of hogs and cattle.

Estimates of the average monthly price-elasticity of supply were obtained for pork and beef at the retail level. The average supply elasticity for pork was derived directly from the estimated pork supply equation. The average

Table 5-1.   Average Monthly Elasticities and Cross Elasticities of Demand at the Retail and Farm Levels for Pork, Beef, and Broilers

Normalized Variable	Elasticities or Cross Elasticities with Respect to:					
	$PP\nabla$	$PB\nabla$	$PCH\nabla$	I	$PH\nabla$	$PC\nabla$
$QPD\nabla$	−0.787	0.207	0.301	0.500	−0.440[a]	0.142
$QBD\nabla$	0.139	−0.571	0.113	0.889	0.078	−0.392
$QCHD$	0.312[b]	0.696	−8.126	11.280	0.175	0.479

[a]Farm level elasticities and cross elasticities were computed by using the margin Equations (5-18) and (5-19). For instance, the farm price elasticity of demand for pork was computed as follows:

$$e^{pdf} = \frac{\overline{PH}\nabla}{\overline{QPD}\nabla} \cdot \frac{\partial QPD\nabla}{\partial PH\nabla} \text{ where } \frac{\partial QPD\nabla}{\partial PH\nabla} = \frac{\partial QPD\nabla}{\partial PP\nabla} \cdot \frac{\partial PP\nabla}{\partial PH\nabla}$$

[b]Elasticities for broilers were computed by solving the estimated retail demand equations simultaneously for $QPD\nabla$, $QBD\nabla$ and $QCHD$ in terms of $PP\nabla$, $PB\nabla$, $PCH\nabla$, I and POP. The transformed broiler demand equation is:

$$QCHD = A + 1.672\,PP\nabla + 2.870\,PB\nabla - 55.358\,PCH\nabla + 22.166\,I - 60.426\,POP$$

where A is the constant term which varies from month to month.

supply elasticity for beef was derived from the estimated cattle supply equation, the beef margin equation, and the identity which converts liveweight of cattle slaughtered to quantity of beef meat.[19] The derived price elasticities of supply are 0.073 for pork and -0.615 for beef for the period of analysis.

The Influence of Time on Elasticity Estimates.   Estimates of the price-elasticity of demand for a commodity or commodities may be useful to policymakers for evaluating the implications of alternative programs. The ultimate policy decision may depend upon the specific elasticity estimate which, in turn, is a function of the length of the observation period from which it was derived. Since different conclusions may be reached depending upon whether the elasticity estimate was short- or long-term, it is desirable to take a closer look at the differences in elasticity estimates because of the time element.

There are two main factors that tend to influence elasticities differently in the short-term than in the long-term. First, during short time periods the demand for storage tends to increase elasticities relative to elasticities for longer-time periods, especially for products which can be stored for only a limited time. Second, ease of substitution during longer-time periods tends to increase longer-term elasticities relative to short-term elasticities.[20]

Quarterly and annual elasticity estimates for pork, beef, and broilers obtained by other researchers are presented in Table 5-2. The monthly price elasticities of demand estimated in this study are more inelastic than the quarterly and annual estimates presented in Table 5-2 for beef and pork. Evidently the lack of substitution in the short-term by consumers appears to be an important factor for beef and pork. The situation is opposite for broilers in that the short-run elasticity is much more elastic than the estimates based on more aggregate, time periods. Also, the inclusion of data for the 1960s and early 1970s could be responsible for the difference.

Beef is usually considered to have a more price elastic demand than pork. Yet results of both this study and the one by Logan and Boles (Table 5-2) indicate a more price elastic demand for pork than for beef during monthly and quarterly time periods. Evidently the length of the time period involved is an important factor in this relationship. The fact that the demand for beef goes from being more price inelastic than pork in the long-term is evidence that consumers are less willing to substitute for beef given short-term changes in beef prices. This indicates that the adjustment period to price changes is longer for beef than for pork. These results coincide with estimates for short- and long-run price elasticities of demand for beef and pork that Tomek and Cochrane [21] obtained using a distributed lag model. Based on data from 1948 through 1958, they estimated the short- and long-run price elasticities of demand for pork to be -0.74 and -0.83 respectively, and for beef to be -0.55 and -1.00 respectively. In further analysis, they estimated the adjustment period to a price change to be about three quarters of a year for beef and one quarter, or less, for pork. It is

Table 5-2.   Retail Price and Income Elasticities of Demand for Pork, Beef, and Broilers from Selected Studies

Study	Meat	Years	Data	Elasticities		Method
				Price	Income	
Logan & Boles [9]	Pork	1948–59	Quarterly-actual	−0.91 to −1.25	Neg.[a]	Indirect L.S.
Stanton [18]	Pork	1953–59	Quarterly-logs	−0.71 to −1.83	.20 to −1.85	Indirect L.S.
Maki [10]	Pork	1949–56	Quarterly-actual	−0.62	Pos.[a]	L.S.
Fox [6]	Pork	1922–41	Annual-logs	−0.81	Pos.[a]	L.S.
Logan & Boles [9]	Beef	1948–59	Quarterly-actual	−0.62 to −0.64	Pos.[a]	Indirect L.S.
Stanton [18]	Beef	1953–59	Quarterly-logs	−0.95 to −1.76	−0.41 to −0.83	Indirect L.S.
Maki [10]	Beef	1949–56	Quarterly-actual	−0.85	Pos.[a]	L.S.
Langemeier & Thompson [8]	Fed beef	1947–63	Annual-actual	−0.98	2.20	Sim. Eq. - TSLS
Logan & Boles [9]	Broilers	1948–59	Quarterly-actual	−2.54 to −3.07	Pos.[a]	Indirect L.S.
Stanton [18]	Broilers	1953–59	Quarterly-logs	−1.26 to −2.24	0.31 to 3.36	Indirect L.S.
Farris & Darley [5]	Broilers	1953–63	Monthly-actual	−0.84 to −1.41	N.S.[a]	L.S.[c]

[a] Actual value not computed. N.S. indicates nonsignificance.

[b] Indirect L.S. refers to the use of least-squares on just-identified reduced-form equations.

[c] Elasticities are for farm level relationships.

Source: [11; p. 24]

interesting to note the similarities between the short-run price elasticies obtained by Tomek and Cochrane and those obtained in this study. The fact that they are nearly identical suggests rather stable relationships over time.

Reduced Form Equations

Structural relationships and estimates are useful for evaluating the cross-effects between related products and market channels, however, a literal interpretation of the coefficients is risky because of the implied ceteris paribus assumption. For example, from the structural equation (5–16) it could be inferred that if corn prices increase ten cents per bushel, live hog slaughter per month will increase 27.5 million pounds, other factors constant. In a simultaneous system other factors are not constant and it is unrealistic to assume that the 27.5 million pound increase in hog slaughter could be observed in the real world, given the ten cent increase corn prices.

In order to evaluate the net changes in endogenous variables, given unit changes in selected exogenous variables, the analytical or derived reduced form equations are needed. To obtain the derived reduced form equation let the estimated ten equation model be expressed in matrix form as follows:

$$\hat{\beta} Y + \hat{\Gamma} Z = \hat{U}$$

where:

β = the 10 by 10 matrix of estimated coefficients associated with the endogenous variables;

Y = the 10 by 1 vector of endogenous variables;

$\hat{\Gamma}$ = the 10 by 24 matrix of estimated coefficients associated with the predetermined variables, including the constant terms.

Z = the 24 by 1 vector of predetermined variables; and

$\hat{U}$ = the 10 by 1 vector of disturbance terms where $\hat{\mu}_9 = \hat{\mu}_{10} = 0$.

Then the derived reduced form equations are obtained by solving the above system for the endogenous variables.

$$Y = \hat{\beta}^{-1} \hat{\Gamma} Z + \hat{\beta}^{-1} \hat{U}$$

where:

$\hat{\beta}^{-1}$ is the inverse of the $\hat{\beta}$ matrix and $-\hat{\beta}^{-1} \hat{\Gamma}$ represents the 10 X 24 matrix of derived reduced form coefficients.

Structural estimates of the behavioral equations and two identities were used.[21] Coefficients for the reduced form equations indicate the net effect of a unit change in an exogenous variable after the system again reaches equilibrium. The reduced form coefficients, therefore, allow for the simultaneous interaction in the system and the a priori zero parameter restrictions placed on the structural model.

Table 5-3 illustrates the difference between structural and reduced form estimates for selected exogenous variables. Except for the cattle and beef relationships, the reduced form estimates are consistent with the structural estimates and across market channels. The effect of simultaneity within the system is evident from the several coefficients presented in Table 5-3. For example, given a ten cent per bushel increase in corn prices, the structural estimates indicate a 27.5 million pound increase in live hog slaughter. However, the net change in live hog slaughter can be expected to be only 14.5 million pounds because of secondary interactions within the system. Reduced form coefficients also allow one to analyze the secondary effects of exogenous variables on those endogenous variables for which the exogenous variable does not appear in the structural equation. For example, if corn prices increase ten cents per bushel, retail meat prices can be expected to increase 1.0, 6.3, and 0.4 cent per pound for pork, beef, and broilers, respectively.

Reduced form equations were used to forecast endogenous variable values and the results were less than satisfying. While the primary purpose of developing and estimating this model was not to generate a forecasting model, monthly values of endogenous variables were forecasted for 1971 and 1972 using the derived reduced form equations and observed monthly values of the predetermined variables. The average percent error in forecasting the endogenous variables for the estimation period, 1949-70, and for two years beyond the estimation period, 1971-72, are pesented in Table 5-4. In general the model did not forecast values of the endogenous variables very accurately. The model tended to forecast quantity variables more accurately than price variables and hog and pork variables more accurately than cattle and beef variables. Furthermore the model simply was unable to account for the changes in the livestock-meat sector which were beginning to occur in 1972.

For quantity variables such as live hog and cattle slaughter, pork quantities and beef quantities, the forecasted values exceeded the observed values for the 1971-72 period. Forecasted values of price variables were seriously lower than observed values. The forecasted prices of live cattle and beef were extremely low with the forecasts for the latter part of 1972 being over $20 per hundredweight below observed prices of live cattle and $50 per hundredweight below observed prices of beef. The forecasted prices of live hogs and pork were also low but the deviations were not as large as for live cattle and beef.

The price of broilers was forecasted more accurately than any other variable during the 24 month period, 1971-72. The largest percent error was about 10 percent of the observed price and this occurred in the middle of the

Table 5–3. Evaluation of Assumed Changes in Selected Exogenous Variables on the Endogenous Variables in the System—Structural vs. Reduced Form Coefficients

Endogenous Variable	Per +10 cents/bc.		R +0.5%		NH +1000 Hogs		NC +1000 Cattle		I +10/capita/mo.		POP +1 mil. people	
	STR[a]	RF[b]	STR	RF	STR	RF	STR	RF	STR	RF	STR	RF
QH (mil. lbs)	+27.5	+14.5	+14.8	+3.1	+0.009	+0.013	—	-0.106	—	+88.0	—	+13.5
PH (cents/lb)	—	+0.5	—	+0.48	—	0	—	0	—	-3.6	—	-0.55
QC (mil. lbs)	+22.1	-94.7	+16.3	-65.4	—	-0.008	0.094	-0.302	—	+692.6	—	+43.2
PC (cents/lb)	—	+2.8	—	+2.0	—	0	—	+0.010	—	-16.6	—	-1.0
QPS (cents/lb)	—	+5.6	+0.13	+2.0	—	+0.004	—	-0.025	—	+21.1	—	+3.2
QPD (mil. lbs)	—	+5.6	—	+2.0	—	+0.004	—	-0.025	+27.8	+21.1	+5.1	+3.2
QB (mil. lbs)	—	-54.0	—	-37.3	—	-0.004	—	-0.172	+68.5	+394.8	+10.0	+24.6
PP (cents/lb)	—	+1.0	—	+0.8	—	—	—	0	—	-5.9	—	-0.91
PB (cents/lb)	—	+6.3	—	+4.4	—	0	—	+0.02	—	-36.6	—	-2.3
PCH (cents/lb)	—	+0.4	—	+0.25	—	0	—	0	+4.8	+1.9	-1.05	-1.24

[a] STR = response based on structural coefficient.
[b] RF = response based on reduced form coefficient.

Table 5–4. Average Percent Error in Forecasting the Prices and Quantities of Hogs, Cattle, Pork, Beef, and Broilers, 1949–1970 and 1971–1972*

Time Period	Variables								
	$QH\triangledown$	$PH\triangledown$	$QC\triangledown$	$PC\triangledown$	$QP\triangledown$	$QB\triangledown$	$PP\triangledown$	$PB\triangledown$	$PCH\triangledown$
1949–70	6.6	15.3	13.1	32.6	4.2	12.5	7.9	20.8	5.1
1971	4.9	16.8	13.3	40.3	4.9	8.9	6.1	24.0	3.5
1972	10.0	27.4	29.4	81.7	6.1	23.2	10.5	55.6	4.8
1971–72	7.4	22.1	21.4	61.0	5.5	16.1	8.3	39.8	4.1

*The average percent error is obtained by first calculating the percent error of each predicted value in the following way:

$$P_{ij} = \left[\frac{Y_{ij} - \hat{Y}_{ij}}{Y_{ij}} \right] \times 100,$$

where:

P_{ij} = percent error for the ith endogenous variable in the jth month.
Y_{ij} = observed value of the ith endogenous variable in the jth month.
$\hat{Y}_{ij}$ = predicted value of the ith endogenous variable in the jth month using observed values of all predetermined variables.

The average percent error is then obtained by:

$$\bar{P}_i = \frac{\sum_{j=1}^{N} P_{ij}}{N}$$

where:

$\bar{P}_i$ = average percent error for the ith endogenous for the various time periods considered.

N = number of months in each of the various time periods considered.

24 month period. On the average forecasted broiler prices were within one cent per pound of the observed prices.

The cattle-beef component of the model exhibited the greatest deviations between predicted and observed values. This suggests that there may be some model specification problems particularly in the cattle-beef component. The addition of a beef supply function would allow relaxing the assumption that monthly domestic production is entirely consumed during the same month and it would introduce imports and exports of beef which might improve the forecasting ability of the cattle-beef component of the model.

Concluding Remarks

This study represents an effort to model the monthly structure of the livestock-meat sector of the U.S. Ten simultaneously determined variables are explained in a model consisting of eight behavioral equations and two identities. Structural parameters were estimated using two-stage least squares techniques and data consisted of monthly observations for the period February 1949 through December 1970.

Except for the coefficients of the cattle cycle variable in the cattle supply equation and the population variable in the broiler demand equation, the signs of the estimated structural parameters were consistent with a priori expectations based on theoretical concepts, previous studies, and knowledge of behavior in the livestock-meat sector. All except three estimated coefficients of variables (excluding intercepts) were larger than their respective estimated standard errors. Computed price elasticities and income elasticities of demand indicated the demand for pork and beef to be inelastic and the demand for broilers to be elastic. Pork is least responsive to changes in income. Computed cross-price elasticities indicate that pork, beef, and broilers are substitutes and provide numerical values of the substitution interrelations among them. In addition cross-price elasticities between quantities consumed of the three meats and farm prices of cattle and hogs were derived from the structural estimates and provide some insights with regard to the effects of changes in hog and cattle supplies on prices and quantities consumed of each of the three meats. For example, a 10 percent increase in cattle prices is associated with a 4 percent decrease in beef consumption, 1.4 percent increase in pork consumption, and a 4.8 percent increase in broiler consumption during the same month, other factors nonvariant.

Ex post predictions for the 24 month period 1971–72, based on analytically derived reduced form equations, revealed that the model left a lot to be desired in terms of forecasting. The model tended to predict quantity variables more accurately than price variables and the largest forecast errors occurred near the latter part of the 24 month period. Thus, the strength of the model is not in its forecasting ability but rather in the delineation of the interactions among market levels and kinds of meats within the livestock-meat sector.

Table 5A-1. Monthly Intercept Values for Six Endogenous Variables

	QH $\triangledown$		QC $\triangledown$		QPS $\triangledown$	
	(mil. lbs)	(index)[a]	(mil. lbs)	(index)[a]	(mil. lbs)	(index)[b]
Jan.	1139	119	1702	101	-23	106
Feb.	879	92	1412	84	-80	28
Mar.	1005	105	1602	95	-21	109
April	908	95	1562	92	-61	54
May	879	92	1699	100	-47	73
June	864	90	1727	102	-47	73
July	809	85	1765	104	-41	81
Aug.	845	88	1830	108	-13	120
Sept.	874	91	1824	108	-4	132
Oct.	1049	110	1934	114	28	177
Nov.	1073	112	1645	97	-14	119
Dec.	1149	120	1594	94	-8	127

	QPD $\triangledown$		QBD $\triangledown$		PCH $\triangledown$.	
	(mil. lbs)[c]	(index)	(mil. lbs)	(index)[d]	(cents/lb)	(index)
Jan.	-149	130	-1165	106	174	100
Feb.	-286	59	-1353	91	173	99
Mar.	-181	113	-1269	98	176	101
April	-255	75	-1301	95	176	101
May	-247	80	-1234	100	175	100
June	-248	79	-1237	100	175	100
July	-272	66	-1236	100	176	101
Aug.	-231	88	-1206	103	177	101
Sept.	-199	104	-1207	102	176	101
Oct.	-109	151	-1140	92	175	100
Nov.	-169	120	-1264	102	172	98
Dec.	-139	135	-1255	101	172	98

[a] Monthly value divided by average monthly value for the year.
[b] Monthly values inflated by 100 prior to calculation of average to eliminate negative values.
[c] Monthly values inflated by 400 prior to calculation of average to eliminate negative values.
[d] Monthly values inflated by 2480 prior to calculation of average to eliminate negative values.
Source: Estimates of constant terms and coefficients of dummy variables.

NOTES

1. EPH_{jk} is the expected price of slaughter hogs in the $(j + 1)^{\text{th}}$ month of the kth year when $j = 1, 2, \ldots, 11$ and it is the expected price of slaughter hogs in the first month of the $(k + 1)^{\text{th}}$ year when $j = 12$.

2. A more detailed discussion of the theoretical development of the slaughter hog supply model is given in a paper by Myers and Havlicek entitled, "Some Theoretical Aspects of Short-term Hog Supply."[12, p. 1396–99]

3. Throughout the remainder of this chapter the subscripts j and k are dropped for convenience and clarity. All observations pertain to the jth month and k^{th} year unless denoted otherwise.

4. Nonsystematic margins are not functions of prices or volumes but instead originate from pricing policies designed to "follow the leader," "meet or beat competition," etc.[4, p. 1]

5. Population is introduced as an explicit variable in the demand relationships, as opposed to expressing quantity demanded on a per capita basis, to eliminate nonlinear supply-demand identities.

6. This is not to imply that the absolute levels of cold storage holdings of broilers are small, only that the monthly inflow and outflow essentially balance.

7. Death loss may include sampling errors since it is the residual after yearly inventories, commercial slaughter, farm slaughter and breeding adjustments are accounted for on a January 1 to January 1 basis.

8. Although there are individual variations to this length of lag, the average time period from high (low) farrowings to high (low) live hog slaughter has been 6 months for the period of analysis.

9. The adjustment factors ranged from 102.1 percent to 136.8 percent depending upon the number of states reporting.[28]

10. Each of these methods is described by Sosnick.[17, p. 735]

11. Several references are available which present clear, concise descriptions of models using zero-one variables.[1, 19 and 20]

12. All estimated equations presented in this section are from the second stage of the two-stage least-squares procedure. Unless otherwise denoted, the values of endogenous variables on the right hand side of the equality signs refer to estimated values as predicted by the corresponding estimated equation of the first stage.

13. Numerical values of the monthly intercepts are presented in Appendix 5A, Table 5A–1.

14. Coefficients of determination pertain to structural equations with predicted values of the nonnormalized endogenous variables (from first stage equations).

15. The actions of beef producers in withholding cattle from market during the price freezes of 1973 are consistent with the positive price-quantity relationships estimated in this model.

16. About 2.13 pounds of live hog are needed to yield one pound of major pork cuts (ham, bacon, loin, picnic, butt, spareribs, and bacon square) at the retail store.[25, p. 19]

17. The 2.12 figure was derived in the following manner: Carcass yields average 59 pounds per 100 pounds liveweight and retail cuts average 80 pounds per 100 pounds of carcass weight. Therefore, net yield of retail beef per pound of liveweight is about 47.2 percent and its reciprocal is 2.12.[22, p. 14]

18. Elasticity estimates must be interpreted with caution because the underlying *ceteris paribus* conditions usually do not hold for simultaneous systems of equations.

19. From identity (5–13), the total quantity of domestically produced beef supplied for consumption equals $KCQC\nabla$. The price-elasticity of supply for beef was derived using the following formula:

$$e^{bs} = \frac{\overline{PB\nabla}}{KCQC\nabla} \cdot \frac{\partial KCQC\nabla}{\partial PB\nabla} \quad \text{where} \quad \frac{\partial KCQC\nabla}{\partial PB\nabla} = KC \frac{\partial QC\nabla}{\partial PC\nabla} \cdot \frac{\partial PC\nabla}{\partial PB\nabla}$$

and KC = average dressing yield for cattle over the period of study
= 0.57.

20. A detailed treatment of these relationships is given by Pasour and Schrimper [14] and Shepherd [16, pp. 63–67].

21. In order to obtain a linear system, KC from Equation (5–13) was set equal to the constant 0.57 which is the average dressing percentage for beef during the observation period.

REFERENCES

1. Ben-David, S. and W.G. Tomek, 1965. *Allowing for Slope and Intercept Changes in Regression Analysis,* Department of Agricultural Economics, A.E. Res. 179, Cornell University.

2. Breimyer, H.R., 1957. "On Price Determination and Aggregate Price Theory " *Journal of Farm Economics,* 39(3):676–94.

3. Buse, R.C and G.E. Brandow, 1960. "The Relationship of Volume Prices, and Costs to Marketing Margins for Farm Foods," *Journal of Farm Economics,* 42(2):362–70.

4. Dalyrmple, D.G., 1961. *On the Nature of Marketing Margins,* Michigan State University, Agricultural Economics Report 824.

5. Farris, P.L. and R.D. Darley, 1964. "Monthly Price-Quantity Relations of Broilers at the Farm Level," *Journal of Farm Economics,* 46(4):849–56.

6. Fox, Karl A., 1953. *The Analysis of Demand for Farm Products,* U.S. Department of Agriculture, Technical Bulletin 1081.

7. Harlow, A.A., 1962. *Factors Affecting the Price and Supply of Hogs,* Economics Research Service, U.S. Department of Agriculture, Technical Bulletin 1274.

8. Langemeier, L. and R.G. Thompson, 1967. "Demand, Supply and Price Relationships of the Beef Sector, Post-World War II Period," *Journal of Farm Economics,* 49(1, Part 1):169–83.

9. Logan, S.H. and J.N. Boles, 1962. "Quarterly Fluctuations in Retail Prices of Meat," *Journal of Farm Economics*, 44(4):1050–60.
10. Maki, W.R., 1959. *Forecasting Beef Cattle and Hog Prices by Quarter-Years*, Iowa Agricultural Experiment Station Research Bulletin 473.
11. Myers, L.H., Joseph Havlicek, Jr. and P.L. Henderson, *Short-Term Price Structure of the Hog-Pork Sector of the United States*, Research Bulletin 855, Purdue University Agricultural Experiment Station, Lafayette, Indiana, February 1970.
12. Myers, L.H. and J. Havlicek, Jr., 1967. "Some Theoretical Aspects of Short-Term Hog Supply," *Journal of Farm Economics*, 49(5): 1395–1400.
13. National Commission on Food Marketing, 1966. *Organization and Competition in the Livestock and Meat Industry*, Technical Study No. 1, Washington.
14. Pasour, E.C. and R.A. Schrimper, 1965. "The Effect of Length of Run on Measured Demand Elasticities," *Journal of Farm Economics*, 47(3):774–88.
15. Schultz, T.W. and O.H. Brownlee, 1942. "Two Trials to Determine Expectation Models Applicable to Agriculture," *Quarterly Journal of Economics*, 56:487–96.
16. Shepherd, G.S., 1963. *Agricultural Price Analysis*, 5th ed., Iowa State University Press.
17. Sosnick, S.H., 1962. "Orderly Marketing for California Avocados," *Hilgardia*, 33(14).
18. Stanton, B.F., 1961. "Seasonal Demand for Beef, Pork, and Broilers," *Agricultural Economics Research*, 13(1):1–14.
19. Suits, D.B., 1957. "Use of Dummy Variables in Regression Equations," *Journal of the American Statistical Association*, 52:548–51.
20. Tomek, W.G., 1963. "Using Zero-One Variables with Time Series Data in Regression Equations," *Journal of Farm Economics*, 45(4): 814–22.
21. Tomek, W.G. and W.W. Cochrane, 1962. "Long-Run Demand: A Concept and Elasticity Estimates for Meats," *Journal of Farm Economics*, 44(3):717–30.
22. United States Department of Agriculture, 1956. *Beef Marketing Margins and Costs*, Misc., Pub. 710.
23. United States Department of Agriculture, *Livestock and Meat Statistics, 1962*, Agricultural Marketing Service, Statistical Bulletin No. 33. Also Annual Supplements 1964 through 1973.
24. United States Department of Agriculture, *Livestock and Meat Situation*, Economic Research Service, Washington, January 1966 to June 1973.
25. United States Department of Agriculture, 1956. *Pork Marketing Margins and Costs*, Misc. Pub. 711.
26. United States Department of Agriculture, *Poultry and Egg Situation*, Economic Research Service, Washington, February 1968 through May 1973.
27. United States Department of Agriculture, 1966. *Selected Statistical Series For Poultry and Eggs Through 1965*, Economic Research Service, Bulletin No. 232.

28. United States Department of Agriculture, Unpublished Broiler Chick Placement Data, Economic Research Service, Marketing Economics Division.
29. United States Department of Commerce, *Survey of Current Business,* Washington, 1949 to 1973.
30. United States Department of Labor, *Employment and Earnings Statistics for the U.S.,* Washington, 1949 to 1973.

Chapter Six

Estimation of Continuous Time Models with an Application to the World Sugar Market

Clifford R. Wymer

The specification of continuous models is common in economic literature but only in recent years have satisfactory econometric techniques become available for the estimation of such models using discrete data. These techniques seem particularly suited to the estimation of models of commodity markets where the market is represented by a nontatonnement process with both prices and quantities being adjusted at all points of time. This paper discusses a method of estimating general linear stochastic differential equation systems and illustrates the use of this estimator with a model of the world sugar market.

The main reason for considering a set of differential equations rather than a discrete system is based on the proposition that the behavior of the market can be represented, or at least better approximated, by a continuous model.[2] Although individual economic decisions may be made almost continuously or at regular or irregular intervals, the observed variables which are the result of a number of decisions taken by different economic units at different points of time would tend to be continuous. As the intervals between observations need not correspond to the intervals between the corresponding decisions, and as there may be various lags in the system, a continuous model may be more appropriate than a discrete one.

In discrete models it is usually assumed that disturbances in successive observations are independent but this can be maintained only if the basic time unit inherent in the economic system generating the data, such as the reaction period of decision units, is not too small relative to the observation period. The distinction between lagged endogenous and dependent variables appears, therefore, as a matter of degree. The independence assumption implies a lower bound on the size of the inherent time unit thus precluding the correct specification of some economic problems. In many models, and especially in the disequilibrium adjustment models considered here, it is necessary to consider

London School of Economics and Political Science.

distributed time lags with the lower limit of the lags almost zero in some cases. These are more easily specified in a continuous model.

An advantage of differential equation systems is that they may be specified independently of the length of interval between observations in the sample, but once estimated allow the continuous paths of the variables in the model to be predicted. It may be valuable for policy purposes to have forecasts of points on this path at shorter intervals than the observation interval of the sample used to estimate the model.

In such differential equation models it is assumed that the behavior units in the system cannot respond to change instantaneously so that the system is recursive and can be given a causal interpretation. It is also assumed that the system is stable with white noise disturbances and that it cannot be reduced to an equivalent system where any equation is of a lower order so that the model is invariant under a linear transformation of time and the parameters of the differential equations may be identified.

A difference equation model which is observationally equivalent to the continuous model, in that this exact discrete model will be satisfied by any set of equispaced observations generated by the set of differential equations, may be derived; the continuous model can then be estimated from a sample of such observations. An alternative estimator approximates the differential equation system by a nonrecursive discrete model with the same structural form as the continuous model and although this estimator is biased, the bias will be small providing that the interval between observations in the sample is small relative to the mean time lag of the adjustment functions in the model or to the inverse of the real part of the eigenvalues of the system.[8] The disturbances in the discrete model are a moving average process of order one less than the highest order equation in the differential system, but the errors can be approximated by a process which is independent of the coefficients of the model so that the variables of the system may be transformed to give almost serially independent disturbances.

Full information maximum likelihood estimates of the parameters of both the exact and approximate models can be obtained subject to any restriction within and across equations; each coefficient of the model may be specified as any function of the set of parameters. The exact model, however, takes considerably more computing time to estimate than the approximate model. As the bias of the approximate model generally is small, especially for monthly or quarterly data, it is suggested that the approximate model is used for all preliminary work on a particular model and the exact model used only for final estimates and for analysis and forecasting. Estimates of the eigenvalues of the system and of their variance matrices can be obtained for each estimate.

ESTIMATION OF CONTINUOUS SYSTEMS

A model where all equations are of the same order and where all variables can be measured at any instant is considered initially and then extended to more general systems. A detailed analysis has been given by Bergstrom [1], Phillips [4], Sargan [5], and Wymer [8].

A recursive model of rth order stochastic differential equations is

$$D^r y(t) = \sum_{k=1}^{r} A_k D^{k-1} y(t) + Bz(t) + u(t) \qquad (6\text{-}1)$$

where D is an operator equivalent to some form of stochastic differentiation, $y(t)$ is a vector of endogenous variables, $z(t)$ a vector of exogenous variables, $u(t)$ a vector of disturbances, and the A's and B matrices of coefficients. As it is assumed that the disturbances are generated by a stationary process with constant spectral density, the integral

$$\zeta(t) = \int_0^t u(s)ds$$

is a homogenous random process with uncorrelated increments. Since

$$\lim_{h \to 0} E\left\{ \left| \frac{\zeta(t+h) - \zeta(t)}{h} - D\zeta(t) \right|^2 \right\}$$

does not exist, $\zeta(t)$ is nondifferentiable and so the $u(t)$ cannot be rigorously defined. The differential Equation (6-1) may be considered, however, as

$$dD^{r-1} y(t) = \sum_{k=1}^{r} A_k D^{k-1} y(t)dt + Bz(t)dt + d\zeta(t) \qquad (6\text{-}2)$$

where $u(t)$ is replaced by the mean square differential of the process $\zeta(t)$. This may be written as the first order system

$$dy^*(t) = A^* y^*(t)dt + B^* z(t)dt + d\zeta^*(t) \qquad (6\text{-}3)$$

where

$$y^*(t) = \begin{bmatrix} y_1^*(t) \\ \vdots \\ \vdots \\ y_r^*(t) \end{bmatrix}, A^* = \begin{bmatrix} 0 & . & I \\ & \vdots & \\ & \vdots & \\ A_1 & . & A_2 \ldots A_r \end{bmatrix}, B^* = \begin{bmatrix} 0 \\ B \end{bmatrix}, \zeta^*(t) = \begin{bmatrix} 0 \\ \zeta(t) \end{bmatrix}$$

$$Dy_i^*(t) = y_{i+1}^*(t), \quad i = 1, \ldots, r-1$$

$$dy_r^*(t) = \sum_{k=1}^{r} A_k y_k^*(t)dt + Bz(t)dt + d\zeta(t).$$

The exact discrete model derived from the solution to (6-2) is

$$y_\tau^* = e^{\delta A^*} y_{\tau-1}^* + \int_0^\delta e^{sA^*} B^* z(\tau\delta - s)ds + \int_0^\delta e^{sA^*} d\zeta^*(\tau\delta - s) \tag{6-4}$$

where $y^*(\tau\delta) = y_\tau^*$ and $z(\tau\delta) = z_\tau$. As observations generated by (6-2) will satisfy (6-4) irrespective of the length of interval between successive observations, the sampling properties of (6-2) may be studied by considering the sampling properties of (6-4). In general the exogenous variables $z(t)$ will not be analytic functions of time so that the integral $\int_0^\delta e^{sA^*}B^*z(\tau\delta - s)ds$ cannot be evaluated directly; the integral may be approximated, however, by making a quadratic approximation about successive discrete observations of the $z(t)$. Although the spectral density matrix may be diagonal, this will not be true of the variance matrix of the disturbances $\int_0^\delta e^{sA^*}d\zeta^*(\tau\delta - s)$ in (6-4); this variance matrix is usually assumed to be unrestricted. It is however, expensive to estimate (6-4) subject to general restrictions on A^* and B^* so, as an alternative, or at least as a method of finding initial estimates of (6-2), an approximation which maintains the structural form and requires less computing time to estimate can be used.

This approximation to (6-2) is a nonrecursive discrete model derived by integrating (6-2) over the interval $(t - \delta, t)$ such that if $t = \tau\delta$

$$\int_{t-\delta}^t Dx(s)ds = \Delta x_\tau, \quad \int_{t-\delta}^t x(s)ds = Mx_\tau$$

where $\Delta = 1/\delta(1 - L)$, $M = 1/2(1 + L)$ and L is the lag operator. Thus

$$\Delta y_t^* = A^* My_t^* + B^* Mz_t + u_t^* \tag{6-5}$$

where u_t^* is a vector of disturbances depending on the disturbances in (6-2) and the errors of approximation. The approximate estimating equation is

$$\Delta^r y_t = \sum_{i=1}^{r} A_i(M^{r-i+1}\Delta^{i-1})y_t + M^r Bz_t + v_t \tag{6-6}$$

where v_t is a moving average process of order $r - 1$ depending on the coefficients of (6-5) and u_t^*. A covariance function which gives an approximation to the moving average process $v(t)$ can be derived [8] and used to transform the variables in (6-6) which is estimated subject to any a priori restrictions using full information maximum likelihood to give $\hat{A}^*$ as an estimate of A^*. The bias in $\hat{A}^*$ is of order $0(\delta^2)$. An alternative estimator is found by using

$$\hat{A}^\dagger = (I - \tfrac{1}{2}\delta\hat{A}^*)^{-1} (I + \tfrac{1}{2}\delta\hat{A}^*) \tag{6-7}$$

from (6-5) as an estimate of $e^{\delta A^*}$ in (6-4) to give

$$\bar{A}^* = H\left(\frac{1}{\delta}\log P\right)H^{-1} \tag{6-8}$$

where $P = H^{-1}A^\dagger H$ is the canonical form of $A^\dagger$. The bias in the unrestricted elements of $\bar{A}^*$ is of order $0(\delta^3)$. The eigenvalues of $\hat{A}^*$ and $\bar{A}^*$ may be found with their approximate asymptotic variance matrices but these variances are about biased probability limits.

  The estimation technique can be extended to a system of mixed order linear differential equations [9]. This general model is assumed to be recursive in the following sense. The system consists of a set of $r + 1$ groups of stochastic differential equations such that the sth group of equations, corresponding to a vector $y_{r-s+1}(t)$ of endogenous variables, is of order s for $s = 0, \ldots, r$. The matrix of coefficients of the vector $D^s y_{r-s+1}(t)$, or more rigorously $dD^{s-1}y_{r-s+1}(t)$, is diagonal and each element of this vector is a function of $D^i y_{k-i}(t), k = 1, \ldots, r; i = 0, \ldots, k - 1$; and y_{r+1}. The latter holds for all $s = 1, \ldots, r$. The set of variables y_{r+1} are defined by zero order differential equations, or static equations, and so correspond to variables which are always in equilibrium. As well as the behavioral part of the system, there may be some first or zero order equations which are identities such as the definition of flows as the rate of change of stocks, and market clearing equations. The disturbance terms are again assumed to be white noise so that the order of each equation cannot be reduced without losing the white noise properties of these disturbances. The model can be written as in (6-3) by redefining the matrix A^* to allow for the mixed order equations [9] and the exact and approximate estimators derived as above. Although the approximation to the continuous system has been derived under the assumption that the variables in the model can be measured at a point in time, such as stock or price variables, the mixed order system allows the analysis to be extended to either a flow or a mixed stock/flow model.

  Although a flow variable $y(t)$ is generally unmeasurable at a point in time, its integral $y^0(t)$ given by

$$y^0(t) = \int_{t-\delta}^{t} y(s)ds$$

is measurable. (The integral perhaps should be represented by $y^0(t - \frac{1}{2}\delta)$ but this is a matter of definition only). Thus a continuous model containing flow variables must be integrated over the interval $(t - \delta, t)$ to give a model defined in terms of measurable variables $y^0(t)$. If all variables in a model are flow variables, the exact and approximate discrete models (6-4) and (6-6) still hold except that the variables are y_t^0 and z_t^0 instead of y_t and z_t. An rth order flow model will involve error terms which are a moving average of order r.

If the model is a mixed stock/flow system, the flow variables are again replaced by their integral as above, but any stock or price variable $x(t)$ must be approximated by

$$x^0(t) = \int_{t-\delta}^{t} x(s)ds \cong Mx_\tau, \text{ where } t = \tau\delta.$$

Thus a mixed stock/flow differential equation system in terms of flow variables $y(t)$ and stock or price variables $x(t)$ may be estimated using the integrals $y^0(t)$ and $x^0(t)$. The 'exact' discrete model will no longer be exact, however, and the term in an rth order model will be a moving average of order r and not of order $r - 1$ as in a model containing stock and price variables only. These moving averages may be approximated as in [8]. A mixed stock/flow system may be estimated in the usual way after the variables have been transformed appropriately.

The full information maximum likelihood programs used to estimate the approximate discrete model (6-5) are SIMUL, where only linear restrictions are imposed within equations, and RESIMUL where any restrictions may be imposed within and across equations. RESIMUL could also be used to estimate a system with moving average errors but this would be feasible for very small models only; in general the moving average errors are eliminated by transforming the variables as in (6-6). The program used to estimate the exact model (6-4) is DISCON which again can impose any restrictions on the coefficients. The eigenvalues of either the exact estimate of A^* or the approximate estimate of $\hat{A}^*$ are determined by CONTINEST which can also find the eigenvalues of $\hat{A}^\dagger$ in (6-7) and their logarithms as well as the estimate $\bar{A}^*$ from (6-8); the variance matrix of each set of eigenvalues is calculated as well as the variance matrix of the elements of $\bar{A}^*$ [1]

DYNAMIC ADJUSTMENT MODEL OF A
SINGLE COMMODITY MARKET

The model of a single commodity market specified here consists of a set of adjustment functions for prices, futures prices, stocks, production and consumption. The demand and supply functions are assumed to be of a simple form with the emphasis placed on the dynamic structure of the market. This model has been developed along the same lines as the financial model in [7] but with a simple expectations function introduced explicitly into the system. The model, which is assumed to be continuous, is a recursive system of mixed order stochastic differential equations and can be estimated by the procedure described above.

The variables in the model are:

$p(t)$ = spot price at time t

$q(t, s)$ = futures price at time t of futures contracts for delivery at $t + s$

$S(t)$ = stocks at time t

$Q(t)$ = rate of production at time t

$C(t)$ = rate of consumption (or sales) at time t

$F(t, s)$ = futures contracts at time t for delivery at $t + s$.

Other notation used is:

$\hat{X}(t)$ is the desired value of a variable $X(t)$

$\bar{X}(t, s)$ is the expected value in period t of $X(t + s)$

$q(t)$ and $\bar{p}(t)$ is some "average" futures price and expected price respectively.

Economic theory may help in specifying the supply and demand functions of a commodity market but gives little indication of the form of the market adjustment functions. This depends on the institutional structure of the market. Two simple formulations of a type of model which may represent single commodity markets are given below. In Model (a) it is assumed that production and consumption adjust to excess supply and demand and that producers have some desired level of stocks which they wish to maintain. Prices adjust to both excess stocks and the rate of change of stocks; that is, the difference between actual production and consumption.

$$Dp(t) = f_1 [\hat{S}(t) - S(t), Q(t) - C(t)] \tag{6-9a}$$

$$DC(t) = f_2 [\hat{C}(t) - C(t)] \tag{6-10a}$$

$$DQ(t) = f_3 [\hat{Q}(t) - Q(t)] \tag{6-11a}$$

$$DS(t) = Q(t) - C(t) \tag{6-12a}$$

where

$$\hat{S}(t) \quad = h_1 \left[p(t), \tilde{p}(t), C(t) \right] \ , \frac{\partial h_1}{\partial p} < 0 \, , \frac{\partial h_1}{\partial \tilde{p}} > 0 \, , \frac{\partial h_1}{\partial C} > 0$$

$$\hat{C}(t) \quad = h_2 \left[p(t), Z_1(t) \right] \qquad , \frac{\partial h_2}{\partial p} < 0$$

$$\hat{Q}(t) \quad = h_3 \left[p(t), \tilde{p}(t), Z_2(t) \right] \, , \frac{\partial h_3}{\partial p} > 0 \, , \frac{\partial h_3}{\partial \tilde{p}} < 0$$

and $Z_1(t)$ and $Z_2(t)$ are exogenous variables affecting consumption and production. Current consumption will be independent of expected prices if consumers do not hold stocks. This model allows prices to be determined by both stocks and flows, but in any particular market price fluctuations may be dominated by one or the other as, for example, Labys [3, pp. 92–100] has suggested.

The model may be respecified to allow producers to hold buffer stocks to maintain prices with production being adjusted to maintain the buffer stock level. Sales, which are assumed equal to consumption, now adjust to the excess of desired over actual prices while prices are determined in the market by excess demand. It is again assumed in this model that all stocks are held by producers. The model may be written:

$$Dp(t) \quad = f_1 \left[\hat{C}(t) - C(t) \right] \tag{6-9b}$$

$$DQ(t) \quad = f_2 \left[\hat{S}(t) - S(t) \right] \tag{6-10b}$$

$$DC(t) \quad = f_3 \left[\hat{p}(t) - p(t) \right] \tag{6-11b}$$

$$DS(t) \quad = Q(t) - C(t). \tag{6-12b}$$

$\hat{p}(t)$, the desired price function of producers, may be derived formally from profit optimization conditions. It can be seen that whereas in the first model prices adjust to a mixed stock/flow formulation, in the second model prices adjust to a flow formulation.

As the behavior functions will depend in general on futures prices and expected prices as well as current spot price, these prices also should be endogenous to the model. If it is assumed that futures prices adjust according to the difference between expected spot price and futures price, and that expected prices are determined by some distributed lag function of spot prices then

$$Dq(t) = g_1 \left[\tilde{p}(t) - q(t) \right] \tag{6-13}$$

$$\tilde{p}(t) = g_2 [p(t)] . \tag{6-14}$$

The adjustment functions above may be lagged or unlagged with the lag structure being determined according to the empirical evidence. As the model is specified to be recursive and is expected to be stable, a plausible expectations function might be given by defining g_2 as a first order exponentially distributed lag

$$D\tilde{p}(t) = \alpha [p(t) - \tilde{p}(t)] \tag{6-15}$$

or perhaps some higher order exponential lag. If the speed of adjustment of (6-15) is sufficiently fast, however, this function could be replaced by the unlagged function

$$\tilde{p}(t) = p(t) \tag{6-16}$$

to give static expectations. The other adjustment functions in the system, $f_1, f_2,$ f_3, and g_1 will be specified as either first or second order exponentially distributed lag functions in the model of the world sugar market below.

Equations (6-13) and (6-14), however, determine only some "average" of futures and expected prices; in order to explain the whole spectrum of these prices it is necessary to introduce holdings of futures contracts into the model and consider the demand and supply of these contracts. Adjustment functions for holdings of futures contracts and for futures prices of each contract may be specified as

$$DF(t, s) = \phi_1 [s; \tilde{p}(t, s) - q(t, s)] \tag{6-17}$$

$$DQ(t, s) = \phi_2 [s; \hat{V}(t, s) - DF(t, s)] \tag{6-18}$$

$$D\tilde{p}(t, s) = \phi_3 [s; p(t) - \tilde{p}(t, s)] \tag{6-19}$$

where $\hat{V}(t, s)$ is the desired net rate of change at time t of holdings of futures contracts for delivery at $t + s$, that is, the desired rate of change of $F(t, s)$. Each function ϕ_1, ϕ_2, ϕ_3 may be considered as a family of adjustment functions depending on the paremeter s. The time path of holdings and futures prices of a particular futures contract for delivery at time T is given by the family of adjustment functions as t moves to T and s moves to zero such that $t + s = T$ for all t, s. Under the assumption that the set of futures contracts is continuous the adjustment functions (6-13) and (6-14) correspond to a single member of the family (6-17), (6-18), and (6-19) where s is fixed at s_0; thus (6-13) and (6-14) refer to a hypothetical "futures contract" which has delivery at time $t + s_0$ for all t.

In the model specified here no distinction is made between hedgers and speculators since it is assumed that all market operators have the same price expectations, although these are held with uncertainty, and costs of holding stocks or of buying or selling futures contracts are not specified. The rate of capital gain (or loss) at time t on holdings of futures contracts for delivery at $t + s$ is $F(t, s) Dq(t, s)$ and the rate of capital gain on all contracts at time t is

$$\ell(t) = \int_0^\infty F(t, s) Dq(t, s)ds. \tag{6-20}$$

Unliquidated futures contracts at time t will be $F(t, 0)$ with value $p(t)F(t, 0)$. The cost of purchases of a long hedger who holds futures until delivery, or the return to a short hedger who does not buy back, is

$$\int_0^\infty q(t - s, s)DF(t - s, s)ds$$

so that the capital gain by a hedger on contracts for delivery at time t is

$$L(t) = p(t)F(t, 0) - \int_0^\infty q(t - s, s)DF(t - s, s)ds. \tag{6-21}$$

For hedgers who are covering the actual amount of sales or purchases to be made in the spot market the rate of capital gain or loss, $\ell(t)$ may be neglected and the actual capital gain or loss $L(t)$ is relevant. There is, however, a financial constraint on the loss which speculators can absorb, but as speculators can always reverse purchases or sales of futures contracts, for them it is the rate of capital gain $\ell(t)$ which will be relevant. When expected prices and futures prices are falling, $F(t, s)$ will be reduced as speculators cut their losses by making a covering sale or purchase of futures of the same delivery date. There is not such a strong constraint on capital gains as only a proportion of the cost of futures contracts is payable on purchases of the futures, the remainder being payable at delivery; this can always be covered by a reverse transaction in either the futures or spot market. There is still some constraint, however, depending on the cost and ease of financing purchases. This would give a reason for introducing either $L(t)$ or $\ell(t)$ into the functions explaining price and quantity behavior.

In future research using data on holdings of futures contracts the futures price Equation (6-13) could be replaced by an approximation to (6-18). The expected price $\tilde{p}(t, s)$ is unobserved, but using (6-19) to eliminate this variable from (6-17) will give a second order equation for holdings of futures contracts which does not include $\tilde{p}(t, s)$. It is likely, however, that the rate of adjustment of these holdings and of futures prices will be rapid with a mean time lag of less than one month. This suggests that in order to identify the parameters of ϕ_1 and ϕ_2, and to obtain consistent and efficient estimates using the exact estimator, weekly data will be required. Such data will also be required if the bias of the approximate discrete estimator is to be small.

Moreover, the adaptive expectations function used above does not seem particularly plausible in studies of commodity markets. It is suggested that rather than price expectations being determined by past price behavior, current expectations should depend on expected excess demand or on current excess demand in other markets. The latter may be particularly useful for a model of several commodity markets especially where the commodities are substitutes. An excess demand for one commodity not only will cause the spot price of that commodity to increase but also may cause an increase in the expected price of other commodities. This seems a more realistic formulation of price expectations and should allow for the very fast interaction between commodity markets which is difficult to incorporate in a model containing adaptive expectations functions.

A MODEL OF THE WORLD SUGAR MARKET

The world sugar market is used to illustrate the applicability of the continuous time estimator to a single commodity market because active spot and futures markets exist for sugar, the commodity is homogenous with few direct substitutes within the price range of the sample period, and monthly data for consumption and production, as well as prices, is available. The time lags in the adjustment of spot and futures prices, and perhaps in consumption, are likely to be short, but as these are specified as being distributed exponentially, the use of the continuous estimator allows the mean time lag to be close to zero. Providing that the aggregated behavior of the participants in the market can be considered as continuous, the length of decision period of these participants need not be defined but is determined empirically. This would not be true of production which is assumed to be exogenous for reasons discussed below.

The model assumes a single world market for sugar with all sales being made at the world price. Although major spot and futures markets for sugar exist in New York and London, arbitrage between the markets ensures that prices remain close. Thus, for this study, the London daily price (p) and the three month futures price (q) in London (both observed at end of month) are taken as the world prices.[2] As sugar futures contracts on the London market are for delivery in March, May, August, October, and December, with each expiring at the end of month, and futures exist for up to 18 months ahead, it was necessary to use the prices of actual contracts to interpolate prices for three-month futures.

Consumption (C), production (Q) and stock (S) data present more of a problem. The International Sugar Organization (ISO) publishes annual data for seven regions: Europe (including USSR), North America, Central America,

South America, Asia, Oceania, and Africa; and monthly data for individual countries. Some countries, especially those of Eastern Europe, the Middle East, and North Africa supply annual data only. Monthly production and consumption for each region was obtained by allocating the annual total of the region according to the monthly figures for "representative" countries in each region.[3] World production and consumption is the sum of the regional series and World stocks were cumulated from a basis of 21.86 million metric tons in December 1964 as in the ISO Sugar Year Book for 1967. All series refer to centrifugal sugar only and are measured in million metric tons (mmt). Prices are measured as £/ton.

The model adopted for the sugar market corresponds to that expressed in Equations (6-9a), (6-10a), (6-12a), (6-13) and (6-14).

$$Dp(t) = \alpha_1 [\hat{S}(t) - S(t)] - \alpha_2 [Q(t) - C(t)] + u_1(t) \tag{6-22}$$

$$D^2 q(t) = \alpha_3 \gamma [p(t) - q(t)] - (\gamma + \alpha_3) Dq(t) + u_2(t) \tag{6-23}$$

$$D^2 C(t) = \alpha_4 \beta [\hat{C}(t) - C(t)] - \alpha_4 DC(t) + u_3(t) \tag{6-24}$$

$$DS(t) = Q(t) - C(t) \tag{6-25}$$

where the demand functions for stocks and consumption are:

$$\hat{S}(t) = a_0 - a_1 p(t) + a_2 q(t) + a_3 t + w_1(t) \tag{6-26}$$

$$\hat{C}(t) = b_0 - b_1 p(t) + b_2 t + w_2(t). \tag{6-27}$$

All parameters, except the constant terms in (6-26) and (6-27) are positive. The trend terms in these demand functions represent the increase in world income and prices during the sample period. The futures price Equation (6-23) can be interpreted as showing the adjustment of futures prices to expected prices $\tilde{p}(t)$.

$$Dq(t) = \alpha_3 [\tilde{p}(t) - q(t)] \tag{6-28}$$

with expected prices being defined as a first order adaptive expectations function

$$D \tilde{p}(t) = \gamma [p(t) - \tilde{p}(t)] . \tag{6-29}$$

The functions (6-28) and (6-29) may be written as the integral of a first order exponentially distributed lag function with mean time lags $|1/\alpha_3|$ and $|1/\gamma|$. Similarly (6-24) may be interpreted as the rate of change of sales adjusting to an exponentially distributed lag of excess demand with mean time lag $|1/\alpha_4|$.

The assumption of a single commodity market makes the model deficient in a number of ways. In particular aggregation over all countries excludes the effect of international trade and the model does not take account of international sugar agreements.[6] An indication of the magnitude of the international market is given in Table 6-1 which shows production, consumption, exports, and imports of centrifugal sugar (in million metric tons) in each of the ISO regions in 1968. About 30 percent of international trade (or about 10 percent of production) in sugar takes place on the free market. This is mainly sales from cane producers to northern hemisphere countries during the early part of the year. The Commonwealth Sugar Agreement (CSA) covers 3 mmt. of which about 60 percent is bought at a negotiated price and the remainder at free market prices. The USA Sugar Quotas cover 10 mmt. for which prices are negotiated. (Hawaii and Puerto Rico each produce and have quotas for 1 mmt.) The current CSA and International Sugar Agreement (ISA) prices which have effect until 1974 are £60 per ton. Under the ISA this price covers imports of up to 75 percent of historical imports. In 1968 the CSA price was £43.50 per long ton and the average London daily price £21.83 per ton. Over the sample period the London price has varied between £105 per ton (in 1963) and £13 per ton (in 1966) and stocks have fluctuated between 5 mmt. and 30 mmt.

The London daily price as well as futures prices thus feature types of fluctuations which may be described using a differential equation approach. However, it is more difficult to represent production by a continuous process. Centrifugal sugar is produced from both cane and beet with production in Europe and North America being almost entirely from beet and production elsewhere from cane. New cane takes about 18 months to grow to maturity but subsequent crops grown by ratooning take about 12 months to ripen. Cane is usually replanted every five to ten years. Beet takes about 6 months to grow but the sugar content depends to a greater extent on rainfall and other weather conditions than cane.

Table 6-1. Regional Production, Consumption, and Trade in 1968*

	Production	*Consumption*	*Exports*	*Imports*
Europe (inc. USSR)	25	29	4	7
North America	4	11	–	7
Central America (inc. Puerto Rico)	11	3	7	–
South America	8	6	2	–
Asia	10	13	2	5
Oceania (inc. Hawaii)	4	1	4	–
Africa	4	4	2	2
	66	67	21	21

*Net exports of countries in Europe and USSR were 1 mmt. and net imports 4 mmt. Total world production from cane was 37 mmt. and production from beet was 29 mmt.

Even though there are relatively long lags between the planting and harvesting of sugar crops a sufficiently high order continuous lag, for example, might give a reasonably good approximation to the production process. Such a lag could allow for the growing period of the crop and, in the case of cane, could allow for variations in the total life of the cane before replanting. In a world model, however, separate functions would have to be introduced for either beet or cane in each of the major regions. In order to avoid this problem production is assumed to be exogenous.

The price expectations function, and also the futures price function, is particularly unrealistic. It would be more plausible to specify expected prices as a function of expected stocks, or expected rate of change of stocks, rather than as a weighted average of past prices. In the sugar market the consumption function is well defined but production, which is heavily dependent on weather conditions in various parts of the world, is not. During the growing season of both cane and beet, forecasts based on acreage planted and weather patterns are made of the sugar crop, and these forecasts affect expected and futures prices.[4] If production was made endogenous to the model and these explicit forecasts introduced into the expectations process, the form of the futures price functions could be improved.

Full information maximum likelihood estimates of the approximate discrete model equivalent to the continuous system (6-22) to (6-25) were calculated using a sample of monthly observations from 1958 to 1968. As the model is a second order mixed stock/flow system, the variables were transformed to eliminate the second order moving average error process inherent in the discrete model equivalent to such a system.[5] [8, 9] The model to be estimated is:

$$Dp = -\alpha_1 a_1 p + \alpha_1 a_2 q - \alpha_1 S - \alpha_2 (Q - C) + \alpha_1 a_0 + \nu_1 \tag{6-30}$$

$$D^2 q = -(\gamma + \alpha_3) Dq + \alpha_3 \gamma(p - q) + \nu_2 \tag{6-31}$$

$$D^2 C = -\alpha_4 DC - \alpha_4 \beta b_1 p - \alpha_4 \beta C + \alpha_4 \beta b_2 t + \alpha_4 b_0 + \nu_3 \tag{6-32}$$

$$DS = Q - C \tag{6-33}$$

All parameters are identifiable except γ and α_3, which may be identified only pairwise. Estimates of the model are reported in Tables 6-2 and 6-3.

The likelihood ratio test rejects the hypothesis that the over-identifying restrictions on the model are consistent with the data. Although this is an asymptotic test, the sample of 127 observations is sufficiently large not to allow the test to be dismissed as invalid. All parameters have the signs expected a priori except either γ, the rate of adjustment in the price expectations function, or α_3 the rate of adjustment of futures prices. This will tend to make the model unstable. The hypothesis that price expectations, or futures prices, are determined as shown by the model must be rejected.

Table 6-2. Estimates of Structural Model of the World Sugar Market, 1958-1968*

Dp = $-0.85\ p + 1.33\ q - 0.41\ S - 0.31\ (Q - C) - 6.84$
 (8.73)$\quad$(8.82)$\quad$(4.87)$\quad$(0.55)$\qquad\quad$(1.83)

D^2q = $-1.15\ Dq - 0.12\ (p - q)$
 (5.94)$\qquad$(2.47)

D^2C = $-4.66\ DC - 0.02\ p - 4.37\ C + 0.06\ t + 22.09$
 (4.94)$\qquad$(3.53)$\quad$(5.33)$\quad$(5.25)$\quad$(5.22)

DS = $Q - C$

*Chi-square value of likelihood ratio = 52.7 with 14 degrees of freedom. Critical chi-square value at 5 percent level of significance is 23.7.

The partial derivative of consumption with respect to prices is $-b_1$, thus giving a price elasticity of demand for sugar, calculated at sample means, of -0.03. This estimate will be biased towards zero because the London daily price, which was the price series used in this study, has a greater variance than the true average price of world sugar consumption. As mentioned above, only about 10 percent of world sugar output is sold on the free market, although a much larger proportion is sold at prices based, in the long run, on the free market price.

The rate of adjustment of consumption to the excess demand for consumption, α_4, is high indicating a mean time lag of less than one week. This suggests that the rate of change of consumption should depend on current excess demand and not a distributed lag function of past excess demands. Thus the order of the differential equation determining consumption would be reduced to give the first order adjustment process

$$DC(t) = \alpha[\hat{C}(t) - C(t)].\qquad\qquad(6\text{-}34)$$

This means that consumption adjusts to a first order exponentially lagged function of demand for sugar.

Table 6-3. Estimates of Structural Parameters of World Sugar Market, 1958-1968

Rates of adjustment and adjustment coefficients:

$\alpha_1 = 0.409$ (4.87)	$\alpha_2 = 0.315$ (0.55)	α_3 or $\gamma = 1.249$ (6.37)
$\alpha_4 = 4.656$ (4.94)	$\beta = 0.938$ (5.06)	γ or $\alpha_3 = -0.096$ (2.85)

Behavioral parameters:

$a_1 = 2.077$ (6.35)	$a_2 = 3.252$ (5.99)
$b_1 = 0.005$ (4.70)	$b_2 = 0.015$ (30.59)

The eigenvalues of the model given in Table 6-4 provide some indication of the overall dynamic properties of the system. The two large negative eigenvalues have a negligible effect on the complementary function in the solution to the model and suggest that the order of one or more of the equations should be reduced. The negative sign of either α_3 or γ in the futures price function and the high rate of adjustment in the consumption function indicate that it may be these functions which are misspecified. If expected prices three months ahead were assumed to be given by spot prices so that the model would exhibit static expectations, and if sales adjust to demand with a first order lag as in (6-34), the futures price and consumption equations would both be of the first order. Unlike many difference equation systems estimated in economics where lagged variables are included or deleted with little effect on the rest of the structure, the respecification of Equations (6-23) and (6-24) fundamentally alters the whole model. The continuous model would become a first order system instead of a second order one, so that all of the variables in the discrete model would need to be redefined and transformed to eliminate a first order moving average error process instead of the second order process in the model above. When the continuous estimator is used, a change in the dynamic specification in part of the model usually has repercussions on the whole system. It is for this reason that the continuous approach often provides a more rigorous test of the dynamic structure of an economic model than other methods.

The model presented here can be considered as no more than a preliminary attempt to specify the way that the world sugar market determines prices, consumption, and stocks. The purpose of the chapter, however, is to outline and illustrate a relatively new econometric technique which might be useful in the specification, estimation, and analysis of models of commodity markets. If the market can be represented by a continuous model, the exact or approximate estimator can be used to estimate the system directly rather than estimating some form of ad hoc discrete model which may be similar, but perhaps not statistically equivalent, to the continuous model. In particular, the lag structure specified in the continuous model directly establishes the structure of the discrete model. Any restriction imposed on the model, based on economic theory or a knowledge of the institutional structure of the market, can usually

Table 6-4.   Dynamic Characteristics of the Sugar Model

Estimates of Eigenvalues	*Standard Errors*
−4.38	0.67
−3.33	1.39
−1.30	0.54
−0.04	0.21
−0.04	0.23
0.02	0.01

be maintained without modification, thus allowing more explicit estimation and testing of the model.

Moreover, the approach suggested in this chapter allows a more satisfactory treatment of the observation interval of the sample. The exact discrete estimator is independent of the length of the observation period (except perhaps where the system generates high frequency cycles) and although the approximate discrete estimator is biased, with the bias depending on the observation interval, previous empirical and Monte Carlo [4] studies suggest that this bias will be small. As it is much more expensive to use the exact discrete estimator, it is suggested that the approximate estimator is used for all preliminary work on a model and the exact estimates calculated only for the final model. The bias of the approximate estimator will usually be sufficiently small that it can be neglected in such preliminary work but, if necessary, an estimate of the bias can be found for a specific model using the exact estimator.

A model estimated in this way may be useful for policy purposes. A basic feature of the continuous estimator is that the exact approximate discrete model may be used for forecasting at more frequent intervals than the observation interval of the sample. Although only yearly data may be available for a particular commodity market, for example, a model estimated with such data could provide quarterly forecasts. Such forecasts might be valuable for producers or manufacturers, or for the management of buffer stocks.

NOTES

1. These programs are described in a set of manuals available from the author.
2. Sources for data used in this study are:

Sugar Weekly Review	C. Czarnikow Ltd.
Statistical Bulletin	International Sugar Organization
Sugar Year Book	International Sugar Organization
World Sugar Statistics	F.O. Licht, G.m.b.H.

3. The major producing and consuming countries for which monthly data are available were selected as representative countries for the region. The annual production and consumption of each region was serially disaggregated according to the monthly figures for the representative countries of that region. The representative countries used in this study, and the proportion of production and consumption of the region accounted for by these countries is as follows:

Europe

Representative countries:	European Economic Community United Kingdom
Proportion of regional production:	25 percent
Proportion of regional consumption:	35 percent

(The USSR accounts for 40 percent of production and 35 percent of consumption of this region. Other Eastern European countries account for 10 percent of production and 15 percent of consumption.)

North America

Representative countries:	USA (including Hawaii and Puerto Rico)
Proportion of regional production:	98 percent
Proportion of regional consumption:	90 percent

Central America

Representative countries:	Cuba (production only) Dominican Republic Mexico
Proportion of regional production:	80 percent
Proportion of regional consumption:	60 percent

(Cuba accounts for 55 percent of production and 20 percent of consumption of this region.)

South America

Representative countries:	Argentina Brazil Peru
Proportion of regional production:	75 percent
Proportion of regional consumption:	75 percent

Asia

Representative countries:	India Japan (consumption only) Philippines (production only) Taiwan
Proportion of regional production:	45 percent
Proportion of regional consumption:	40 percent

(China accounts for 25 percent of production and 20 percent of consumption of this region.)

Oceania

Representative country:	Australia
Proportion of regional production:	85 percent
Proportion of regional consumption:	80 percent

Africa

Representative countries:	Mauritius
	South Africa
Proportion of regional production:	50 percent
Proportion of regional consumption:	45 percent

4. For example, forecasts by F.O. Licht, G.m.b.H. reported in *World Sugar Statistics.*

5. A detailed explanation of the estimation of both the exact and approximate discrete model and the transformations of the variables in these models is contained in manuals entitled "DISCON Manual" and "Continuous Systems Manual" available from the author.

REFERENCES

1. Bergstrom, A.R., "Non-Recursive Models as Discrete Approximations to Systems of Stochastic Differential Equations." *Econometrica,* 1966, pp. 173–82.

2. Koopmans, T.C., "Models Involving a Continuous Time Variable," in *Statistical Inference in Dynamic Economic Models,* edited by T.C. Koopmans, Cowles Commission for Research in Economics, Monograph 10, New York: John Wiley and Sons, Inc. 1950, pp. 384–89.

3. Labys, W.C., *Dynamic Commodity Models: Specification, Estimation and Simulation.* Lexington, Mass.: Heath Lexington Books, 1973.

4. Phillips, P.C.B., "Some Problems in the Estimation of Continuous Time Models." Unpublished Ph.D. dissertation, University of London, 1973.

5. Sargan, J.D., "Some Discrete Approximations to Continuous Time Stochastic Models." *Journal of the Royal Statistical Society,* 1973 (forthcoming).

6. Snape, R.H., "Some Effects of Protection in the World Sugar Industry." *Economica,* 1963, pp. 63–73.

7. Wymer, C.R., "A Continuous Disequilibrium Adjustment Model of United Kingdom Financial Markets" in *Econometric Studies of Macro and Monetary Relations* edited by A.A. Powell and R.A. Williams, North-Holland, 1972.

8. ——, "Econometric Estimation of Stochastic Differential Equation Systems." *Econometrica,* 1972, pp. 565–77.

9. ——, *"Estimation of General Linear Differential Equation Systems."* Mimeographed, 1971.

Chapter Seven

Evaluating Supply Control Policies for Frozen Concentrated Orange Juice with an Industrial Dynamics Model

Richard C. Raulerson
Max R. Langham

The Florida citrus industry has been characterized by large shifts in supplies of fruit—particularly during and after such freeze years as 1957–58 and 1962–63, when the low supplies caused by the freezes led to high profit levels[1] and subsequently to large investments in new tree plantings. These new plantings are a potential source of excess supplies at prices that would be acceptable to growers.

This chapter reports an investigation into the problem of fluctuating orange supplies and grower profits in the frozen concentrated orange juice (FCOJ) sector of the Florida citrus industry. More specifically, a second generation[2] industrial dynamics[3] model was developed and used to appraise alternative supply control policies which were designed to reduce fluctuations in supplies and grower profits. The study provides an empirical application of industrial dynamics to an industry policy problem.[4]

INDUSTRIAL DYNAMICS

Forrester [4, p. 13] defines industrial dynamics quite broadly as ". . . the study of the information-feedback characteristics of industrial activity to show how organizational structure, amplification (in policies), and time delays (in decisions and actions) interact to influence the success of the enterprise. It treats the interaction between flows of information, money, orders, materials, personnel, and capital equipment in a company, an industry, or a national economy." Emphasis in industrial dynamics is placed upon information-feedback loops which characterize most decision environments. An information-feedback loop exists whenever the environment leads to a decision that results in action that

Richard C. Raulerson is Chief, Marketing Services Division, National Marine Fisheries Service at St. Petersburg, Florida; and Max R. Langham is professor of food and resource economics at the University of Florida.

affects the environment and thereby influences future decisions. Critical to these information-feedback loops are the amplifications and delays present in the decision-making system.

An example of an information-feedback loop is provided by a simplified model of the intrayear pricing of FCOJ (Figure 7-1). The object here is to arrive at an equilibrium price. However, because of delays in the system, the actual price fluctuates about the equilibrium price. The components of the information-feedback loops are connected by material flows and information flows. In the figure, flows of FCOJ are shown as solid lines. This flow begins with growing and processing activities. The rate at which FCOJ becomes part of processed inventory is symbolized as an hourglass-shaped valve. Processed inventory moves into retail inventory at another rate. Then consumption removes FCOJ from retail inventory at still another rate. Information flows, upon which the pricing of FCOJ depends, are shown as broken lines. An FOB price is set by processors after a delay while they consider the level of processed inventory and the rate at which it is disappearing. This FOB price dictates a certain retail price. After a delay in discovering this retail price, consumers adjust their rate of buying according to their demand schedule. Buying reduces retail inventory and after a delay for ordering and shipping, FCOJ moves from processed to retail inventory at some given rate. Then the processors reevaluate the level of inventory and rate of disappearance to consider a new FOB price. Then the pricing process is repeated. The dynamic equilibrium price (shown in Figure 7-1 to be stable) will probably never be reached because the pricing process is continuous. That is, while processors are debating inventories and movements, consumers are still reacting to the old price. By the time the new price reaches the consumer, the inventories and rates will have changed and a new price will be forthcoming.

THE MODEL

Our industrial dynamic model of the FCOJ industry was specified by 137 equations [16, pp. 111-116] written in the DYNAMO[5] simulation language. However, the focus here will be on the major forces that were thought to be operating in the industry at the time of the study rather than on detailed mathematical specification of model structure.

Economic structure generally enters a DYNAMO Model in simple tabular form through what are termed table functions. For example, in the model developed for this study, consumer demand for FCOJ enters as a schedule of quantities demanded at varying retail prices. This schedule was derived from estimates of demand structure by Langham [12] and Riggan.[17] Population and income projections developed by Daly [3] were used to derive estimates of shifts in demand over the period of the simulation. These were introduced into the model as a schedule of values based on time. A presentation of tabled values that reflect model assumptions of the economic structure would be of little use

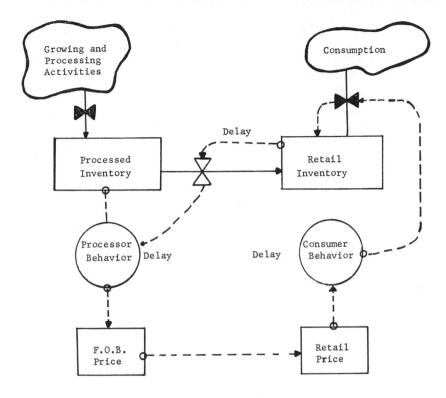

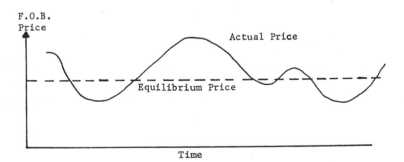

Figure 7-1. Intra-Year Pricing of Frozen Concentrated Orange Juice.

to the reader without added explanation of the research on which such assumptions were based, and space precludes such explanation.[6] Therefore, the underlying economic structure was submerged, and the model was treated in terms of general flows of materials and information.[7]

Major concerns of the detailed specification were determining where to close the model and validating it as an acceptable representation of real world industry behavior. The general criterion used in determining where to close the model was to obtain sufficient detail of industry behavior to accommodate test-ing the marketing policies of interest.[8] General criteria used in validating the model were internal consistency of separate model components and performance of the model in simulating actual industry performance during the period 1961–62 through 1966–67.

The FCOJ industry[9] and the DYNAMO model of it are composed of several interrelated sectors. The major economic forces that integrate the sectors and make the model go are based on the actions of two distinct groups of decision makers. Production and marketing decisions are subject to control by growers and processors, and consumption decisions depend on the behavior of consumers. The model is subjected to external shocks via random freezes which affect both short- and long-run supplies of oranges. These forces combine to determine the behavior of the FCOJ industry, including the level of orange supplies and grower profits over time. The model specification includes informa-tional delays and feedbacks which represent an attempt to capture—in the model—the actual dynamics of individual decision making and overall system behavior. Additionally, the model is extended to include the supply management policies defined in the next section.

Figure 7–2 outlines the *gross* feedback loops affecting supplies for the industry and the model. Long-run supply as a consequence of tree numbers is affected exogenously by weather and endogenously by the level of grower profits. This long-run supply influences the general level of FOB prices. Grower profits are in turn partly dependent on the existing FOB prices. Of special importance is the effect of weather as a source of variation in long-run supplies.

For any given season, the initial estimate of short-run supplies determines the FOB price. The retail price is determined from the FOB price; and through the consumer demand schedule, the retail price determines the level of retail sales. Retail sales and the effects of weather combine to influence short-run supply. In turn, short-run supply, when compared by processors to some desired inventory level, determines whether a change in the FOB price will occur. The short-run supply information-feedback loop prevents stabilization of prices and flows because of delays in information that exist in the system (see discussion of Figure 7–1).

Figure 7–3 summarizes the interaction of major forces hypothesized to be operating in the industry. Implicit in the figure are delays due to time-consuming physical and decision processes. These delays were of course made explicit in the mathematical specification of the model. Symbols used in Figure 7–3 have the following interpretation:

$\bigtimes$ represents a flow variable. It represents the aggregate response resulting from decisions made by growers, processors, or consumers and can be thought of as a value which restricts or increases a given flow.

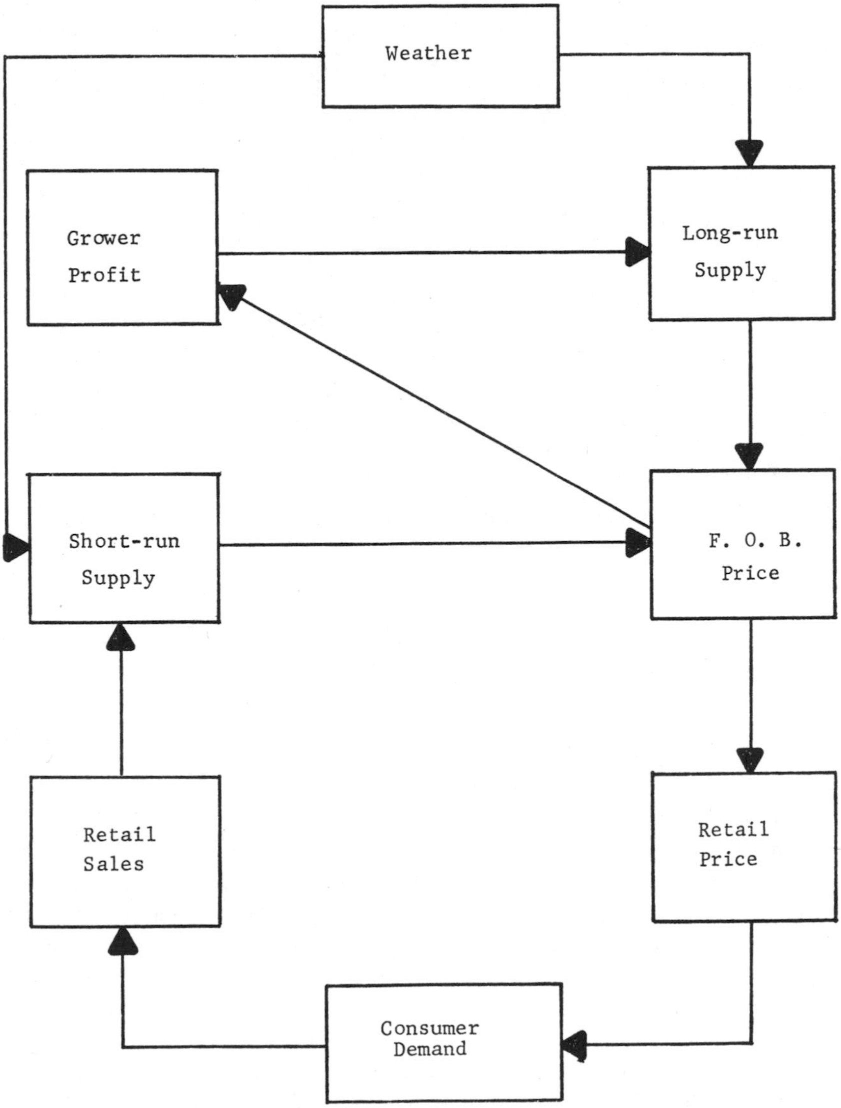

Figure 7-2. Block Diagram of Major Supply Feedback Loops of the Frozen Concentrated Orange Juice Industry.

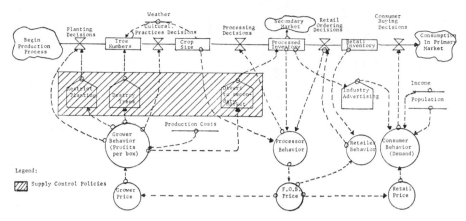

Figure 7-3. Flow Chart Showing the Major Forces Operating in the FCOJ Industry, Including the Hypothesized Supply Policies Considered in the Study.

○   represents variables that provide information for decision making.

▭   represents a stock variable. It is the cumulative result of inflows and outflows.

△   represents a collective decision variable. It depicts an industry policy and is not affected by individuals acting alone.

─○─   represents an exogenous variable.

───   represents flows of orange concentrate.

- - -   represents information flows.

        Since the relationships depicted involve a system of interdependent information-feedback loops, the decision as to where to enter the system in order to examine it is rather arbitrary. The production process begins with the planting of trees and provides a reasonable starting point.
        Following Figure 7-3, individual planting decisions in the model depended on grower profit per box. Grower profit per box equaled the grower (on-tree) price less production costs. The grower price was derived from the FOB price. The model assumed that individual growers increased or restricted the rate at which they planted trees as grower profit rose or fell. Historically, it has been evident that these decisions in the aggregate produce sizable fluctuations in the number of trees. More specifically, growers have tended to overinvest (collectively) in new trees when profits are unusually high. For this reason the model included a policy alternative to restrict new plantings when profits were unusually high.

Over time, the planting rate added to the stock of trees. This stock could be reduced instantly by the effect of weather, freezes in particular. A freeze can affect orange supplies in one of three possible ways, depending on severity and duration: (1) Trees can be killed or so severely damaged that they have to be butt-cut.[10] (2) Trees can be damaged enough so that they have to be hatracked; that is, all but the primary or secondary scaffold branches have to be pruned. (3) Trees may only suffer yield losses in the current year.

The weather assumptions for simulation runs included only the effects of freezes in reducing orange supplies.[11] These assumptions were based on 29 seasons of actual temperature data (1937–38 through 1964–65) obtained from the Federal State Frost Warning Service.[18] Each of these seasons was assigned (according to the severity of the winter and corresponding crop losses) a fraction of trees or fruit lost by each of the three ways discussed above. Random sampling with replacement was used to obtain six sets of 14 years of weather assumptions from the 29. These six sets were used to observe the effects of different numbers, timing, and severity of freezes on model results. Three such sets of weather are presented in Table 7-1.[12] The first two of these are used later in the empirical comparison of the policies.

The stock of trees was also reduced as trees became unproductive. Although this is a natural process, the rate at which trees become unproductive is influenced by cultural practices. Individual decisions concerning cultural practices depended on grower profits. The crop size for any given year was based on the number of trees and their yield. The yield was affected by cultural practices and the influence of weather.

Processed inventory was accumulated as the result of processing rate decisions. Since mature oranges can be stored on the tree, it may be thought that the on-tree price and other factors will influence the processing rate. This may be true to some degree, but historically the processing rate has been quite consistent from year to year. Evidently, the gains from attempting to operate processing facilities at peak capacity outweigh other forces that influence processing decisions. Thus, the schedule of processing rates during a season were fixed in the model. A policy that would divert FCOJ into the secondary market was included. This action was presumed to take place whenever the grower profit per box reached the minimum allowable (for policy purposes) level (15 cents per box). The policy was designed to reduce short-run supplies and to raise the price structure and grower profits.

All disappearing processed inventories not channeled into the secondary market was accumulated as retail inventory. The flow into retail inventory was regulated by retail ordering decisions based on the current FOB price and level of retail inventory. Retail inventory was depleted as consumer buying decisions regulated the outflow of FCOJ into final consumption. The consumer buying decisions were based on an estimated demand function. Demand shifters in the form of income, population, and industry advertising

Table 7-1. Three 20-Year Sets of Weather Effects in Terms of Fraction of Trees Lost, Fraction of Crop Lost, and Fraction of Trees Hatracked[a]

| | Weather condition | | | | | | | | |
| | One | | | Two | | | Three | | |
Season	Lost	Yield	Hat	Lost	Yield	Hat	Lost	Yield	Hat
1961–62	–	–	–	–	–	–	–	–	–
1962–63	0.11	0.15	0.18	0.11	0.15	0.18	0.11	0.15	0.18
1963–64	–	0.3	–	–	0.3	–	–	0.3	–
1964–65	–	0.2	–	–	0.2	–	–	0.2	–
1965–66	–	–	–	–	–	–	–	–	–
1966–67	–	–	–	–	–	–	–	–	–
1967–68	–	–	–	–	–	–	–	–	–
1968–69	–	–	–	0.11	0.15	0.18	–	–	–
1969–70	–	–	–	–	0.2	–	–	–	–
1970–71	–	–	–	–	0.1	–	–	–	–
1971–72	–	–	–	–	–	–	–	–	–
1972–73	–	–	–	–	–	–	–	–	–
1973–74	–	–	–	–	–	–	–	0.13	–
1974–75	–	–	–	–	–	–	0.06	0.12	0.06
1975–76	–	–	–	–	–	–	–	0.05	–
1976–77	–	–	–	–	–	–	0.08	0.15	0.1
1977–78	–	–	–	–	–	–	0.08	0.3	0.1
1978–79	–	–	–	–	–	–	–	0.19	–
1979–80	–	–	–	–	–	–	–	0.04	–
1980–81	–	–	–	–	–	–	–	–	–

[a]Actual freeze effects are shown for seasons 1961–62 through 1966–67; random freeze effects are shown for seasons 1967–68 through 1980–81.

were estimated (the latter quite crudely) and incorporated into the model. Retail price was derived from the FOB price. Industry advertising was specified as a collective decision and its level was tied to a per-box tax on the fruit processed.

This completes discussion of the physical flow of FCOJ in the model, which began with the initial decisions to plant trees and ended with FCOJ flowing into final consumption. Main interest in the study was with grower profits, and all policy decisions added to the model were based on the goal of stabilizing grower profits at acceptable levels. These policies are defined in the next section.

MARKET POLICIES

The model was used to test the effectiveness of the following policies in stabilizing orange supplies and grower profits:

1. "Free market" policy. The FCOJ industry was simulated with its current policy of no explicit supply controls.

2. Allocation of FCOJ to two separate markets. This policy assumed that two separable markets for FCOJ either existed or could be established. The economic reasoning behind this policy was that if different price elasticities of demand existed in two different markets, then total revenue could possibly be increased in the short run by shifting FCOJ from the market with the smaller (in an absolute sense) elasticity coefficient to the market with the higher elasticity coefficient. In this study the two markets were designed as primary and secondary markets, respectively. The normal retail market was considered to be the primary market, while such possible markets as school lunch, vending machines, and relief were considered together as the secondary market. All FCOJ was considered sold in the primary market when grower profits were above 15 cents per box. When profits were below this level, an amount of FCOJ necessary to raise profits to 15 cents per box was shifted to the secondary market. It was assumed that FCOJ moving into the secondary market faced a perfectly elastic demand at a price of $1.00 per box and that entry into and exit from the secondary market was possible.

3. Elimination of fully productive trees. This policy was designed to stabilize profits above the 15 cents per box level. To accomplish this goal, a certain portion of the existing productive trees were destroyed whenever grower profits dropped below 15 cents per box. When the policy was effective, trees were removed at a rate that would eventually raise grower profits to $1.00 per box. However, the policy would never actually bring profits to that level since the policy was no longer effective when grower profits rose above 15 cents per box.

4. Curtailment of new tree plantings. This policy was formulated so that no new orange trees could be planted whenever grower profits were above $1.00 per box. The rationale behind this policy was derived from the known tendency of orange growers to overinvest in new tree plantings when grower profits were at an unusually high level (e.g., following a freeze, when supplies were very low and prices were high). Due to the nature of its control over supplies, this policy was perhaps more forward looking than the other policies. Instead of representing an attempt to correct a low grower profit situation, the policy was designed to help keep such a low profit situation from developing.

5. Allocation of FCOJ to two separate markets, used in conjunction with elimination of fully productive trees.

6. Allocation of FCOJ to two separate markets, used in conjunction with curtailment of new tree plantings.

Simulation runs with alternative sets of randomly selected weather assumptions indicated that weather had little effect on the relative performance of the six policies. Generally, the "best" policy became more valuable as weather increased fluctuations in orange supplies. An empirical comparison of the policies under two sets of weather assumptions is presented in the next section.

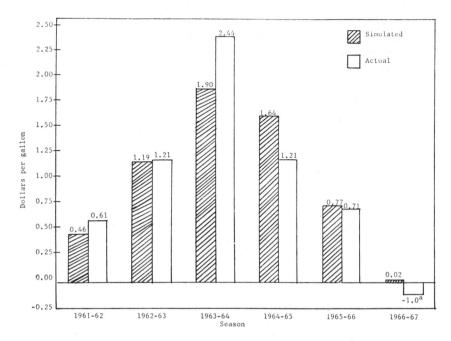

Figure 7–4.   Simulated and Actual Grower Profits of Frozen Concentrated Orange Juice, 1961–1962 Through 1966–1967. Source: *Florida Canners Association Statistical Summary, Season of 1965–66*, Winter Haven, Florida.

[a]Estimated

SIMULATION RESULTS

Validation of Model

Figures 7–4 and 7–5 provide a view of the correspondence of model behavior[13] to that of the actual system with respect to pack of FCOJ and grower profits per gallon. These variables are representative of the other variables in the model insofar as model behavior versus actual industry behavior is concerned. The model and the actual system exhibited the same modes of behavior for the six seasons, 1961–62 through 1966–67. The cycles of the variables have the same periods, and the amplitudes (absolute change from a high point on a curve to a low point) are similar. The ability of the model to represent turning points in the movement of variables during this six-year period supported the notion that the model could satisfactorily simulate the time-varying behavior of the industry system.

Simulation of the "free market" policy with no freezes (weather One) is presented in Figure 7–6.[14] This run, like all runs, was started with the initial conditions corresponding to the start of the 1961–62 season. Crop size

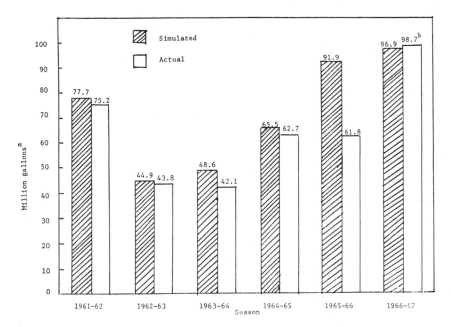

Figure 7-5. Simulated and Actual Retail Pack of Frozen Concentrated Orange Juice, 1961-1962 Through 1966-1967. Source: *Florida Canners Association Statistical Summary, Season of 1965-66.* Winter Haven, Florida.

[a]Based on 45° Brix   [b]Estimated

(for FCOJ only) was 55.9 million boxes, FOB price per dozen six-ounce cans was $1.44, grower profits averaged 73 cents per box, and productive trees (not shown in Figure 7-6) numbered 13.9 million.

Violent shifts in the variables in the early years were a consequence of the 1962-63 freeze. Beginning with the 1964-65 season grower profits fell continuously and reached zero in the 1966-67 season. During this same period crop size rose to 69.7 million boxes, the FOB price fell to about $1.15, and the number of productive trees rose to over 18 million. Grower profits did not become positive again until the 1975-76 season after which they followed a general upward trend with slight seasonal variation.

Analysis of Alternative Policies

Method of Comparing. Supply control policies were compared on the basis of their ability to stabilize supplies and grower profits at acceptable levels. Weather conditions One and Two (Table 7-1) were each used to simulate each of the six policies. As indicated earlier, different weather conditions had little effect on the desirability of the six policies in terms of an ordinal ranking.

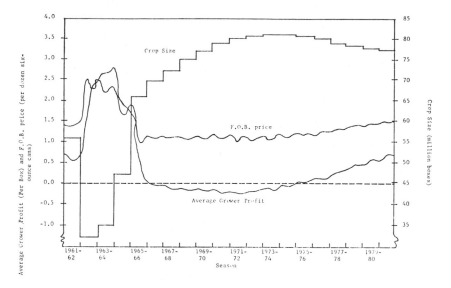

Figure 7-6. Average Grower Profit, FOB Price, and Crop Size for a 20-Year Simulation with Weather Assumption One and a "Free Market" Policy, 1961-62 Through 1980-1981.

However, as will be shown later, the absolute performance of the six policies was sensitive to the number and severity of freezes that occurred.

Policy comparisons were made on the level and relative variability of grower profits.[15] The comparison used assumed that industry utility (from the grower's point of view) was an increasing function of total grower profits and a declining function of variability of profits.

Comparison Using Weather One. The "free market" policy appeared to be the least desirable of the six studied from the growers' point of view. It produced the lowest total grower profits and had the highest rel-variance (Table 7-2). However, at the end of the simulation it ranked third in the level of grower profits. This result is consistent with the well-known facts that a free market is capable of correcting a low grower profit situation without the aid of supply-oriented policies but that the time required to correct such a situation can be quite long. The hypothesized utility function suggests that some type of direct program would be preferred. The time required for profits to recover in a "free market" environment if no freezes occur can be seen in Figure 7-6. Note that the period of high profits following the freeze lasted only four years, while it took twelve years for profits to come back to prefreeze levels once they declined. This situation is common among several important tree crops (see Bateman [2]). The difference in investment between a nursery tree and a fully productive tree probably contributes to the longer period of depressed prices and grower profits.

Table 7-2.   Total Grower Profits, Rel-Variances, Grower Profits for the 20th Year, and Total Retail Sales for 20-Year Simulations of the Frozen Concentrated Orange Juice Industry, 1961–1962 Through 1980–1981

	Weather condition	
Policy[a]	One	Two
	Total grower profits (million dollars)	
PRSM	773.9	1159.1
PR	771.0	1152.6
TRSM	699.8	905.5
TR	694.5	899.4
SM	509.7	722.3
FM	431.6	684.5
	Rel-variances	
TRSM	0.56	0.45[c]
TR	0.58	0.46[c]
PRSM	0.61	0.23
PR	0.72	0.24
SM	1.46	1.01
FM	2.83	1.18
	20th year grower profits (million dollars)	
PR	69.9	69.3
PRSM	66.5	69.1
FM	49.8	24.0[c]
TR	44.6	26.9
TRSM	44.3	26.3
SM	31.6	15.1
	Total retail sales (million cases)[b]	
FM	886.0	823.4
SM	852.3	816.1
TR	827.4	790.5
TRSM	826.9	789.7
PR	816.8	754.3
PRSM	816.5	752.2

[a]Policies are ranked according to their performance under weather One. FM = "free market," policy 1 (as defined in text); SM = secondary market, policy 2; TR = tree removal, policy 3; PR = planting restriction, policy 4; TRSM = tree removal and secondary market, policy 5; PRSM = planting restriction and secondary market, policy 6.

[b]Each case contains 48 six-ounce cans of concentrate.

[c]Ranks differ from weather assumption One.

Growers seem to be more willing to plant new trees during periods of high profits than to destroy productive trees during periods of low profits. These differences in growers' response substantiate the proposition that large fluctuations in crop size and grower profits tend to lower long-run profits because of the stimulant to planting during periods of high grower profits.

The two policies, planting restriction (PR) and planting restriction combined with secondary market (PRSM), produced similar total grower profits. However, the behavior of industry variables for the two policies was somewhat different over the 20-year simulation period. Yearly grower profits were higher for PRSM during seasons 1966–67 through 1972–73. This occurred because the secondary market part of the policy limited supplies earlier than a planting policy by itself. However, for the balance of the simulation the policy (PR), which called for planting restrictions, alone had higher yearly profits. Since no immediate supply removal policy was used to raise the grower profits, with this single policy, the planting restriction was in effect longer. In addition, the lower profits restricted the planting of more trees, which resulted in lower supplies and higher profits later. An examination of the profits for the latter years of the simulation revealed that the planting restriction only policy (PR) was gaining on the dual policy (PRSM) at the rate of over three million dollars per year. Since the total grower profits were 773.9 and 771.0 million dollars for the dual and single policy, respectively, grower profits for the single policy would probably be greater had the simulation been extended one more year.

The policies that included removal of productive trees—tree removal (TR) and tree removal combined with secondary market (TRSM)—had rel-variances slightly lower than the policies that restricted plantings, but produced lower grower profits. Total grower profits for TRSM were almost identical to those for the single tree removal policy, TR (Table 7-2). Other major industry variables reacted analogously over time for TR and TRSM. The tree removal and secondary market policies were both designed to bring grower profits up to 15 cents per box. Thus, the addition of the secondary market policy added very little to the short-run effects of the tree removal policy. In later years of the simulation the grower profits were above 15 cents per box so that the secondary market part of the policy was not in effect. Thus, it appears that a secondary market policy used in tandem with a tree removal policy has little advantage over a tree removal policy used by itself.

The secondary market policy (SM) used by itself had the lowest total grower profits and the highest rel-variance of all policies except the "free market" policy. At the end of the simulation it produced lower grower profits than any other policy (Table 7-2). Its influence on industry variables was to raise profits in the short run while limiting long-run gains. This type of policy attacks only the symptoms of the problem and allows the cause to go unchecked. A secondary market policy adjusts supplies on a year-to-year basis. However, only oranges are removed. In order to affect future supplies, the trees must be controlled in some manner. Model experimentation showed that curtailing short-run supply with a secondary market scheme encouraged the planting of trees; hence long-run supply problems were actually magnified.

Comparison Using Weather Two.   The relative desirability of the six policies studied under weather assumption One remained unchanged under weather condition Two. However, the absolute and percentage differences in grower profits between the leading policies showed some increase under weather assumption Two.

Under weather condition One, the total grower profits for the policies involving the removal of productive trees were about 90 percent of the total grower profits for the policies that restricted new plantings. However, this figure dropped to about 78 percent for weather condition Two (Table 7-3). This implies that the more exogenous fluctuations in supply (freezes) that occur, the more valuable the planting policy becomes. This is reasonable, considering the argument presented earlier that growers are more responsive to high than to low prices. Consequently, intermittent periods of high grower profits induced larger supplies unless a restriction on planting was imposed.

Relative Costs of Alternative Policies

The policies discussed have been judged only on their capability to stabilize grower profits and supplies of oranges at specified levels. Implementing any policy program will necessitate some costs. The two dual policies—planting restrictions plus secondary market, and tree removal plus secondary market— would certainly cost more than their counterparts—planting restrictions and tree removal. Since the single policies performed as well as the dual policies, the single policies would probably be preferred on the basis of cost considerations.

The elimination of dual policies leaves four policies—"free market" policy, the secondary market, tree removal, and planting restrictions—to be considered. Of these, the "free market" policy is obviously the least expensive to employ, but it produced the highest rel-variance and the lowest total grower profits. The planting restriction policy added most to grower profits and would probably be the least expensive to administer. The secondary market idea would probably be the most expensive to administer because of the record supervision required to assure that supplies would be channeled into the correct market. This policy also ranked third among the four single policies in terms of total grower

Table 7-3. Simulated Total Grower Profits for Six Policy Decisions Under Two Weather Conditions Expressed as a Percent of Total Grower Profits of Leading Policy Under Each Weather Assumption

| Policy | *Weather condition* | |
	One[a]	*Two[a]*
PRSM	100.0	100.0
PR	99.6	99.4
TRSM	90.4	78.1
TR	89.7	77.6
SM	65.9	62.3
FM	55.8	59.1

[a]Total grower profits as percent of PRSM under each weather assumption.

profits and variability of profits. The tree removal policy probably falls between the planting restriction and secondary market policies in terms of cost, as well as in terms of grower profits. Thus, it appears that a consideration of the cost of alternative supply policies probably would not alter the relative desirability of these policies.

CONCLUDING REMARKS

Before the FCOJ industry adopts any supply-oriented policy, it should resolve some basic conflicts of interest regarding the desired level of orange supplies and the length of time the proposed policy should be in effect. Furthermore, it should also recognize that any policy will undoubtedly change the industry environment which created the need for the policy. The industry should therefore be cautioned to continually evaluate both the tangible benefits of any policy and the structural changes in the industry resulting from such a policy.

The price elasticity of demand is more elastic for the processor than for the grower sector of the FCOJ industry at any given level of crop size. This situation is common in agriculture and results from the addition of processing and marketing charges to the value of raw fruit. These different price elasticities imply that a crop size that maximizes net revenue for the grower may produce less than the maximum net revenue for the processor.

One solution to any conflict that may exist or arise between growers and processors concerning optimum crop size is vertical integration in the FCOJ industry. Historically, vertical integration has been occurring in the industry. The continuation of a "free market" policy will probably provide greater impetus to more integration than the other policies considered in this study.

The study shows that policies designed to control supplies on a year-to-year basis may create additional supply problems in the future. If so, there may be a general conflict between short- and long-run policy goals. The implication for the industry is that careful study should be given to any policy to determine whether such a conflict exists.

Even though a supply policy is successful in stabilizing grower profits and supplies of oranges at an acceptable level, industry decision makers should be aware of possible unforeseen dangers. It was pointed out earlier that a policy may change the industry environment in such a way that producers will respond in an unpredicted or unpredictable manner. For example, when the Israeli government established a program of guaranteed forward prices to help the poultry industry, farmers increased egg production an estimated 81.3 percent above normal production for that price because the price was no longer uncertain (Mundlak, [13, p. 98]). If such a situation developed in the FCOJ industry, the results of this study would tend to be optimistic for all policies tested, except "free market."

A final word of caution. Before the FCOJ industry adopts any policy it must recognize the irreversibility of the industry supply function. The time lag of grower response to price increases is much shorter than to price decreases. Thus, any policy that improves prices in the short run and does not attempt to control tree numbers appears to lower average grower profits in the long run.

NOTES

1. "High profit levels" refers to total industry profits without regard to the distribution of these profits. It is certainly recognized that some growers suffered severe economic losses.
2. The first generation model was developed by Jarmain.[10]
3. The industrial dynamics approach has been well documented by its developer, J.W. Forrester. [4] Ansoff and Slevin [1] developed an expository paper on industrial dynamics under a joint commission by the Office of Naval Research and the Army Research Office. Forrester has published a response to this expository paper [5] and a review article on industrial dynamics after the first decade [6].
4. Halter and Dean have reported an application of industrial dynamics to a decision problem of a firm.[8, 9] For examples of some problems in industrial dynamics, see Jarmain.[11]
5. The DYNAMO language was developed by Alexander Pugh.[15] We found the language to be a flexible instrument for translating a real world problem into a mathematical model. There are 58 different types of equations permitted, but these can be used in combination for additional model building flexibility.
6. A detailed discussion of each equation in the model may be found in Raulerson.[16, ch. 3]
7. Our approach is not inconsistent with the philosophy of industrial dynamics. This approach allows a view of system flows and feedbacks that appear to be only indirectly connected to the underlying economic structure while the onus of system "performance" ultimately falls on that underlying structure. Even so, our choice has led to the charge by one anonymous reviewer that we have tended to abandon our role as economists writing for other economists.
8. In reviewing the original article, Professor Ray A. Goldberg cautioned in a letter to the Associate Editor of the AJAE ". . . that there are so many limiting factors that were not taken into consideration in the model, such as the impact of synthetics, major institutional changes such as the growth of cooperatives, long-term contractual arrangements, the advent of the futures market, and the importance of market orientation of the total industry. If you isolate the producer from these other interrelated participants and institutions, you will be doing both the producer and the total industry a great disservice. This approach is an important step forward in the thinking of producer groups and public policy makers. Therefore, I would be disappointed to see it put forth without talking about the importance

of the other participants and the market orientation. Otherwise, producers might get the mistaken idea that they do not have to worry about pricing themselves out of the market, and that they don't have to learn how to be their own best competitors by developing their own synthetic products to compete with themselves."

An anonymous reviewer indicated that evaluation completely from the growers' viewpoint was myopic.

The comments by both reviewers have validity and represent criticisms of the point at which the model was closed. Research is under way to expand the model to include other variables and the interests of the other participants in the subsector system. However, any model must remain an abstraction, and a major benefit of constructing a model is not the numbers that it generates but the understanding of the system that the effort gives to those involved in constructing it. This understanding may in turn become a valuable resource for decision makers. The comments by the reviewers serve to emphasize the degree of abstraction in the model and to help caution the reader in evaluating the actual numbers generated by the model.

9. Goldberg [7] has published a description of the Florida orange industry system.
10. Butt-cut trees take about as long to come back into production as newly planted trees and were treated in the model as trees completely lost.
11. Droughts, hurricanes, and other weather conditions also have their effect on orange supplies. The effects of weather on orange supplies is currently undergone more intensive study by David W. Parvin, Jr.[14] since the present study was completed.
12. All simulation runs actually had a duration of 20 years (1961–62 through 1980–81). Actual weather for the first six years (through 1966–67) was used in order to provide a basis for validation of the model.
13. All simulation runs were identical during the first six years.
14. The behavior of only three variables is traced. The DYNAMO simulation program will plot and present in tabular form the data that traces the movement of any variable in the model.
15. Grower profits were defined as on-tree price less average production cost of 85 cents per box.

REFERENCES

1. Ansoff, H.I., and D.P. Slevin, "An Appreciation of Industrial Dynamics." *Mgt. Sci.* 14 (March 1968): 383–97.
2. Bateman, M.J., "Aggregate and Regional Supply Functions for Ghanaian Cocoa, 1946–1962." *J. Farm Econ.,* 47 (May 1965): 384–401.
3. Daly, R.F., "Agriculture in the Years Ahead," paper presented at the Association of Southern Agricultural Workers Conference in Atlanta, February 1964.
4. Forrester, J.W., *Industrial Dynamics,* Cambridge: M.I.T. Press, 1965.

5. ———, "Industrial Dynamics—A Response to Ansoff and Slevin." *Mgt. Sci.* 14 (May 1968): 601–18.

6. ———, "Industrial Dynamics—After the First Decade." *Mgt. Sci.* 14 (March 1968): 398–415.

7. Goldberg, R.A., *Agribusiness Coordination, A Systems Approach to Wheat, Soybeans, and Florida Orange Economics,* Boston, Division of Research, Harvard Business School, 1968.

8. Halter, A.N., and G.W. Dean, *Simulation of a California Range Feedlot Operation,* Giannini Foundation Res. Rep. 282, University of California, May 1965.

9. ———, "Use of Simulation in Evaluating Management Policies Under Uncertainty: Application to a Large-Scale Ranch." *J. Farm Econ.* 47 (August 1965): 557–73.

10. Jarmain, W.E., "Dynamics of the Florida Frozen Orange Concentrate Industry," unpublished M.S. thesis, Massachusetts Institute of Technology, 1962.

11. ———, ed., *Problems in Industrial Dynamics.* Cambridge: M.I.T. Press, 1963.

12. Langham, M.R., "On-Tree and In-Store Citrus Price Relationships," in *Proceedings of the Second Annual Citrus Business Conference,* Florida Citrus Commission, November 1965.

13. Mundlak, Y., *An Economic Analysis of Established Family Farms in Israel, 1953–58, The Folk Project for Economic Research in Israel.* Jerusalem: The Jerusalem Post Press, July 1964.

14. Parvin, D.W., Jr., "Effects of Weather on Orange Supplies," unpublished Ph.D. thesis, University of Florida, 1970.

15. Pugh, A.L., III, *DYNAMO User's Manual,* 2nd ed., Cambridge: M.I.T. Press, May 1963.

16. Raulerson, R.C., "A Study of Supply-Oriented Marketing Policies for Frozen Concentrated Orange Juice: An Application of DYNAMO Simulation," unpublished M.S. thesis, University of Florida, 1967.

17. Riggan, W.B., "Demand for Florida Oranges," unpublished Ph.D. thesis, North Carolina State University, 1965.

18. U.S. Department of Commerce, Weather Bureau, *Winter Minimum Temperatures in Peninsular Florida, Summary of 20 Seasons, 1937–57,* and *Annual Reports,* 1958 through 1965, Federal-State Frost Warning Service, Lakeland, Florida.

Chapter Eight

Dynamics of the International Lauric Oils Market

Walter C. Labys

     The major coconut oil exporting countries of Southeast Asia have suffered from problems of instability in the fluctuations of exports and prices, caused by adverse climatic conditions as well as by weaknesses in productivity programs. These have led to a reduction in the usage of coconut oil to minimum levels in certain products and have encouraged industrial users to look towards synthetics to substitute for coconut derivatives. In an effort to surmount such difficulties, these countries have organized the Asian Coconut Community, which is currently investigating policy alternatives which could best rejuvenate the industry and provide for future market growth.

     This chapter summarizes the dynamic characteristics and policy applications of an econometric model of the international lauric oils market which has been used to analyze some of those alternatives.[1] The model features dynamic explanations of import, export, and price behavior based on the premise that an economic system can be more realistically described as a system of first or higher order difference equations. Both linear and nonlinear versions are presented, utilizing annual data which span the years 1953-1967. Dynamic aspects of the market are discussed using stability analysis, multiplier analysis, and simulation analysis. Simulation analysis of a nonstochastic nature provides results concerning the validity of the model as well as the impact which an export norm scheme or buffer stock scheme might have on stabilizing prices. To reflect the impact of random changes in the surrounding climatic conditions on market prospects, stochastic simulation is used to generate a set of long run projections.

THE MARKET

Lauric oils represent a typical world primary product since supply originates almost entirely in developing countries and consumption takes place largely in

Visiting Professor, Graduate Institute of International Studies, Geneva.

developed countries. Although lauric oils also form part of a larger market featuring trade in desicated coconut and copra meal and cake, the majority of trade pertains to the oils, which have many specialized uses. In fact, lauric oils constitute an important link in the world's supply of oils and fats, ranking second in both volume and value of output. Table 8-1, summarizing the quantity and percentage composition of world trade, shows the Philippines, Sri Lanka, and Indonesia to be the principal exporting countries; the U.S., U.K., and the E.E.C. constitute the principal importing countries.

The economic character of the lauric oils market is a highly competitive one, not hampered by severe government price regulations or other constraints. Accordingly, the major firms which exist on the export and the import side of the market have roughly the same bargaining power. Nyberg [15] has counted 30 export firms in the Philippines with the 4 largest copra firms shipping about 70 percent of copra exports and the two largest oil firms shipping about 75 percent of oil exports. He also reports 12 dealers and about 20 crushers handling imports in Western Europe and 3 large crushers in the U.S. The 2 major European importers are responsible for more than 70 percent of total imports, while the 3 U.S. firms account for about 20 percent.

Lauric oil price determination is in terms of coconut oil prices, particularly as they are formed in New York, Rotterdam, and Manila. The New York price used in the model best appears to reflect adjustments in world market equilibrium. The price of palm kernel oil, a near perfect substitute for coconut oil, is determined by the latter.

THE MODEL

Market behavior within the above framework can be described using a market form of econometric model where price adjustment normally is reached through the simultaneous interaction of supply and demand. However, since the short run behavior of the supply and demand for lauric oils is relatively price-inelastic, price adjustment also relates to fluctuations in stock levels in both exporting and importing countries. The resulting price mechanism which represents a form of combined stock and flow adjustment can be understood more readily by examining Figure 8-1, where the model is shown to consist of 22 equations divided into three major blocks. Definitions for the variables appear in Table 8-2.[2] The Recursive Block 1 contains lauric oils export Equations 1-7 and precedes the other blocks because exports are often influenced more strongly by climatic conditions than by market prices. The Simultaneous Block which includes stock and price Equations 8-14 indicates that prices depend on the exports forthcoming in a year as well as on current adjustments in stocks. The Recursive Block 2, featuring the consumption and import Equations 15-21 together with the market clearing identity, appears last since the inelastic demand situation implies that demand adjusts somewhat independently of short run price changes. Also

Table 8-1. Composition of Net Lauric Oil Exports and Imports, 1951-1970[a], (000 metric tons)

Distribution of Exports	Quantity	%	Distribution of Exports	Quantity	%
Coconut oil and copra			Palm kernel and palm kernel oil		
Philippines	13316	54.9	Nigeria	3655	48.8
Sri Lanka	2111	8.7	Sierra Leone	546	7.3
Indonesia	3196	13.2	Congo (Kins)	1080	14.4
Oceania	3301	13.6	French W. and Eq. Africa	1120	14.9
ROW[b]	2344	9.6	ROW	1096	14.6
Total	24267	100.0	Total	7497	100.0
			Combined oils exports	31764	

Distribution of Imports	Quantity	%
Combined lauric oils		
U.S.	6910	21.8
E.E.C.	10606	33.4
U.K.	4096	12.8
Japan	1144	3.6
ROW	9008	28.4
Total imports	31764	100.0

[a] All data includes quantities of copra, palm kernels, or both in oil equivalent.
[b] Rest of world residual.

Source: *World Oils and Fats Statistics*, Prepared by Economics and Statistics Department, Unilever Limited, for the Congress of the International Association of Seed Crushers, various issues.

Recursive Block 1—Oils Exports

1. $\Delta x_t^{ph} = f(x_{t-1}^{ph}, p_{t-1}^{ph}, \Delta p_t^{ph}, r_{t-2}^{ph}, \Delta r_{t-1}^{ph})$

2. $\Delta x_t^{sr} = f(x_{t-1}^{sr}, p_{t-1}^{sr}, \Delta p_t^{sr}, r_{t-2}^{sr}, \Delta r_{t-1}^{sr})$

3. $\Delta x_t^{in} = f(x_{t-1}^{in}, p_{t-1}^{in}, \Delta p_t^{in}, r_{t-2}^{in}, \Delta r_{t-1}^{in})$

4. $\Delta x_t^{oc} = f(x_{t-1}^{oc}, \Delta p_t^{x}, p_{t-1}^{x})$

5. $\Delta x_t^{rw} = f(x_{t-1}^{rw}, \Delta p_t^{x}, p_{t-1}^{x})$

6. $x_t^{pk} = f(x_{t-1}^{pk}, p_t^{x}, p_{t-1}^{x}, p_{t-2}^{x})$

7. $x_t^{w} = x_t^{ph} + x_t^{sr} + x_t^{in} + x_t^{oc} + x_t^{rw} + x_t^{pk}$

Simultaneous Block—Oils Stocks and Prices

8. $s_t^{us} = f(\Delta y_{t+1}^{us}, p_t^{w}, \Delta p_t^{w}, D_t^{us})$

9. $s_t^{uk} = f(s_{t-1}^{uk}, \Delta y_t^{uk}, p_t^{w}, \Delta p_t^{w}, D_t^{uk})$

10. $\Delta s_t^{ec} = f(s_{t-1}^{ec}, \Delta y_t^{ec}, \Delta p_t^{w}, D_t^{ec})$

11. $s_t^{sr} = f(p_t^{w}, p_{t-1}^{w}, p_{t-2}^{w}, D_t^{sr})$

12. $s_t^{ph} = 0.10 \, x_t^{ph}$

13. $s_t^{w} = s_t^{us} + s_t^{uk} + s_t^{ec} + s_t^{sr} + s_t^{ph}$

14. $p_t^{w} = f(p_{t-1}^{w}, s_t^{w}, s_{t-1}^{w}, x_t^{w})$

Recursive Block 2—Oils Consumption and Imports

15. $c_t^{us} = f(c_{t-1}^{us}, y_t^{us}, p_t^{w})$

16. $c_t^{uk} = f(c_{t-1}^{uk}, y_t^{uk}, p_t^{w}, Z_t^{uk})$

17. $c_t^{ec} = f(y_t^{ec}, \Delta y_t^{ec}, p_t^{w}, Z_t^{ec})$

18. $m_t^{jp} = f(m_{t-1}^{jp}, y_t^{jp}, p_t^{w}, Z_t^{jp})$

19. $m_t^{us} = c_t^{us} \pm \Delta s_t^{us} - s_t^{gsa}$

20. $m_t^{uk} = c_t^{uk} \pm \Delta s_t^{uk}$

21. $m_t^{ec} = c_t^{ec} \pm \Delta s_t^{ec}$

22. $m_t^{rw} = x_t^{w} - m_t^{us} - m_t^{uk} - m_t^{ec} - m_t^{jp}$

Figure 8-1. Block Structure of the Linear Version of the Lauric Oils Model.

Table 8-2.   Classification and Definition of Variables

Endogenous Variables

1	x_t^{ph}	Philippine coconut oil exports
2	x_t^{in}	Indonesia coconut oil exports
3	x_t^{sr}	Sri Lanka coconut oil exports
4	x_t^{oc}	Oceania coconut oil exports
5	x_t^{rw}	Rest of world coconut oil exports
6	x_t^{pk}	World palm kernel oil exports
7	x_t^{w}	World lauric oil exports
8	s_t^{us}	U.S. lauric oil stocks
9	s_t^{uk}	U.K. lauric oil stocks
10	s_t^{ec}	E.E.C. lauric oil stocks
11	s_t^{sr}	Sri Lanka coconut oil stocks
12	s_t^{ph}	Philippine coconut oil stocks
13	s_t^{w}	World lauric oil stocks
14	p_t^{w}	World (N.Y. crude) coconut oil prices
15	c_t^{us}	U.S. lauric oil consumption
16	c_t^{uk}	U.K. lauric oil consumption
17	c_t^{ec}	E.E.C. lauric oil consumption
18	m_t^{us}	U.S. lauric oil imports
19	m_t^{uk}	U.K. lauric oil imports
20	m_t^{ec}	E.E.C. lauric oil imports
21	m_t^{jp}	Japan lauric oil imports
22	m_t^{rw}	Rest of world lauric oil imports

Exogenous Variables

1	y_t^{jp}	Japan output index
2	z_t^{jp}	Japan substitution effect ratio
3	RT	Reverse trend
4	y_t^{us}	U.S. output index
5	y_t^{uk}	U.K. output index
6	z_t^{uk}	U.K. substitution effect ratio

(continued)

Table 8–2 continued

	Exogenous Variables	
7	y_t^{ec}	E.E.C. output index
8	z_t^{ec}	E.E.C. substitution effect dummy
9	D_t^{us}	U.S.G.S.A. stockpile release dummy
10	D_t^{uk}	U.K. stock adjustment dummy
11	D_t^{ec}	E.E.C. stock adjustment dummy
12	D_t^{sr}	Sri Lanka export tax dummy
13	p_t^p	Philippines copra export price
14	r_t^{ph}	Philippines dry season rainfall
15	p_t^{sr}	Sri Lanka coconut oil price
16	r_t^{sr}	Sri Lanka rainfall
17	p_t^{in}	Indonesia copra export price
18	r_t^{in}	Indonesia rainfall
19	p_t^x	Philippine implicit coconut oil price

providing for the simulation of the model, this form of block structure has been confirmed elsewhere [8] through examination of the estimated Jacobian matrix and the variance-covariance matrix of equation disturbance terms.

Concerning the geographical coverage and equation structure of the model, it would have been best to explain total market behavior in terms of consumption, production, and stock changes for each of the major countries included in Table 8–1, but the lack of complete commodity balance sheets precluded the specification of production and consumption equations for the exporting countries and of stock equations for Japan, Indonesia, Philippines, Oceania, and the rest of the world.

Recursive Block 1—Export Equations

Coconut oil and palm kernel oil derive from perennial tree crops, which require several time periods for production and exports to respond to changed agronomic and economic conditions. Coconut trees have a regular gestation pattern with effective yields reached approximately 8 years after planting and then continuing for 50 to 60 years; also the growth of coconuts depends heavily on rainfall with the response extending for a period of 2 years from blossom to nut. The output of such crops best can be described using the method of capital stock supply adjustment as witnessed in the works of Ady [2], Bateman [3], and Behrman [4]. In short, this method involves a two-stage procedure.

One begins with a relationship which describes the decision to plant as a function of the existing stock of trees, future price expectations, and agronomic variables. At a subsequent stage, this relationship is combined with one which links output to the history of plantings, the latter based on tree numbers and yields. Only the final forms of relationships are reported, as estimated for the Philippines, Sri Lanka, and Indonesia.[3,4]

$$\Delta x_t^{ph} = 133.29 - 0.854 x_{t-1}^{ph} + 3.62 p_{t-1}^{ph} + 3.85 \Delta p_t^{ph} + 0.129 r_{t-2}^{ph}$$
$$\qquad\qquad (-3.09)\qquad (2.37)\qquad (1.15)\qquad\quad (1.31)$$

$$\qquad + 0.182 \Delta r_{t-1}^{ph} \qquad\qquad\qquad\qquad\qquad\qquad\qquad (8\text{-}1)$$
$$\qquad\quad (4.37)$$

$$\bar{R}^2 = 0.82$$

$$\Delta x_t^{sr} = 1.40 - 1.29 x_{t-1}^{sr} - 579.64 p_{t-1}^{sr} - 298.98 \Delta p_t^{sr} + 0.113 r_{t-2}^{sr}$$
$$\qquad\quad (-8.50)\qquad (-3.34)\qquad\quad (-2.28)\qquad\quad (7.94)$$

$$\qquad + 0.63 \Delta r_{t-1}^{sr} \qquad\qquad\qquad\qquad\qquad\qquad\qquad (8\text{-}2)$$
$$\qquad\quad (7.02)$$

$$\bar{R}^2 = 0.93$$

$$\Delta x_t^{in} = -388.35 - 1.312 x_{t-1}^{in} + 11.89 p_{t-1}^{in} - 17.31 \Delta p_t^{in} + 0.153 r_{t-2}^{in}$$
$$\qquad\qquad (-5.41)\qquad\quad (3.50)\qquad\quad (-2.59)\qquad\quad (2.29)$$

$$\qquad + 0.037 \Delta r_{t-1}^{in} \qquad\qquad\qquad\qquad\qquad\qquad\qquad (8\text{-}3)$$
$$\qquad\quad (0.55)$$

$$\bar{R}^2 = 0.69.$$

It has been shown elsewhere [9] that the negative sign found on the lagged exports variable and several of the price variables are not unusual for equations of this type. The more positive results are those of the significant rainfall coefficients; they agree with the statistical results of Abeywardena [1] who demonstrates that rainfall exerts a strong influence on coconut production up to two years prior to the year of harvest. The relatively inelastic response of exports to prices also agrees with prior expectations. Comparison to other results is possible only for the Philippines; Nyberg [15] reports an elasticity of 0.29 based on an equation linking tree numbers and current prices, which is reasonably close to the lagged price elasticity of 0.11 found here.

Of several different forms of distributed lag equations based on an implicit Philippines export price, the following were selected as best explaining coconut oil exports for Oceania and rest of the world and for total palm kernel oil exports.

$$\Delta x_t^{oc} = 147.45 - 0.846 x_{t-1}^{oc} + 0.096 \Delta p_t^x - 0.012 p_{t-1}^x \qquad (8\text{-}4)$$
$$(-3.55) \qquad (0.48) \qquad (-0.12)$$

$$\bar{R}^2 = 0.51$$

$$\Delta x_t^{rw} = 169.04 - 1.261 x_{t-1}^{rw} - 0.463 \Delta p_t^x - 0.395 p_{t-1}^x \qquad (8\text{-}5)$$
$$(-4.55) \qquad (-1.78) \qquad (-2.15)$$

$$\bar{R}^2 = 0.66$$

$$x_t^{pk} = 422.67 + 0.163 x_{t-1}^{pk} - 0.769 p_t^x + 1.045 p_{t-1}^x - 1.498 p_{t-2}^x \qquad (8\text{-}6)$$
$$(0.47) \qquad (-1.60) \qquad (1.81) \qquad (-3.38)$$

$$\bar{R}^2 = 0.70.$$

$$x_t^w = x_t^{ph} + x_t^{sr} + x_t^{in} + x_t^{oc} + x_t^{rw} + x_t^{pk} \qquad (8\text{-}7)$$

Simultaneous Block—Stock and Price Equations

The functional specification of the equations explaining the levels of stocks held in importing countries is based on the theory of the modified flexible accelerator as proposed first by Lovell [13] and later applied to commodity behavior.[17] The demand for stocks would be a function of levels of output, changes in output, changes in prices, and previous stock levels. By utilizing closing stocks, the equations finally reached for the U.S. and U.K. indicate a cyclical proportionality between stocks and output, the latter variable being retained only in the form of changes. The dummy variable included in the U.S. equation represents those releases from the G.S.A. coconut oil stockpile which occurred between 1960-1964. The equation obtained for the E.E.C. verified the linear accelerator but in flow rather than stock form. The negative sign on the change in price variable suggests a speculative phenomenon whereby stock holders react as if the most recent change in price would be reversed.

$$s_t^{us} = -1.28 + 0.142 \Delta y_{t+1}^{us} + 146.29 p_t^w - 257.88 \Delta p_t^w + 69.94 D_t^{us} \qquad (8\text{-}8)$$
$$(0.80) \qquad (1.01) \qquad (-2.02) \qquad (5.87)$$

$$\bar{R}^2 = 0.83$$

$$s_t^{uk} = -25.06 + 0.550s_{t-1}^{uk} + 0.087\Delta y_t^{uk} + 132.28p_t^w - 93.88\Delta p_t^w$$
$$\quad\quad\quad\ (5.19)\quad\quad\ (1.04)\quad\quad\ (2.91)\quad\ (-2.46)$$

$$-21.38D_t^{uk} \tag{8-9}$$
$$(-6.18)$$

$$\bar{R}^2 = 0.89$$

$$\Delta s_t^{ec} = 29.09 - 0.100s_{t-1}^{ec} + 0.005\Delta y_t^{ec} + 101.39\Delta p_t^w - 49.59D_t^{ec} \tag{8-10}$$
$$\quad\quad\quad\ (-0.49)\quad\quad\ (0.40)\quad\quad\ (0.50)\quad\quad\ (-2.14)$$

$$\bar{R}^2 = 0.42.$$

It is believed that stocks held by lauric oils exporters are retained primarily for price speculation. Though such behavior can be described for Sri Lanka through the use of a distributed lag on prices, only a crude technical approximation based on an assumption of 10 percent carryover was possible for the Philippines.

$$s_t^{sr} = -13.57 - 8.44p_t^w + 35.74p_{t-1}^w + 39.27p_{t-2}^w + 5.75D_t^{sr} \tag{8-11}$$
$$\quad\quad\ (-0.47)\quad\ (2.49)\quad\quad\ (2.11)\quad\quad\ (2.29)$$

$$\bar{R}^2 = 0.42$$

$$s_t^{ph} = 0.10x_t^{ph} \tag{8-12}$$

$$s_t^w = s_t^{us} + s_t^{uk} + s_t^{ec} + s_t^{sr} + s_t^{ph}. \tag{8-13}$$

The above equations account for roughly 70 percent of the world lauric oil stocks. Because of the inadequacy of the data for compiling a world balance sheet whereby stock changes could be defined as the difference between exports and imports, the stock equations are utilized only to help explain price behavior. Closing the model has been possible solely through the import and export identity.

This situation also dictated that one include an explicit price equation in the model rather than trying to solve for prices from the stock equations. A linear price equation explaining prices as a function of world stock changes, world exports, and previous prices has been used for the stability and multiplier analysis. It reflects a form of flow relationship in which prices adjust to current stock changes and exports play a greater role in periods when they deviate from their normal or average levels.

$$p_t^w = 0.657 + 0.227p_{t-1}^w - 0.0046s_t^w - 0.00028s_{t-1}^w - 0.00014x_t^w \qquad (8\text{-}14a)$$
$$(2.46) \qquad (-1.50) \qquad (-1.11) \qquad (-1.98)$$

$$\bar{R}^2 = 0.61.$$

For purposes of simulation analysis, it was possible to introduce into the model a nonlinear equation based more realistically on a combined stock and flow adjustment. The world stock variable now defined as closing stocks in importing countries is also formed into a ratio with consumption so as to more appropriately reflect inventory coverage. Both price equations, although having only a low multiple correlation and several insignificant coefficients, were retained because they describe well the actual price-making process.

$$p_t^w = 0.575 + 0.535p_{t-1}^w - 0.680\frac{s_t^m}{c_t^m} - 0.00019x_t^w \qquad (8\text{-}14b)$$
$$(2.38) \qquad (-2.08) \qquad (-2.32)$$

$$\bar{R}^2 = 0.45.$$

Recursive Block 2—Consumption and Import Equations

The demand for lauric oils is a derived demand, depending on its rate of usage in a number of inedible products such as detergents, cosmetics, and synthethic lubricants as well as edible products such as margarine, confectionaries, and artificial dairy creams. Thus, one must consider the demand for lauric oils not only a function of prices and the output of manufacturers and processors but also of substitution possibilities with other oils and fats depending on the different end uses. It has been shown elsewhere [11, 14] that substitution possibilities are limited, confirming the model's relative independence of the influence of the total oils and fats market. This is consistent with the findings of a relative price inelasticity of demand. To account for whatever limited substitutability might exist, it was decided to include in the demand equation a variable describing the price differential between lauric oils and their possible nearest competitors, palm oil and marine oil. This price differential is defined as a ratio for the U.K. and Japan and as a dummy for the E.E.C. Neither form of variable proved significant in the U.S. equation.

The estimated equations reveal magnitudes of price inelasticity similar to those found elsewhere. For the U.S., the short run elasticity of -0.16 and the long run elasticity of -0.25 resemble the values of -0.19 and -0.25 found by Nyberg.[14] For the U.K., the E.E.C., and Japan, demand is shown to be slightly less inelastic, with long-run values of - 1.00, -0.31, and -1.59 approximating the values of -0.84 to -1.32 obtained by Librero [12] for aggregate Philippine export demand.

$$c_t^{us} = 89.77 + 0.379c_{t-1}^{us} + 0.100y_t^{us} - 165.87p_t^{w} \qquad (8\text{-}15)$$
$$\phantom{c_t^{us} = 89.77 + }(2.37) \qquad\quad (3.80) \qquad (-2.25)$$

$$\delta = 0.621, E_{ps} = -0.155, E_{pl} = -0.249 \qquad\qquad \bar{R}^2 = 0.96$$

$$c_t^{uk} = 76.73 + 0.588c_{t-1}^{uk} + 0.307y_t^{uk} - 259.25p_t^{w} - 36.42Z_t^{uk} \qquad (8\text{-}16)$$
$$\phantom{c_t^{uk} = 76.73 + }(4.32) \qquad\quad (2.78) \qquad (-2.57) \qquad (-2.52)$$

$$\delta = 0.412, E_{ps} = -0.441, E_{pl} = -1.00 \qquad\qquad \bar{R}^2 = 0.89$$

$$c_t^{ec} = 658.33 + 0.028y_t^{ec} - 0.196\Delta y_t^{ec} - 507.22p_t^{w} + 22.73Z_t^{ec} \qquad (8\text{-}17)$$
$$\phantom{c_t^{ec} = 658.33 + }(11.19) \qquad (-3.07) \qquad (-4.11) \qquad (2.11)$$

$$\delta = 1.0, E_{ps} = -0.306 = E_{pl} \qquad\qquad \bar{R}^2 = 0.73$$

$$m_t^{jp} = 13.75 + 0.587m_{t-1}^{jp} + 0.244y_t^{jp} - 118.66p_t^{w} + 35.83Z_t^{jp} \qquad (8\text{-}18)$$
$$\phantom{m_t^{jp} = 13.75 + }(3.76) \qquad\quad (1.67) \qquad (-1.39) \qquad (2.09)$$

$$\delta = -0.656, E_{ps} = 0.656, E_{pl} = 1.590 \qquad\qquad \bar{R}^2 = 0.84.$$

Consumption estimates for the U.S., U.K., and the E.E.C. are adjusted subsequently for stock changes to provide estimates of country imports. While the relationship for Japan already explains imports, rest of the world imports are determined as a residual from the world market-clearing identity.

$$m_t^{us} = c_t^{us} \pm \Delta s_t^{us} - s_t^{gsa} \qquad\qquad (8\text{-}19)$$

$$m_t^{uk} = c_t^{uk} \pm \Delta s_t^{uk} \qquad\qquad (8\text{-}20)$$

$$m_t^{ec} = c_t^{ec} \pm \Delta s_t^{ec} \qquad\qquad (8\text{-}21)$$

$$m_t^{rw} = x_t^{w} - m_t^{us} - m_t^{uk} - m_t^{ec} - m_t^{jp} \qquad\qquad (8\text{-}22)$$

DYNAMIC POLICY APPLICATIONS

The dynamic properties and applications of the lauric oils model have been considered in terms of the information which can be derived from examining its stability, the response of the endogenous to the exogenous variables over time, and its functioning as an evolutionary simulation. To perform dynamic analysis, one must formulate the structural form of the above model as a system of first order difference equations

$$\Gamma Y_t = B_1 Y_{t-1} + B_2 X_t + U_t$$

where Y_t = a $G \times n$ matrix of current endogenous variables, Y_{t-1} = $G \times n$ matrix of lagged endogenous variables, $X_t = M \times n$ matrix of exogenous variables, U_t = a $G \times n$ matrix of stochastic disturbance terms, Γ and $B_1 = G \times G$ matrices of coefficients on the endogenous variables and their lagged values, and B_2 = a $G \times M$ matrix of the coefficients on the exogenous variables. The corresponding reduced form is given by

$$Y_t = \Gamma^{-1} B_1 Y_{t-1} + \Gamma^{-1} B_2 X_t + \Gamma^{-1} U_t$$

or

$$Y_t = \pi_1 Y_{t-1} + \pi_2 X_t + V_t$$

where π_1 is a $G \times G$ matrix of reduced form coefficients on the lagged endogenous variables and π_2 is a $G \times M$ matrix of multipliers of coefficients on the exogenous and policy variables. For the stability analysis, we concentrate only on the subset of the reduced form corresponding to the Simultaneous Block.

Stability Analysis

Zusman [18], Reutlinger [16], and others have shown that determining the stability of an econometric commodity model requires examining the characteristic roots of the analytical solution to the nonstochastic reduced form. The analytical solution to the reduced form is given by

$$|\pi_1 - \lambda I| = 0$$

which for the Simultaneous Block of the lauric oils model is

$$\begin{vmatrix} 0.119-\lambda & 0.119 & 0.119 & 0.119 & 340.59 \\ 0.017 & 0.591-\lambda & 0.017 & 0.017 & -48.71 \\ 0.019 & 0.019 & 0.919-\lambda & 0.019 & -55.14 \\ 0.017 & 0.017 & 0.017 & 0.017-\lambda & -50.11 \\ 0.001 & 0.001 & 0.001 & 0.001 & 0.349-\lambda \end{vmatrix} = 0$$

The characteristic roots obtained are: $\lambda_1 = 0$, $\lambda_2 = 0.857$, $\lambda_3 = 0.313 + 0.635i$, $\lambda_4 = 0.313 - 0.635i$, and $\lambda_5 = 0.513$. None of the real roots has a value greater than 1, nor do the complex roots have a modulus greater than or equal to 1. Thus, the validity of the lauric oils model is confirmed with regard to stability where all endogenous variables converge in the limit to what can be considered their equilibrium values.

Multiplier Analysis

Multiplier analysis represents the first step to determining the response that the endogenous variables such as lauric oils prices or stocks have to changes in the exogenous of policy variables of concern to the exporting countries. Only a sample of the results obtained from computing static and dynamic multipliers for the lauric oils model can be reported here. See Table 8-3 for the delay and cumulative dynamic multipliers defining the impact on a subset of endogenous variables of an increase in exports. In terms of policy applications, for example, one can observe that the impact of an increase of lauric oils exports of 100,000mt would be to decrease prices about 1.2 cents/kg in the same year, the cumulative change amounting to the 1.6 cents/kg reached after 2 years.

Simulation Analysis

The response of the endogenous to the exogenous variables can be measured more comprehensively using simulation analysis. This approach also has been shown [7, 8] to be preferred to multiplier analysis when the model of interest contains dynamic lags and nonlinearities in endogenous variables as well as when it features stochastic variations. The simulation analysis of the lauric oils model is based more realistically on the nonlinear price equation, follows the final or evolutionary form of simulation using the Gauss-Seidel algorithm, and later includes stochastic variations. The final form of simulation requires providing starting values for the variables Y_t, Y_{t-1}, and X_t; the values of Y_{t-1} generated in one period are then fed back into the model in succeeding periods to generate Y_t based on given values of X_t. Actual values of X_t are used for historical verification, values of X_t reflecting alternative policies are used for market stabilization analysis, and projected values of X_t are used for short and long run policy forecasts.

Table 8-3. Delay Multipliers: Philippines Exports

	Time Period in Years Following the Initial Change in Exports				
Endogenous Variables	*Same Year*	*1*	*2*	*3*	*4*
Prices	-0.011900	-0.003700	-0.000300	0.000400	0.000500
World stocks	0.025510	-0.037808	-0.023978	-0.006234	0.000159
U.S. consumption	0.019727	0.013531	0.004602	0.000312	-0.000631
U.K. consumption	0.030832	0.027595	0.015405	0.006819	0.002837
E.E.C. consumption	0.060323	0.018533	-0.001594	-0.004374	-0.002292

	Cumulative Multipliers: Philippine Exports				
	Time Period in Years Following the Initial Change in Exports				
Endogenous Variables	*Same Year*	*1*	*2*	*3*	*4*
Prices	-0.011900	-0.015600	-0.015900	-0.015400	-0.014900
World stocks	0.025510	-0.012297	-0.036275	-0.042509	-0.042550
U.S. consumption	0.019727	0.033258	0.037860	0.038172	0.037541
U.K. consumption	0.030832	0.058427	0.073832	0.080651	0.083488
E.E.C. consumption	0.060323	0.078856	0.077261	0.072887	0.070595

Source: W.C. Labys, *Dynamic Commodity Models: Specification, Estimation and Simulation,* Lexington, Mass.: Heath Lexington Books, 1973, p. 198. Reprinted by permission of the publisher.

Validation. Let us first examine the simulation results obtained from operating the simulation over the latter part of the historical period 1960–1967 as well as over the forecast period 1968-1969 to provide further evidence as to the model's validity. Based on *ex post* mean percentage absolute forecast errors as reported in Table 8-4, Recursive Block 1 explains lauric oils exports emanating from the various countries with reasonably low percentage errors except for Indonesia. The percentage errors obtained for the Simultaneous Block are somewhat higher, but the stock equations especially for the U.K. and the E.E.C. were difficult to specify and only now is information available which could revise and improve the equations. The Recursive Block 2 explained consumption and imports with the lowest percentage errors. When the simulation was continued through 1968-69 based on projected values for X_t, the *ex ante* percentage errors proved to be considerably higher. However, these years represented a period of severe change in the market. Due to unusual climatic con-

Table 8-4. Lauric Oils Simulation (Ex post and Ex ante Mean Percentage Absolute Forecast Errors)

Model Variables	% Error (1960–1967)	% Error (1968–1969)
Recursive Block 1		
Philippine exports	3.67	9.50
Sri Lanka exports	6.53	10.80
Indonesia exports	13.21	23.50
Oceania exports	2.95	11.70
Rest of world exports	10.51	43.76
World palm kernel oil exports	3.74	8.56
Simultaneous Block		
U.S. stocks	12.95	14.20
U.K. stocks	9.13	52.20
E.E.C. stocks	30.83	3.20
Sri Lanka stocks	14.03	11.70
World stocks	8.50	1.58
Prices	2.91	12.50
Recursive Block 2		
U.S. consumption	2.09	0.10
U.S. imports	5.19	2.02
U.K. consumption	6.72	2.38
U.K. imports	6.13	8.85
E.E.C. consumption	2.76	2.34
E.E.C. imports	3.95	3.98
Japan imports	8.68	7.52
Rest of world imports	5.18	14.00

Source: W.C. Labys, *Dynamic Commodity Models: Specification, Estimation and Simulation,* Lexington, Mass.: Heath Lexington Books, 1973, p. 229. Reprinted by permission of the publisher.

ditions, levels of lauric oils exports fell back from 1,769,000 mt in 1966 to 1,552,000 mt in 1968 and 1,415,000 mt in 1969. In the Philippines, the dry season lasted as long as 5 months in 1968 and 8 months in 1969; typhoons also occurred during those two years and the production areas suffered two earthquakes of intensity VI. That even reasonable forecasts could be obtained for prices and consumption results from the various stock forecasts summing such that the percentage error for world stocks amounted to only 1.6 percent.

Stabilization. A first application of simulation analysis to policy questions faced by the exporting countries has been to determine whether or not market stabilization using the instrument of an export norm scheme or a buffer stock scheme could stabilize prices, thus helping to check the market deterioration previously mentioned. The export norm scheme would require that each country enlarge or deplete oil stocks in such a way as to maintain exports at a predetermined level each year. Three different export norm levels of 1,225,000 mt, 1,255,000 mt, and 1,275,000 mt have been tested, centering upon the average level of coconut oil exports supplied over the period 1960-1969. To determine the impact of the norms, the simulation has been operated such that the world stock variable adjusted according to excesses or deficiencies in annual exports, an initial stock being required for the highest norm level.

The buffer stock which would be internationally controlled operates such that lauric oils stocks are purchased from the market when price falls towards the minimum or floor price set for the scheme. Conversely, stocks are sold from storage when price rises towards the maximum or ceiling price. The volume of stocks bought or sold also has been computed from simulation of the model, depending on two different price ranges. A ceiling price of 33.8 ¢/kg and a floor price of 28.6 ¢/kg corresponds to a reduction in price fluctuations of three-fourths of a standard deviation of prices, based on the same ten-year period. The alternate range of 32.9 ¢/kg to 29.5 ¢/kg corresponds to one-half of a standard deviation.

Tables 8-5 and 8-6 contain the simulation results demonstrating that the standard deviation of world price fluctuations could be lowered only slightly with the instigation of the export norm schemes, but it could be lowered much more with the buffer stock schemes. The net gains anticipated from using either instrument could be positive or negative. With initial stocks required for the only norm level showing positive gains, the buffer stock schemes would be the more useful.

Conditional Projections. Simulation analysis also has been performed to determine levels of lauric oils demand and prices which might be reached over the period 1972-1987, given conditional forecasts of country export levels. Although analysis of this type has been performed to provide a market outlook, it could also be employed to assess the impact of different productivity and planting programmes as reflected in changing supply. Performing long run simu-

Table 8-5. Coconut Oil Price Levels, Actual and Stabilized
Estimates, 1960-1969*

	Actual	*Norm I*	*Norm II*	*Norm III*	*Stock I*	*Stock II*
1960	35.5	36.2	35.8	35.6	33.8	32.9
1961	28.0	28.1	27.7	27.5	28.6	29.5
1962	26.0	27.9	27.5	27.3	28.6	29.5
1963	27.0	31.9	31.5	31.2	28.6	29.5
1964	30.4	34.5	34.1	33.9	30.4	30.5
1965	35.1	35.0	34.6	34.3	33.8	32.9
1966	29.3	33.6	33.2	32.9	29.3	29.5
1967	32.1	32.4	32.0	31.8	32.1	32.1
1968	36.8	34.9	34.5	34.2	33.8	32.9
1969	30.4	38.9	38.5	38.4	30.4	30.5
Std. Dev.	3.24	2.88	2.88	2.86	2.20	1.52

*New York, Crude in Tanks, U.S. cents/kg.
Source: W.C. Labys, *Feasibility of Operating a Supply Stabilization Scheme for the Lauric Oils Market: Returns, Costs and Financing,* UNCTAD/CD/Misc. 41, Geneva, March 1971, p. 13.

lation analysis with the present medium term model requires two critical assumptions: (1) The market underlying the model's parameters will retain its present structure, and (2) the short run substitution effect described by the price-differential variables will be applicable in the long run. While the first assumption has been verified to some extent in discussions with market experts, the second assumption is not as reliable requiring price projections for the other oils. Instead, it was simply assumed that no major substitution variations would occur during that period. To provide greater realism with respect to possible changes in climatic conditions, stochastic shocks of type II were imposed on the export projections. As suggested by Adelman and Adelman [2] and later by Desai [6], shocks of this type imposed on several variables all at once can also yield information regarding the validity or long run stability properties of a model. Table 8-7 summarizes the resulting demand forecasts, including rates of changes based on conditional export levels cumulating to 1,538,000 mt, 1,908,000 mt, and 2,470,000 mt by 1987. Details regarding the assumptions which underlie these projections as well as an interpretation of results are provided elsewhere.[10] In general, one can conclude that the model is stable in the long run and, more importantly, that lauric oils demand will remain constant or grow slightly over this period should the exporting countries be able to meet the medium or high export projections.

CONCLUSIONS

Of course the model and its applications as reported above are limited in many respects. A more accurate lauric oils model is currently being devised featuring improved export, stock, and price equations, distinct links to the total oils and

Table 8-6. Returns, Costs, and Net Gains from Operating Alternative Stabilization Schemes, 1960-1969,[a] U.S. $(000)

	Returns	*Storage Costs*	*Handling Costs*	*Total Costs*	*Net Gains*	*Cumulative Stocks*[b]
Export norm						
Norm I	-90,734	53,926	317	54,243	-144,977	292,000
Norm II	9,254	27,768	294	28,062	-18,808	48,000
Norm III	71,778	36,118	299	36,417	35,361	—
Buffer stock						
Stock I	23,998	15,672	144	15,816	8,182	3,000
Stock II	21,671	25,608	225	25,833	-4,162	26,000

[a]*Returns:* positive or negative revenues obtained from selling and buying stocks to maintain export norm levels or to achieve the degree of price stabilization required for operating the buffer stocks schemes.

Costs: storage and handling costs represent a combination of cost estimates received: storage costs = $2/mt/month = $24/mt/year; handling costs = $0.50/mt.

Net Gains: difference between returns and total costs.

[b]Metric tons.

Source: W.C. Labys, *Feasibility of Operating a Supply Stabilizing Scheme for the Lauric Oils Market: Returns, Costs and Financing,* UNCTAD/CD/Misc. 41, Geneva, March 1971, p. 18.

fats market, and different elasticities of demand reflecting periods of lesser or greater lauric oils availabilities. Testing these modifications is important, given the current possibility of greater exports coming from the Philippines. Substitution effects featured need to be improved, particularly with respect to the impact of the changing technology of synthetic derivatives. Better and more data are available permitting the dynamic equations to be estimated using more sophisticated methods. The possible application of control theory could improve the ability of the simulation to respond to sudden shocks of an episodic nature such as, for example, the export deficiencies of 1968-1969. Nonetheless, the model can already provide a reasonable explanation of a complex market, and it would be appropriate to broaden the types of policies examined. These include not only tests of export quotas and tariffs but also of new programs regarding productivity and plantings.

NOTES

1. Lauric oils are defined here as consisting of coconut oil and palm kernel oil. The data used also contain quantities of copra and palm kernels in oil equivalent.

2. Sources of data for the variables include: "World Oils and Fats Statistics," Congress of the International Association of Seed Crushers, London; "Agricultural Statistics of the European Communities," Luxembourg; "Fats and Oils Situation," Economic Research Service,

Table 8-7. Projections for Lauric Oil Demand Including Rates of Change,[a] 1972-1987

Year	U.S.			E.E.C. Countries			World[b]		
	Low	Medium	High	Low	Medium	High	Low	Medium	High
1972	486	492	492	510	527	545	1464	1606	1689
1977	547	561	575	495	526	568	1409	1665	1984
1982	607	624	648	507	536	595	1561	1773	2232
1987	659	684	717	502	552	620	1538	1908	2470
Annual percent change in growth									
1972-77	2.4	2.7	3.2	-0.6	0.0	0.7	-0.8	0.8	3.2
1977-82	2.2	2.2	2.5	0.6	0.4	0.9	2.0	1.2	2.3
1982-87	1.8	2.0	2.2	0.0	0.9	0.9	-0.5	1.5	1.6
1972-87	2.1	2.2	2.6	0.0	0.3	0.9	0.3	0.8	2.6

[a]Demand figures represent 2 year average taken over indicated and succeeding year except for 1987.
[b]Imports for consumption.
Source: W.C. Labys, "Projections and Prospects for the Lauric Oils, 1972-1987," Journal of the American Oil Chemists' Society 49 (June 1972), pp. 232A-233A.

U.S.D.A., Washington, "FAO Statistical Yearbook," Rome; "FAO Coconut Situation," Rome; and private government and industry documents.
3. A more complete description of the construction of these relationships can be found in Labys.[9] Ordinary least-squares are provided for the equations in Recursive Blocks 1 and 2. The shortness of the time series together with the relative noncorrelation of the disturbance terms did not warrant using more sophisticated methods. Two-stage principal-components estimates based on all exogenous variables are provided for the Simultaneous Block. The Durbin-Watson statistic is not reported, since it is biased when applied to dynamic equations.
4. The following equations as well as some of the tabular material used are reprinted from *Dynamic Commodity Models: Specification, Estimation and Simulation* by W.C. Labys with the permission of Heath Lexington Books, Lexington, Mass.

REFERENCES

1. Abeywardena, V. "Forecasting Coconut Crops Using Rainfall Data–A Preliminary Study." *Ceylon Coconut Quarterly* 19 (1968): 161–76.
2. Adelman, I. and Adelman, F. "The Dynamic Properties of the Klein Goldberger Model." *Econometrica* 27 (1959): 596–625.
3. Ady, Peter. "Supply Functions in Tropical Agriculture." *Bulletin of the Oxford University Institute of Economics and Statistics* 30 (1968): 157–88.
4. Bateman, Merrill J. "Aggregate and Regional Supply Functions for Ghanian Cocoa." *J. Farm Econ* 47 (1965): 384–401.
5. Behrman, Jere R. "Monopolistic Pricing in International Commodity Agreements: A Case Study of Cocoa." *American Journal of Agricultural Economics* 50 (1968): 702–19.
6. Desai, M. "An Econometric Model of the World Tin Economy, 1948–1961." *Econometrica* 34 (1966): 105–34.
7. Klein, L.R. and Evans, M.K. *Econometric Gaming.* London: The Macmillan Co., 1969.
8. Labys, W.C. *Dynamic Commodity Models: Specification, Estimation and Simulation.* Lexington, Mass.: Heath Lexington Books, 1973.
9. Labys, W.C. "A Lauric Oil Exports Model Based on Capital Stock Supply Adjustment." *Malayan Economic Review* 18 (April 1973): 1–10.
10. Labys, W.C. "Projections and Prospects for the Lauric Oils, 1972–1987." *Journal of the American Oil Chemists Society* 49 (1972): 228A–33A.
11. Labys, W.C. "The Nature, Analysis and Future of Lauric Oil Substitution." UNCTAD/CD/Misc.42, Geneva, 1971.
12. Librero, A.D. "The International Demand for Philippine Coconut Products: An Aggregate Analysis." *The Philippine Economic Journal* 10 (1971): 1–22.
13. Lovell, M.C. "Manufacturers' Inventories, Sales Expectations, and the Accelerator Principle." *Econometrica* 29 (1961): 293–314.

14. Nyberg, A. "The Demand for Lauric Oils in the United States." *American Journal of Agricultural Economics* 52 (1970): 97–120.

15. Nyberg, A. "The Philippine Coconut Industry." Unpublished Ph.D. dissertation, Cornell University, 1968.

16. Reutlinger, S. "Analysis of a Dynamic Model, With Particular Emphasis on Long Run Projections." *J. Farm Econ* 48 (1966): 88–107.

17. Witherell, W.H. "Dynamics of the International Wool Market: An Econometric Analysis." Research Memorandum No. 91, Econometric Research Program, Princeton University, 1967.

18. Zusman, G.P. "Econometric Analysis of the Market for California Early Potatoes." *Hilgardia* 33 (1962): 539–668.

Chapter Nine

Feedback Control Rule for Cocoa Market Stabilization

Han K. Kim
Louis M. Goreux
David A. Kendrick

Commodity stabilization problems are characterized by uncertainty in weather and demand conditions, by lagged responses to price changes, and by nonlinear supply and demand relationships. These attributes of uncertainty, dynamics, and nonlinearities make stochastic control theory a useful tool for analyzing problems of commodity stabilization. In this study, the effect of weather on yield was modeled as an additive noise (shock) to the supply response equations, the dynamics were captured by third and higher order difference equations in prices on both the supply and demand sides, and the nonlinearities were included via nonlinear supply and demand response functions. Finally, stabilization policy was undertaken in the name of a rather specific goal.

Control theory provides a means of specifying the objective or goal and of searching for the policy or policies which cause the market to most closely approach this objective.

It thus seems reasonable that the application of stochastic control theory to the world cocoa market could provide useful decision rules for stabilization policy. To test this proposition we applied the approximation techniques discussed by Kendrick (1970) to the world cocoa model developed by Goreux (1972).

In our presentation, we outline the theoretical procedure for optimal policy determination under uncertainty. We present the problems to be investigated and give a brief description of the econometric model of the world cocoa market. The optimization procedure is then applied to the cocoa market model. The outcome is fully evaluated and conclusions given.

Prepared for the Development Research Center, International Bank for Reconstruction and Development, Washington, D.C. We are indebted to R. Muralidharan, A. Meeraus and M. Parthasarathy for programming assistance.

SOLUTION PROCEDURE FOR OPTIMAL POLICY
DETERMINATION UNDER UNCERTAINTY

The *stochastic* nonlinear optimization problem is very hard, if not impossible, to solve. Thus, we are forced to resort to approximation methods until better methods can be found. The traditional procedure for decision-making under uncertainty is to employ Monto Carlo methods. This approach of simulating different possible outcomes may lead to a prohibitively large number of solutions if there are several stochastic variables in the model. Rather than simulating a large number of outcomes, Kendrick first solves the problems with expected values and then derives rules for the variation in target and instrument variables caused by deviations in structural variables.[1] In control theory, this rule is called a "feedback stochastic controller."

The solution procedure consists of two parts:

1. *Deterministic Solution.* Determine nominal optimum paths of the state variables and the control variables assuming no disturbances in the system.

2. *Feedback Stochastic Control Law.* Approximate the system and the welfare function by first-order and second-order Taylor series expansions, respectively, about the deterministic nominal paths; determine a linear decision rule (the deviation of the control variables from their nominal values as a linear function of the deviation of the state variables from their nominal values) using the "certainty equivalence theorem."

The quality of the approximation depends on how well the deterministic econometric model represents the real economy, i.e., the magnitude of random shocks and errors in estimation of parameters. The advantage of this approach is that although it is a formidable work to compute all the second-order partial derivatives of the Hamiltonian and the system equations, the numerical solution for the "feedback stochastic control law" itself involves no more than adding and multiplying matrices.

To obtain the deterministic optimum solution, we postulate the existence of a collective welfare function and specify it as a weighted sum of differing conflicting targets. Instead of arbitrarily fixing the constant weights, we allowed the weights to vary within certain ranges so that we could trace out the "tradeoff possibility frontier" among conflicting targets. The advantage of this approach is that the policy-maker could be presented with a set of tradeoff possibilities so that he could choose among alternatives.[2] Marglin (1967) has demonstrated that the "tradeoff possibility frontier" also can be obtained by maximizing one target subject to a constraint on the other target and varying constraint levels. It should be remarked that if the set of alternative feasible combinations of contributions to the multiple targets of policy instruments is not strictly convex, then maximization of a weighted sum of differing targets may lead to a nonoptimal solution.

THE WORLD COCOA MODEL

For the period 1950-1967, cocoa prices (expressed in terms of export unit-values in 1963 prices) fluctuated widely around an average of U.S. 27¢ per pound. During the same period, world cocoa production grew at approximately 3.5 percent per year, while export earnings declined annually at about 0.5 percent. The decline in export earnings is due to the decline in long-run cocoa prices at the annual rate of 4 percent. In this situation, the future cocoa markets would very likely become increasingly worse.

The unfavorable trends of export earnings and the wide fluctuations of prices and earnings are the main features of the commodity problems for developing countries. While there is no doubt that the two objectives of high level export earnings and *earnings* stability are highly desirable,[3] some people argue that *price* stability is not such an important economic objective. In the period 1950-1967, major cocoa exporters (Ghana and Nigeria) experienced small earnings fluctuations and large price fluctuations, while minor cocoa exporters (Brazil and Togo) experienced large earnings fluctuations and small price fluctuations. Thus, policies which reduce earnings fluctuations may harm major exporting countries and benefit minor exporting countries. Moreover, since widely fluctuating prices cannot provide adequate signals for resource allocations and may generate wasteful commodity cycles, reductions in price fluctuations may also be considered an important goal. Finally, the international buffer stock operation is a technique which attacks the problems of instability from the price angle.

For these reasons, the three objectives of export earnings, price stability and earning stability are chosen. The policy instruments we model are:

1. Export tax.
2. Purchases or sales of buffer stock.

A dynamic model of the supply and demand for cocoa and the resulting dynamic price equations is employed to study the optimum operating procedure for an international buffer stock agency. Here we convert Goreux's econometric model to an optimizing model by adding a preference function and by transforming the model into control theory format (i.e., a set of first order difference equations). We first deduce a dynamic system from the cocoa model. Next, we define a criterion function.

The Dynamic System
The cocoa model can be written as follows:

Distribution Equation from (22) in Goreux[4]

$$S_t - S_{t-1} + Dd_t + Ds_t + Dgc_t + Dge_t + Bf_t \equiv Q_t, \tag{9-1}$$

where

S_t = the level of inventory,

Dd_t = consumption of grindings in the developed countries,

Ds_t = consumption of grindings in the socialist countries,

Dgc_t = consumption of grindings in the developing countries for domestic use,

Dge_t = consumption of grindings in the developing countries for export,

Bf_t = purchases or sales of stocks by an international buffer stock agency,

Q_t = world cocoa production. (Prefix D = difference operator.)

Private Stocks (see (48) and (49) on p. 24 in Goreux)

$$\frac{S_t}{S_{t-1}} = \left(\frac{\hat{D}_t}{D_{t-1}}\right)\left(\frac{P_{nt}}{P_{n,t-1}}\right)^{-0.91896} , \tag{9-2}$$

D_t = total world demand,

$\hat{D}_t$ = total world demand when export unit-value for the previous year prevails,

P_{nt} = spot price in New York.

The simplest motivation for this equation is that private stocks will grow with demand if prices hold constant. That is, when $P_{nt} = P_{n,t-1}$, the price term will be equal to one and stocks will change in the same ratio as demand. Furthermore, the function requires that stocks fall when prices rise, and conversely. The argument for using a function of this form in an annual model is that in years when the crop is short, forward sales exceed the new cocoa harvested and delivery has to be made by drawing down stocks. For projecting one year ahead, one can use the forecasts of production and grindings regularly published by Gill and Duffus. However, since these forecasts are published less than a year in advance, they cannot be used in a long-term projection model.

Demand (see (43)–(47) on p. 24 in Goreux)

$$Dd_t = \alpha_{1t} P_{t-1}^{-0.1817} P_t^{-0.2365} ,$$

$$Ds_t = \alpha_{2t} (P_{t-2} - L_{t-2})^{-0.2}$$

$$Dgc_t = \alpha_{3t} \, (P_{t-1} - L_{t-1})^{-0.2} \, (P_{t-2} - L_{t-2})^{-0.2} \, ,$$

$$Dge_t = \alpha_{3t} \, P_{t-1}^{-0.2} \, P_{t-2}^{-0.2} \, , \tag{9-3}$$

where

P_t = export unit-value, deflated,

L_t = export tax,

$\alpha_{1t} = $ antilog$_{10}$ $(3.553028 + 0.00787 \, t - 0.00007 \, t^2)$,

$\alpha_{2t} = $ antilog$_{10}$ $(2.453479 + 0.038067 \, t - 0.00064 \, t^2)$,

$\alpha_{3t} = $ antilog$_{10}$ $(2.663385 + 0.03265 \, t - 0.00047 \, t^2)$.

The price effect was important for the developed countries and a distinction could clearly be made between the impact of the current year's price and of the previous year's price. These two values of the price elasticity were -0.24 and -0.18 respectively. For the developing countries, the price effect was lagged one or two years but not very significantly. For the socialist countries price effect was lagged two years.

Supply (see Goreux (13a) and (13b) on p. 10)

Cocoa production in year "t" is a function of two factors. The first is the capacity existing in year "t" which depends on the tree population of bearing age (say between 6 and 50). The second is the rate of utilization of the capacity, which is affected by the frequency of picking and by the application of purchased inputs such as fertilizers and pesticides. The impact of prices on capacity creation corresponds to the long-term supply elasticity. The impact of prices on the rate of capacity utilization corresponds to the short-term supply elasticity.

Let us consider first the short-term elasticity. When prices fall sharply, the rate of capacity utilization also falls. Since it is always possible not to use existing capacity, supply will always disappear before prices reach zero. When prices rise, the rate of capacity utilization increases up to a point. But once the capacity is fully used, supply cannot respond in the short-term to any further rise in prices. The short term supply response to price changes is therefore asymmetrical. This applies not only to tree crops, such as coffee and cocoa, but also to minerals, such as copper and tin. To reflect this asymmetry, the short term price response was expressed in the form of b/P_{t-1}^2 .

Let us now turn to the long-term elasticity. Let us assume that capacity increases by 3 percent a year at a price of 30. When the price reaches 40, planting will increase and capacity will rise rapidly. When the price falls to 20, the cultivator will probably abstain from planting new trees. He will probably also give little care to the trees already planted, but he will not generally uproot them. He will rather wait for better years to come. To reflect this asymmetry, the rate of growth of capacity in year "*t*" was related to the square of the price in year "*t-τ*". During this century, such a relation appeared remarkably stable.

We begin statement of the supply portion of the model with:

$$C_t = C_{t-1} + I_{t-\tau} , \qquad\qquad\qquad (9\text{-}4a)$$

$$I_{t-\tau} = b\,[(P_{t-\tau} - L_{t-\tau})^2 - \pi^2]\,C_{t-2},\, b > 0, \pi > 0 , \qquad (9\text{-}4b)$$

where

C_t = capacity,

I_t = net investment,

τ = lag from the planting to first crop (six years),

π = price at which the tree population would remain stationary.

The form (9-4b) relates the percentage of capacity changes to price changes in an asymmetric fashion so that a given price increase produces a larger capacity expansion than the corresponding price decrease produces capacity contraction. (See Figure 9-1.)

Solving the difference Equation (9-4a) and substituting (9-4b) into the solution yields

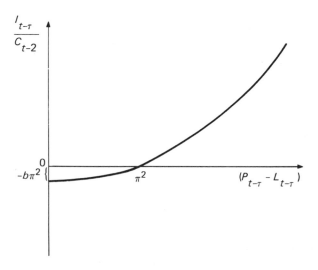

Figure 9-1. Relation of Capacity Changes to Price Changes.

$$C_t = C_0 + b \sum_{\Theta=1-\tau}^{\Theta=t-\tau} [(P_\Theta^2 - L_\Theta^2) - \pi^2].$$ (9-4c)

This gives capacity as a function of price but not output. To capture the effect of short-run price changes on the care and harvesting of the trees, Goreux uses

$$C_t - Q_t = \frac{\mu_1 C_{t-2}}{(P_{t-1} - L_{t-1})^2} + \frac{\mu_2 C_{t-2}}{(P_{t-2} - L_{t-2})^2} + \frac{\mu_3 C_{t-3}}{(P_{t-3} - L_{t-3})^2} \, ,$$ (9-4d)

for $C_t > Q_t$.

Here the amount of unused capacity decreases with increases in current prices. Since some of the effects of better care may last for several years, a distributed lag over three years is used. Solving (9-4d) for Q_t and substituting (9-4c) into it for a lag of $\tau = 6$ years yields:

$$Q_t = C_0 + b \sum_{\Theta=-5}^{t-6} [(P_\Theta - L_\Theta)^2 - \pi^2] \, C_{\Theta+4}$$

$$- \mu_1 C_{t-2} (P_{t-1} - L_{t-1})^{-2} - \mu_2 C_{t-2} (P_{t-2} - L_{t-2})^{-2}$$

$$- \mu_3 C_{t-3} (P_{t-3} - L_{t-3})^{-2} \, ,$$ (9-4e)

$$C_t = \frac{Q_{t-1} + Q_t + Q_{t+1}}{3} \, ,$$ (9-4f)

$$\pi = 20.5 \, ,$$

and the coefficients estimated by Goreux [see (51-III) on p. 24] are

$C_0 = 989.6$,

$b \ = 0.00007302$,

$\mu_1 = 30.39$,

$\mu_2 = 30$,

$\mu_3 = 20$.

Spot Price to Export Unit-Value Relationship

The spot price in the New York market is related to the average deflated export unit-value with the function

$$P_t = 0.69005 P_{nt} + 0.19403 P_{n,t-1} \ . \tag{9-4g}$$

Buffer Stock Accumulation Equation

The accumulated buffer stock is simply last year's buffer stock plus buffer stock purchases (or minus buffer stock sales):

$$N_{t+1} = N_t + Bf_{t+1} \ . \tag{9-4h}$$

Also, we require that the accumulated buffer stock be nonnegative,

$$N_t \geqslant 0 \text{ for all } t \ . \tag{9-4i}$$

The Complete Model

In summary, the complete set of systems equations may be written:

Distribution

$$S_t - S_{t-1} + Dd_t + Ds_t + Dgc_t + Dge_t + Bf_t \equiv Q_t \ , \tag{9-1}$$

Private stocks

$$\frac{S_t}{S_{t-1}} = \left[\frac{\alpha_{1t} P_{t-1}^{-0.4182} + \alpha_{2t}(P_{t-2} - L_{t-2})^{-0.2}}{\alpha_{1,t-1} P_{t-2}^{-0.1817} P_{t-1}^{-0.2365} + \alpha_{2,t-1} (P_{t-3} - L_{t-3})^{-0.2}} \right.$$

$$\left. \frac{+ \alpha_{3t} (P_{t-2} - L_{t-2})^{-0.2} (P_{t-1} - L_{t-1})^{-0.2} + \alpha_{3t} P_{t-2}^{-0.2} P_{t-1}^{-0.2}}{+ \alpha_{3,t-1} (P_{t-3} - L_{t-3})^{-0.2} (P_{t-2} - L_{t-2})^{-0.2} + \alpha_{3t} P_{t-3}^{-0.2} P_{t-2}^{-0.2}} \right] \left(\frac{P_t}{P_{t-1}} \right)^{-0.91896} \tag{9-2a}$$

Demand

$$Dd_t = \alpha_{1t} P_{t-1}^{-0.4182} \ ,$$

$$Ds_t = \alpha_{2t} (P_{t-2} - L_{t-2})^{-0.2} \ ,$$

$$Dgc_t = \alpha_{3t} (P_{t-1} - L_{t-1})^{-0.2} (P_{t-2} - L_{t-2})^{-0.2} \ ,$$

$$Dge_t = \alpha_{3t} P_{t-1}^{-0.2} P_{t-2}^{-0.2} \ , \tag{9-3}$$

Supply

$$Q_t = C_0 + b \sum_{\Theta=-5}^{t-6} [(P_\Theta - L_\Theta)^2 - \pi^2] \, C_{\Theta+4} - \mu_1 \, C_{t-2} \, (P_{t-1} - L_{t-1})^{-2}$$

$$- \mu_2 \, C_{t-2} \, (P_{t-2} - L_{t-2})^{-2} - \mu_3 \, C_{t-3} \, (P_{t-3} - L_{t-3})^{-2} , \qquad \text{(9-4e)}$$

$$C_t = \frac{Q_{t-1} + Q_t + Q_{t+1}}{3} , \qquad \text{(9-4f)}$$

Export unit-value

$$P_t = 0.69005 \, P_{nt} + 0.19403 \, P_{n,t-1} , \qquad \text{(9-4g)}$$

Accumulated buffer stock

$$N_{t+1} = N_t + Bf_{t+1} , \qquad \text{(9-4h)}$$

$$N_t \geqslant 0 \text{ for all } t. \qquad \text{(9-4i)}$$

The System of First Order Difference Equations

Since most control theory algorithms are written for systems of first order difference equations, we convert our set of difference equations to first order.

Substituting (9-4f) in (9-4e) and using the fact that

$$P_{t+1}^* - P_t^* = [(P_{t-5} - L_{t-5})^2 - \pi^2] \, C_{t-1} ,$$

where P_t^* is defined as

$$P_t^* = \sum_{\Theta=-5}^{t-6} [(P_\Theta - L_\Theta)^2 - \pi^2] \, C_{\Theta+4} ,$$

we obtain

$$Q_{t+1} = A_{0t} \, Q_t + A_{1t} \, Q_{t-1} + A_{2t} \, Q_{t-2} + A_{3t} \, Q_{t-3} + A_{4t} \, Q_{t-4} \qquad \text{(9-5)}$$

where

$$A_{0t} = \left[1 - \frac{0.00007302\ \pi^2}{3} - 10.13\ (P_t - L_t)^{-2} - 10\ (P_{t-1} - L_{t-1})^{-2} \right.$$

$$\left. + \frac{0.00007302}{3}\ (P_{t-5} - L_{t-5})^2 \right],$$

$$A_{1t} = \left[-\frac{0.00007302\ \pi^2}{3} - 10.13\ (P_t - L_t)^{-2} + 0.13\ (P_{t-1} - L_{t-1})^{-2} \right.$$

$$\left. + \frac{10}{3}\ (P_{t-2} - L_{t-2})^{-2} + \frac{0.00007302}{3}\ (P_{t-5} - L_{t-5})^2 \right],$$

$$A_{2t} = \left[-\frac{0.00007302\ \pi^2}{3} - 10.13\ (P_t - L_t)^{-2} + 0.13\ (P_{t-1} - L_{t-1})^{-2} \right.$$

$$+ \frac{10}{3}\ (P_{t-2} - L_{t-2})^{-2} + \frac{20}{3}\ (P_{t-3} - L_{t-3})^{-2}$$

$$\left. + \frac{0.00007302}{3}\ (P_{t-5} - L_{t-5})^2 \right],$$

$$A_{3t} = \left[10.13\ (P_{t-1} - L_{t-1})^{-2} + \frac{10}{3}\ (P_{t-2} - L_{t-2})^{-2} \right.$$

$$\left. + \frac{20}{3}\ (P_{t-3} - L_{t-3})^{-2} \right],$$

$$A_{4t} = \frac{20}{3}\ (P_{t-3} - L_{t-3})^{-2}\ .$$

Substituting Equations (9–2a), (9–3), and (9–5) into (9–1) and using Equation (9–4g), we derive the following spot price dynamic equation:

$$B_{0t}\ (0.19403\ P_{nt} + 0.69005\ P_{n,t+1})^{-0.2365} + B_{1t}\ P_{n,t+1}^{-0.91896} \tag{9-6}$$

$$= A_{0t}\ Q_t + A_{1t}Q_{t-1} + A_{2t}Q_{t-2}$$

$$+ A_{3t}\ Q_{t-3} + A_{4t}Q_{t-4} + S_t$$

$$- \alpha_{2,t+1}(P_{t-1} - L_{t-1})^{-0.2}$$

$$- \alpha_{3,t+1}\ P_{t-1}^{-0.2}\ P_t^{-0.2}$$

$$- \alpha_{3,t+1}(P_{t-1} - L_{t-1})^{-0.2} (P_t - L_t)^{-0.2}$$

$$- U_t,$$

where

$$B_{0t} = \alpha_{1,t+1} P_t^{-0.1817},$$

$$B_{1t} = \left[\frac{\alpha_{1,t+1} P_t^{-0.4182} + \alpha_{2,t+1} (P_{t-1} - L_{t-1})^{-0.2}}{\alpha_{1t} P_{t-1}^{-0.1817} P_t^{-0.2365} + \alpha_{2t} (P_{t-2} - L_{t-2})^{-0.2}} \right.$$

$$\left. \frac{+ \alpha_{3,t+1} (P_{t-1} - L_{t-1})^{-2} + \alpha_{3,t+1} P_{t-1}^{-0.2} P_t^{-0.2}}{+ \alpha_{3t} (P_{t-2} - L_{t-2})^{-0.2} + \alpha_{3t} P_{t-2}^{-0.2} P_{t-1}^{-2}} \right] P_{nt}^{0.91896} S_t,$$

and where we have defined the control variable

$$Bf_{t+1} = U_t. \tag{9-7}$$

Export unit-value dynamic equation (9-4g) can be rewritten as (9-8).

$$P_{t+1} = 0.69005 P_{nt} + 0.19403 P_{n,t-1}. \tag{9-8}$$

From Equation (9-2), we derive the inventory accumulation Equation (9-9).

$$S_{t+1} = B_{1t} P_{n,t+1}^{-0.91896}, \tag{9-9}$$

where

B_{1t} is as defined in (9-6).

Buffer stock accumulation Equation (9-4h) can be rewritten using (9-7) as (9-10).

$$N_{t+1} = N_t + U_t, \tag{9-10}$$

where

N_t = cumulated buffer stocks.

Finally, we define:

$$P_{t-1} = X_{1t}, P_{t-2} = X_{2t}, P_{t-3} = X_{3t}, P_{t-4} = X_{4t}, P_{t-5} = X_{5t}, \tag{9-11}$$

$$L_{t-1} = Y_{1t}, L_{t-2} = Y_{2t}, L_{t-3} = Y_{3t}, L_{t-4} = Y_{4t}, L_{t-5} = Y_{5t}, \tag{9-12}$$

and

$$Q_{t-1} = Z_{1t}, Q_{t-2} = Z_{2t}, Q_{t-3} = Z_{3t}, Q_{t-4} = Z_{4t}. \tag{9-13}$$

Substituting (9-11), (9-12), and (9-13) into (9-5) and (9-6), Goreux's cocoa model can be converted into the following system of first-order difference equations:

(A) Lagged Price Subsystem:

$$
\begin{bmatrix} X_{1,t+1} \\ X_{2,t+1} \\ X_{3,t+1} \\ X_{4,t+1} \\ X_{5,t+1} \end{bmatrix}
=
\begin{bmatrix} 0&0&0&0&0 \\ 1&0&0&0&0 \\ 0&1&0&0&0 \\ 0&0&1&0&0 \\ 0&0&0&1&0 \end{bmatrix}
\begin{bmatrix} X_{1t} \\ X_{2t} \\ X_{3t} \\ X_{4t} \\ X_{5t} \end{bmatrix}
+
\begin{bmatrix} 1 \\ 0 \\ 0 \\ 0 \\ 0 \end{bmatrix} P_t ,
\begin{bmatrix} \bar{X}_{10} \\ \bar{X}_{20} \\ \bar{X}_{30} \\ \bar{X}_{40} \\ \bar{X}_{50} \end{bmatrix} ,
$$

(B) Lagged Export Tax Subsystem:

$$
\begin{bmatrix} Y_{1,t+1} \\ Y_{2,t+1} \\ Y_{3,t+1} \\ Y_{4,t+1} \\ Y_{5,t+1} \end{bmatrix}
=
\begin{bmatrix} 0&0&0&0&0 \\ 1&0&0&0&0 \\ 0&1&0&0&0 \\ 0&0&1&0&0 \\ 0&0&0&1&0 \end{bmatrix}
\begin{bmatrix} Y_{1t} \\ Y_{2t} \\ Y_{3t} \\ Y_{4t} \\ Y_{5t} \end{bmatrix}
+
\begin{bmatrix} 1 \\ 0 \\ 0 \\ 0 \\ 0 \end{bmatrix} L_t ,
\begin{bmatrix} \bar{Y}_{10} \\ \bar{Y}_{20} \\ \bar{Y}_{30} \\ \bar{Y}_{40} \\ \bar{Y}_{50} \end{bmatrix} , \bar{L}_0 ,
$$

(C) Lagged Output Subsystem:

$$
\begin{bmatrix} Z_{1,t+1} \\ Z_{2,t+1} \\ Z_{3,t+1} \\ Z_{4,t+1} \end{bmatrix}
=
\begin{bmatrix} 0&0&0&0 \\ 1&0&0&0 \\ 0&1&0&0 \\ 0&0&1&0 \end{bmatrix}
\begin{bmatrix} Z_{1t} \\ Z_{2t} \\ Z_{3t} \\ Z_{4t} \end{bmatrix}
+
\begin{bmatrix} 1 \\ 0 \\ 0 \\ 0 \end{bmatrix} Q_t ,
\begin{bmatrix} \bar{Z}_{10} \\ \bar{Z}_{20} \\ \bar{Z}_{30} \\ \bar{Z}_{40} \end{bmatrix} ,
$$

(D) Output Subsystem:

$$Q_{t+1} = A_{0t} \, Q_t + A_{1t} \, Z_{1t} + A_{2t} \, Z_{2t} + A_{3t} \, Z_{3t} + A_{4t} \, Z_{4t} , \bar{Q}_0 \, ,$$

where

$$A_{0t} = [0.98977111 - 10.13 \, (P_t - L_t)^{-2} - 10 \, (X_{1t} - Y_{1t})^{-2}$$
$$+ \, 0.00002434 \, (X_{5t} - Y_{5t})^2] \, ,$$

$$A_{1t} = [-0.01022889 - 10.13 \, (P_t - L_t)^{-2} + 0.13 \, (X_{1t} - Y_{1t})^{-2}$$
$$+ \, 3.3333334 \, (X_{2t} - Y_{2t})^{-2} + 0.00002434 \, (X_{5t} - Y_{5t})^2] \, ,$$

$$A_{2t} = [-0.01022889 - 10.13 \, (P_t - L_t)^{-2} + 0.13 \, (X_{1t} - Y_{1t})^{-2}$$
$$+ \, 3.3333334 \, (X_{2t} - Y_{2t})^{-2} + 6.6666667 \, (X_{3t} - Y_{3t})^{-2}$$
$$+ \, 0.00002434 \, (X_{5t} - Y_{5t})^2] \, ,$$

$$A_{3t} = [10.13 \, (X_{1t} - Y_{1t})^{-2} + 3.3333334 \, (X_{2t} - Y_{2t})^{-2}$$
$$+ \, 6.6666667 \, (X_{3t} - Y_{3t})^{-2}] \, ,$$

$$A_{4t} = 6.6666667 \, (X_{3t} - Y_{3t})^{-2} \, .$$

(E) Spot Price Subsystem:

$$B_{0t} \, (0.19403 \, P_{nt} + 0.69005 \, P_{n,t+1})^{-0.2365} + B_{1t} \, P_{n,t+1}^{-0.91896}$$
$$= A_{0t} \, Q_t + A_{1t} \, Z_{1t} + A_{2t} \, Z_{2t}$$
$$+ \, A_{3t} \, Z_{3t} + A_{4t} \, Z_{4t} + S_t$$
$$- \, \alpha_{2,t+1} \, (X_{1t} - Y_{1t})^{-0.2} - \alpha_{3,t+1} \, X_{1t}^{-0.2} \, P_t^{-0.2}$$
$$- \, \alpha_{3,t+1} \, (X_{1t} - Y_{1t})^{-0.2} \, (P_t - L_t)^{-0.2}$$
$$- \, U_t , \bar{P}_{n0} \, ,$$

where

$$B_{0t} = \alpha_{1,t+1} \, P_t^{-0.1817}$$

$$B_{1t} = [\alpha_{1,t+1} \, P_t^{-0.4182} + \alpha_{2,t+1} \, (X_{1t} - Y_{1t})^{-0.2}$$

$$+ \alpha_{3,t+1} \, (X_{1t} - Y_{1t})^{-0.2} \, (P_t - L_t)^{-0.2}$$

$$+ \alpha_{3,t+1} \, X_{1t}^{-0.2} \, P_t^{-0.2}] \, [\alpha_{1t} \, X_{1t}^{-0.1817} \, P_t^{-0.2365} + \alpha_{2t} \, (X_{2t} - Y_{2t})^{-0.2}$$

$$+ \alpha_{3t} \, (X_{2t} - Y_{2t})^{-0.2} \, (X_{1t} - Y_{1t})^{-0.2} + \alpha_{3t} \, X_{2t}^{-0.2} \, X_{1t}^{-0.2}]^{-1} \, P_{nt}^{0.91896} \, S_t \,,$$

$$\alpha_{1t} = \text{antilog}_{10} \, (3.553028 + 0.00787 \, t - 0.00007 \, t^2),$$

$$\alpha_{2t} = \text{antilog}_{10} \, (2.453579 + 0.038067 \, t - 0.00064 \, t^2) \,,$$

$$\alpha_{3t} = \text{antilog}_{10} \, (2.663385 + 0.03265 \, t - 0.00047 \, t^2) \,.$$

(F) Export Unit-Value Subsystem:

$$P_{t+1} = 0.19403 \, P_{nt} + 0.69005 \, P_{n,t+1}, \bar{P}_0 \,.$$

(G) Inventory Subsystem:

$$S_{t+1} = B_{1t} \, P_{n,t+1}^{-0.91896} \,, \bar{S}_0 \,.$$

(H) Buffer Stock Subsystem:

$$\begin{bmatrix} Bf_{t+1} \\ N_{t+1} \end{bmatrix} = \begin{bmatrix} 0 & 0 \\ 0 & 1 \end{bmatrix} \begin{bmatrix} Bf_t \\ N_t \end{bmatrix} + \begin{bmatrix} 1 \\ 1 \end{bmatrix} U_t \,, \begin{bmatrix} Bf_0 \\ \bar{N}_0 \end{bmatrix} \,.$$

The logical interdependence of subsystems is shown in Figure 9-2.

The Criterion Function

We wish to compute the optimal mix of policy instruments (export tax and purchases or sales of buffer stock) to serve desired goals:

(i) maximizing the sum of discounted export earnings plus tax proceeds minus costs of the schemes;

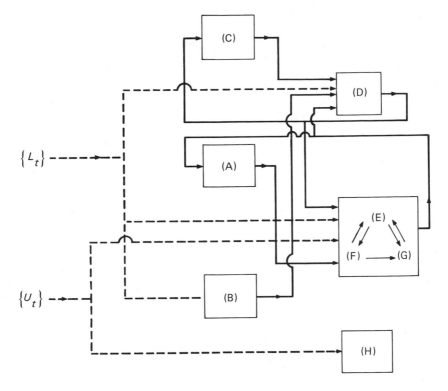

Figure 9-2. Subsystems Diagram.

(ii) minimizing the sum of squared relative price fluctuations from a seven year moving average; and,

(iii) minimizing the sum of squared relative earnings fluctuations from a seven year moving average.

That is, the criterion function is to maximize a weighted sum of (i), (ii), and (iii):

$$W = \sum_{t=1}^{T} \left\{ (1 + \rho)^{-t} (E_t + T_t - C_t) - \alpha \left(\frac{P_t - L_t - PE_t}{PE_t} \right)^2 - \beta \left(\frac{E_t + T_t - YE_t}{YE_t} \right)^2 \right\}, \quad (9\text{--}14)$$

where

E_t = export earnings

$\quad = g \, (P_t - L_t) \, [Q_t - Dgc_t]$

$$= g \left(P_t - L_t\right) \left[Q_t - \alpha_{3t} \left(P_{t-1} - L_{t-1}\right)^{-0.2} \left(P_{t-2} - L_{t-2}\right)^{-0.2}\right]$$

$$= g \left(P_t - L_t\right) \left[Q_t - \alpha_{3t} \left(X_{1t} - Y_{1t}\right)^{-0.2} \left(X_{2t} - Y_{2t}\right)^{-0.2}\right] \,,$$

T_t = tax proceeds

$$= gL_t \left[Q_t - Ds_t - Dgc_t - Bf_t\right]$$

$$= gL_t \left[Q_t - \alpha_{2t} \left(P_{t-2} - L_{t-2}\right)^{-0.2} - \alpha_{3t} \left(P_{t-1} - L_{t-1}\right)^{-0.2} \left(P_{t-2} - L_{t-2}\right)^{-0.2} - Bf_t\right]$$

$$= gL_t \left[Q_t - \alpha_{2t} \left(X_{2t} - Y_{2t}\right)^{-0.2} - \alpha_{3t} \left(X_{1t} - Y_{1t}\right)^{-0.2} \left(X_{2t} - Y_{2t}\right)^{-0.2} - Bf_t\right] \,,$$

C_t = cost attached to buffer stock operation

$$= 0.5\, \delta + g \left(N_t + P_{nt}\, Bf_t\right), \qquad \delta = 0 \quad \text{if } N_t = 0,$$
$$\delta = 1 \quad \text{if } N_t > 0,$$

g = a conversion factor from (¢/lb) to (million $/1,000 metric ton),

ρ = rate of discount,

α, β = weights attached to differing objectives,

$P_t - L_t$ = producer's price,

PE_t = seven year moving average of the producer's price which would be prevailing without policy interventions,

YE_t = seven year moving average of export earnings plus tax proceeds.

The optimality problem is then posed as one of choosing L_t and U_t for all t so as to maximize the criterion function (9–14), subject to the system of first order difference Equations (A)–(H).

OPTIMIZATIONS

In this section the stochastic nonlinear optimization problem is approached by, first, solving the deterministic version of the problem which substitutes zero for random disturbances and, second, tracking the deviations of endogenous variables from the deterministic optimal path. This approach enables us to derive a simple linear feedback decision rule under uncertainty. That is, the optimal policy variables would be determined by observed endogenous variables via the linear feedback control rule which reflects the social welfare. To make this section self-contained and to simplify the ensuing discussion, we state the stochastic non-linear optimization problem symbolically.

The world cocoa market model defined in terms of the above subsystems represents a full system of 20 first-order stochastic difference equations where new state variables are specified for the lagged variables:

$$x_{t+1} = f_t(x_t, u_t, \xi_t),$$ (9-15)

where

$x_t = 20 \times 1$ column vector of endogenous variables

$$= (P_{t-1} \cdots, P_{t-5}, L_{t-1} \cdots, L_{t-5}, Q_{t-1} \cdots, Q_{t-4},$$

$$Q_t, P_{nt}, P_t, S_t, Bf_t, N_t)',$$

P_t = export-unit value,

L_t = export tax,

Q_t = world cocoa production,

P_{nt} = spot price,

S_t = the level of private inventory,

Bf_t = purchases or sales of buffer stock,

N_t = cumulated buffer stock,

$u_t = 2 \times 1$ column vector of policy variables

$$= (L_t, Bf_{t+1})',$$

ξ_t = a serially uncorrelated vector with mean zero and covariance matrix Γ,

and

f_t is a vector-valued function.

It should be remarked that the world cocoa market model involves an implicit equation. Thus, the model should be written as

$$g_t\left(x_{t+1}, x_t, u_t, \xi_t\right) = 0. \tag{9-16}$$

Since for given values of x_t, u_t, and ξ_t the corresponding values of x_{t+1} and of its derivatives with respect to x_t and u_t are uniquely determined and depend only on the values of x_t and u_t, the implicit dynamic system (9-16) can be rewritten as (9-15).[5]

The optimality problem is now posed as one of choosing L_t and Bf_{t+1} for all t so as to maximize (9-14) subject to (9-15). We first solve the deterministic version of the problem. With the deterministic solution, the dynamic feedback coefficients are then computed. Finally, we consider the possible welfare gains of the feedback control policy over the deterministic policy.

Deterministic Solution

We have developed new programs for deterministic control based on the first-order differential dynamic programming algorithms of Jacobson and Mayne (1970)[6] and used these for solving a 20-state variable nonlinear optimization problem. The two main features of our new solution algorithms can be made here:

1. Since the world cocoa market model developed by Goreux includes an implicit dynamic equation, it is necessary for optimization to go through a root-finding procedure. Thus, we have integrated the Newton-Raphson method into the first-order DDP;

2. A negative export tax has no economic meaning. Also, cumulated buffer stocks cannot be negative. Thus, we have modified the first-order DDP to allow for nonnegativity constraints both on state and control variables. Specifically, we have multiplied the gradient of the Hamiltonian by the adjustment coefficient and chosen the proper value of this adjustment coefficient so that nonnegativity constraints could be satisfied for all iterations. More intuitively, we start with the given nominal control and compute the gradient of the Hamiltonian. To obtain an improved control when the gradient turns out to be negative, we descend along the gradient from the current nominal control until nonnegativity constraints are binding.

Computational Details[7]

We have experimented with the following three alternative sets of weights on price stability and earnings stability relative to high level export earnings in the welfare functional (9-14):

Case I: $\alpha = 5,000$ and $\beta = 5,000$;

Case II: $\alpha = 10,000$ and $\beta = 5,000$;

Case III: $\alpha = 5,000$ and $\beta = 10,000$.

Using the CDC 6600, we obtained convergent solutions for the 20-

state variable, thirty-three period nonlinear model of the world cocoa markets in 313 iterations (Case I); in 268 iterations (Case II); in 347 iterations (Case III). It took between seven and nine system minutes. The number of iterations required for an optimal solution obviously depends upon the starting nominal path chosen and the convergence criterion. Our criterion was that computation was halted when no further improvement in the welfare functional could be made with the first order DDP. And the initial nominal path was chosen from our simulation experimentations on the model. It should be pointed out that while the actual improvement in welfare was negligible at the final iteration, the estimated improvement in welfare turned out to be sizable. Thus, we would be forced to resort to the second-order differential dynamic programming algorithms to go the remaining distance to optimality. The second-order DDP, however, requires large inputs of human skills and computation time. In view of the high marginal costs of these inputs, we have settled on our convergent solutions obtained from the first-order DDP.

If the Hamiltonian is a strictly concave function of endogenous variables, our solution is globally optimal. However, price stability and earnings stability are alternatively conflicting and complementary. Thus, our Hamiltonian very likely is nonconcave. In this case, extensive search techniques must be employed to find the maximum among the multiple local stationary points. However, great expense in obtaining the global optimum is not justified in our case since the deterministic solution is not used directly but only as a path about which to expand the model for the stochastic solution.

Numerical Solutions

The optimal policy results for the three cases would provide useful insights on the "tradeoff" possibility frontier among our three objectives. For each case, there are two sets of calculations to be presented in Table 9–1, the first obtained before control and the second after control. Estimates in Table 9–1 are the welfare function (Column 4), the sum of discounted export earnings plus tax proceeds minus costs attached to buffer stock operation (Column 5), the sum of squared relative price fluctuations from the trend value (Column 6) and finally the sum of squared relative earnings fluctuations from the trend value (Column 7). Numbers in parentheses under Column 6 denote price fluctuations from the seven year moving average before control.

As far as the three experiments are concerned, the welfare gain varies between about 17 to 20 percent of the welfare function before control. While the improvement in export earnings is approximately 9 to 10 percent, price and earnings fluctuations are substantially reduced after control.

In considering possible "tradeoffs" between high level export earnings and price stability or between high level export earnings and earnings stability, it would be proper to measure price fluctuations from the seven-year moving average before control. While we have updated the seven-year moving

Table 9-1.   Measuring Welfare Gains Before and After Control with Three Alternative Sets of Marginal Weights

Case	Marginal Weights on Levels of σ^2_{P-L}	σ^2_{E+T}		$W = (E + T + C) - \alpha\sigma^2_{P-L} - \beta\sigma^2_{E+T}$ (4)	$E + T - C$ (5)	σ^2_{P-L} (6)		σ^2_{E+T} (7)
I	5,000	5,000	Before control	9,432	10,051	0.0832		0.0407
			After control	11,007	11,081	0.0071	(0.1723)	0.0078
II	10,000	5,000	Before control	9,016	10,051	0.0832		0.0407
			After control	10,793	10,901	0.0066	(0.0763)	0.0084
III	5,000	10,000	Before control	9,228	10,051	0.0332		0.0407
			After control	10,955	11,067	0.0083	(0.1770)	0.0071

Notes: Estimates of Columns 4 and 5 in U.S. million dollars; numbers in parentheses represent fluctuations from seven year moving averages before control.

average of export earnings, we have stuck to the original seven-year moving average of producer's price for all iterations.

As Columns 5, 6 and 7 of Table 9-1 show, when a weight on price stability relative to export earnings is increased from 5,000 to 10,000 with the same weight on earnings stability, price fluctuations are substantially reduced from 0.1723 to 0.0763 at the cost of less export earnings and wider earnings fluctuations. As a weight on earnings stability is increased from 5,000 to 10,000 with the same weight on price stability of 5,000, on the other hand, earnings fluctuations are very slightly reduced from 0.0078 to 0.0071 and the resulting decreases in export earnings and increases in price fluctuations are negligible. Thus, price stability is more costly than earnings stability in terms of export earnings.

The general conclusion from our three experiments is that fluctuations and export earnings increase go hand in hand and that price stability and earnings stability are conflicting.

The optimal policy results for the three cases are shown in Table 9-2. Note that Columns 1 and 5 refer to "before control"; Columns 2 and 6, Case I; Columns 3 and 7, Case II; Columns 4 and 8, Case III. As Table 9-2 shows, tax policy turns out to be active, the level of export tax uniformly rises during the first half of the planning period and then declines for the rest of the period, thereby reflecting cocoa cycles. A proportional tax policy would thus be a first-order approximation to optimality. On the other hand, buffer stock operation becomes inactive. This phenomenon is obvious because we have assumed no random disturbances. The main function of buffer stock operation is to eliminate short-term fluctuations.

Finally, producer's price is substantially stabilized around the seven-year moving average after control. For further illustration, producer's prices before

Table 9-2. Optimal Paths of Policy Instruments When α = 5,000 and β = 5,000 (Case I); α = 10,000 and β = 5,000 (Case II); α = 5,000 and β = 10,000 (Case III)

	L_t				Bf_t			
	0	*I*	*II*	*III*	*0*	*I*	*II*	*III*
Year	*(1)*	*(2)*	*(3)*	*(4)*	*(5)*	*(6)*	*(7)*	*(8)*
1968	0.	5.7	5.4	5.8	0.	0.	0.	0.
1972	0.	6.0	5.0	5.7	0.	0.5	0.1	0.3
1976	0.	11.6	9.0	11.7	0.	0.4	0.1	-0.4
1980	0.	14.5	11.4	14.4	0.	-0.1	0.1	-0.2
1984	0.	15.7	12.4	15.6	0.	-0.4	-0.1	-0.2
1988	0.	14.7	12.4	14.3	0.	-0.4	-0.2	-0.4
1992	0.	11.4	10.8	11.0	0.	-0.3	-0.2	-0.3
1996	0.	7.8	8.8	7.3	0.	-0.1	-0.1	-0.1
2000	0.	4.4	6.6	4.3	0.	0.1	-0.1	-0.1

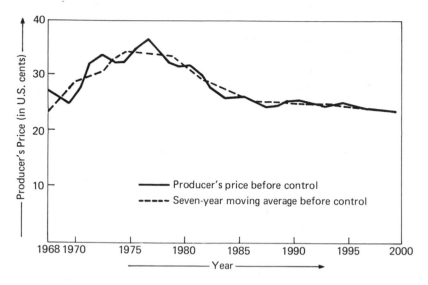

Figure 9-3.   Projected Producer's Price Without Policy Interventions.

and after control are drawn on Figures 9-3 through 9-6. The dotted graph corresponds to the seven-year moving average before control. The short-term fluctuations from the seven-year moving average are almost eliminated. Since we are interested not only in price stability but also in high level export earnings and earnings stability, however, producer's price after control turns out to be uniformly lower during the first twelve years and higher for the rest of the planning

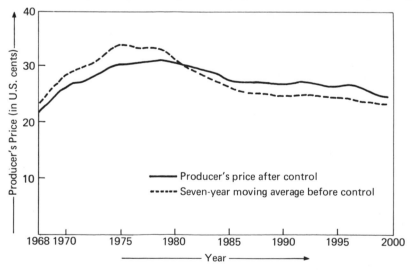

Figure 9-4.   Optimal Path for Producer's Price When $\alpha = 5,000$ and $\beta = 5,000$ (Case I).

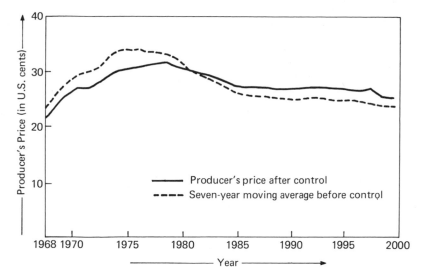

Figure 9-5. Optimal Path for Producer's Price When $\alpha = 10{,}000$ and $\beta = 5{,}000$ (Case II).

period than the original seven-year moving average before control. It is quite interesting to observe that the larger the relative weight on price stability is, the narrower the distance between these two price series becomes.

Feedback Stochastic Control Law

With the deterministic solution in hand, we compute the dynamic feedback coefficients (shown in (9-19)) which can be used to track the deterministic optimal path. To facilitate our expositions, we define the Hamiltonian of the system symbolically

$$H^t\left(x_t, u_t, \lambda_{t+1}\right) = (1 + \rho)^{-t}\left(E_t + T_t - C_t\right) - \alpha\left(\frac{P_t - L_t - PE_t}{PE_t}\right)^2$$
$$- \beta\left(\frac{E_t + T_t - YE_t}{YE_t}\right)^2$$
$$+ \lambda'_{t+1} f_t\left(x_t, u_t\right), \tag{9-17}$$

where λ_t is the 20×1 vector of auxiliary variables associated with the system Equation (9-15). Also, we denote the deterministic optimal paths for the state and control variables as x_t^* and u_t^*, respectively. This control is no longer optimal if random disturbances are included. Since the stochastic nonlinear optimization problem is very hard, if not impossible, to solve, we are forced to resort to a first-order approximation. That is, we approximate the system Equation (9-15)

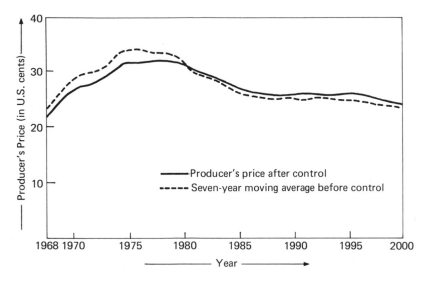

Figure 9-6. Optimal Path for Producer's Price When $\alpha = 5{,}000$ and $\beta = 10{,}000$ (Case III).

and the welfare function (9-14) by a first-order and a second-order Taylor series expansions, respectively, about the deterministic paths. The resulting problem has a quadratic welfare function and a linear stochastic model in the variables,

$$dx_t = x_t - x_t^* \text{ and } du_t = u_t - u_t^* . \tag{9-18}$$

The solution to this quadratic-linear perturbation problem, using the "certainty equivalence theorem," yields a linear feedback control law,[8]

$$du_t = -C_t \, dx_t \,, \tag{9-19}$$

where

$$C_t = [H_{uu}^t + (f_u^t)' \, S_{t+1} \, f_u^t]^{-1} \, [H_{ux}^t + (f_u^t)' \, S_{t+1} \, f_x^t] \tag{9-20}$$

and S_t is the solution of the matrix Ricatti equation,

$$S_t = [f_x^t - f_u^t \, (H_{uu}^t)^{-1} \, H_{ux}^t]' \, [S_{t+1} - S_{t+1} \, f_u^t (H_{uu}^t + (f_u^t)' \, S_{t+1} \, f_u^t)^{-1}$$

$$(f_u^t)' \, S_{t+1}] \, [f_x^t - f_u^t (H_{uu}^t)^{-1} \, H_{ux}^t] + H_{xx}^t - H_{xu}^t \, (H_{uu}^t)^{-1} H_{ux}^t \tag{9-21}$$

with terminal condition

$$S_T = (1 + \rho)^{-T} (E_T + T_T - C_T) - \alpha \left(\frac{P_T - L_T - PE_T}{PE_T} \right)^2$$

$$- \beta \left(\frac{E_T + T_T - YE_t}{YE_T} \right)^2 \tag{9-22}$$

Note that all partial derivatives are evaluated on deterministic optimal paths.

Thus, the solution procedure is to evaluate all first-order and second-order partial derivatives of the Hamiltonian and the system equation on the deterministic path and use these values first in (9-21) to integrate the matrix Ricatti equation backward from the terminal condition (9-22). The S_t matrix is then used in (9-20) to compute the feedback coefficients C_t.

The Dynamic Feedback Multipliers

Using the CDC 6600, we obtained the solution of this quadratic-linear problem in 38 system seconds. The solution of the matrix Ricatti equation required no more than multiplying and adding matrices. The only computational problem was that errors were accumulated from the inner product operation over time. As iterations increased, therefore, the symmetric matrix turned out to be nonsymmetric. So we took advantage of the symmetry of the matrix by computing only the upper triangle.

While the quadratic-linear perturbation problem looks simple and actually was easy to solve, it was a formidable work to compute all second-order partial derivatives of the Hamiltonian—in total about 300. We did our best in correctly computing all partial derivatives and checked them several times. However, we are not assured of perfect accuracy. The accuracy of our computations can be determined by actually implementing our feedback stochastic control law, which requires extensive Monte Carlo evaluations.

The dynamic feedback multipliers for a few selected years (i.e., some elements of the matrix C_t) are shown in Table 9-3 (for export tax) and in Table 9-4 (for purchases of sales of buffer stock). In order to check the numerical results obtained, one would like to compare them with those found in similar studies. However, there are no existing studies of this type in the literature that we know about. Therefore, the only check against numerical error which is available to us is the question of whether or not the coefficient signs conform to common sense judgments. In order to do this it is useful to look in detail at the feedback control function (9-19) for a single control variable namely buffer stock purchases and sales:

$$Bf_{t+1} = Bf_{t+1}^* - [c_{21t} (P_t - P_t^*) + \ldots + c_{26t} (P_{t-5} - P_{t-5}^*)$$

$$+ c_{27t} (L_{t-1} - L_{t-1}^*) + \ldots + c_{2,11,t} (L_{t-5} - L_{t-5}^*)$$

Table 9-3. Dynamic Feedback Multipliers for Export Tax When $\alpha = 5,000$ and $\beta = 5,000$ (Case I)

Tracking Deviations of Endogenous Variables	Year			
	1968	1976	1984	1992
$P_t - P_t^*$	-1.407	-1.798	1.533	-1.513
$P_{t-1} - P_{t-1}^*$	0.087	-0.248	-3.623	-0.143
$P_{t-2} - P_{t-2}^*$	0.666	1.054	3.731	0.072
$P_{t-3} - P_{t-3}^*$	0.420	0.535	-2.986	0.403
$P_{t-4} - P_{t-4}^*$	-0.251	-0.544	-0.343	-0.476
$P_{t-5} - P_{t-5}^*$	-0.183	-0.388	-0.227	-0.463
$L_{t-1} - L_{t-1}^*$	-0.253	0.004	3.038	0.098
$L_{t-2} - L_{t-2}^*$	-0.723	-1.248	-2.997	-0.100
$L_{t-3} - L_{t-3}^*$	-0.420	-0.538	2.986	-0.403
$L_{t-4} - L_{t-4}^*$	0.251	0.544	0.343	0.476
$L_{t-5} - L_{t-5}^*$	0.188	0.388	0.277	0.463
$P_{nt} - P_{nt}^*$	-0.616	-1.236	3.638	-0.472
$S_t - S_t^*$	-0.193	-0.767	0.421	0.516
$Bf_t - Bf_t^*$	0.004	-0.012	-0.038	0.005
$N_t - N_t^*$	0	0	0	0
$Q_t - Q_t^*$	-0.050	-0.036	0.040	-0.061
$Q_{t-1} - Q_{t-1}^*$	0.003	0.004	-0.001	-0.001
$Q_{t-2} - Q_{t-2}^*$	-0.004	-0.003	-0.001	-0.002
$Q_{t-3} - Q_{t-3}^*$	-0.004	-0.002	-0.001	-0.002
$Q_{t-4} - Q_{t-4}^*$	-0.001	-0.001	0	-0.001

$$+ c_{2,12,t} (P_{nt} - P_{nt}^*) + c_{2,13,t} (S_t - S_t^*) + c_{2,14,t} (B_t - B_t^*)$$

$$+ c_{2,15,t} (N_t - N_t^*) + c_{2,16,t} (Q_t - Q_t^*) + \ldots$$

$$+ c_{2,20,t} (Q_{t-4} - Q_{t-4}^*)] \tag{9-23}$$

where

c_{2jt} = coefficient in the second row (buffer stock row) and j^{th} column of the matrix C_t

* = deterministic path values.

With this function in hand, we can discuss whether or not the signs of the coefficients are predominantly of the sign one would expect. Consider the P_t coefficient c_{21t}. It is negative for all four years shown in Table 9-4. From (9-23) we can then obtain the feedback rule: if price one year ago was higher than the deterministic path, make a purchase ($Bf_{t+1} > 0$) for the buffer stock. At first glance this violates common sense—if the price was high then buy. However, the result is consistent with Goreux's model in that increases in prices in any of the three years preceding the current period will result in greater output in the current period. This is thought to model the fact that fertilizing and care of the existing trees can increase output over a period of several years. Thus a price higher than the deterministic solution price a year ago will result in greater output than the deterministic solution in the current period and will therefore require buffer stock purchases in order to hold the price up to the deterministic solution level.

This phenomenon holds for three years and in fact the sign of this

Table 9-4. Dynamic Feedback Multipliers for Purchases or Sales of Buffer Stock When $\alpha = 5,000$ and $\beta = 5,000$ (Case I)

Coefficient Number	Tracking Deviations of Endogenous Variables	Year			
		1968	1976	1984	1992
1	$P_t - P_t^*$	−2.827	−1.447	−37.234	−0.546
2	$P_{t-1} - P_{t-1}^*$	−6.448	−3.349	43.054	−7.608
3	$P_{t-2} - P_{t-2}^*$	−3.455	−4.140	−51304	0.900
4	$P_{t-3} - P_{t-3}^*$	6.518	0.609	42.585	0.926
5	$P_{t-4} - P_{t-4}^*$	2.753	2.372	4.216	4.656
6	$P_{t-5} - P_{t-5}^*$	−2.183	−4.286	−5.853	−4.623
7	$L_{t-1} - L_{t-1}^*$	5.929	3.100	−36.152	5.718
8	$L_{t-2} - L_{t-2}^*$	3.696	4.739	42.058	−0.747
9	$L_{t-3} - L_{t-3}^*$	−6.518	−0.609	−42.585	−0.926
10	$L_{t-4} - L_{t-4}^*$	−2.753	−2.372	−4.216	−4.656
11	$L_{t-5} - L_{t-5}^*$	2.138	4.286	5.853	4.623
12	$P_{nt} - P_{nt}^*$	−1.625	1.714	−52.116	−1.493
13	$S_t - S_t^*$	−0.169	1.197	−6.883	−7.570
14	$Bf_t - Bf_t^*$	−0.027	−0.040	0.473	−0.057
15	$N_t - N_t^*$	0.	0.	0.	0.
16	$Q_t - Q_t^*$	−0.435	−0.638	−1.474	−0.342
17	$Q_{t-1} - Q_{t-1}^*$	−0.005	−0.014	0.012	0.017
18	$Q_{t-2} - Q_{t-2}^*$	0.026	0.004	0.007	0.009
19	$Q_{t-3} - Q_{t-3}^*$	−0.146	−0.014	−0.012	−0.009
20	$Q_{t-4} - Q_{t-4}^*$	−0.012	−0.006	−0.005	−0.005

coefficient is predominantly negative for the first three lags (consider the values of C_t for all 30 years). It then becomes predominantly positive for P_{t-3} and P_{t-4} and then sharply turns back to negative (for 28 of 30 years) on the coefficients for P_{t-5}. The reason for the sharp change back to negative on P_{t-5} is that buffer stock purchases in year $t+1$ need to reflect the fact that a high price six years ago would have resulted in greater plantings than the deterministic solution and, therefore, more output in the current period. So buffer stock purchases are in order to keep price from falling below the deterministic solution. So our numerical results seem to be consistent with Goreux's model.

Finally, it should be pointed out that while buffer stock operations were inactive in the deterministic world, they turn out to be very active in a stochastic environment. The feedback coefficients for buffer stock operations vary more widely from year to year than for export tax.

CONCLUSIONS

A feedback stochastic decision rule has been developed for potential buffer stock agencies in cocoa. This rule prescribes the values of policy variables as a linear function of actually observed endogenous variables with time-varying coefficients which reflect the social welfare, and was derived by, first, solving the deterministic nonlinear optimization problem, and, second, by tracking the deviations of endogenous variables from their deterministic optimal paths. The welfare function was chosen as a weighted sum of the three eminently desirable objectives, high level export earnings, price stability and earnings stability. Instead of arbitrarily fixing the weights, we varied them within certain ranges so that policy-makers could be presented with a set of "possibility tradeoffs" among our three objectives. The weights on price stability and earnings stability were inferred from simulation results. All of these results should be considered demonstrative rather than prescriptive.

We have also developed new solution algorithms for the deterministic control based on Jacobson's and Mayne's (1970) first-order DDP which allow for both nonnegativity constraints and implicit dynamic systems and applied these to solve the 20-state variable, thirty-three period nonlinear model of the world cocoa markets developed by Goreux (1972). Since our algorithms converged slowly near the optimum, we employed the convergence criterion that computation is halted when no further improvement in the welfare functional can be made. As far as our experiments are concerned, the welfare gain varied from 17 to 20 percent of the welfare function computed before control.

Our original intent in the research described in this chapter was to see if the application of a stochastic control technique to a commodity stabilization model was a practical undertaking and whether or not it would prove to be a useful policy instrument. Our conclusions are as follows:

1. The most time consuming part of the project was the calculation

of the derivatives. We have subsequently learned that the NBER Computer Research Center has a program which will perform this function. We would advise others who undertake the solution of sizeable nonlinear models to be sure they can obtain and use such a program and/or that they have available substantial help to do the task of taking the derivatives.

2. Though we do not think the problem of the nonconvex welfare function resulted in an optimal first stage path which was far from the global optimum, we do not know that this is the case. As work progresses in this field it will be necessary to check that the local optimum solutions are not so far from the global optimum solutions as to result in the expansion for the second stage problem about a path distant from the true optimum. This checking can be done by starting the first stage gradient method from many different points to see if better solutions can be obtained.

3. Other approximate stochastic control methods than the one used here may prove desirable to use. One such method is that developed by Denham (1964) in which the two stages of our approach are combined and the nominal path is chosen with consideration of the random properties of the model.

4. To be operational, the feedback rule must provide guidance to traders who operate on a day-to-day basis in the market rather than on the annual basis used in our model. Yet they must continually gage the effects of their day-to-day actions on plantings and.production several years hence. Thus one probably needs a hierarchy of models with different time periods, viz., annual, monthly, and daily if operational rules are to be obtained.

5. The welfare function used in our study should be disaggregated in future studies to explicitly include the export earnings and fluctuations in export earnings of each country. This is necessary because price stabilization in the world market will have different effects on the export earnings level and fluctuation of different countries.

6. Finally, one can check the computational results of a model such as ours by performing simulations with the optimal feedback rule. We did not have the resources to do this, but we would regard it as an important part of the development of operational feedback rules.

NOTES

1. Kendrick's development is based on that of Bryson and Ho (1967).
2. DePrano's and Nugent's approach (1967) is similar to ours.
3. The orthodox view has long held that developing countries suffer greater fluctuations in their export earnings than do developed countries and that, furthermore, their unusually high fluctuations cause damage to domestic stability and to prospects for sustained growth. Although entirely plausible counter arguments can be offered to show that export fluctuations have either no effect or even a positive effect up-

on an economy, wide fluctuations of export earnings very likely cause developing countries a short-term liquidity crisis for debt repayments.
4. We suppress the disposal variable W_t which Goreux uses.
5. For details, see Kim (1972).
6. As an alternative to this we could have used the conjugate gradient algorithm used by Kendrick and Taylor (1970).
7. All our computational works were done on the CDC 6600.
8. For details, see Kendrick (1970).

REFERENCES

Bryson, A.E., Jr. and Yu-Chi Ho. *Applied Optimal Control.* Waltham, Massachusetts: Blaisdell Publishing Company, 1969.

DePrano, M.E. and J.B. Nugent. "The Effects of Long-Run and Short-Run Planning Goals on Economic Policy Instruments." Presented at the Econometric Society, Washington, D.C., 1967.

Denham, W.F. "Choosing the Nominal Path for a Dynamic System with Random Forcing Functions to Optimize the Statistical Performance." Technical Report No. 449, Division of Engineering and Applied Physics, Harvard University, Cambridge, Massachusetts, 1964.

Goreux, L.M. "Price Stabilization Policies in World Markets for Primary Commodities: An Application to Cocoa." Working Paper, The Development Research Center, IBRD, 1972.

Jacobson, D.H. and D.Q. Mayne. *Differential Dynamic Programming,* New York: American Elsevier Publishing Company, Inc., 1970.

Kendrick, D.A. and L. Taylor. "Numerical Solution of Nonlinear Planning Models." *Econometrica* 38 (May 1970): 453–67.

Kendrick, D.A. "Numerical Methods for Planning Under Uncertainty." Technical Report No. 33, Institute for Mathematical Studies in the Social Sciences, Stanford University, Stanford, California, 1970.

Kim, H. "Notes on the Necessary Conditions for Optimality in Simultaneous, Implicit Economic Systems." Working Paper, the Development Research Center, IBRD, 1970.

Little, I.M.D. and J.A. Mirrlees. *Manual of Industrial Project Analysis in Developing Countries,* Paris, 1964.

Loucks, D. "Conflict and Choice: Planning for Multiple Objectives." Working Paper, The Development Research Center, IBRD, 1972.

Marglin, S.A. *Public Investment Criteria,* London, 1967.

Norman, A.L. and M.R. Norman. "Behavioral Consistency Test of Econometric Models." *IEEE Transactions on Automatic Control* AC-18 (5) (October, 1973): 465–72.

Pindyck, R.S. *Optimal Planning for Economic Stabilization.* Amsterdam: North Holland Publishing Company, 1973.

Theil, H. *Optimal Decision Rules for Government and Industry.* Amsterdam: North Holland Publishing Company, 1964.

Theil, H. "Linear Decision Rules for Macro-dynamic Policy Problem." *Quantitative Planning of Economic Policy.* Washington, D.C.: The Brookings Institute, 1965.

United Nations Industrial Development Organization. New York: *Guidelines for Project Evaluation,* 1972.

Van Eijk, C.J. and J. Sandee. "Quantitative Determination of an Optimum Economic Policy." *Econometrica* 27 (1) (1959).

Chapter Ten

Application of a Planning–Decision Model for Surplus Commodity Removal Programs

Richard C. Haidacher
R.C. Kite
Jim L. Matthews

Most quantitative models for commodities concentrate on a mathematical-statistical description of the economic structure of a particular market and its behavior. In some cases interest may center on the isolation of various structural parameters or relationships. In others, interest may be in aspects of market equilibrium or forecasting where the focus is on the reduced form of the system. In all of these cases the main focus is on quantitatively describing and understanding the economic behavior of the market.

There is another area in which quantitative commodity models are of interest and have relevance, namely, in the operation and administration of programs whose explicit purpose is to alter, alleviate, or otherwise change the economic impact or effects that would occur in commodity markets in the absence of such programs. In this context the focus on commodity models is much different than in the previous cases, in that this effort requires the synthesis of a model and program, with its inherent objectives, characteristics, and constraints. That is, not only does one need a quantitative description of the commodity market behavior of interest, but one needs to integrate this model with the program characteristics to obtain a larger model framework that can be used in administering the program. It is in this general context that the model presented here is developed.

MODEL DEVELOPMENT

This chapter reports on a modification and extension of a prototype decision model reported in an earlier paper.[1] The model is based on the assumption that the primary purpose of a commodity removal program is price and income enhancement. Single minded pursuit of this goal is, however, limited by two

The authors are with the Pricing, Policy and Program Analysis Section, National Economic Analysis Division, Economic Research Service, U.S. Department of Agriculture, Washington, D.C.

kinds of restrictions. One class of restrictions, which may be termed legal-administrative, arise from the general legal-administrative environment within which the removal program must operate. A second class of restrictions, which may be termed economic restrictions, arise from the character of the general economic system surrounding the commodity removal program.

The Legal-Administrative Environment—Section 32

Section 32 of the Agricultural Adjustment Act of 1935, as amended, provides authorization and funds for the Department of Agriculture to encourage exportation and domestic consumption of agricultural products for the purpose of contributing to market price stabilization. This is accomplished in practice through actual market entry or announcements that the Department stands ready to enter the market.[6]

Over the period of years since the inception of Section 32 certain specifications and restrictions have evolved which influence the implementation characteristics of the program. For example, the principal use of funds has been restricted to perishable, nonbasic, commodities which do not have in operation a price support program. The major restriction on expenditures is that no more than 25 percent of total available funds may be used for any one commodity.[2]

As the operation of Section 32 programs have evolved over time, they have been operated in conjunction with various food distribution programs such that surpluses removed from the market are donated to schools, institutions, and needy persons. Section 32 funds are being used for (1) child feeding programs and nutritional programs authorized by the School Lunch Act and the Child Nutrition Act, (2) financial assistance to enable certain low income counties to operate food distribution programs, and (3) a food certification program and special supplementary food packages for expectant mothers, new mothers, and infants.[3]

The basic goal of the Section 32 commodity removal program, and its evolved connection with food assistance programs is seen as an attempt to correct politically perceived inequities at the two ends of the food production-consumption chain. Although the legislation related to Section 32 provides for alternative ways to support commodity markets, the primary support activity has been the acquisition of "surplus" commodities which are then distributed by the food assistance programs. Thus, the operation of the Section 32 program, and related programs, spans the food economy from production to consumption.

Since Section 32 activities are specifically aimed at support of the production end of the system, the development of the decision model focuses on that level of the total system. This concentration excludes a large part (but not all) of the complicating aspects of the acquisition-distribution problem. We specifically exclude, for example, all consideration of the geographic source and disposition of surplus commodities. On the other hand, it is not possible to develop the decision model in complete isolation from the distribution programs; first, because the intended disposition of an acquired commodity will condition the form in which it is purchased, and second, this determines the level in the economic system at which purchases are made. One is left with the necessity of allowing for interaction between one or more levels of the food economy.

The Economic Environment

The two most important economic factors are economic interdependence and the nature of the market mechanism. Economic interdependence derives from the theoretical assumption in economics that prices of all goods are related to a greater or lesser degree. Thus, relationships may exist among prices of specific commodities under Section 32, between Section 32 commodities and other commodities, and between various levels in the market from farm to retail. At any given level the interrelations among various commodity prices can be taken into account by a complete set or matrix of demand parameters (elasticities or flexibilities) which show the quantitative relation between commodity prices and quantities. Conceptually, a set of these parameters exists at each level in the system and a relationship between each level is implied. For Section 32 activities this is important because purchases are generally made at several stages removed from the farm level, whereas a major objective relates to the benefits accruing at or near the farm level.

Assumptions regarding the nature of the market mechanism are important in designing the decision model from both the economic and administrative viewpoint. From the administrative view the issue is one of what the appropriate planning horizon is, while from the economic aspect the issue is one of specifying the behavior assumptions most appropriate for the selected period. In this study the planning period was specified to be a year, largely on the grounds that the major planning and budget allocation decisions are made on an annual basis. In conjunction with this, it was assumed that total quantities available for market were given for the period and not subject to change in response to prices or other economic determinants. Thus, it is assumed that quantities are given and the price mechanism makes the necessary adjustments to allocate the fixed quantities among alternative outlets or uses. Consequently, there is implied a complete system of inverse demand functions which express each price as a function of all of the given quantities and income. From a theoretical viewpoint, the interdependencies among the various commodities and prices can be represented by a complete matrix of price flexibilities, where the latter are defined as the elements of the inverse of the matrix of demand elasticities.[3]

An additional assumption regarding economic behavior in the market is that the existing demand for commodities is independent of government program activities. Essentially, this says that government purchase activity largely operates outside the regular market channels, etc., and therefore has a negligible effect on existing demand. While this assumption is consistent with the wording and intent of the legislation itself, the reality of this assumption remains doubtful.

A final economic consideration concerns the calculation of benefits, or the impact of the various purchases. This includes consideration of which beneficial impacts are to be considered, at what level in the system, etc. Indeed, it raises the more basic question of what constitutes a benefit. In the present study a pragmatic approach was adopted. The approach is based on the implied program objective of price and/or income enhancement to the commodity subsectors. Briefly, given the particular purchase strategy specifying commodities, expenditure, etc., an attempt is made to calculate a measure of dollar benefit and impute the allocation by geographic region.

The list of additional considerations in model development, having some relevance in the operation of programs such as Section 32, could probably be extended indefinitely. As with the present study, the delineation can be narrowed substantially by selection of the specified annual time period and by focusing on the "plan selection" part of the planning-decision process as opposed to the "implementation" and "evaluation" parts of the process. The list includes the program decisions and constraints mentioned previously, in addition to the following important considerations.

A major consideration concerns the selection of a decision rule or criterion that can be used as a basis for developing alternative plans from which a choice can be made. A necessary condition in selecting such a rule is that it be directly related to the objective or goal to be achieved. When more than one objective exists, or the objective is not explicit and consequently leads to more than one implied objective, the selection of a single rule is open to choice. This is the situation in the present problem. That is, it is not clear whether major emphasis should be focused on relative commodity price levels or on returns to producers.

One of the most important considerations in developing a model to aid in this type of administrative decision process is the recognition that a formal model cannot capture all aspects of the decision process that are relevant to program planning. This results because the factors are too numerous and many of them are either qualitative or lack sufficiently precise definition such that they cannot be formally introduced in a model. For example, such factors would include possible conflict with other programs, agencies, or administrative policies, in addition to adverse political repercussions.

These considerations have important implications for developing a formal system to aid in the decision process. For example, these factors augur strongly against the use of a strict optimizing model framework from the standpoint that it purports to come up with a single plan which is "best," even though many factors have not been taken into account. Rather than a framework that attempts to select a single optimum plan, one needs a framework which incorporates the more important aspects that can be formally introduced to generate alternative plans that indicate the tradeoff between alternatives. Selection among these alternatives can then be made in view of the qualitative and other factors not formally included in the model. The model presented here provides two means through which alternative plans can be generated.

One method of generating alternative plans is obtained by recognizing that there are two aspects to the operation of the Section 32 program. One aspect is that some minimum purchases may be required in conjunction with the operation of food assistance programs. In the terminology of the model this provision is called "stage one" or "required purchases." Purchases beyond the minimum requirements are referred to as "discretionary" or "stage two" purchases. The stage one feature, beyond securing a means for generating alternative plans by varying the required purchase quantities, provides a direct link between the Section 32 program and the food assistance programs.

Alternative plans can also be generated through the use of different decision rules which provide a means for ranking the commodities. One rule ranks commodities according to their price relative to a "normal" price. Provision is made for use of alternative rules by allowing entry of other rankings of commodities. This aspect of the model is discussed further in the following section.

Formal Statement of the Model

The variables and relationships used in the model are defined as follows:

R = list (set) of all commodities to be included in the model

n = number of commodities included in R

S_k = the kth subset of R ($k = 1, \ldots, K$). These sets are used to specify commodity groups for which some minimum, required, purchases must be made

MIN_k = quantity of the kth subset which must be purchased in stage one. That is, some combination of the commodities contained in S_k must be purchased such that their combined quantity is MIN_k at the purchase level

Q_i^1 = purchase, stage one, of commodity i

Q_i^2 = purchase, stage two, of commodity i

TS_i = total supply of the ith commodity, at the impact level

$W = [w_{ij}]$ = an $n \times n$ matrix of price flexibilities at the purchase level

PW_i = initial equilibrium purchase level price for the ith commodity

APW_i^1 = adjusted purchase level price, end of stage 1

APW_i^2 = adjusted purchase level price, end of stage 2

$LOTS_i$ = purchase lot size

MAX_i = maximum allowed purchase of commodity i

FFP_i = initial (forecasted) equilibrium impact level price

FP_i^1 = impact level price, end of stage 1

FP_i^2 = impact level price, end of stage 2

η_{kj} = partial elasticity of price transmission indicating the percent change in purchase level price of a commodity (k) for each one percent change in the price of commodity j at the impact level. *(1), (4)*

$CONV_{mj}$ = factor for converting purchase level quantities of commodity m into an equivalent quantity for commodity j at the impact level. When only one impact level commodity is involved, this is written $CONV_j$

T_j = impact level equivalent of the purchase level quantities
$$T_j = Q_j(CONV_j) + \Sigma_{m=1}^M Q_m(CONV_{mj})$$

M = number of commodities that have more than one impact level commodity

PFP_i = specified limit on impact level price for commodity i

PN_i = "normal price" for commodity i at impact level

$PFACT$ = proportion for adjusting price eligibility

$IOBJ$ = commodity ranking according to specified criteria

TF = funds available for purchase of all commodities

STF = funds which may be used for purchase of commodities in R.

There are three basic operations performed in the model: One is determination of purchase eligibility, another is price adjustment due to purchase impact, and the third is a mechanism to insure that constraints are not violated. The major determinant of the structure of any purchase strategy is the rule used to determine eligibility.

However, in the first stage, where required purchases (MIN_k) have been specified for commodity groups, within group purchases are determined by a commodity ranking. Thus, we define $X(S_k)$ as a process which ranks the commodities in S_k such that

$$IOBJ = X(S_k)$$

where the process $X(..)$ may be any rule which assigns weights to the commodities contained in S_k. Since we have chosen to use the ratio of the "normal" price (PN_i) to the forecasted price (FFP_i),

$$IOBJ = X(PN_j/FFP_j \mid j\epsilon S_k)$$

and *IOBJ* will contain a ranking of commodities in S_k according to decreasing values of the ratio.

We then proceed with the stage one solution. Thus we choose from *IOBJ* the first ranked commodity (i), purchase commodity i until either MIN_k is satisfied or MAX_i is exceeded. If MAX_i is exceeded we move to the next element of *IOBJ*. If MIN_k is satisfied we move to the next subset (S_k). The result is a schedule of stage one purchases (Q_i^1) from which the price adjustments, expenditures, and impacts are calculated. First define,

$$\Delta FP_i^1/FFP_i = \sum_{j=1}^{n-M} (T_j/TS_j)\,(w_{ij}/\eta_j); \quad i = 1,\ldots,n-m$$

then the impact level price adjustment is,

$$FP_i^1 = FFP_i(1 + \Delta FP_i/FFP_i); \quad i = 1,\ldots,n-m.$$

Purchase level prices for products having a single input are calculated,

$$APW_i^1 = PW_i[1 + (\Delta FP_i/FFP_i)\eta_i]; \quad i = 1,\ldots,n-m$$

Purchase level prices for products having more than one input are calculated,

$$APW_m^1 = PW_m[1 + \sum_{j=1}^{n-m} (\Delta FP_j/FFP_j)\eta_{mj}]; \quad m = 1,\ldots,M$$

Given the schedule of purchases and adjusted prices as calculated above, we then proceed to determine expenditure and income impacts according to the following relations:

$$C_1 = 1/2 \sum_{j}^{n} Q_j^1\,(PW_j + APW_j^1)$$

Impact:

$$AR_1 = 1/2 \sum_{j=1}^{n-m} (FP_j^1 - FFP_j)(TS_j + T_j)]$$

We then reduce TS_j by the quantity removed and proceed to the second stage. In the second stage we take account of the funds and price eligibility constraints which were ignored in the first stage. The general procedure, however, is much the same as for stage one. We begin with the commodity ranking procedure,

$$IOBJ = X(R)$$

In this stage, like stage one, the process $X(..)$ must rank the commodities in the set R according to some rule. Here again, we have chosen to rank them according to PN_i/FP_i. However, provision is made for entry of either a different function or an outright user ranking of the commodities.

In this second stage we consider the price and funds constraints. The price constraint is formulated so that a commodity is ineligible for purchase if $FP_i > (PFACT)(PFP_i)$. By varying $PFACT$ we may generate purchase strategies in addition to those methods discussed previously. There are two funds constraints to be considered: One fund constraint is that total expenditures be less than STF; the other is that funds expended on a single commodity not exceed $0.25TF$. These constraints are checked each time a provisional purchase is made.

The stage two process can be described as follows. We select the first commodity from $IOBJ$, call it (i). Commodity i is purchased if it is eligible; if it is not, then select the next element of $IOBJ$. A provisional purchase of commodity i is made in amounts of $LOTS_i$, prices are updated and MAX_i and funds limits are checked. If no restrictions are violated, we rerank according to $X(..)$ and repeat the process. If restrictions are violated we do not purchase this LOT. Termination occurs when either funds are expended or no commodities are eligible for purchase. The result is a schedule of stage two purchases, (Q_j^2), price changes, income impacts and expenditures. The values for these variables are calculated for stage two according to the relationships described as for stage one, except that the variables in those relations are replaced as shown in Table 10–1.

Total expenditure is then $C = C_1 + C_2$, and total impact is $AR = AR_2$. In actual application of the model we calculated C and AR for each commodity included in the analysis.

Application: Some Economic Implications of AMS Purchases in Fiscal Year 1973

Background.   Twenty-seven commodities were included in an analysis of the commodity removal program conducted by the Agricultural

Table 10-1. Variable Replacement Index

Replace variable	with variable
FFP_i	FP_i^1
TS_j	$TS_j - T_j$
ΔFP_i^1	ΔFP_i^2
FP_i^1	FP_i^2
APW_i^1	APW_i^2
PW_i	APW_i^1
C_1	C_2
AR_1	AR_2
Q_j^1	Q_j^2

Marketing Service in 1973. The selected commodities were specified by AMS personnel as being of major importance, and were selected from a total set which in some years contained over a hundred items. Table 10-3 shows the selected commodities and some related information.

Total expenditure (excluding transportation) for the twenty-seven commodities was 179 million dollars for fiscal 1973 (Table 10-2). This amounted to 97.8 percent of expenditure for all commodities in FY 1973.

Fiscal year 1973 purchases by major groups are shown in Table 10-4 while Table 10-5 shows individual purchases for the twenty-seven commodities examined. These tables present the data as tons purchased by disposition to needy families, schools, and institutions as well as tons purchased using Section 32 and FNS funds. The major activity occurred for poultry and poultry products which were purchased primarily for distribution to schools and institutions (72.2 percent of all poultry products). The same general relationship also held for vegetables. Fruits and juices, dry beans, prunes, raisins, shortening, and

Table 10-2. AMS Expenditures, Fiscal Year 1973, Twenty-Seven Commodities

	Million Dollars
Total expenditures—all commodities	183
Twenty-seven commodities:	
Distributed to needy families	80
Distributed to schools, institutions	99
Total	179

Source: Derived from Table 10-4 and data supplied by AMS.

Table 10-3. Commodities Included in Removal Impact Analysis

Commodity Description			
Purchase Level		*Impact Level*	
Name	*Specification*	*Name*	*Specification*
Beef (frozen)	Ground frozen beef, carlots of 700/55 lb boxes	Steers/heifers	Minimum grade U.S. utility
Beef (canned)	Beef in natural juices, carlot of 1600/43-1/2 lb boxes of cans, wt. 24–29 oz.	Cows	Minimum grade U.S. canner
Pork (frozen)	Ground frozen pork, carlot of 700/55 lb boxes	Hogs	
Pork (canned)	Pork in natural juices, 1600/43-1/2 lb boxes of cans, wt. 24–29 oz.	Hogs	
Canned meat	Luncheon meat, 1600/45 lb boxes of cans, wt. 24–30 oz. 85% beef (cows) 15% pork	Cows/hogs	
Lard	Carlot of 60,000–63,000 lbs, approx. 1250 boxes of 48/1 lb ctns.	Lard	Bulk lard
Vegetable shortening	Carlot 60,000–54,000 lbs, approx. 1250 boxes 48/1 lb ctns.	Soybean oil	
Chicken (RTC)	Ready-to-cook chicken— 72,000 lbs/carlot	Broilers	
Chicken (canned)	Canned boned chicken— 73950 lbs/carlot	Chickens excluding broilers	
Turkey (RTC)	Ready-to-cook turkey— 70,000 lb/carlot, frozen, young, 12–24/lbs	Turkey	
Turkey (canned)	Canned boned turkey	Turkey	
Egg mix	Carlot/36,000 lbs 51% whole egg solids	Eggs	N.Y. wholesale graded eggs 10% AA large
Corn (canned)	Carlot of 2,200 cases, 6/#10 cans whole kernel	Sweet corn	U.S. Grade A
Snap beans	Carlot of 2,200 cases 6/#10 cans, whole, French or cut style	Snap beans	U.S. Grade A
Peas (canned)	Carlot of 2,200 cases 6/#10 cans	Peas	U.S. Grade B top of range
Potatoes (frozen)	Frozen french fries carlot of 2,000 cases 6/5-lb cartons	Potatoes	U.S. Grade A medium or longer
Tomatoes (canned)	Canned tomatoes carlot of 2,200 cases 6/#10 cans	Tomatoes	U.S. Grade B (modified for color)
Sweet potatoes	Sweet potatoes canned, carlot of 2,200 cases 6/#10 cans	Sweet potatoes	U.S. Grade A wholes and/or cuts

Table 10–3 continued

Commodity Description			
Purchase Level		*Impact Level*	
Name	*Specification*	*Name*	*Specification*
Beans (northern)	Northern beans	Same	U.S. #2 or better
Beans (pea)	Pea beans	Same	U.S. #2 or better
Beans (pinto)	Pinto beans 2 & 25 lb packages	Same	U.S. #1 or better
Apple Sauce	Canned applesauce cases 6/#10 cans	Applesauce	
Peaches (canned)	Canned peaches case 6/#10's	Peaches	
Pears (canned)	Canned pears case 6/#10's	Pears	
Frozen O.J.	Frozen concentrated orange juice, case 12/32 oz. cans	Oranges	
Raisins	Carlot 48/1# package 15–75 cases	Dry raisins	
Prunes	Carlot 24/1 lb packages, 3080 cases	Dry prunes	

Table 10–4. AMS Purchases, Major Food Groups, Fiscal Year 1973, Twenty-Seven Commodities

	Quantity Purchased (tons)				
	Disposition			*Source of funds*	
Group	*Needy Families*	*Schools, Institutions*	*Total*	*Section 32*	*FNS*
Meat/products	20,041	447	20,488	11,556	8,932
%	(97.82)	(2.18)	(100)	(56.40)	(43.60)
Poultry/products	31,311	81,440	112,751	65,102	47,649
%	(27.77)	(72.23)	(100)	(57.74)	(42.26)
Vegetables	12,353	37,852	50,205	38,247	11,958
%	(24.61)	(75.39)	(100)	(76.18)	(23.82)
Dry beans	24,826	15,445	40,271	40,271	–
%	(61.65)	(38.35)	(100)	(100)	(0.0)
Fruit & juices	28,950	11,949	40,899	39,736	1,163
%	(70.78)	(29.22)	(100)	(97.16)	(2.84)
Raisins & prunes	–	–	–	–	–
%	(0.0)	(0.0)	(0.0)	(0.0)	(0.0)
Shortening & lard	2,425	128	2,553	2,553	–
%	(94.99)	(5.01)	(100)	(100)	(0.0)
Total	119,906	147,261	267,167	197,465	69,702
%	(44.88)	(55.12)	(100)	(73.91)	(26.09)

Source: Derived from Table 10–4.

lard were all purchased primarily for distribution to needy families. The total of the twenty-seven commodities was distributed 45 percent to needy families and 55 percent to schools and institutions.

The distribution of purchases by source of funds was 74 percent from Section 32 funds and 26 percent from FNS funds. The meat and poultry food group was most evenly distributed between the two fund sources (58 percent Section 32, 42 percent FNS), all other food group purchases drew largely on Section 32 funds (Table 10-4).

Analysis for Fiscal 1973. The data presented in Table 10-5 was used to analyze the impact of fiscal 1973 purchases. The analysis concentrates on the price and income impacts of the purchase activities. Several cases were considered, referred to as Solutions I-IV. The major price, lot size and maximum purchase data for the four Solutions are shown in Table 10-6. Beginning with Solution I, the four cases introduce increasing flexibility to the model choices. Basic characteristics of the four runs are as follows:

Solution I—required purchases for each commodity set at actual total for fiscal 1973 (see Column 3, Table 10-5). Maximum purchases also set at actual total purchases.

Solution II—required purchase for each commodity set at quantity purchased using FNS funds (see column 7, Table 10-5). Maximum purchases same as Solution I.

Solution III—same minimum required purchases as for Solution II. Maximum allowed purchases for each commodity set at 48,000 tons (an arbitrary large upper limit).

Solution IV—no required purchases specified. Maximum allowed purchases set at 48,000 tons for each commodity. Since the average price paid by AMS was used for the purchase level prices for the four Solutions, the purchase level price changes were not allowed. Only impact level prices were allowed to vary.

Total funds available, funds used, excess funds and purchase impact of commodity removal from the four Solutions are shown in Table 10-7. The percentage distribution of expenditures on major commodity groups (for each of the four Solutions) are shown in Table 10-8.

The model behavior, as restrictions are relaxed, manifests itself in a reduction in the income-impact/expenditure ratio (Table 10-7). The ratio declines from a value of $7.00 income per dollar expenditure for Solution I to a value of $2.57 for Solution IV. From the data in Table 10-8 we can infer that the reduction in the ratio is due to a shift in the composition of purchases, specifically, from meat and poultry products to vegetables and fruit products.

The effects of the shift in purchase composition may be seen by comparison of Solutions I and II. Solution I forces both required and maximum purchases to equal AMS reported purchases for fiscal year 1973. In effect, this

Table 10–5. AMS Purchases by Disposition and Source of Funds, Fiscal Year 1973

	Disposition			Cost 1/		Source of Funds	
Commodity	Needy Families (ton)	Schools, Institutions (ton)	Total (ton)	Total/Cost ($)	Cost/ton ($)	Section 32 (ton)	FNS (ton)
Beef (frozen)							
Beef (canned)[b]							
Pork (frozen)[b]	8,485	447	8,932	12,502,659	1399.80		8,932
Pork (canned)	11,556		11,556	13,587,566	1175.80	11,556	
Total	20,041	447	20,488	26.09		11,556	8,932
Chicken (RTC)		47,124	47,124	33,794,000	717.13		47,124
Chicken (canned)	20,151	1,997	22,148	35,723,000	1612.92	22,148	
Turkey (RTC)		29,050	29,050	20,998,000	722.82	28,525	525
Turkey (canned)	11,160	2,552	13,712	20,096,000	1465.58	13,712	
Egg mix		717	717	1,426,000	1990.23	717	
Total	31,311	81,440	112,751	112.04		65,102	47,649
Corn (canned)	3,159	7,113	10,272	2,179,401	212.18	3,159	7,113
Snap beans	391		391	121,486	311.02	391	
Peas (canned)	3,831	851	4,682	1,196,692	255.63	3,831	851
Potatoes (frozen)		12,480	12,480	3,160,919	253.28	9,300	3,180
Tomatoes (canned)	4,972	16,594	21,566	5,548,576	257.28	21,566	
Sweet potatoes		814	814	243,386	299.08		814
Total	12,353	37,852	50,205	12.42		38,247	11,958
Beans (northern)							
Beans (pea)						970	
Beans (pinto)						39,301	
Total	24,826	15,445	40,271	9.67	240.06	40,271	
Applesauce		8,542	8,542	1,922,614	255.09	8,542	
Peaches (canned)	18,426		18,426	5,056,146	274.40	18,426	
Pears (canned)	5,124	2,244	7,386	2,683,861	364.24	7,368	
O.J. (frozen)	5,400	1,163	6,563	8,038,171	1224.86	5,400	1,163
Total	28,950	11,949	40,899	17.70		39,736	1,163
Shortening							
Lard[b]	2,425	128	2,553	1,200,967	420.60	2,553	
Total	2,425	128	2,553	1.20		2,553	
Grand total	119,906	147,261	267,167	179.12		197,465	69,702

[a]Commodity cost only—excludes transportation costs. Total cost is million dollars.
[b]95 percent to needy families, 5 percent to schools and institutions. Canned meat is considered 85 percent pork and 15 percent beef.

Table 10–6.   Major Data, Four Runs, Fiscal Year 1973

No.	Commodity	Forecasted Farm Price	Normal Farm Price	Parity Farm Price	Wholesale Price	Solutions I and II		Solutions III and IV	
						Lot Size	Maximum Purchase	Lot Size	Maximum Purchase
		($/ton)				(tons)			
1	Beef (frozen)	780.00	597.20	828.00	1400.00	100.	1	200	48000
2	Beef (canned)	601.03	405.20	560.00	1600.00	100.	1	200	48000
3	Pork (frozen)	580.00	438.66	634.00	1399.00	100.	8932	200.	48000
4	Chicken (RTC)	310.00	276.00	477.00	717.03	100.	47124	200.	48000
5	Chicken (canned)	252.39	173.20	291.00	1612.02	100.	22148	200.	48000
6	Turkey (RTC)	606.80	452.00	724.00	722.02	100.	29050	200.	48000
7	Egg mix	553.00	445.33	772.00	1990.23	100.	717	200.	48000
8	Corn (canned)	30.85	24.03	38.70	212.18	100.	10272	200.	48000
9	Snap beans	125.55	97.73	184.00	311.02	100.	391	200.	48000
10	Peas (canned)	133.92	109.33	171.00	255.63	100.	4682	200.	48000
11	Potatoes (frozen)	78.43	44.54	70.20	253.28	100.	12480	200.	48000
12	Tomatoes (canned)	42.09	34.90	58.20	257.28	100.	21567	200.	48000
13	Sweet potatoes	147.71	127.05	168.10	290.08	100.	814	200.	48000
14	Beans (northern)	204.30	175.86	260.00	240.00	100.	1	200.	48000
15	Beans (pea)	210.14	196.80	200.00	245.60	100.	970	200.	48000
16	Beans (pinto)	193.22	177.80	260.00	240.00	100.	39301	200.	48000
17	Applesauce	61.26	45.13	76.60	225.09	100.	8542	200.	48000
18	Peaches (canned)	84.80	77.73	109.00	274.40	100.	18426	200.	48000
19	Pears (canned)	130.29	108.03	190.00	364.24	100.	7369	200.	48000
20	O.J. (frozen)	35.60	37.40	79.00	1224.86	100.	6563	200.	48000
21	Raisins	513.16	363.33	407.00	800.00	100.	1	200.	48000
22	Prunes (dried)	368.01	272.00	437.00	300.00	100.	1	200.	48000
23	Shortening	447.37	238.80	342.21	632.00	100.	1	200.	48000
24	Lard	274.39	218.26	322.72	470.60	100.	2553	200.	48000
25	Pork (canned)	661.20	500.07	652.00	1600.00	100.	1	200.	48000
26	Canned meat	583.15	433.64	433.64	1175.00	100.	11556	200.	48000
27	Turkey (canned)	1189.33	885.92	712.00	1465.58	100.	13712	200.	48000

Table 10–7. Expenditure and Impact, Four Solutions, Fiscal Year 1973

	Solution			
	I	*II*	*III*	*IV*
(million dollars)				
Funds available	215.0	215.0	215.0	215.0
Funds used	179.2	104.2	215.0	215.0
Excess funds	35.8	110.8	0.0	0.0
Purchase impact	1254.8	364.4	611.5	552.2
$Impact/$expenditure	7.00	3.50	2.84	2.57

formulation ignores all of the constraints and conditions and indicates the impact of the reported purchases. Results for individual commodities are shown in Tables 10–9 and 10–10.

The most striking elements of the results from Solution I revolve around some rather large impact-level price changes and the income impact/ expenditure ratio. The largest impact level price change was for pinto beans at 41.9 percent (Table 10–10). This price change is the result of two forces: The purchase of 17.5 percent of the total supply of pinto beans and the cross price effects of other purchases. The direct price flexibility of pinto beans was 2.19, which, when combined with the 17.5 percent of supply purchased, accounts for a 38.4 percent change in price, leaving 3.5 percent due to purchase of other commodities.[4] This induced price change may be compared with the price change for steers and heifers (beef, frozen) and cows (beef, canned). The changes in price for these two commodities were, respectively, 4.3 and 15 percent. The price change for frozen beef was indirect, while the change in price of canned beef was due primarily to purchase of canned meat.

The second Solution retains the maximum allowed purchases used in the first Solution but sets minimum or required quantities at the levels reported as purchases using FNS funds. This change in required purchases allows more

Table 10–8. Percent Distribution of Expenditures, Four Solutions, Fiscal Year 1973

Food Group	Solution			
	I	*II*	*III*	*IV*
	(%)	*(%)*	*(%)*	*(%)*
Meat/products	14.56	12.00	5.82	0.0
Poultry/products	62.54	55.47	44.12	47.80
Vegetables	6.95	9.63	10.30	10.44
Dry beans	5.40	4.82	2.93	3.16
Fruit/juice	9.08	16.95	35.30	36.33
Dry fruit	0.0	0.0	0.0	0.74
Lard/shortening	0.67	1.13	1.53	1.53

Table 10-9.   Required, Discretionary, and Total Purchases: Four Solutions for Fiscal Year 1973 Commodity Removal (purchase level)

(thousand tons)

Commodity	Required Purchases				Discretionary Purchases			
	I	II	III	IV	I	II	III	IV
Beef (frozen)								
Beef (canned)								
Pork (frozen)	8.932	8.932	8.932	8.932				
Pork (canned)								
Canned meat	11.566							
Subtotal	20.498	8.932	8.932	8.932				
Chicken (RTC)	47.124	47.124	47.124				0.800	48.000
Chicken (canned)	22.148					1.000	8.800	20.200
Turkey (RTC)	29.050	0.525	0.525			28.500		
Turkey (canned)	13.712					0.700	27.000	27.000
Egg mix	0.717							
Subtotal	112.751	47.649	47.649			30.200	36.600	95.200
Corn (canned)	10.272	7.113	7.113			3.100	6.400	0.200
Snap beans	0.391					0.300		9.400
Peas (canned)	4.682	0.851	0.851			3.800	15.000	22.000
Potatoes (frozen)	12.480	3.180	3.180				48.000	48.000
Tomatoes (canned)	21.567					21.500		5.000
Sweet potatoes	0.814	0.814	0.814				4.000	
Subtotal	50.206	11.958	11.958			28.700	73.400	84.600
Beans (northern)	0.970						2.000	2.000
Beans (pea)	39.301					0.900	11.000	12.000
Beans (pinto)						20.000	13.000	14.000
Subtotal	40.271					20.900	26.000	28.000
Applesauce	8.542					8.500	48.000	48.000
Peaches (canned)	18.426					18.400	25.000	31.000
Pears (canned)	7.369					7.300	42.600	43.800
Orange juice (frozen)	6.563	1.163	1.163			5.400		
Subtotal	40.900	1.163	1.163			39.600	115.600	122.800
Raisins								
Prunes (dry)								2.000
Subtotal								2.000
Shortening								
Lard	2.553					2.500	7.000	7.000
Subtotal	2.553					2.500	7.000	7.000

	Total Purchases (thousand tons)				Percent of Expenditures (percent)			
	I	II	III	IV	I	II	III	IV
Beef (frozen)	8.932	8.932	8.932			12.00	5.82	
Beef (canned)								
Pork (frozen)								
Pork (canned)	11.566				6.97			
Canned meat				48.000	7.58			
Subtotal	20.498	8.932	8.932	48.000	14.55	12.00	5.82	
Chicken (RTC)	47.124	47.124	47.924	48.000	18.86	32.44	15.99	16.01
Chicken (canned)	22.148	1.000			19.94	1.54		
Turkey (RTC)	29.050	29.025	9.325	20.200	11.72	20.14	3.14	6.79
Turkey (canned)	13.712				11.21			
Egg mix	.717	.700	27.000	27.000	.79	1.33	24.99	24.99
Subtotal	112.751	77.849	84.249	95.200	62.50	55.47	44.12	47.80
Corn (canned)	10.272	10.213	7.113	.200	1.21	2.08	.70	.02
Snap beans	.391	.300	6.400	9.400	.06	.09	.93	1.36
Peas (canned)	4.682	4.651	15.851	22.000	.66	1.14	1.89	2.61
Potatoes (frozen)	12.480	3.180	3.180		1.76	.77	.37	
Tomatoes (canned)	21.567	21.500	48.000	48.000	3.09	5.31	5.75	5.74
Sweet potatoes	.814	.814	4.814	5.000	.13	.23	.67	.69
Subtotal	50.206	40.658	85.358	84.600	6.95	9.63	10.30	10.44
Beans (northern)	.970	.900	2.000	2.000	.13	.21	.22	.22
Beans (pea)		20.000	11.000	12.000		4.61	1.26	1.37
Beans (pinto)	39.301		13.000	14.000	5.26		1.45	1.56
Subtotal	40.271	20.900	26.000	28.000	5.39	4.82	2.93	3.16
Applesauce	8.542	8.500	48.000	48.000	1.07	1.84	6.13	6.13
Peaches (canned)	18.426	18.400	25.000	31.000	2.82	4.85	4.24	5.25
Pears (canned)	7.369	7.300	43.763	43.800	1.49	2.55	24.94	24.95
Orange juice (frozen)	6.563	6.563			4.48	7.72		
Subtotal	40.900	40.763	116.763	122.800	9.08	16.95	35.30	36.33
Raisins								
Prunes (dry)				2.000				.74
Subtotal				2.000				.74
Shortening								
Lard	2.553	2.500	7.000	7.000	.67	1.13	1.53	1.53
Subtotal	2.553	2.500	7.000	7.000	.67	1.13	1.53	1.53

Table 10-10. Prices, Percent Price Changes, Percent of Supply Taken and Purchase Impact for Fiscal Year 1973 Commodity Removal (impact level)

Commodity	Initial Price	Maximum Allowed Change	Percent Change				Percent of Supply Taken			
			I	II	III	IV	I	II	III	IV
	($/ton)		(percent)				(percent)			
Beef (frozen)	78.00	—	4.32	0.92	0.80	0.62				
Beef (canned)	601.03	—	14.97	3.20	3.15	2.50				
Pork (frozen)	580.00	—	6.40	1.89	1.89	0.82	0.22			
Subtotal							0.49	0.23	0.23	
Chicken (RTC)	310.00	38.48	16.42	4.37	3.78	3.62	1.68	1.68	1.71	1.71
Chicken (canned)	252.39	3.77	25.28	4.08	3.09	2.89	11.31	0.51		
Turkey (RTC)	606.80	7.38	12.33	4.04	1.98	2.85	6.60	3.42	1.10	2.38
Egg	553.00	25.64	2.16	.82	7.76	7.72	0.04	0.04	1.39	1.39
Subtotal							0.15			
Corn (canned)	30.85	12.90	18.66	12.37	15.27	12.01	1.21	1.21	0.83	0.02
Snap beans	125.55	17.56	3.33	1.50	5.76	6.86	0.04	0.03	0.64	0.94
Peas (canned)	133.92	14.92	7.42	4.73	10.49	12.19	0.62	0.62	2.10	2.92
Potatoes (frozen)	78.43	—	3.48	1.00	1.92	1.33	0.26	0.07	0.06	
Tomatoes (canned)	42.09	24.45	3.56	2.62	6.19	6.53	0.50	0.50	1.10	1.10
Sweet potatoes	147.71	2.42	2.35	0.96	3.53	3.43	0.15	0.15	0.88	0.91
Subtotal										
Beans (northern)	204.30	14.54	13.97	7.67	17.17	17.49			3.11	3.11
Beans (pea)	210.14	11.35	15.08	8.39	19.30	20.12	0.34	0.32	3.89	4.25
Beans (pinto)	193.22	21.11	41.86	21.93	22.29	23.23	17.54	8.91	5.80	6.25
Subtotal										
Applesauce	61.26	12.54	2.53	1.88	4.81	4.81	0.38	0.38	3.27	3.27
Peaches (canned)	84.80	15.68	4.23	4.02	11.58	12.37	1.26	1.25	3.45	4.28
Pears (canned)	130.29	31.25	4.29	3.85	12.08	13.86	1.02	1.01	4.31	4.32
Orange juice (frozen)	35.60	99.72	3.07	2.50	12.60	12.55	0.65	0.65		
Subtotal										
Raisins	513.16	—								
Prunes (dry)	368.01	6.87				1.98				1.25
Subtotal										1.25
Shortening	447.37	—	2.23	0.94	2.30	2.26	0.33	0.33	0.91	
Lard	274.39	5.85	4.38	2.38	6.19	6.07				
Subtotal							0.33	0.33	0.91	0.91
Total										

| | Purchase Impact | | | |
	I	II	III	IV
		(Million Dollars)			
Beef (frozen)	316.203	67.308	58.403	46.669
Beef (canned)	168.944	36.173	35.565	29.216
Pork (frozen)	245.680	72.805	72.618	31.564
Subtotal	730.827	176.286	166.586	107.449
Chicken (RTC)	197.002	52.491	45.291	43.386
Chicken (canned)	36.382	6.185	4.710	4.409
Turkey (RTC)	77.035	25.644	12.703	18.223
Egg	51.708	19.571	184.875	183.839
Subtotal	362.127	103.891	247.579	249.857
Corn (canned)	12.630	8.374	10.350	8.176
Snap beans	2.859	1.286	4.927	5.862
Peas (canned)	5.407	3.449	7.589	8.779
Potatoes (frozen)	32.542	9.368	17.949	12.468
Tomatoes (canned)	10.139	7.461	17.586	18.555
Sweet potatoes	2.168	.883	3.246	3.159
Subtotal	65.745	30.821	61.647	56.999
Beans (northern)	1.837	1.009	2.224	2.265
Beans (pea)	8.926	4.972	11.225	11.682
Beans (pinto)	16.537	9.073	9.375	9.746
Subtotal	27.300	15.054	22.824	23.693
Applesauce	4.509	3.357	8.581	8.589
Peaches (canned)	4.374	4.153	11.849	12.664
Pears (canned)	4.021	3.616	11.197	12.796
Orange juice (frozen)	6.695	5.453	26.972	26.867
Subtotal	19.599	16.579	58.599	60.916
Raisins	–	–	–	–
Prunes (dry)	–	–	–	1.159
Subtotal	–	–	–	1.159
Shortening	39.913	16.792	41.216	40.362
Lard	9.249	5.026	13.023	12.765
Subtotal	49.162	21.818	54.239	53.127
Total	1,254.769	364.448	611.474	552.202

constraints to become operative. The result is elimination of purchases of canned meat and canned turkey and a reduction in quantities of canned chicken, frozen potatoes, and pinto beans. Purchase of these commodities continued until they were no longer eligible for purchase. All other commodities were purchased at maximum levels, subject to the lot size constraint. The reduction in purchases naturally resulted in lower total expenditures for the second Solution. The total expenditure was $104.2 million with a purchase impact of $364.4 million. This difference in purchase impact is primarily due to the reduced purchase of red meats.

The effects of relaxing maximum purchase restrictions and required purchase quantities are shown in Solutions III and IV. Solution III maintains minimum purchase requirements at the same levels used for Solution II but sets the maximum purchase at 48,000 tons and lot size for each commodity at 200 tons. For Solution IV the required purchases are set at zero. This increased flexibility permits the purchase of commodities until all funds are used, or until no price is below its eligibility limit. In both Solutions III and IV prices of some commodities were sufficiently below the eligibility limit to allow either maximum purchase of 48,000 tons or expenditure of the 25 percent limit on a given commodity. The four Solutions exhibit a positive correlation between the number of effective constraints and impact/expenditure ratio.

Regional Distribution of Income Impacts. An item of frequent interest to program administrators is the distribution of the purchase impact to various regions in the U.S., as shown in Table 10-11. The income impact generated by the model for each Solution and commodity was used in conjunction with income distribution data from the 1964 Census of Agriculture to impute a regional distribution of the removal impacts.

Table 10-11. Distribution of Purchase Impact, Six Regions, Fiscal Year 1973

Region*	Solution					Solution		
	(million Dollars)					*(percent)*		
1	71.5	22.8	58.2	53.5	5.7	6.2	9.5	9.8
2	170.1	55.6	96.1	83.4	13.5	15.3	15.7	15.1
3	362.9	97.3	114.9	88.3	28.9	26.7	18.8	16.0
4	171.6	53.0	110.6	106.4	13.7	14.6	18.1	19.3
5	266.7	69.9	111.1	102.7	21.3	19.2	18.2	18.6
6	211.9	65.9	120.5	117.5	16.9	18.0	19.7	21.3

*Regions are defined as follows: (1) Minnesota, Iowa, Missouri, North Dakota, South Dakota, Nebraska, Kansas; (2) Ohio, Indiana, Illinois, Michigan, Wisconsin; (3) Montana, Idaho, Wyoming, Colorado, New Mexico, Arizona, Utah, Nevada, Washington, Oregon, California, Alaska, Hawaii; (4) Kentucky, Tennessee, Alabama, Mississippi, Arkansas, Louisiana, Oklahoma, Texas; (5) Delaware, Maryland, Virginia, West Virginia, North Carolina, South Carolina, Georgia, Florida; and (6) New England, New York, New Jersey, Pennsylvania.

The results from Solution I, which indicate benefits due to actual operation of the commodity removal program, indicate that Region 3 (Western States) received the greatest benefit at 362.9 million dollars added income. This amounts to nearly 29 percent of all benefits and is due primarily to the location of animal production in that region. As the restrictions are relaxed so that the program constraints become effective, the percentage distribution of impact benefits assumes a more even character.

CONCLUSION

The foregoing discussion describes a model developed as a decision aid for use in planning decisions related to surplus commodity removal. Essentially the model is constructed to develop and evaluate the impact of a set of alternative purchase strategies from which a choice can be made, where the alternative strategies take into account the various program objectives and constraints. The model is also designed to permit interaction between the model and the decisionmaker.

Several planning and decision strategies have been examined in this paper in the operation of a surplus commodity removal and purchase program. The strategies discussed emphasize situations where commodity surpluses exist and where the primary objective of the purchase program is to enhance producer prices and income. Of equal interest at times is the determination of purchase strategies where commodity shortages prevail and food assistance programs are still maintained. In such a situation, the objective of the program can switch to one of minimizing price impacts for required purchases. While this concern was not highlighted in the chapter, information summarized in Tables 10-7 to 10-10 is of value in considering either the objectives of minimum price impact or maximum price impact.

APPENDIX 10A

Table 10A-1.   Price Transmission Elasticities for Included Commodities

Commodity	Elasticity of Price Transmission	Conversion Factor*
Beef (frozen)	0.64691	2.382
Beef (canned)	0.86362	2.382
Pork (frozen)	0.58322	1.727
Pork (canned) Canned meat	⎫ See Table 10A-2	
Chicken (RTC)	0.77489	1.389
Chicken (canned)	0.54200	3.086
Turkey (RTC)	0.87839	1.256
Turkey (canned)	⎫ See Table 10A-2	
Egg mix	0.40443	2.234
Corn (canned)	0.96060	2.604
Snap beans	0.91891	0.687
Peas (canned)	0.97955	0.725
Potatoes (frozen)	0.48479	2.500
Tomatoes (canned)	0.82791	1.561
Sweet Potatoes	0.95368	1.144
Beans (northern)	1.0	1.000
Beans (pea)	1.0	1.000
Beans (pinto)	1.0	1.000
Applesauce	0.88492	1.292
Peaches (canned)	0.63248	0.836
Pears (canned)	0.65245	1.000
Orange Juice (frozen)	1.14453	6.060
Raisins	1.0	1.000
Prunes (dry)	1.0	1.000
Shortening	0.50289	1.040
Lard	0.65388	1.000

*Tons of purchase level commodity to tons impact level commodity.

Table 10A-2.   Quantity Conversion and Price Transmission Coefficients for Special Commodities

Purchase Commodity	Impact Level Commodity		Factor to Convert Purchase Level Commodity To Impact Level Commodity		Price Transmission from Impact Level Commodity to Purchase Level Commodity	
	C_1	C_2	F_1	F_2	B_1	B_2
Pork (canned)	Hogs	—	1.14	—	0.44304	—
Canned meat	Cows	Hogs	0.15	0.85	0.35826	0.30598
Canned turkey	Turkey	—	1.961	—	0.6790	—

Table 10A-3. Price Flexibilities—Retail (percent change in price for each one percent change in quantity)

| Commodity | | 1 | 25 | 2 | 3 | 26 | 4 | 5 | 6 | 7 | 8 |
Number	Description	Beef (frozen)	Beef (canned)	Pork (frozen)	Chicken (RTC)	Chicken (canned)	Turkey (RTC)	Egg Mix	Corn (canned)	Snap Beans	Peas (canned)
1	Beef (frozen)	-1.74608	-0.63415	-0.52649	-0.20921	-0.14633	-0.02245	-0.01023	-0.00253	-0.00192	-0.00166
25	Beef (canned)	-1.65877	-2.33097	-1.65877	-0.72763	-0.50894	-0.07164	-0.11870	-0.03642	-0.02325	-0.03391
2	Pork (frozen)	-0.49670	-0.66308	-2.77769	-0.21494	-0.15034	-0.02478	-0.02805	-0.00694	-0.00527	-0.00453
3	Chicken (RTC)	-0.62628	-0.63415	-0.71297	-1.44683	-0.56505	-0.08476	-0.01904	-0.00470	-0.00358	-0.00308
26	Chicken (canned)	-0.96349	-0.39823	-0.96138	-0.96138	-1.01198	-0.12495	-0.06021	-0.01851	-0.01181	-0.01720
4	Turkey (RTC)	-0.29831	-0.24730	-0.34163	-0.39721	-0.27783	-0.66753	-0.00837	-0.00207	-0.00158	-0.00136
5	Egg Mix	-0.05614	-0.32146	-0.17617	-0.03453	-0.05018	-0.00314	-1.89113	-0.05155	-0.03340	-0.04996
6	Corn (canned)	-0.24080	-0.29095	-0.36008	-0.09345	-0.06537	-0.01745	-0.21838	-4.40385	-0.11297	-0.63415
7	Snap beans	-0.21794	-0.23945	-0.32536	-0.08454	-0.05913	-0.01597	-0.20065	-0.08960	-4.06317	0.09831
8	Peas (canned)	-0.17937	-0.17852	-0.26522	-0.06946	-0.04859	-0.01339	-0.16936	-0.55547	-0.12820	-2.58654
9	Potatoes (frozen)	-0.13373	-0.13841	-0.21838	-0.05101	-0.03568	-0.00933	-0.13307	-0.01138	-0.00865	-0.00742
10	Tomatoes (canned)	-0.10368	-0.22262	-0.14815	-0.03990	-0.02791	-0.00837	-0.10822	-0.09483	-0.26968	-0.43383
11	Sweet potatoes	-0.16676	-0.10856	-0.24930	-0.06192	-0.04331	-0.01199	-0.18271	-0.01650	-0.01254	-0.01075
22	Beans (northern)	-0.08132	-0.15152	-0.25834	-0.05039	-0.03525	-0.00456	-0.24280	-0.63415	-0.08562	-0.63415
23	Beans (pea)	-0.11385	-0.15198	-0.36168	-0.07055	-0.04935	-0.00638	-0.33992	-0.63415	-0.11986	-0.63415
24	Beans (pinto)	-0.11385	-0.15198	-0.36168	-0.07055	-0.04935	-0.00638	-0.33992	-0.63415	-0.11986	-0.63415
12	Applesauce	-0.06787	-0.09581	-0.21470	-0.04195	-0.01912	-0.00381	-0.21284	-0.04396	-0.02844	-0.04158
13	Peaches (canned)	-0.02549	-0.03403	-0.02709	-0.00926	-0.00647	-0.00307	-0.04577	-0.01115	-0.00848	-0.00727
21	Pears (canned)	-0.03014	-0.04024	-0.09723	-0.01891	-0.01323	-0.00169	-0.09717	-0.02844	-0.01854	-0.02725
14	O.J. (frozen)	-0.05548	-0.07374	-0.17733	-0.03456	-0.01456	-0.00312	-0.17659	-0.05640	-0.3667	-0.05476
19	Raisins	-0.02212	-0.02952	-0.07112	-0.01385	-0.00969	-0.00124	-0.05089	-0.01545	-0.01057	-0.01268
20	Prunes (dry)	-0.02212	-0.02952	-0.07112	-0.01385	-0.00969	-0.00124	-0.05089	-0.01545	-0.01057	-0.01268
15	Shortening	-0.15946	-0.21287	-0.23442	-0.06170	-0.04316	-0.01219	-0.15231	-0.05064	-0.03851	-0.03298
16	Lard	-0.26349	-0.35175	-0.39530	-0.10239	-0.07162	-0.01908	-0.23217	-0.04843	-0.03681	-0.03154

Table 10A–3 continued

Number	Commodity Description	9 Potatoes (frozen)	10 Tomatoes (canned)	11 Sweet Potatoes	22 Beans (northern)	23 Beans (pea)	24 Beans (pinto)	12 Apple-sauce	13 Peaches (canned)	21 Pears (canned)	14 O. Juice (frozen)
1	Beef (frozen)	−0.00461	−0.00165	−0.00086	−0.00108	−0.00108	−0.00108	−0.00258	−0.00111	−0.00114	−0.00632
25	Beef (canned)	−0.04990	−0.01176	−0.00888	−0.00380	−0.00380	−0.00380	−0.00958	−0.00482	−0.00402	−0.02212
2	Pork (frozen)	−0.01262	−0.00458	−0.00237	−0.00300	−0.00300	−0.00300	−0.00712	−0.00313	−0.00322	−0.01765
3	Chicken (RTC)	−0.00856	−0.00310	−0.00160	−0.00203	−0.00203	−0.00203	−0.00482	−0.00211	−0.00217	−0.01191
26	Chicken (canned)	−0.02493	−0.00593	−0.00432	−0.00308	−0.00308	−0.00308	−0.00478	−0.00229	−0.00331	−0.01092
4	Turkey (RTC)	−0.00378	−0.00136	−0.00071	−0.00089	−0.00089	−0.00089	−0.00212	−0.00091	−0.00094	−0.00520
5	Egg Mix	−0.07748	−0.01916	−0.01519	−0.01770	−0.01770	−0.01770	−0.04434	−0.01350	−0.02024	−0.11037
6	Corn (canned)	−0.04015	−0.10975	−0.00735	−0.57611	−0.57611	−0.57611	−0.03880	−0.02434	−0.02510	−0.14933
7	Snap beans	−0.03820	−0.53063	−0.00686	−0.03750	−0.03750	−0.03750	−0.03560	−0.02250	−0.02321	−0.13769
8	Peas (canned)	−0.02916	−0.36498	−0.00532	−0.17397	−0.17397	−0.17397	−0.02937	−0.01866	−0.01925	−0.11602
9	Potatoes (frozen)	−3.85790	−0.00753	−0.44531	−0.00494	−0.00494	−0.00494	−0.01180	−0.00517	−0.00533	−0.02975
10	Tomatoes (canned)	−0.01538	−2.73213	−0.00278	−0.02808	−0.02808	−0.02808	−0.01794	−0.01208	−0.01247	−0.07495
11	Sweet potatoes	−0.63415	−0.01093	−2.28261	−0.00716	−0.00716	−0.00716	−0.01711	−0.00751	−0.00775	−0.04320
22	Beans (northern)	−0.03943	−0.06819	−0.00817	−0.63415	−0.63415	−0.63415	−0.03926	−0.01959	−0.02780	−0.16740
23	Beans (pea)	−0.05520	−0.09547	−0.01144	−2.19205	−2.19205	−0.63415	−0.05496	−0.02743	−0.03893	−0.23436
24	Beans (pinto)	−0.05520	−0.09547	−0.01144	−0.63415	−0.63415	−2.19205	−0.05496	−0.02743	−0.03893	−0.23436
12	Applesauce	−0.03297	−0.01525	−0.00683	−0.01374	−0.01374	−0.01374	−1.56768	−0.14142	−0.06645	−0.63415
13	Peaches (canned)	−0.00113	−0.00740	−0.00016	−0.00484	−0.00484	−0.00484	−0.09987	−1.39247	−0.63415	−0.18777
21	Pears (canned)	−0.01490	−0.01060	−0.00309	−0.00973	−0.00973	−0.00973	−0.06645	−0.63415	−1.43644	−0.13394
14	O.J. (frozen)	−0.02772	−0.02123	−0.00575	−0.01953	−0.01953	−0.01953	−0.36342	−0.08863	−0.04465	−2.80000
19	Raisins	−0.01089	−0.00549	−0.00226	−0.00506	−0.00506	−0.00506	−0.11505	−0.24903	−0.25689	−0.10769
20	Prunes (dry)	−0.01089	−0.00549	−0.00226	−0.00506	−0.00506	−0.00506	−0.11505	−0.24903	−0.25689	−0.10769
15	Shortening	−0.09201	−0.03366	−0.01721	−0.02204	−0.02204	−0.02204	−0.05271	−0.02318	−0.02391	−0.13383
16	Lard	−0.08800	−0.03217	−0.01647	−0.02107	−0.02107	−0.02107	−0.05032	−0.02215	−0.02285	−0.12735

Table 10A-3 continued

Commodity		19 Raisins	20 Prunes (dry)	15 Short- ening	16 Lard
Number	Description				
1	Beef (frozen)	−0.00071	−0.00071	−0.00578	−0.00177
25	Beef (canned)	−0.00251	−0.00251	−0.06669	−0.02395
2	Pork (frozen)	−0.00201	−0.00201	−0.01580	−0.00488
3	Chicken (RTC)	−0.00135	−0.00135	−0.01073	−0.00331
26	Chicken (canned)	−0.00206	−0.00206	−0.03380	−0.01219
4	Turkey (RTC)	−0.00059	−0.00059	−0.00477	−0.00146
5	Egg Mix	−0.00901	−0.00901	−0.09941	−0.03294
6	Corn (canned)	−0.01159	−0.01159	−0.16135	−0.03155
7	Snap beans	−0.01124	−0.01124	−0.14914	−0.02894
8	Peas (canned)	−0.00761	−0.00761	−0.12648	−0.02416
9	Potatoes (frozen)	−0.00331	−0.00331	−0.10059	−0.01870
10	Tomatoes (canned)	−0.00549	−0.00549	−0.08337	−0.01507
11	Sweet potatoes	−0.00481	−0.00481	−0.13634	−0.02587
22	Beans (northern)	−0.01230	−0.01230	−0.19726	−0.04100
23	Beans (pea)	−0.01722	−0.01722	−0.27617	−0.05740
24	Beans (pinto)	−0.01722	−0.01722	−0.27617	−0.05740
12	Applesauce	−0.09779	−0.09779	−0.16514	−0.03427
13	Peaches (canned)	−0.14949	−0.14949	−0.03885	−0.00576
21	Pears (canned)	−0.21836	−0.21836	−0.07492	−0.01556
14	O.J. (frozen)	−0.03051	−0.03051	−0.13977	−0.02891
19	Raisins	−1.58514	−0.63415	−0.05468	−0.01136
20	Prunes (dry)	−0.63415	−1.58514	−0.05468	−0.01136
15	Shortening	−0.01483	−0.01483	−1.19232	−0.20080
16	Lard	−0.01418	−0.01418	−0.63415	−2.70894

Note: Developed from George and King [1].

NOTES

1. Primary developmental work on the prototype model was done by Richard Haynes and reported by Haidacher, Haynes, Culver, and Matthews in [2].
2. Funds are obtained from custom receipts on imports. The amount available for use under Section 32 is equal to 30 percent of such duties, collected during the preceding calendar year, plus unused balances of up to 300 million dollars. Funds actually obligated and expended on commodities depends on the market situation, volume of surpluses, and availability of potential outlets.

   The original legislation and subsequent amendments give authorization and responsibility to the Secretary of Agriculture and the Department of Agriculture for the various programs and activities. Responsibility for carrying out the programs and coordinating the various activities, however, has been delegated to the Agricultural Marketing Service of the Department and its Administrator.
3. Responsibility for the various food distribution programs is delegated to the Food and Nutrition Service (FNS) of the Department.

4. The price flexibilities and price transmission elasticities are given in the Appendix 10A tables. It should be noted that the procedure used to derive the flexibilities assumes consumers are at an equilibrium point and that the flexibilities remain constant in the neighborhood of that point. Thus, when large relative quantity changes occur for a given commodity, one needs to take account of this assumption in interpreting the results.

REFERENCES

1. George, P.S., and G.A. King. "Consumer Demand for Food Commodities in the United States with Projections for 1980." Giannini Found. Monog. 26, Calif. Agr. Exp. Sta., March 1971.
2. Haidacher, R.C. et al. "A Planning-Decision Model for Surplus Commodity Removal Programs." *Agricultural Economics Research* 26(1) (January 1974): 1.
3. Houck, J.P. "A Look at Price Flexibilities and Elasticities." *J. Farm Econ.* 48(1) (1966): 225–32.
4. Hildreth, C., and E.G. Jarrett. *A Statistical Study of Livestock Production and Marketing.* New York: John Wiley and Sons, Inc., 1955.
5. Naylor, Thomas H. *Computer Simulation Experiments with Models of Economic Systems.* New York: John Wiley and Sons, Inc., 1971.
6. U.S. Senate, "Department of Agriculture–Environmental and Consumer Protection Appropriation Bill, 1974." 93d Cong., 1st Sess., Rep. 93–253, Calendar No. 239.

Chapter Eleven

A World Model of Living Marine Resources

Frederick W. Bell
Darrel A. Nash
Ernest W. Carlson
Frederick V. Waugh
Richard K. Kinoshita
Richard F. Fullenbaum

In an industry based upon a relatively fixed (but renewable) resource, it is especially urgent that we be able to predict the economic impact of demand pressures on that resource. Many important public policy questions arise: Will there be enough of the resource to satisfy human needs? Will prices rise substantially? Are we about to overexploit our resources?

The world fishery resource is not only relatively fixed, but is common property in nature.[1] When no one owns scarce fishery resources, government regulations are often necessary to prevent wasteful exploitation, or overfishing. This is an additional reason to project the future course of demand so that overfishing may be avoided. Finally, demand and supply projections serve as a useful input into a broad range of policy foundation regarding fishery resources.

One aspect of world fishery consumption since World War II has been its propensity to increase at a greater rate and, for some periods, at a considerably greater rate than the increase in world population.[2] [4] Between 1958 and 1965, world fishery consumption (or utilization) increased at an annual rate of 7.0 percent per year. Over this same period, the consumption of no other basic food commodity increased at anything approaching this rate, and the rate of increase in human population was of the order of 2.0 percent per annum.

The world is presently consuming approximately 62 percent of maximum sustainable yield (*MSY*) for finfish. Shellfish is consumed at 23 percent of its potential yield. However, there are wide variations as to the extent of utilization of the stocks within these categories. Many of the stocks are fully utilized and have already attracted excess capital and labor.

The authors are respectively: Professor of Economics, Florida State University; Economist, Atomic Energy Commission; Economist, Office of Management and Budget (Executive Office of the President); Professor of Agricultural Economics, University of Maryland; Economist, National Marine Fisheries Service; and Economist, Office of Management and Budget (Executive Office of the President). The contents represent the opinions of the authors and in no way reflect the policy position of the affiliated organizations cited above.

291

The situation is likely to get worse if free access to the resource is allowed to persist. The rising world demand will contribute to the problem. The principal factor influencing further exploitation of the fishery resources is market demand, the main determinants of which are the growth in population and income (assuming tastes and preferences constant). This is true both for fishmeal as well as fish used directly as human food. The demand for fishmeal is derived indirectly through demand for poultry products, which depends in turn upon the growth of population and income.

For the above reasons, we have constructed a "bioeconomic model" to determine more about future impact of world population and income upon the available supplies of fish. This model is essentially a set of relationships describing the main biological and economic forces that determine the maximum sustainable supply of fish from the ocean, the amounts caught and consumed, the prices, the costs of production, and consumer income and population. Its contribution to commodity modeling methodology is that it integrates relevant biological and utilization factors into a single system structure.

CATCH AND UTILIZATION OF FISHERY PRODUCTS IN THE UNITED STATES AND THE WORLD 1950-1967[3]

When catch and consumption of fishery products were compared on a value basis, rather than the traditional volume basis, some very important factors were revealed. There were 16 countries in 1967 which caught over $100 million worth of fish and shellfish. The U.S. was third, ranked at $440 million, behind Japan with $2 billion and the U.S.S.R. with $1 billion. On this basis, Peru ranked thirteenth in 1967.

After World War II many countries made substantial percentage increases in fish and shellfish catch. However, in terms of absolute volume there were three countries which recorded phenomenal increases in fish catch. These were Peru, which increased catch from almost zero to 4 billion pounds; the U.S.S.R., where catch almost tripled; and Japan, where it doubled between 1950 and 1967. The U.S.S.R. and Japan are perhaps most important to the U.S. because of the increase in catch of high-valued species in areas traditionally fished by U.S. fishermen. As an example, groundfish catch by the U.S.S.R. tripled during this time, while Japan's catch of groundfish doubled (primarily Alaskan pollock). Japan and the U.S. made substantial gains in the catch of tuna. Also, the crab catch made by the U.S. was up 250 percent, while both Japan and the U.S. made notable increases in the catch of clams. Surprisingly, the U.S. ranked first in production of all shellfish except lobsters; it was second in the catch of tuna, salmon, and halibut. Thus, out of 12 species considered, the U.S. was first in five and second in three others.

On the consumption side, the U.S. is even more important because

Americans are the leading consumers of 10 of the 12 species considered. It is common to assume that fish consumption per person in the U.S. is remaining quite static over time. However, the species mix has been extremely changeable during the postwar period. The per capita consumption of crabs, tuna, fishmeal, shrimp, clams, lobsters, groundfish, and scallops has increased at the rate of more than 2 percent per year since 1950. Counterbalancing this has been the decrease in per capita consumption of halibut, oysters, sardines, and salmon.

With these dynamic changes in catch and consumption levels, the question immediately arises as to what the maximum potential production from the oceans is in order to fulfill the future increases in consumption of fish products. For some of our popularly consumed species, i.e., groundfish, salmon, and halibut, the catch is now near *MSY*. Salmon may be an exception if hatchery programs are fully developed to supplement the existing supply. In addition, tuna, crabs, lobsters, and shrimp are experiencing a rapid growth in catch, thus hastening the day when they too will be nearly fully utilized. Within these major groups there are species which are being fished at or beyond *MSY* in certain fishing grounds. The ratio of present landings of commonly consumed species of fish and shellfish to potential yield, assuming a world *MSY* of 120 million metric tons, is 62 percent.

It should be clearly pointed out that there is no consensus among scientists with respect to estimates of *MSY*. As a result, there may be a great deal of disagreement for any given estimate. The figure of 120 million presents a somewhat middle ground of various expert judgments as to the level of total *MSY*. Further biological research, which will ultimately reduce the range of estimates, is now being undertaken by the National Marine Fisheries Service. However, the authors assume sole responsibility for the figures used; the numbers in no way should be construed as official estimates of the *NMFS*.

DEMAND RELATIONSHIPS FOR
FISHERY PRODUCTS

The primary interest in this study is to project fish consumption and prices by species for the United States. In order to accomplish this, however, we must take the rest of the world into account. The analysis showed that the demand for some fish products will be increasing more rapidly in other countries than in the U.S. Thus, the availability of imports of several fish products for the domestic market will not increase, and within a decade total availability to the U.S. market is likely to decline.

The demand estimates are based on economic theory relating the consumption of any good to its price relative to other prices in the market and the disposable income of consumers. The most simplified model available was used in this study because the data at our disposal were rather inexact. Estimates were made for each of 13 fish product categories for each country producing significant quantities utilizing the following nonlinear demand relationship:

$$Q/N = A \, (P_0/CPI)^{\alpha} \, (Y/N)^{\beta} \tag{11-1}$$

where

Q = quantity of a product consumed per year in a country

N = population in a given year for a given country

P_0 = price per unit of Q

CPI = consumer price index for given years in a country

Y = per capita consumption per year in a country deflated by CPI

A = a constant

α = price elasticity

β = income elasticity.

The estimated elasticities were adjusted according to a priori theory where it was clear that they were incorrect in terms of sign and magnitude to be used in making the long term projections. The adjustments that were made are more precisely explained in Appendix 11A.

      Lobsters, shrimp, and groundfish generally have high income elasticities. Salmon and clams are lowest in income elasticities, with sardines falling in this category for all but the United Kingdom, Spain, and Portugal, which do not comprise a large percent of world population.

      Price elasticities generally are highest for groundfish, with shrimp also showing higher than average price elasticities. All other products generally fall within a common price elasticity range of -0.2 to -1.0. Except for extraordinarily unusual price and income elasticities, the main determinants of a country's consumption of a fish product revolves around the size of the population. Because of this, Japan, the U.S.S.R., and the U.S. are and will remain the major consumers.

BIOLOGICAL GROWTH, YIELD, AND SUPPLY

The derivation of supply schedules for fish products is necessarily based upon very strong assumptions that are necessitated in part because most of the world's fish populations have not been subjected to an analysis of their internal dynamics. Virtually the only information that is available for a large part of the world's fishery resources is species identification by area and estimates of MSY often based upon "best guesses" of interested experts. This section will establish the theoretical foundation for the supply side of the projection model which is presented later on in "The Mechanics of Projection." The model is essentially a variant of that developed by Milner B. Schaefer.[4] [6] The models assume logistic growth of the biomass of fish and decreasing returns from effort. We call it the logistic-decreasing returns (*LDR*) model.

First, consider biological growth. The *LDR* model assumes the simple logistic growth curve

$$M_t = \frac{M_s}{1 + \delta e^{-\gamma t}} \tag{11-2}$$

where M_t is the biomass at time t, M_s is the stable biomass that would be approached from biological causes alone (recruitment, growth, and mortality), e is the base of natural logarithms ($e \sim 2.718$), and δ and γ are constants.

The logistic in population studies has been used to describe the numbers in a population and not its weight. The extension to weight may be unwarranted, but it has been used extensively by biologists, notably Schaefer. The logistic curve rises throughout, the rate of increase first increases, then declines; and it approaches the upper limit, M_s. The maximum size of the biomass is limited by food, space, and other environmental parameters.

More specifically, the rate of increase (found by differentiating (11-2)) is

$$\frac{\Delta M_t}{\Delta t} = \gamma M_t (1 - M_t/M_s) \tag{11-3}$$

Second, consider the effect of fishing effort upon the population.

Ideally, fishing effort is an index of inputs, including ships, gear, labor, and time used to catch fish. In practice, we usually must be content with some proxy, such as the number of ship-days spent fishing. Corresponding to any given effort, there is a sustainable yield, i.e., an average yield that could be maintained indefinitely.

Assume that the first unit of effort takes some proportion of the biomass, say pM_t, leaving $(1 - p)M_t$, where p is the fraction of the biomass taken by a unit of effort ($0 < p < 1$) and M_t is the biomass at time t. We shall now assume with Beverton and Holt[5] [2] that a second unit of effort would take $p(1 - p)M_t$, leaving $(1 - p)^2 M_t$. Then X_t units of effort would leave $(1 - p)^{X_t} M_t$, or $Z^{X_t} M_t$ (where $Z = (1 - p)$). The yield would then be

$$Y_t = M_t (1 - Z^{X_t}) \tag{11-4}$$

where Y_t is yield, X_t is effort, and where Z is the proportion of the biomass that would be left after removals by one unit of effort.[6] If (11-4) holds,

$$Y_t = \gamma M_t (1 - M_t/M_s) = (1 - Z^{X_t})M_t \tag{11-5}$$

from which we find that

$$M_t = M_s [1 - (1 - Z^{X_t}/\gamma)] \tag{11-6}$$

and inserting (11-6) into the righthand side of (11-5),

$$Y_t = M_s \left[(1 - Z^{X_t}) - \frac{(1 - Z^{X_t})^2}{\gamma} \right] \tag{11-7}$$

Since $0 < Z < 1$, Equation (11-7) shows that the annual yield would approach $M_s(1 - 1/\gamma)$ if fishing effort were increased indefinitely. It also indicates that with no effort there would be no yield. As effort increased, yield would increase until it reached a maximum, and then depending upon the value of γ, it might fall.

The derivation of our yield function utilizes (11-7) together with landings and price in a base period, and biologists' estimates of *MSY*. We used (11-7) to estimate relative yield Y_t/Y_1 associated with relative effort X_t/X_1, where Y_1 and X_1 are averages of some base period such as the last 5 years. Various biologists have estimated *MSY*, Y_m, for various fish stocks using a variety of technical methods and guesses. A survey of these was published by Gulland.[7] [5]

The *LDR* yield function can be derived in the following way. If we are given only the yield (i.e., catch) in the base period, Y_1, and the *MSY*, Y_m, and if we assume some value of γ in (11-2), we can estimate the relative yields, Y_t/Y_1. Thus, if we believe that the yield would approach zero if effort became very large, we are implying that $\gamma = 1$; in this study assume $\gamma = 1$. Equation (11-7) can then be written

$$Y_t/Y_1 = M_s Z^{X_t/X_1} (1 - Z^{X_t/X_1}) \tag{11-8}$$

Equation (11-8) is maximized when $Z^{X_t/X_1} = 1/2$; therefore the maximum ratio Y_m/Y_1 is reached when $Y_m/Y_1 = 1/4 M_s$, or $M_s = 4 Y_m/Y_1$. Thus (11-8) is equivalent to

$$Y_t/Y_1 = 4(Y_m/Y_1) Z^{X_t/X_1} (1 - Z^{X_t/X_1}) \tag{11-9}$$

Since Y_1, X_1, and Y_m are known, and since in the base period

$$Y_1/Y_1 = 1 = 4 (Y_m/Y_1) Z(1 - Z) \tag{11-10}$$

we can compute

$$Z = \frac{1 \pm [(1 - Y_1)/Y_m]^{1/2}}{2} \tag{11-11}$$

We use the smaller root when there is current overfishing and the larger root otherwise.

To derive cost curves, we assume that total cost of harvesting, C_t, varies with effort, X_t, so that the relative cost in any region is proportional to relative effort (i.e., if effort should increase by 10 percent, total cost would increase by 10 percent as well).

We can rewrite (11-8) as

$$Y_t/Y_1 = M_s \left(Z^{X_t/X_1} - Z^{2X_t/X_1} \right) \tag{11-12}$$

Thus

$$Z^{X_t/X_1} = \frac{1 \pm \sqrt{4Y_t/Y_1 \cdot M_s}}{2} \tag{11-13}$$

and, assuming that $C_t/C_1 = X_t/X_1$, we can solve (11-13) for C_t/C_1 as shown below:

$$C_t/C_1 = \frac{\log \left[\dfrac{1 \pm \sqrt{1 - 4Y_t/Y_1 \cdot M_s}}{2} \right]}{\log Z} \tag{11-14}$$

Equation (11-14) gives total cost. Average cost is, as before, $(C_t/C_1)/(Y_t/Y_1)$;

$$\frac{C_t/C_1}{Y_t/Y_1} = \frac{\log \left[\dfrac{1 \pm \sqrt{1 - 4Y_t/Y_1 \cdot M_s}}{2} \right]}{\log Z \cdot Y_t/Y_1} \tag{11-15}$$

Equation (11-15) is a curve of average cost as a function of landings.

Under conditions of perfect competition, increasing costs, and free access to the resource, production is increased up to the point where price, P_t, equals average cost. This condition should apply, at least approximately, to fisheries. In any case, we will assume $P_t/P_1 = C_t/C_1$, so that should average costs rise 10 percent, we would expect production to be adjusted so that the price of fish would rise by 10 percent as well.

The supply curve for the *LDR* model is

$$\frac{P_t/P_1}{Y_t/Y_1} = \frac{\log \left[1/2 \pm (\sqrt{1 - 4Y_t/Y_1 \cdot M_s})/2 \right]}{Y_t/Y_1 \cdot \log Z} \tag{11-16}$$

Thus far we have discussed the supply curve in any region; i.e., the amount that

the region could be expected to supply at various assumed prices. Next we need
to combine these regional supply functions into a world supply function.

World sustainable supply at any specified price is the total amount
that would be supplied by all regions at that price. Figure 11-1 illustrates the
procedure for the case of three regions.

First we estimate each of the three regional supply curves (the heavy
lines in the diagram). In the case illustrated, region 1 may be a region near the big
market center, where fish may be caught at little expense but where the stock is
soon reduced by overfishing. Regions 2 and 3 are further removed from the
market; the potential supplies from these regions are large, but can be obtained
only at greater expense. We shall assume that all three regions sell at the "world
price" minus transportation; thus, supplies in all three regions respond to the same
world price.

The curve of world sustainable supply is obtained by summing the
regional supplies at any given price. For example, the diagram illustrates the case
where the world price is P. (The price in each region is assumed to be some
known percentage of the world price.) When the world price is P, the regional

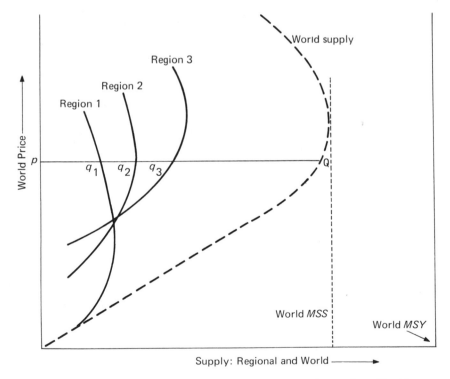

Figure 11-1. Aggregating Regional Supply Curves into World
Supply.

amounts supplied are q_1, q_2, q_3. Their sum, $Q = q_1 + q_2 + q_3$, is the world supply at price P. Similarly, the world sustainable supply at any other price can be found by adding the curves horizontally.

We note that the world *MSY* is the sum of the *MSY*'s for the individual regions. It is indicated by the vertical line to the right of Figure 11-1. This *MSY* would not be attainable without maintaining each region at *MSY*. However, this is economically untenable under competitive conditions.

The dashed curve indicates the response of world supply to changes in world price. It assumes no controls in addition to the ones already in effect, only the normal competitive responses of the fishing industry to prices and costs. The maximum of this function—maximum sustainable supply (*MSS*)—is, in general, less than *MSY*.

THE PROJECTION TECHNIQUE

In this section we shall discuss the general procedure adopted for empirically deriving the world demand and supply projections for fish products. For a given species *i* and country *j*, the demand relationship is given as

$$(Q^*/N)_{ij} = A_1 \, (P_i/CPI)^{-a(i)} \, (Y^*/N)^{\beta(ij)} \tag{11-17}$$

where (Q^*/N) is projected per capita consumption, and (Y^*/N) is projected per capita income. (Q^*/N) was then multiplied by projected population, N^*, to obtain projected aggregate consumption for the ith species in the jth country. Demand was estimated for the most significant consumers (i.e., countries) under the assumption that their collective share out of world consumption would remain the same as it was in the 1965–1967 base period. Thus, we may define net world demand, *QNDW*, as the summation of the projected demand for each species across *j* countries and gross world, *QGDW*, as

$$QGDW = 1/k \cdot QNDW \tag{11-18}$$

where *k* is equal to the ratio of net to gross world demand during the base period, and is assumed to remain constant during the forecasting period.

Within the context of the general demand projection model, there are three different assumptions: (1) the income elasticity estimated in (11-17) is constant over the forecasting period; (2) the income elasticity declines at some exponential rate for the period of projection; (3) the income elasticity is constant and equal to zero.

Assumption (2) requires some further explanation. The initial income elasticity estimated in (11-17), $\beta(ij)$, decays in the following manner:

$$\beta(t) = \beta(ij) \, (1 + 0.4)^{-t} \tag{11-19}$$

where each t represents a 5-year interval. We have observed a tendency for income elasticities for fish to decline with rising incomes; such a decline appears theoretically appropriate. The decay rate of $1/1.4$ each 5-year interval is a rough estimate based upon studies of tuna and other species. Assumption (2) was employed in making the demand projections. On the supply side, regional supply functions for a given species were summed across j regions to obtain a world supply function.

The projected world demand, $QGDW$, is then compared to world supply, Y_w, at the given weighted world price (base period price). If $QGDW > Y_w$, prices are automatically increased in each of the countries by an arbitrary percentage. A new weighted world price is obtained after the first iteration. Then, a new supply response is obtained. This iterative procedure is carried out until projected demand and supply are equal at a projected equilibrium world price, POW, or

$$(QGDW)^* = Y_w^*$$

(11-20)

Through the use of this technique, the following projections can be obtained:

1. Projected world demand, $(QGDW)^*$.
2. Projected world supply, Y_w^*.
3. Projected equilibrium world weighted price, $(POW)^*$.

The only other assumptions included in the world demand-supply model are listed below:

1. No change in the existing degree of fishery management.
2. Input prices to the fishing industry increase at the same rate as all consumer prices.
3. No change in the level of pollution.
4. No major disruptions in international trade or production.
5. No significantly high cross-elasticities between fish product groups selected for projection.

COMPARISON OF 1970 PROJECTIONS WITH ACTUAL REPORTED DATA

We begin by comparing our 1970 projections of production with the actual production as reported by FAO. Before examining the data the reader should be cautioned that projections for any one year could be at great variance with reported data, even if the model and data were absolutely correct. Projection errors constantly arise because of random biological and economic fluctuations. Of course we are not so naive that we believe that the model used was more than a convenient abstraction, or that the production data used were more than a crude first cut at ascertaining real production by FAO. In addition, many of the key numbers, such as *MSY*'s, are no more than the grossest approximations to the productivity of many resources, especially in currently lightly exploited areas.

Many of these sources of error could of course have been corrected; but we felt it best that we publish so that others might exploit the technique if they wished.

We made projections for 13 different fish product groups. The geometric mean error for the 13 groups is only 1.5 percent; the standard deviation, however, is approximately 13 percent. Although our mean error of prediction is quite low, the standard deviation is moderately large.

Table 11-1 compares actual and projected values. For six of our species groups, the projected and actual were within 10 percent in 1970. However, some of our projections (B group) missed the mark by a considerable margin. The differences between the actual and projected may be explained by various factors that may not hold over our 30-year projection period. Let us consider each species in group B in order of degree of divergence.

Tuna production was probably underestimated because of the accelerated growth in demand over the 1965–1967 period since there was no appreciable change in the resource constraint. This may be a temporary phenomenon that cannot continue over the next 30 years. However, we do believe that the demand for tuna will remain strong, but it cannot grow at the pace recently exhibited.

Table 11-1. Comparisons Between Projections of World and Actual Production Reported by FAO

Species Group	Projection	Actual	Ratio of Projection to Actual
	(millions of pounds)		
A. Species with error less than 10 percent			
Crabs	870	882	0.986
Lobsters	330	342	0.965
Other food fish	62,000	59,579	1.041
Salmon	1,051	1,007	1.044
Shrimp	1,970	1,858	1.060
Clams	1,060	1,168	0.908
B. Species with error greater than 10 percent			
Tuna	2,900	3,338	0.869
Halibut	129	150	0.860
Fishmeal	50,000	61,180	0.817
Groundfish	15,400	19,427	0.793
Oysters	2,127	1,609	1.322
Sardines	2,570	1,930	1.332
Scallops	440	309	1.424

The *Pacific halibut* resource has been subject to fishing pressure by the Japanese and Russians since the 1965–1967 base period. This catch is incidental to other species fished by these nations. In the short run, however, this incidental catch would increase world landings above *MSY* or lower the productivity of the resource. The International Pacific Halibut Commission has already moved to lower annual quotas in the face of increased foreign fishing effort. This measure has been instituted to conserve the stock while international negotiations are carried on.

Fishmeal is very difficult to predict since it may contain so many different species. We grossly underprojected the actual production of fishmeal. Most of the increase in production over the 1965–1967 base period was accounted for by Peru, which has been attempting to gain increasing foreign exchange. Peru may have increased landings by overfishing since production has recently plummeted. There is a controversy as to the cause of this decline in production: some authorities maintain that it was due to overfishing, while others maintain that it was primarily due to a temporary shift in the Humbolt current.

Groundfish production was underestimated by over 20 percent in 1970. This was probably due to an underestimate of the potential of the Alaskan pollock, which has been increasingly fished by the Russians and Japanese. A check of FAO data revealed that increases in groundfish production came principally in this area.

Oysters were overprojected probably because of two factors: (1) poor aquaculture season in Japan in 1970, and (2) an overestimate of the strength of demand for oysters. We substituted a judgment that zero was a better estimate of the income elasticity, and, as it turns out, it looks as though the data knew better.

Sardines were overestimated primarily because of two factors: (1) an overestimate of the resource potential of the Northwest Atlantic, and (2) an optimistic view of demand elasticities which, for many countries, are probably much lower than the ones used in the model.

Scallops were probably overprojected due to failure of year-class strength in the Northwest Atlantic.

Our estimate of *total* fish production (food and industrial) was low by less than 8 percent, which is not too bad considering the many shortrun factors that the model has no capacity to handle.

ECONOMIC PROJECTIONS OF DEMAND, SUPPLY, AND PRICES FOR SELECTED FISH PRODUCTS TO THE YEAR 2000

Economic projections of world supply, demand, and prices for selected fish products were made using the model outlined above. As indicated, we have decided to present the declining income elasticity (*DIE*) demand model and the logistic diminishing returns to scale, or *LDR* supply model (see discussion under biology), which we believe represent the most reasonable assumptions regarding supply and demand. The only exceptions to this general procedure are found in the cases of oysters, clams, and salmon. Oysters are assumed to possess infinitely elastic supply (*IES*) functions because of the introduction of artificial techniques of cultivation. The same is true of clams and salmon; however, because of more uncertainty, we have presented two sets of projections for each of these two species: one with the *LDR* model and one under the assumption of *IES* functions. Figures 11–2 through 11–14 show projected supply and demand.

Table 11–2 presents projections for the world which were used for the graphs and for the United States for two points in the forecasting period—1975 and 2000.

After making the aforementioned projections, the following basic conclusions were reached.

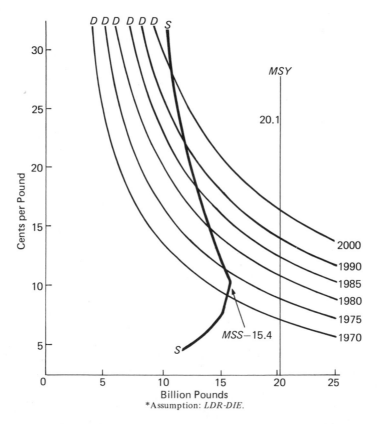

Figure 11–2. World Demand and Supply Functions for Groundfish, 1970–2000.*

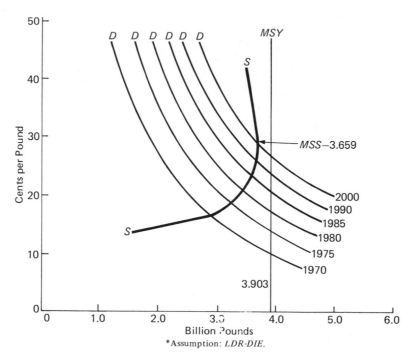

Figure 11-3. World Demand and Supply Functions for Tuna, 1970-2000.*

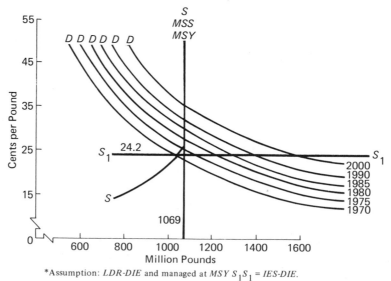

Figure 11-4. World Demand and Supply Functions for Salmon 1970-2000.*

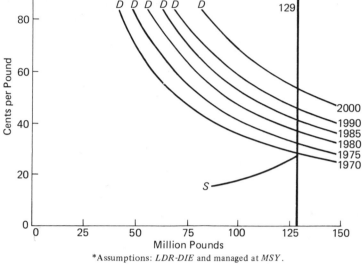
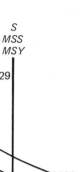

*Assumptions: LDR-DIE and managed at MSY.

Figure 11-5. World Demand and Supply Functions for Halibut, 1970-2000.*

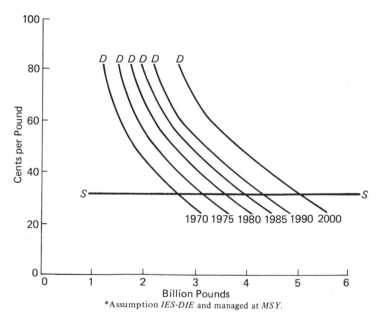

*Assumption IES-DIE and managed at MSY.

Figure 11-6. World Demand and Supply Functions for Sardines, 1970-2000.*

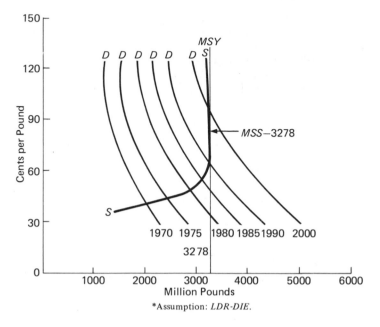

Assumption: LDR-DIE.

Figure 11-7. World Demand and Supply Functions for Shrimp, 1970–2000.*

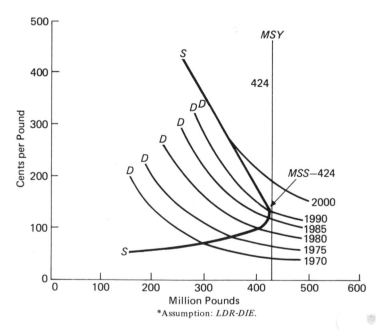

Assumption: LDR-DIE.

Figure 11-8. World Demand and Supply Functions for Lobster, 1970–2000.*

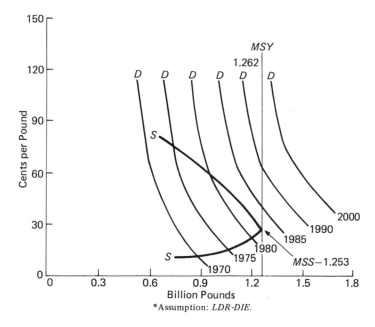

Figure 11-9. World Demand and Supply Functions for Crabs, 1970–2000.*

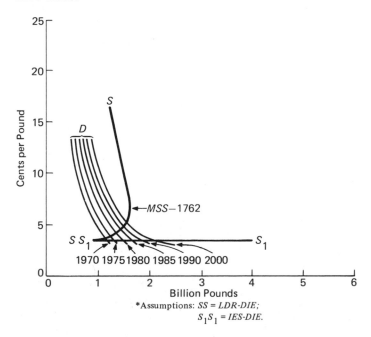

Figure 11-10. World Demand and Supply Functions for Clams, 1970–2000.*

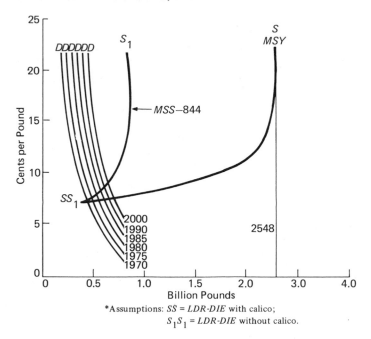

Figure 11-11.   World Demand and Supply Functions for Scallops, 1970-2000.*

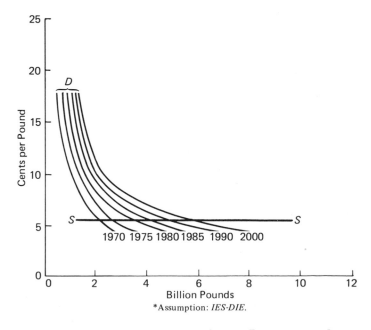

Figure 11-12.   World Demand and Supply Functions for Oysters, 1970-2000.*

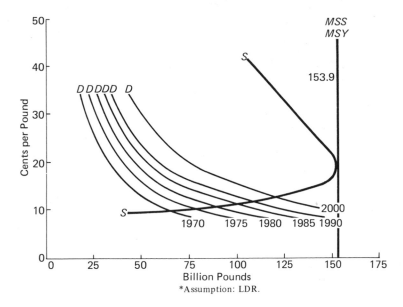

Figure 11-13. World Demand and Supply Functions for Other Food Fish, 1970-2000.*

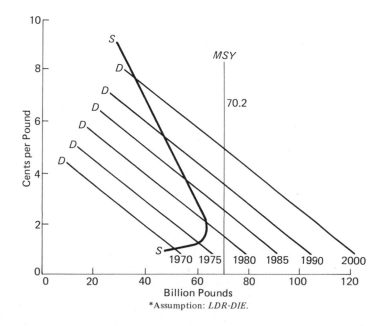

Figure 11-14. World Demand and Supply Functions for Fish Meal, 1970-2000.*

Table 11-2. Projections[a] for 1975 and 2000

(round weight)

Year	World				United States			
	Quantity Million Pounds	Real Price ¢/lb	% of MSY	% of MSS[c]	Quantity Million Pounds	Per Capita Consumption in lbs.	Real Price ¢/lb	U.S. Consumption as % of World
Species: Groundfish								
1975	15,300	11.3	76	99	1,250	5.69	12.7	8.2
2000	10,500	28.3	52	68[b]	830	2.69	31.8	7.9
Species: Tuna								
1975	3,210	18	82	88	1,215	5.54	14	38
2000	3,650	30	94	100	1,395	4.53	23	38
Species: Salmon (LDR)								
1975	1,069	25.5	100	100	325	1.48	19.0	30.4
2000	1,069	37.7	100	100	346	1.12	28.1	32.4
Species: Salmon (elastic supply)								
1975	1,126	24.2			338	1.54	18.0	30.0
2000	1,590	24.2			474	1.54	18.0	29.8
Species: Halibut[d]								
1975	129	32	100	100	88	0.40	23	68
2000	129	52	100	100	89	0.29	38	69
Species: Sardines (elastic supply)								
1975	3,228	31			148	0.67	36	4.6
2000	5,225	31			208	0.68	36	4.0
Species: Shrimp								
1975	2,350	46	72	72	840	3.83	41	36
2000	3,260	94	99	99	1,320	4.29	84	40
Species: Lobster								
1975	383	81	90.3	90.3	258	1.18	87	67.4
2000	320	311	75.5	75.5	242	0.79	336	75.6
Species: Crabs								
1975	1,060	15	84	85	520	2.37	9.8	49
2000	850	114	67	68	425	1.38	114.0	50

Species / Year	Quantity Million Pounds	Real Price ¢/lb	World Consumption of Sardines Million Pounds	% of MSY[f]	% of MSS[f]	Quantity Million Pounds	Real Price ¢/lb	Real Price ¢/lb	U.S. Consumption as % of World
Species: Clams (LDR)									
1975	1,180	3.6		67	67	560	2.55	3.6	47
2000	1,530	4.8		87	87	690	2.24	4.8	45
Species: Clams (elastic supply)									
1975	1,210	3.5				570	2.60	3.5	47
2000	1,970	3.5				840	2.73	3.5	43
Species: Scallops (with calico scallops)									
1975	520	7.3		20	20	335	1.53	6.8	65
2000	710	7.6		28	28	500	1.62	7.0	70
Species: Scallops (without calico scallops)									
1975	490	7.8		54	58	320	1.46	7.3	65
2000	650	9.0		71	77	450	1.46	8.3	69
Species: Oysters (elastic supply)									
1975	2,686	5.3				639	2.91	5.5	23.8
2000	5,409	5.3				896	2.91	5.5	16.6
Species: Other Food Fish									
1975	72,000	10.4		47	47	1,380	6.29	10.4	1.9
2000	118,000	12.4		77	77	1,623	5.27	12.4	1.4
Species: Fish Meal									
1975	59,900	1.3	3,228	90	95	9,250	1.3		15.4
2000	33,500	7.8	5,225	55	58	5,700	7.8		17.0
All Seafood (inclusive of fish meal)									
1975	163,003.71					7,568			
2000	184,154.64					8,714			

[a] LDR function used unless otherwise specified.

[b] It is important to note that the reason for the low rate of utilization is that the fishery is operating on the other side of MSS.

[c] Maximum Sustainable Supply. This represents the maximum point of the world supply function, which, in some instances, may be less than MSY because of different rates of regional exploitation.

[d] Since 1933, the catch of most of the world's halibut has been regulated under a treaty between the United States and Canada.

[e] Included here to show utilization of the herringlike resource.

[f] Including utilization of the resource for sardines.

The World

1. The world demand for species fished by U.S. fishermen will, in many cases, outstrip the maximum world supply potential before 1985. Table 11-3 indicates the year in which certain species will attain *MSS*.[8] Critical problems of an increase in resource supply are occurring or are about to occur for groundfish, salmon, halibut, lobsters, crabs, and fishmeal. Unless proper management policies are adopted, overfishing for crabs, lobsters, groundfish, and fishmeal on a world basis is possible within the next 15 years.

2. Aggregate fish consumption (including fishmeal) for the world will expand from approximately 125.8 billion pounds in the 1965-1967 base period to 184.1 billion pounds (round weight) by the year 2000, an increase of 46.3 percent. In contrast, FAO projects that by the year 1985, aggregate fish consumption will attain a level of 234.8 billion pounds—an increase of 86.5 percent over the 1965-1967 base period. The major reason for this higher level of projected consumption is accounted for by the lack of incorporation of supply constraints into the FAO projections. As a result, real prices are held constant and resource scarcities are not introduced in the forecasting period. (See Figure 11-15.)

The United States

1. Aggregate consumption of food fish for the United States will expand from approximately 2.2 billion pounds in the 1965-1967 base period to almost 2.9 billion pounds (edible weight) in the year 2000, an increase of 33 percent.

Table 11- 3. Projected Data of Maximum Sustainable Supply

Species*	*Year World Will Reach Maximum Sustainable Supply*
Salmon[a]	1970
Halibut	1970
Groundfish[b]	1970
Crabs	1980-85
Fishmeal (i.e., species for reduction)	1980
Lobsters	1985
Tuna[c]	2000
Shrimp	2000
Sardines	2000+
Scallops[d]	2000+
Clams	2000+

*Aquaculture not assumed in these projections.

[a]Does not include the possibility of expanded supply through hatchery operations and stream improvements.

[b]Excludes hake and hake-like fish.

[c]Excludes Central Pacific skipjack.

[d]Includes recent discovery of calico scallops.

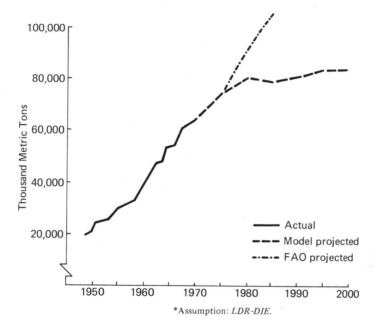

Figure 11-15. Historical and Projected World Aggregate Consumption of Fishery Products.*

2. Because of resource supply problems and declining income elasticities for fish products, per capita consumption of all food fish in the United States is expected to decline from 11.02 pounds in the base period to 9.38 pounds by the year 2000, a decrease of 14.9 percent.

IMPLICATIONS OF THE DEMAND AND SUPPLY PROJECTIONS FOR PUBLIC POLICY

The following discussion represents the opinions of the authors and in no way reflects a policy determination by the federal government. We shall outline four policies which could be pursued with respect to fishery resources; the consequences of these policies will be discussed.

A Fishery Management Policy

Our projections indicate that the process of exploiting (and overexploiting) fishery resources will continue and worsen for many species in the next 30 years. Without fishery management, fishing effort will increase to the point where physical output will be reduced for groundfish (before 1975), crabs (1980), fishmeal (1980), lobsters (1985), and tuna (before 2000); these species therefore require immediate attention, and other species need attention in some areas of the world. The ranking of fisheries on the basis of projected utilization is shown in Table 11-4.

Potential benefits from fishery management are thus substantial. Fishing beyond *MSY* is counterproductive in the sense that the marginal product of effort is negative. A policy directed toward preventing overfishing can, if properly administered, prevent the negative contribution of further inputs into the fishery.

An Antipollution Policy

This study indicates that future world sustainable supplies of fish will be utilized rapidly and that fish prices will rise appreciably. However, projected price increases may even be exacerbated and future fish supplies reduced still further if our current estimates of *MSY*'s are lowered. This may occur if the ecological parameter—assumed fixed in our analysis—is changed because of increased water pollution. Although a serious problem now, further uncontrolled pollution could lower the *MSY*'s of some of the principal species of commercial fish.

Aside from prohibitory legislation, much could be done through the use of economic incentives and penalties aimed at internalizing pollution costs and thus reducing the pollution level relative to its "zero cost" state.

Table 11-4. Ranking of Fisheries on the Basis of Projected Utilization

Species	Year Fully Utilized at MSS	Region Problems
Halibut	Presently	At *MSY* and inefficiently utilized[a]
Salmon	Presently	At *MSY* and inefficiently utilized[a]
Groundfish	1970	Overfishing in Northwest and Northeast Atlantic
Crabs	1980	Overfishing in North Pacific; near *MSY* in West Central Atlantic
Lobsters	1985	Nearly at *MSY* in Southwest Atlantic and Southwest Pacific
Shrimp	Before 2000	
Tuna	Before 2000	Eastern tropical yellowfin nearly at *MSY*
Scallops	b	At *MSY* in Northeast Atlantic
Clams	c, d	
Sardines	e	
Oysters	d	
Fishmeal	1980	Northwest Atlantic at *MSY*

[a]Inefficient fishery management policies in effect.

[b]By 2000 only 28 percent of *MSY* is expected to be utilized when calico scallops are included.

[c]By 2000 only 87 percent of *MSY* is expected to be utilized without additional aquaculture.

[d]Infinitely elastic supply, within relevant range, with additional aquaculture.

[e]Infinitely elastic supply, within relevant range, as food fish.

A Fish Farming Policy

Effective control over water pollution could probably prevent future drops in the *MSY*'s of many species of fish. However, rapidly rising populations and real incomes will mean a substantial increase in the demand for fish. To satisfy an increasing world demand, we need to explore feasible methods of increasing supply through pond culture and supplementation of wild stocks.

A recent study by Bardach et al. referred to the farming of plaice, sole, shrimp, crabs, abalone, sea bream, puffer fish, carp, and mullet in various parts of the world.[9] [1] They concluded that,

> The practice of aquaculture may not only be greatly expanded, particularly in those parts of the world most in need of its products, but also that its yields may be very appreciably increased through the use of modern science and technology.[10] [1]

The Japanese have led the way in fish farming. Not only have they developed commercial oyster farming, but they are now producing a substantial percentage of their fresh water fish from farming. Brown stated that in Japan in 1965, "The following percentages of fish produced were cultured: 100 percent of the trout, 88 percent of the eel, 72 percent of the carp, 14 percent of the Crucian carp, and 10 percent of the ager."[11] [3]

Although more work needs to be done in this area, in general, it is doubtful whether many of the presently commercial species would be successful candidates for fish culture.

An Underutilized Species Policy

Our projections indicate that supplies of some of the principal market species of fish will soon be fully utilized and that their prices will rise. But if consumers prove willing to buy some of the presently less preferred species, total per capita supplies of fish need not decline much, at least for many decades. Also, such a switch in buying would tend to dampen the increases in prices of the more preferred species. Although we have not found evidence of switching or of substitution of less preferred species, it is likely that this would occur given sufficient price disparities.

CONCLUSION

While refinements will certainly be needed in future work, the central thrust of this study is that we are fast approaching a period of scarcity with respect to the more traditionally consumed species of fish. However, there are two factors, at a minimum, which may lessen these anticipated scarcities: (1) the adoption of one or a combination of the policies outlined in the previous section, and/or (2) a secular change in tastes—not incorporated into our model—away from the more popularly consumed species and toward other presently less preferred species.

Although long run forecasting is replete with pitfalls, and definitive pronouncements about the state of the world in the year 1990 or 2000 should properly be viewed with suspicion, our results indicate that the popular notion that the world's oceans have the potential to supply all of man's food needs is, at best, highly questionable, and, at worst, incorrect. On the other hand, the alarmist view that the oceans will soon be depleted of fish is shown to be equally false because rising costs place a limit upon expansion.

APPENDIX 11A
EQUATIONS USED IN THE PROJECTION MODEL

Tables 11A-1, 11A-2, and 11A-3 present the estimated regression equations for three of the more important species: groundfish, tuna, and shrimp. Tables 11A-4, 11A-5, and 11A-6 indicate the actual parameters used in making the demand projections. Following these tables, we present explanatory notes and reasons for adjustments made in the regression results to obtain the forecast parameters.

Groundfish, tuna, and shrimp were selected for illustrative purposes for two reasons: (1) they are the more popularly consumed species of fish; (2) one can obtain some insight into the array of adjustments that were made in the originally estimated regression equations.

The two most common reasons for changing the estimated parameters were (1) the elasticities had the "wrong" sign from a theoretical standpoint, and (2) the elasticities were obviously incorrect in terms of magnitude. General solutions for this study were to use the elasticity of a similar fishery product, or to use the elasticity of the same product from a country with similar consuming habits.

It should be pointed out that even with ideal data there would be sufficient "noise" in the system to make some of the estimates highly suspect. However, the data obtained from FAO on landings, consumption, and prices are far from ideal. Product definitions were not uniform across countries, and, in general, FAO must use considerable judgment in combining individual country reports which come to them in diverse forms and with different bases for reporting weight. More work is needed to improve these basic data, but, for now, they are the only sources available for many countries. The study would not have been possible without FAO data.

Finally, although several of the parameters used were 'subjectively' chosen, we do not feel that the changes made distort the general thrust of the overall demand projections.

EXPLANATORY NOTES FOR TABLES 11A-4
THROUGH 11A-6

[a]Constant changes so that equation goes through the 1965–67 value of each variable after the elasticity coefficients are changed and where original equations did not approximate 1965–67 base.

[b]Price elasticity has "wrong" sign, assumed to be –1.

[c]Low relative to other countries. U.S. was unrealistically losing share of world consumption.

[d]Elasticity "too high," and low *t* value; assumed to be –1.

[e]Income elasticity taken from U.S. groundfish.

[f]Magnitude of elasticities unacceptable; those for United Kingdom used.

Table 11A–1.   Regression Results of Groundfish Demand Equations by Selected Countries (in logarithms)

Country	Constant	Price Elasticity	Income Elasticity	R^2	D–W	Period
U.S.A.	-2.0145 (-6.7514)	0.1014 (0.7541)	0.8518 (9.1877)	0.84	2.23	1948–68
Japan	-1.6923 (-3.4357)	0.2767 (0.7008)	1.0467 (6.5060)	0.83	1.05	1956–67
Canada	6.6006 (0.4757)	-3.6297 (-0.7904)	-1.2045 (-0.2481)	0.30	2.37	1953–66
Korea[a]	2.2774 (1.6845)	0.7873 (0.8476)	-1.0595 (-1.6433)	0.26	1.33	1956–67
Denmark[b]	-3.9025 (-4.1255)	-0.3016 (-0.4763)	1.9469 (5.8995)	0.83	0.93	1956–67
France[b]	-10.3194 (-1.5965)	-7.1220 (-1.8019)	6.5998 (2.7293)	0.46	2.76	1956–67
Netherlands	-.6.9719 (-4.8273)	-0.0783 (-0.2316)	2.6716 (4.6651)	0.88	1.86	1956–67
United Kingdom	-4.1534 (-2.1125)	-1.3952 (-1.6296)	2.1924 (2.5550)	0.55	2.06	1955–66

[a]Japanese price data were used in the equation.

[b]U.S. price data were used in the equation.

Dependent variable is per capita consumption of groundfish in round weight.

Notes: Prices are ex vessel deflated by the individual country's *CPI* and converted into U.S. cents per pound by the exchange rates.

Income is deflated by the individual country's *CPI* and converted into U.S. dollars per capita by the exchange rates.

Table 11A-2. Regression Results of Tuna Demand Equations by Selected Countries (in logarithms)

Country	Product Form	Constant	Price Elasticity	Income Elasticity	R^2	D-W	Period
U.S.A.	Can	-2.6099 (-2.3862)	-0.8632 (-4.9220)	1.1675 (4.1626)	0.94	1.44	1947-67
Canada	Can	0.3115 (0.1151)	-0.1353 (-0.6090)	-0.0868 (-0.1068)	0.04	1.77	1956-67
United Kingdom	Can	3.0045 (0.9403)	0.8675 (2.0944)	-1.4787 (-1.4950)	0.45	1.92	1956-67
EEC	Can	-1.9451 (-1.1439)	-0.3524 (-0.9966)	0.8313 (1.6023)	0.32	1.14	1956-67
Spain	Raw	-2.2564 (-1.0961)	-0.4058 (-0.5344)	1.0425 (1.6359)	0.29	2.33	1956-67
	Can	-0.3610 (-0.3273)	0.5865 (1.4416)	-1.3867 (-0.0406)	0.20	1.85	1956-67
Turkey	Raw	13.8698 (1.4047)	-0.2453 (-0.1720)	-5.7316 (-1.4898)	0.22	2.06	1956-67
Japan	Raw	-0.4085 (0.4439)	-0.5095 (-0.6674)	0.3434 (1.2366)	0.15	1.59	1956-67
	Can	2.4965 (2.4297)	0.9953 (1.1675)	-1.3954 (-4.5004)	0.70	1.65	1956-67
Taiwan	Raw	-0.2467 (-0.2561)	-0.2190 (-0.9106)	0.4926 (1.2008)	0.23	2.89	1956-67
	Can	-10.5766 (-5.2343)	-0.0583 (-0.1155)	5.5071 (4.7395)	0.78	1.87	1956-67
Peru	Raw*	0.1854 (0.0274)	0.1392 (0.0485)	0.2715 (0.1299)	0.002	1.29	1956-67

*U.S. price data were used in the equation.

Notes: Dependent variable is per capita consumption of tuna in round weight, except for the U.S. which is in edible weight.
Prices are ex-vessel deflated by the individual country's CPI and converted into U.S. cents per pound by the exchange rates.
Income is deflated by the individual country's CPI and converted into U.S. dollars per capita by the exchange rates.
T values in parentheses.

Table 11A-3. Regression Results of Shrimp Demand Equations by Selected Countries (in logarithms)

Country	Constant	Price Elasticity	Income Elasticity	R^2	D-W	Period
U.S.A.	-4.8075 (-12.0400)	-0.3099 (-2.7001)	1.6999 (11.5558)	0.91	0.80	1948-67
Mexico	-11.5852 (-5.2599)	-1.6584 (-3.1705)	5.2396 (5.8561)	0.84	2.15	1958-67
India*	-1.0936 (-0.7041)	0.4761 (1.7194)	-0.0133 (-0.0157)	0.31	1.72	1958-67
Japan	-0.0306 (-0.0589)	-0.1492 (-0.4616)	0.1350 (1.1603)	0.11	0.62	1953-67
Pakistan*	-4.5177 (-5.2110)	0.1692 (0.5791)	2.0226 (4.5649)	0.65	1.61	1953-67
Thailand*	-8.8344 (-14.4455)	0.6047 (2.3746)	3.9753 (14.4492)	0.97	1.50	1958-67

*U.S. price data were used in the equation.

Notes: Dependent variable is per capita consumption of shrimp in round weight.

Prices are ex vessel deflated by the individual country's CPI and converted into U.S. cents per pound by the exchange rates.

Income is deflated by the individual country's CPI and converted into U.S. dollars per capita by the exchange rates.

T values in parentheses.

Table 11A-4. Groundfish Equations Used for Making Projections

Country	Constant	Price Elasticity	Income Elasticity
		(logarithms)	
United States	-1.0919^a	-1.0^b	0.8518^c
Canada	-2.7681^a	-1.0^d	1.211^e
Denmark	-2.3922^a	-1.3952^f	1.9469_f
France	-4.4452^a	-1.3952^f	2.1924^f
Netherlands	-3.9736^a	-1.3952^f	2.1924^f
United Kingdom	-4.1534	-1.3952	2.1924
Japan	-0.9106^a	-1.0^b	1.0467
Korea	-1.1102^a	-1.0^b	1.0467^g

Table 11A-5. Tuna Equations Used for Making Projections

Country	Constant	Price Elasticity	Income Elasticity
		(logarithms)	
U.S.-canned	-2.3164^a	-0.8632_h	1.1675_i
Canada-canned	-3.1757^a	-0.8632^h	1.1675^i
U.K.-canned	-3.4410^a	-0.8632^i	1.1675^i
EEC-canned	-2.3904^a	-0.8632^i	1.1675^i
Spain-not canned	-2.2564	-0.4058	1.0425
Spain-canned	$1.4874^{a,j}$	-1.0000	0^k
Turkey-not canned	0.3720^a	-0.2453	0^k
Japan-not canned	0.4085	-0.5095	0.3434
Japan-canned	$0.8389^{a,j}$	-1.0000^b	0^k
Taiwan-not canned	-0.2467	-0.2190_l	0.4926
Taiwan-canned	-3.4832^a	-1.0000^l	2.0000^m
Peru-not canned	-1.2773^a	-0.4058^n	2.0425^o

Table 11A-6. Shrimp Equations Used for Making Projections

Country	Constant	Price Elasticity	Income Elasticity
		(logarithms)	
United States	-4.8075	-0.3099	1.6999
Mexico	-8.2105^a	-1.6584	4^m
India	-3.0222^a	-1^b	2.0226^p
Japan	-0.0306	-0.1492	0.135
Pakistan	-2.8301^a	-1^b	2.0226
Thailand	-2.3305^a	-1^b	2.0226^q

[g]Elasticities have "wrong" signs and low t values; those for Japan used.
[h]Elasticity "too low" and had low t value; U.S. coefficient used.
[i]Elasticity has "wrong" sign; U.S. coefficient used.
[j]Constant term changed to put equation in round weight.
[k]Income elasticity has "wrong" sign, assumed to be zero.
[l]Price elasticity "too low," and had low t value; assumed to be –1.
[m]Income elasticity too large, felt to result partially from other time-related changes.
[n]Elasticity has "wrong" sign and low t value; Spain coefficient used;
[o]Elasticity "too low" and low t value; Spain coefficient used.
[p]Elasticity had "wrong" sign and low t value; elasticity of Pakistan used.
[q]Data unreliable; elasticity of Pakistan used.

NOTES

1. We are referring here to fishery stocks in the wild state which are renewable but nevertheless fixed on a sustainable yield basis for a given level of fishing effort.
2. *The Prospects for World Fishery Development in 1975 and 1985,* FAO Indicative World Plan (June 1969).
3. The following discussion excludes Mainland China.
4. The rationale behind this assumption was supplied by M.B. Schaefer in "Some Aspects of the Dynamics of Populations Important to the Management of Commercial Marine Fisheries," *Inter-American Tropical Tuna Commission Bulletins 1 and 2,* 1954.
5. R.J.H. Beverton and S.V. Holt, "On the Dynamics of Exploited Fish Populations." *Fisheries Investigations* 19, Sec. 2. London: Ministry of Agriculture, Fisheries and Food, 1957.
6. An alternative to this model is the LCR, or logistic constant returns model, in which catch per unit time was assumed to be equal to

$$Y_t = kX_tM_t, 0 \leqslant kX_t \leqslant 1.$$

When this is combined with (11–2), and the similar assumptions are used, we have the following:

$$Y_t/Y = a(X_t/X_1) - (a - 1)(X_t/X_1)^2$$

where

$$a = 2Y^*/Y_1 [1 \pm \sqrt{1 - (Y_1/Y^*)}].$$

7. John A. Gulland, *The Fish Resources of the Ocean,* FAO Technical Paper No. 97, Rome, 1971.
8. For halibut and salmon, projections cannot go below MSY because of existing regulations to protect the resource from overfishing. Oysters were

excluded from the above list because of aquaculture augmenting natural stock supplies.

9. John E. Bardach et al., *The Status and Potential of Aquaculture*, Vol. II (particularly Fish Culture). American Institute of Biological Sciences, Washington, D.C., May 1968.
10. Ibid., p. 10.
11. E.E. Brown, *The Fresh Water Cultured Fish Industry of Japan*, University of Georgia, Agricultural Experiment Station Research Report 41, March 1969.

REFERENCES

1. Bardach, John E., et al. *The Status and Potential of Aquaculture*. Vol. II, particularly Fish Culture. American Institute of Biological Sciences, Washington, D.C., May 1968.
2. Beverton, R.J.H. and S.V. Holt. "On the Dynamics of Exploited Fish Populations." *Fisheries Investigations* 19, Sec. 2. Ministry of Agriculture, Fisheries, and Food, London, 1957.
3. Brown, E.E. *The Fresh Water Cultured Fish Industry of Japan*. Agricultural Experiment Station Research Report 41, University of Georgia, March 1969.
4. FAO. *The Prospects for World Fishery Development in 1975 and 1985*. FAO Indicative World Plan, June 1969.
5. Gulland, John A. *The Fish Resources of the Ocean*. FAO Technical Paper No. 97. Rome, 1971.
6. Schaefer, Milner B. "Some Aspects of the Dynamics of Populations Important to the Management of Commercial Marine Fisheries." *Inter-American Tropical Tuna Commission Bulletins 1 and 2*, 1954.

Chapter Twelve

Trade Flows in the Grain–Livestock Economy of the European Economic Community

William E. Kost

The objective of this study is to develop an international trade model that will represent the grain-livestock sector of the EEC and then utilize the model to project the grain-livestock trade pattern for that region. Since international trade in agricultural commodities is not completely transacted within a competitive framework, an important aspect of this study will be the incorporation of institutionally controlled policy variables into the model. A secondary modeling objective will be to develop a simplistic, practical model structure, requiring only easily available data.

A recent Michigan State University-U.S. Department of Agriculture research project focused on the effects of the implementation of the EEC's agriculture policy on the grain-livestock economy.[7, 10, 12, 14, 16] Their analysis is summarized in the form of supply-demand balances for the EEC member countries. By utilizing the data and projections presented in their study as a data base, a spatial equilibrium analysis can be employed to generate grain-livestock trade flows for the EEC countries.

Spatial equilibrium analysis is a broad methodology covering a wide range of techniques: from fixed production-fixed consumption models at one end of a continuum to supply-demand models at the other end. While there have been numerous interregional studies, using the full range of spatial equilibrium techniques, there have been few spatial equilibrium models applied to international trade.

Dean and Collins [6] used a fixed production-fixed consumption (transportation) model to analyze the effects of EEC tariff policies on world trade in fresh oranges. They estimated production and wholesale demand curves for each country. Given these estimated demand curves, existing price levels were

The author is an agricultural economist with the Foreign Demand and Competition Division, Economic Research Service, U.S. Department of Agriculture.

adjusted until world demand equaled world production. These quantities demanded, with the estimates of production, transportation costs and tariff rates, were used in a transportation model to determine the optimum trade pattern. The solution to the transportation model implied a set of price differentials based on transportation rates and tariff rates. These price differentials were compared with the original adjusted prices, and the quantities demanded were readjusted until world demand again equaled world production and until the newly adjusted prices were consistent with those implied in the transportation model solution. A second transportation model was solved, using the readjusted estimates of world demand and production. This procedure was repeated until a consistent set of prices, consumption and trading patterns was obtained.

Fox [8], in his study of the EEC's grain trade, employed activity analysis models—linear programming production models augmented by international transfer activities. Unlike Dean and Collins, he assumed grain prices were predetermined—mainly by political factors. Given these prices and demand and resource levels, he estimated trade patterns between countries and resource use and production levels for each country for food wheat, feed wheat and feed grain.

In his study of international trade in feed grain, Bjarnason [5] employed a supply-demand spatial equilibrium model. He used regression techniques to estimate demand and, indirectly, supply via separate acreage and yield functions. Given the supply functions, the demand functions and a transportation cost matrix, Bjarnason maximized international consumer surplus or what Samuelson [15] called "net social pay-off" to determine the optimum production, consumption, prices and trade patterns for each country. Utilizing the same basic spatial equilibrium model as Bjarnason, Bates and Schmitz [1] analyzed international trade in sugar, making use of a transportation model to study the efficiency of the world sugar trade.

In 1964, Takayama and Judge [17, 18, 19] developed an interregional supply-demand spatial equilibrium model involving several interrelated commodities. By including trade policies, Bawden [2, 3, 4, 22] adapted this interregional model to international trade. Bawden's model was utilized to analyze the effect of domestic and foreign trade policies on production, consumption, prices and trade patterns.

THE MODEL

The approach used was to start at the simplest end of the continuum of spatial equilibrium models and increase the model complexity only to the point where the major relationships in the grain-livestock sector could be represented. Thus this model starts from a fixed production-fixed consumption or transportation model base.

Since one of the objectives of this study is to incorporate institutionally controlled policy variables into the model, the next step involves defining what forms these institutionally controlled policy variables will take. They can be incorporated into a basic transportation model in one of two ways. Some can be incorporated in the form of additional restrictions in the model; the rest can be incorporated in the objective function (the transportation costs function) which is to be minimized. Thus, the objective function must be redefined as minimization of total transfer, not transportation, costs. Transfer costs are all (including transportation) costs involved in moving a commodity from one country to another.

This model is still defined in terms of a particular commodity; no direct interrelationships between commodities are yet included. However, inter-relationships do exist between these grain and livestock commodities: i.e., food grain can be utilized as feed grain. The relationship between veal and beef must be considered; should one market his calves in the form of veal or beef? A third complication enters since the demand for feed grain is a derived demand. These interrelationships are production oriented. They involved modifying what was initially final commodities in a transfer cost model to what is, in part at least, intermediate commodities. That is, some of the grain and livestock commodities are inputs in the production process for other commodities. These interrelation-ships can be included by changing the minimum transfer costs model into a minimum total cost model where total costs include transfer costs and production costs. This model would include not only transfer activities but also production activities for all commodities. In this total costs model, optimum trade patterns and production levels will be determined simultaneously for all commodities.

This is a partial equilibrium world trade model for the grain-livestock sectors of the world. Since the primary interest of this study is the grain-livestock sector of the EEC, production levels in non-EEC countries and trade patterns between these countries are not within the scope of this study. Thus, production activities for outside countries and transfer activities between outside countries are unnecessary. The model thus includes four types of activities for each commodity: (1) production activities for the EEC countries, (2) transfer activities for trade between any two EEC countries, (3) purchase activities for imports from outside countries and (4) sale activities for exports to outside countries. This model then lies somewhere between the transfer cost model and the general (world) total cost model on the continuum of spatial equilibrium models.

Another question needs to be asked now. Is the relevant optimizing criterion minimization of total costs? Three alternative optimizing criteria come to mind: (1) cost minimization, (2) revenue maximization and (3) profit maxi-mization. Microeconomic theory tells us that economic man maximizes profit. This might logically be the best criteria. However, the model being developed here is not a microeconomic model but a macroeconomic model. While not a model of the total economy of the EEC, it is a model of one sector—the grain-livestock sector—of that economy rather than a model of a firm. Therefore, the relevant objective criteria should be the macroeconomic equivalent to profit maximization. Profits are the returns to that factor of production called entrepreneurship. Under competition the other factors—land, labor, and capital—earn their marginal product. This is the maximum that they can earn. Thus, all factors of production are earning the maximum possible returns. At a macroeconomic level, one definition of national income is the sum of the returns to all factors of production. It follows then that a relevant macroeconomic decision criteria comparable to profit maximization at the microeconomic level would be national income maximization.

The microeconomic decision criteria of profit maximization is a special case of this macroeconomic criteria. Under competition the scarcity of the other factors assures them of receiving their maximum returns (their marginal product); therefore, the decision criteria is maximization of the residual—profits. Maximizing national income will still be the relevant decision criteria even if the economy isn't competitive. Under conditions of less than perfect competition, some factors of production are able to extract some of the returns to other factors of production. Maximizing national incomes maximizes the sum of these returns and does not consider the welfare question of how this maximum bundle of returns is distributed among the factors of production. Any welfare considerations could be included in this national income maximizing model by placing additional restrictions on the distribution of resources on the model.

This specific model of the EEC grain-livestock sector incorporates the following interrelationships between commodities:

1. the utilization of food grain as feed grain for livestock on a farm;
2. the utilization of food grain as feed grain, via a denaturing process;
3. the derivation of feed grain consumption (by livestock);
4. the production of a joint product: milk, beef and feeder calves;
5. the derivation of feeder calf consumption;
6. the production of beef by alternative production techniques;
7. the satisfaction of a commodity consumption level by either domestic production (utilizing domestically produced and/or imported inputs in the case of the livestock commodities), transfer from another EEC country, and/or purchase from an outside country of that commodity;
8. the export of surplus production of any commodity by a transfer to another EEC country and/or sale to an outside country.

Only one type of external input restriction exists for the production activities: a land restriction. Crop land is a limiting factor on the production of grain in a country and forage land is a limiting factor on the livestock production in a country. Feed grain is a second input for the livestock production activities, but it in turn is limited by the amount of crop land available in the country. It is assumed that capital and labor are not limiting factors of production for the agricultural sectors of the EEC. These two factors can be obtained from the other sectors of the economy, at least to the point where the land restrictions become operative. As an example, the interrelationships for one country are shown in Figure 12-1.

The following notation is used in the formal model:

(1) The subscripts i and j represent countries or regions included in the model, where

i, j = 1 = France
2 = Italy
3 = Germany-Benelux
4 = Eruopean Free Trade Area
5 = Eastern Europe
6 = Other Europe
7 = United States
8 = Canada
9 = Latin America
0 = Africa and Mid East
A = Other Asia
B = Australia, New Zealand, and South Africa

(2) The superscripts k and h represent the commodities, intermediate and final, included in the model, where

k, h = 1 = food grain
2 = denatured food grain
3 = feed grain
4 = total feed grain equivalent
5 = the joint product, milk-beef-feeder calf[1]
6 = feeder calves
7 = beef (cull dairy cows)
8 = beef (fed more than one year)
9 = beef (fed less than one year)
0 = total beef
A = veal
B = pork
C = eggs
Z = poultry

(3) R = returns to the grain-livestock sector.

(4) P_i^k = the price of commodity k in country i.

(5) P_j^k = the price of commodity k in country j.

(6) S_i^k = the level of production of commodity k in country i.

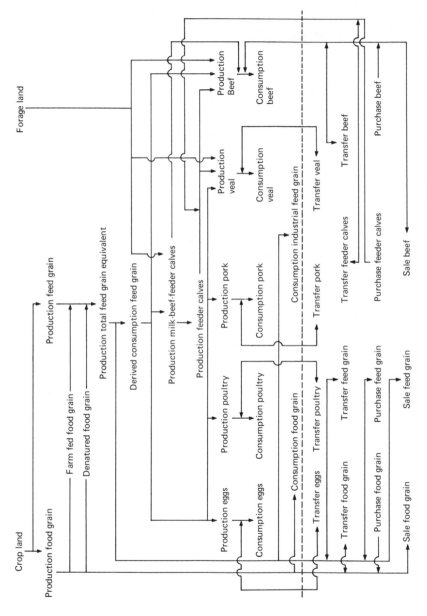

Figure 12-1. A Schematic Diagram for a One Country Segment of the EEC Grain-Livestock Trade Model.

(7) T_{ij}^k = the unit transportation cost of moving commodity k from country i to country j.

(8) X_{ij}^k = the quantity of commodity k transferred from country i to country j (when $i = j$, X_{ij}^k = the quantity of commodity k that is produced in country i and consumed in country i).

(9) ID_{ij}^k = the per unit fixed or specific import duty on commodity k from country i imposed by country j.

(10) IDR_{ij}^k = the ad valorem import duty rate on commodity k from country i imposed by country j.

(11) ES_{ij}^k = the per unit export subsidy granted by country i on commodity k exported to country j.

(12) ED_{ij}^k = the per unit fixed or specific export duty on commodity k imposed by country i on exports to country j.

(13) EDR_{ij}^k = the ad valorem export duty rate on commodity k imposed by country i on exports to country j.

(14) F_i = the quantity of forage land in country i.

(15) f_i^k = the number of units of forage land necessary to produce one unit of commodity k in country i.

(16) L_i = the quantity of crop land in country i.

(17) l_i^k = the number of units of crop land necessary to produce one unit of commodity k in country i.

(18) w_i^{14} = the percentage of food grain production in country i that is fed to livestock on the farm (without going through a market).

(19) M_i^k = the minimum production of commodity k in country i.

(20) N_i^k = the maximum production of commodity k in country i.

(21) r_i^{k5} = the proportion of commodity k that can be produced from the joint product milk-beef-feeder calves in country i.

(22) D_j^k = the level of consumption of commodity k in country j.

(23) $D_j^{4'}$ = the level of consumption of total feed grain equivalent for industrial and seed purposes in country j.

(24) s_j^{kh} = the number of units of commodity k necessary to produce one unit of commodity h in country j.

(25) G = net revenue or expenditure by the European Agricultural Guidance and Guarantee Fund.

(26) E_i^2 = the cost of denaturing food grain in country i.

(27) $\%_{ij}^k$ = the historical minimum percentage of commodity k transferred from country i to country j.

The object of the model is to maximize returns to the grain-livestock sector of the EEC where[2]

$$R = \sum_i \sum_j \sum_k \left[[(P_i^k - E_i^k) S_i^k] + [T_{ij}^k X_{ij}^k] + [(T_{ij}^k - ID_{ij}^k - IDR_{ij}^k P_i^k) X_{ij}^k] \right.$$
$$\left. - [(P_i^k + T_{ij}^k + \left\{ P_j^k - P_i^k \right\} - ES_{ij}^k + ED_{ij}^k + EDR_{ij}^k P_i^k) X_{ij}^k] \right].$$

The term in the first pair of brackets represents the production activities in the model. Internal EEC transfer activities are represented by the second term. For these two terms $i, j \leqslant 3$. The terms in the third bracket represent sale activities. In these terms $i \leqslant 3$ and $j > 3$. The final bracketed terms represent purchase activities. Here $i > 3$ and $j \leqslant 3$.

This objective function allows for import duties, both fixed or specific and ad valorem, imposed on EEC sales by outside countries (see the sale activity term). Export duties, both fixed or specific and ad valorem, on sales by outside countries to members of the EEC are included in the purchase activity term. This purchase activity term also includes an export subsidy imposed on EEC purchases by outside countries; hence, it also is incorporated into the production activity term. Prices in the above equation are internal, domestic prices rather than world prices; therefore, an export subsidy is implicit in all EEC sales. For the same reason, variable import levies and variable export subsidies on transfers between EEC members are implicit in the production activity term. The variable levy imposed by EEC members on outside imports is included in the purchase term.

This objective function is subject to the following restrictions:

(1) There is a maximum amount of forage land in country i ($i \leqslant 3$) available for production of the joint product milk-beef-feeder calves, beef and veal.

$$F_i \geqslant f_i^5 S_i^5 + f_i^8 S_i^8 + f_i^9 S_i^9 + f_i^A S_i^A$$

(2) All crop land in country i ($i \leqslant 3$) is used in the production of food grain, denatured food grain and feed grain.

$$L_i = l_i^1 S_i^1 + l_i^2 S_i^2 + l_i^3 S_i^3$$

(3) The amount of total feed grain equivalent produced in country i ($i \leqslant 3$) is

the sum of the amount of farm fed food grain, denatured food grain production and feed grain production.

$$S_i^4 = w_i^{14} S_i^1 + S_i^2 + S_i^3$$

(4) The amount of feed grain produced in country i ($i \leqslant 3$) is at least as great as the level of consumption of total feed grain equivalent for industrial and seed purposes.[3]

$$S_i^3 \geqslant M_i^3$$

(5) The amount of the joint product milk-beef-feeder calves produced in country i ($i \leqslant 3$) is at least as great as that necessary for country i to be self-sufficient in milk but no greater than that amount required to produce the surplus of milk projected in the MSU-USDA study.

$$N_i^5 \geqslant S_i^5 \geqslant M_i^5$$

(6) The amount of feeder calves produced in country i ($i \leqslant 3$) equals the amount that is produced from the joint product milk-beef-feeder calves.

$$S_i^6 = r_i^{65} S_i^5$$

(7) The amount of beef (cull dairy cows) produced in country i ($i \leqslant 3$) equals the amount that is produced from the joint product milk-beef-feeder calves.

$$S_i^7 = r_i^{75} S_i^5$$

(8) The total amount of beef produced in country i ($i \leqslant 3$) equals the amounts of beef produced by the different production processes in country i.

$$S_i^0 = S_i^7 + S_i^8 + S_i^9$$

(9) The total production of commodity k in country i ($i \leqslant 3$) is transferred (or sold) to country j. For $k = 1$

$$S_i^1 - w_i^{14} S_i^1 = \sum_j X_{ij}^1$$

and for $k = 4, 6, 0, A, B, C, Z$

$$S_i^k = \sum_j X_{ij}^k$$

(10) The total consumption of commodity k ($k = 1, 4, 6, 0, A, B, C, Z$) in country j ($j \leqslant 3$) is equal to the amounts of commodity k transferred from country i to country j.

$$D_j = \sum_i X_{ij}$$

The consumption levels of food grain, total beef, veal, pork, eggs and poultry are predetermined as this represents the demand for final products. The consumption levels for the total feed grain equivalent and feeder calves are not predetermined and represent a derived demand. Total feed grain equivalent in an EEC country ($j \leqslant 3$) is utilized by livestock and for industrial and seed uses.

$$D_j^4 = s_j^{45} S_j^5 + s_j^{48} S_j^8 + s_j^{49} S_j^9 + s_j^{4A} S_j^A + s_j^{4B} S_j^B + s_j^{4C} S_j^C + s_j^{4Z} S_j^Z + D_j^{4'}$$

Feeder calves in an EEC country ($j \leqslant 3$) are utilized in some beef production activities and in the veal production activity.

$$D_j^6 = s_j^{68} S_j^8 + s_j^{69} S_j^9 + s_j^{6A} S_j^A$$

(11) There is a maximum amount of net expenditures by the European Agricultural Guidance and Guarantee Fund.[4]

$$G \leqslant \sum_i E_i^2 S_i^2 + \sum_i \sum_j \sum_k [(P_i^k - P_j^k) - IDR_{ij}^k - IDR_{ij}^k P_i^k + ES_{ij}^k - ED_{ij}^k$$

$$- EDR_{ij}^k P_i^k] X_{ij}^k,$$

where $i \leqslant 3, j = 4$ to $B, k = 1, 4, 6, 0, A, B, C, Z$.

(12) In order to simulate trade patterns more accurately it is necessary to place additional restrictions on the transfer activities, particularly the purchase and sale activities. Because the model is linear, no more than one purchase or sale activity will enter the solution at a positive level for each commodity traded.[5] The restrictions in this model are in terms of minimum quantities of commodity k ($k = 1, 4, 6, 0, A, B, C, Z$) transferred between countries. This minimum quantity is based on historical trade patterns. The most logical method of determining

this minimum is to base it on a historical percentage of consumption in the country.

$$X_{ij}^k \geqslant \%_{ij}^k D_j^k$$

This formulation will be sufficient in defining the minimum X_{ij}^k ($j \leqslant 3$) for all internal EEC transfer activities and for all purchase activities.[6] For sale activities the minimum quantity of commodity k ($k = 1, 4, 0$) transferred between countries will be based on a historical percentage of production in a country ($i \neq j$ and $i \leqslant 3$).

$$X_{ij}^k \geqslant \%_{ij}^k S_i^k$$

This minimum percentage can be determined by solving the above equations for $\%_{ij}^k$ and substituting historical data into the right hand side of the equation.[7] It will be based on an average of percentages for a predetermined historical time period.

How will this last restriction affect the results of the model? This is a method by which certain rigidities in the economic system can be incorporated in the model. That is, a certain portion of trade will be allocated on the basis of historical trading patterns and the rest will be allocated on the basis of the internal criteria of the linear programming model. If a time dimension were added to this model, this historical minimum percentage would take the form of a moving average of past trading patterns. This, *ceteris paribus,* would cause the solution over time to converge toward the linear programming solution for the model without this set of restrictions.

THE EEC TRADE MODEL—A TEST

In order to test the EEC grain-livestock trade model postdictions were made for 1964 and 1968. The 1964 base was selected since it served as the base period for the MSU-USDA production and consumption projections. The 1968 model provided a further test of the model's structure. The model structure remained the same for both years. Only the input coefficients were changed. The endogenous variables include production levels and trade levels for the EEC countries. For food grain, feed grain and beef, internal transfer, purchase and sale activities were allowed. Only internal transfer and purchase activities were allowed for feeder calves, while internal transfer activities alone were permitted for veal, pork, eggs and poultry.

Several criteria were used in evaluating the goodness of fit of this model. Four separate approaches were used in this evaluation process. The first was a subjective appraisal of the errors for the various classes of activities in the model. The next three more quantitative tests involved the Theil inequality coefficient [20, pp. 31–48] , the sign test, and regression analysis. The results for these three tests are summarized in Table 12-1. Average percentage errors are not shown for the activity classes listed in these tables since for some activities either the actual or the predicted values were zero. In lieu of this a general discussion of where the major differences in actual-predicted values occurred is included. Following this is a brief discussion of the results of the three quanti-tative tests for each year.

The 1964 Model

Predicted production levels for the EEC when compared with actual levels showed errors varying from less than one percent for eggs to twelve percent for poultry and averaged about five percent for the five product categories (total grain, beef and veal, pork, eggs and poultry) in Table 12-2. The predicted production levels for France, Italy and Germany-Benelux also showed errors of a similar magnitude. The one exception being beef and veal production. The model shows France becoming the major EEC beef producer instead of the other members, particularly Germany-Benelux.

The trade patterns resulting from these production patterns are presented in Tables 12-3 to 12-7. With two exceptions predicted total grain transfer levels have the same order of magnitude as actual transfers. The two ex-ceptions being French exports to Eastern Europe and French imports from Germany-Benelux. The model does show increases in German-Benelux total grain imports, primarily from the United States over actual imports. The difference in beef and veal production is carried over to the transfer sector of the model. The beef that was more profitable to produce in France is now shipped to Germany-Benelux and Italy. The predicted transfer patterns for pork, eggs and poultry are close to actual levels. For both production and transfer activities the predicted values are generally of the same order of magnitude as the actual values.

The deviations from what actually happened in 1964 primarily revolve about shifting production patterns and the resulting trade changes. The model showed an increase in meat production in France of over 1.7 million metric ton. Over 75 percent of this increase was increased beef production which was exported to Germany-Benelux and Italy. French pork production in the model was also up by over 200 thousand metric ton. The bulk of this excess pork production was shipped to Germany-Benelux to replace their decrease in pork production. Poultry production for France exceeded actual production by over 100 thousand metric ton. There was also a slight increase in the French egg pro-duction which was exported to Italy.

To achieve their increased beef production, France imported large numbers of feeder calves from both Germany-Benelux and Italy. Almost two-thirds of their production was shipped to France. These feeder calf imports were

Table 12-1.   Goodness of Fit Criteria

	Theil's Inequality Coefficient	The Sign Test ($\alpha = 0.05$)	Regression: $p_i = \beta_0 + \beta_i \hat{q}_i$				
			$\hat{\beta}_0$	$\hat{\sigma}_{\beta_0}$	$\hat{\beta}_1$	$\hat{\sigma}_{\beta_1}$	$\hat{\sigma}_{p_i \hat{q}_i}$
The 1964 model							
Production activities	0.15	Accept	715.70	1,108.77	0.89	0.07	4,598.71
Transfer activities:							
Food grain	0.38	Accept	30.46	72.54	1.12	0.27	260.44
Feed grain	0.23	Accept	4.76	132.88	1.17	0.15	475.78
Total grain	0.08	Accept	27.95	85.39	1.12	0.02	455.36
Feeder calves	0.77	Reject	543.28	636.70	0.48	0.14	2,049.19
Beef and veal	0.37	Reject	589.27	575.20	0.56	0.15	2,252.45
Pork	0.05	Accept	257.61	238.97	0.94	0.04	621.02
Eggs	0.02	Accept	40.86	27.84	0.99	0.01	70.17
Poultry	0.07	Accept	70.91	81.37	1.07	0.05	200.15
All transfer activities	0.54	Accept	183.71	122.32	0.86	0.04	1,331.13
The complete model	0.29	Accept	211.85	204.65	0.91	0.03	2,437.10
The 1968 model							
Production activities	0.17	Accept	1,372.40	1,801.07	0.84	0.10	6,132.06
Transfer activities:							
Food grain	0.65	Accept	34.72	62.72	0.81	0.17	243.19
Feed grain	0.40	Accept	447.97	189.54	0.38	0.15	691.34
Total grain	0.12	Accept	-86.97	183.38	1.15	0.04	971.36
Feeder calves	0.73	Accept	1,358.95	671.26	-0.92	0.77	1,615.22
Beef and veal	0.38	Accept	783.32	596.71	0.55	0.15	2,364.08
Pork	0.19	Accept	633.11	432.18	0.67	0.05	1,133.17
Eggs	0.37	Accept	241.98	144.36	0.81	0.05	364.61
Poultry	0.08	Accept	169.55	105.63	0.88	0.05	258.67
All transfer activities	0.23	Accept	235.34	132.24	0.84	0.04	1,438.27
The complete model	0.18	Accept	298.52	240.22	0.88	0.03	2,796.92

Table 12-2. 1964 Production Levels

Commodity	Units	France Actual	France Model	Italy Actual	Italy Model	Germany-Benelux Actual	Germany-Benelux Model	European Economic Community Actual	European Economic Community Model
Total grain	1,000 m.t.	27,364.0	28,288.3	13,955.0	14,160.8	19,841.0	20,574.3	61,160.0	63,023.4
Food grain	1,000 m.t.		13,776.1		8,862.4		5,282.8		27,921.3
Denatured food grain	1,000 m.t.		12,815.2		0		12,418.5		25,233.7
Total food grain[a]	1,000 m.t.	13,980.0	26,591.3	9,198.0	8,862.4	10,367.0	17,701.3	33,545.0	53,155.0
Feed grain[a]	1,000 m.t.	13,384.0	1,697.0	4,757.0	5,298.4	9,474.0	2,873.0	27,615.0	9,868.4
Total feed grain equivalent	1,000 m.t.		17,267.4		6,007.4		15,714.1		38,988.9
Beef and veal	1,000 m.t.	1,428.3	2,809.7	540.5	390.6	1,550.7	621.8	3,519.5	3,822.1
Milk-beef-feeder calves	1,000 head	11,472.0	9,501.2	4,483.7	4,522.0	8,538.1	8,504.2	24,493.8	22,527.4
Feeder calves[b]	1,000 head	8,917.9	6,413.3	2,647.0	3,052.4	6,924.0	5,740.3	18,488.9	15,206.0
Beef (cull cows)	1,000 m.t.		551.1		275.8		467.7		1,294.6
Beef (≥ 1 year)	1,000 m.t.		1,848.2		0		10.0		1,858.2
Beef (< 1 year)	1,000 m.t.				0				0
Total beef	1,000 m.t.	1,066.8	2,399.3	464.9	275.8	1,362.2	477.7	2,893.9	3,152.8
Veal	1,000 m.t.	361.5	410.4	75.6	114.8	188.5	144.1	625.6	669.3
Pork	1,000 m.t.	1,203.1	1,439.0	396.9	364.1	2,419.8	2,293.4	4,019.8	4,096.5
Poultry	1,000 m.t.	550.0	655.2	340.0	322.5	363.0	434.2	1,253.0	1,411.9
Eggs	1,000 m.t.	560.0	581.4	458.0	463.1	1,100.0	1,092.6	2,118.0	2,137.1

[a]Actual and predicted food grain and feed grain production levels are not strictly comparable. No distinction is made between food grain produced for human consumption and for livestock consumption in the published data as was the case in this model.

[b]A cull rate for dairy cattle of 0.2 is assumed in calculating the actual number of feeder calves.

Source (actual): [16].

Table 12-3. 1964 Transfer Levels: Total Grain

Exporter	Importer	France	Italy	Germany-Benelux	EFTA	Eastern Europe	Other Europe	Africa & Mid East	Other Asia
				(1,000 metric tons)					
France	Actual	20,385.9	434.9	1,394.1	1,832.6	676.1	722.4	682.9	619.9
	Model	21,066.7	426.1	2,567.3	1,104.0	1,849.5	172.4	551.0	551.0
Italy	Actual	55.3	13,572.9	170.3		32.5		106.4	
	Model	343.3	13,640.2	0		0		177.2	
Germany-Benelux	Actual	0.9	1.3	18,172.6	695.6	600.9		189.6	94.3
	Model	686.7	85.8	18,642.2	525.6	211.3		211.3	211.3
EFTA	Actual			258.8					
	Model			464.2					
United States	Actual	602.0	1,108.9	4,062.5					
	Model	403.1	1,043.3	5,929.9					
Canada	Actual	184.0	66.3	1,000.3					
	Model	119.5	177.1	1,242.7					
Latin America	Actual	249.6	2,489.9	1,202.1					
	Model	231.5	1,720.3	1,723.6					
Africa & Mid East	Actual	119.6		24.8					
	Model	291.2		232.1					
Australia, New Zealand, South Africa	Actual		157.3	294.4					
	Model		343.3	696.4					

Source (actual): [16].

Table 12-4. 1964 Transfer Levels: Food Grain

Exporter / Importer		France	Italy	Germany-Benelux	EFTA	Eastern Europe	Africa & Mid East	Other Asia
				(1,000 metric tons)				
France	Actual		202.0	371.8	880.3	676.1	682.9	619.9
	Model	5,616.5	168.6	1,870.9	413.3	1,849.5	551.0	551.0
Italy	Actual	0	7,976.2	0		32.5	106.4	
	Model	0		0		0	177.2	
Germany-Benelux	Actual	0.5	1.3	4,014.9	364.1	600.9	189.6	94.3
	Model	0	0		211.3	211.3	211.3	211.3
United States	Actual	195.0	112.9	851.1				
	Model	59.8	442.7	828.9				
Canada	Actual	184.0	66.0	1,000.3				
	Model	179.5	177.1	1,242.7				
Latin America	Actual	191.0	151.0	292.0				
	Model	59.8	88.5	331.6				
Africa & Mid East	Actual	96.0						
	Model	119.5						

Source (actual): [16], [21].

Table 12-5. 1964 Transfer Levels: Feed Grain

Exporter	Importer	France	Italy	Germany-Benelux	EFTA	Other Europe
			(1,000 metric tons)			
France	Actual		232.9	1,022.3	952.3	722.4
	Model	15,450.2	257.5	696.4	690.7	172.7
Italy	Actual	55.3		170.3		
	Model	343.3	5,664.0	0		
Germany-Benelux	Actual	0.4	0		331.5	
	Model	686.7	85.8	14,627.3	314.3	
EFTA	Actual			258.8		
	Model			464.2		
United States	Actual	407.0	996.0	3,211.4		
	Model	343.3	600.6	5,101.0		
Latin America	Actual	58.6	2,338.9	910.1		
	Model	171.7	1,631.8	1,392.3		
Africa & Mid East	Actual	23.6		24.8		
	Model	171.7		232.1		
Australia, New Zealand, South Africa	Actual		157.3	294.4		
	Model		343.3	696.4		

Source (actual): [16], [21].

in lieu of producing these calves domestically. With fewer calves being produced fewer cows were required in France. Thus the model postulated a sixty percent lower milk surplus in France than that predicted in the MSU-USDA study. The model predicted a milk self-sufficiency position for Italy and a milk surplus level equal to that predicted in the above study for Germany-Benelux. Since France increased their beef production at the expense of Italian and German-Benelux production, EFTA and Eastern Europe exports of feeder calves to Germany-Benelux and Italy dropped accordingly.

This increased meat production required increased feed grain consumption in France. This demand was met through an increase in the production of feed grain in France by over one million metric ton and through a one million metric ton increase in imports. These imports came from Germany-Benelux, Italy, Africa and the Mid East and Latin America. Germany-Benelux and Italy filled their resulting shortage of food grain by also increasing their imports: the former from France and Canada, and the latter from North America.

These differences all hinge on one central point. The model shows France developing into the major agricultural center of the EEC. It is already the major grain producer and to utilize this grain most efficiently it also became a major producer of livestock. Italy and Germany-Benelux supported this shift by becoming major input suppliers for France (particularly for feeder calves). With

Table 12-6. 1964 Transfer Levels: Beef and Veal

Exporter		France	Italy	Germany-Benelux	All Other Countries
			(1,000 metric tons)		
France	Beef and veal: actual	1,358.1	2.6	54.8	10.6
	Beef and veal: model	1,385.3	350.5	1,073.8	0
	beef: model	1,003.4	337.9	1,058.0	0
	veal: model	381.9	12.6	15.8	
Italy	Beef and veal: actual	0.1	1,090.4	0	0
	Beef and veal: model	0	390.4	0	0
	beef: model	0	275.8	0	0
	veal: model	0	114.8	0	
Germany-Benelux	Beef and veal: actual	27.2	39.5	1,472.6	9.7
	Beef and veal: model	10.1	14.2	597.5	0
	beef: model	10.1	14.2	453.4	0
	veal: model	0	0	144.1	
EFTA	Beef and veal: actual	4.4	58.9		
	Beef and veal: model	0	21.3		
	beef: model	0	21.3		
Eastern Europe	Beef and veal: actual	0.5	16.2		
	Beef and veal: model	0	7.1		
	beef: model	0	7.1		
Latin America	Beef and veal: actual	26.9	114.2	93.4	
	Beef and veal: model	0	55.0	46.7	
	beef: model	0	55.0	46.7	

Source (actual): [16], [21].

France assuming this new role the EEC moved to virtual self sufficiency in livestock production. With the shift from food grain to the feed grain production necessary for the livestock production, the net exports of food grain by the EEC decreased. This shifting production mix between grains, however, was not adequate to meet consumption requirements under livestock self-sufficiency and net EEC imports of feed grains increased.

A final difference should be pointed out. The composition of the grain fed is different from what the model predicts. The model shows that a substantial portion of the grain fed in France and in Germany-Benelux is denatured food grain rather than feed grain. In fact, only that amount of feed grain required for seed and industrial purposes is produced in these two regions.

Theil's Inequality Coefficient—the 1964 Model. The Theil inequality coefficient is a type of correlation coefficient used to measure the goodness of fit of predicted to actual outcomes. This coefficient ranges from zero (a perfect fit) to one (no correlation) in value. The calculated coefficients for the 1964 model are presented in Table 12-1. Coefficients are given for the production and transfer subsections of the model as well as for the complete model.

Table 12–7.   1964 Transfer Levels: Feeder Calves, Pork, Eggs, Poultry

Exporter	Importer	France	Italy	Germany-Benelux
feeder calves (1,000 head)				
France	Actual	8,540.6	330.9	46.4
	Model	6,374.9	38.9	0
Italy	Actual	0	2,647.0	0
	Model	2,001.9	1,050.5	0
Germany-Benelux	Actual	27.3	174.2	6,722.5
	Model	3,796.6	38.9	1,904.8
EFTA	Actual		418.0	2,290.7
	Model		103.8	291.4
Eastern Europe	Actual	0	434.4	204.0
	Model	0	64.8	44.8
pork (1,000 metric tons)				
France	Actual	1,199.6	0.2	2.6
	Model	1,153.8	36.0	249.2
Italy	Actual	0	396.9	0
	Model	0	364.1	0
Germany-Benelux	Actual	51.0	3.9	2,363.6
	Model	23.5	4.0	2,265.8
eggs (1,000 metric tons)				
France	Actual	552.2	0.2	5.6
	Model	545.9	35.5	0
Italy	Actual	0	457.4	0.1
	Model	0	463.1	0
Germany-Benelux	Actual	1.5	10.5	1,072.7
	Model	11.1	15.4	1,066.0
poultry (1,000 metric tons)				
France	Actual	525.7	0	15.5
	Model	572.0	35.5	47.8
Italy	Actual	0	339.6	0.2
	Model	0	322.5	0
Germany-Benelux	Actual	0.2	0	354.0
	Model	0	0	434.2

Source (actual): [16], [21].

One problem with Theil's inequality coefficient is that the predicted and actual values must be additive. The values presented in Tables 12-2 to 12-7 obviously are not additive. In order to convert these data to a scale that was additive a conversion factor was defined for use throughout the testing of this basic model. A commonly accepted conversion factor in economic literature is price (the additive scale then being dollars). The 1964 price, however, could not be used to convert the production and transfer data to common units because the levels of the activities in 1964 are functions of these prices. Thus a change in the conversion factors would cause not only immediate changes in Theil's inequality coefficient but also changes in the activity levels. These changing activity levels would again alter the value of the coefficient.

The 1960–1968 average world price for the grain-livestock products was used to convert the 1964 results to common units. This is still a price but it is as far removed as possible from being an exogenous variable in the model. It will be used throughout wherever a scale conversion is necessary in order to carry out any goodness of fit test. Thus any changes in the test results will be due only to changes in the levels of the activities.

The inequality coefficient does not provide a test of the goodness of fit of the total model. However, it does provide a relative measure of the goodness of fit of separate portions of the model, permitting sectors of the model to be ranked according to their goodness of fit. As can be seen from Table 12-1, the transfer sections for eggs, pork, poultry and total grain have the best fit of all sections. A second grouping—consisting of the production activities, feed grain transfer, and the total model (all production and transfer activities)—fall into a second best fit category. The third best fit grouping includes beef and veal transfer, food grain transfer, and total transfer activities. Finally, come the feeder calf transfer activities. This ordered ranking of the coefficients agrees with the points in the model where the major variations between the 1964 predicted results and the 1964 actual results occurred: a shift in beef production and the resulting shifts in feeder calf production and transfer.

The Sign Test—the 1964 Model. The hypothesis that the predicted and actual quantities for sections of the 1964 model were distributed equally was tested by sign tests. All parts of the model, except the feeder calves transfer and beef and veal transfer activities, were accepted as being equally distributed with their actual counterparts at the 0.05 level (see Table 12-1).

This again is consistent with a visual inspection of the data. Beef is, in the model, produced in France from feeder calves imported from Germany-Benelux and Italy. This is not what actually happened in 1964; therefore, these two parts of the model were rejected by the sign test.

Regression—the 1964 Model. A third test of goodness of fit centers around a regression of predicted values of the activities on actual values. A perfect fit would be one where all predicted values equaled actual values. This is equivalent to a regression equation with parameters zero and one.[8] Regression coefficients, and their standard errors, for different parts of the 1964 model are presented in Table 12-1. The regression results are not based on the data in Tables 12-2 to 12-7. This data have been converted on the basis of 1960–1968 average world prices in order to provide an additive scale.

The hypothesis that the intercept of the regression equations equaled zero was accepted at a significance level of 0.05 for all groupings of activities on the basis of a *t*-test. Using the same type of test, the hypothesis that the slope of the regression equations equaled one was rejected for total grain transfer, feeder calves transfer, beef and veal transfer, all transfer and the complete model. The hypothesis was accepted for the other divisions of activities. This implies that the predictions of the total grain activities are overestimated; while the whole model, particularly the feeder calves and beef and veal transfer activities, are under-estimated.

Again the results of the regression analysis are consistent with the points where the predicted and actual variations occur in the 1964 model.

The 1968 Model

Predicted production levels for 1968, when compared with actual levels showed errors ranging from less than one fourth of one percent to eighteen percent and averaging about five percent for total grain, beef and veal, pork, eggs, and poultry (see Table 12-8). As with 1964, with the exception of beef and veal, the predicted production levels for the three EEC regions were close to the actual production levels.

The resulting 1968 transfer patterns are shown in Tables 12-9 to 12-13. With the exception of French-Eastern Europe, Italian-French, United States-German-Benelux and Australian, New Zealand, South African-German-Benelux trade, predicted total grain shipments were similar to actual shipments. Again trade patterns for beef and veal depended on production patterns. With the exception of French beef exports to Germany-Benelux and Italy and a slight tendency for a similar pattern in other livestock products the predicted trade levels for all the livestock products were also close to actual levels.

The 1968 model shows the same type of deviation as the 1964 model. France is still the major livestock producer in the EEC. This is particularly true for beef and veal. The 1968 model shows that 75.3 percent of the EEC's beef and veal production (rather than the actual 41.7 percent) is produced in France. This excess production is shipped to Germany-Benelux and Italy, with France supplying over two-thirds of the beef consumed in Germany-Benelux and over a third of that consumed in Italy. French exports of beef and veal are increasing (from 59.6 to 134.7 thousand metric ton during the 1964-1968 period), however, not as fast as the model predicts.

What is true for beef and veal is true, to a lesser extent for the other livestock products in the model. French pork production is twenty percent over what it really was in 1968. The model shows this extra production being shipped primarily to Germany-Benelux with some to Italy. Total pork production in the EEC was larger than predicted. Over a 200 thousand metric ton increase above actual in egg production is indicated for France. This is in large part at the expense of German-Benelux production with France supplying about fifteen percent of both Italian and German-Benelux demand. The model's poultry pro-

Table 12-8. 1968 Production Levels

Commodity	Units	France		Italy		Germany-Benelux		European Economic Community	
		Actual	Model	Actual	Model	Actual	Model	Actual	Model
Total grain	1,000 m.t.	32,704.0	34,238.2	14,331.0	15,443.8	22,153.0	22,855.1	69,188.0	72,537.1
Food grain	1,000 m.t.		13,811.6		9,163.3		5,345.4		28,320.3
Denatured food grain	1,000 m.t.		18,542.6		0		12,726.7		31,269.3
Total food grain[a]	1,000 m.t.	14,842.0	32,354.2	9,590.0	9,163.3	11,166.0	18,072.1	35,598.0	59,589.6
Feed grain[a]	1,000 m.t.	17,862.0	1,884.0	4,741.0	6,280.5	10,987.0	4,783.0	33,590.0	12,947.5
Total feed grain equivalent	1,000 m.t.		23,188.9		7,013.6		17,937.0		48,139.8
Beef and veal	1,000 m.t.	1,648.0	3,019.6	590.0	438.7	1,714.0	550.7	3,952.0	4,009.0
Milk-beef-feeder calves	1,000 head	8,762.0	10,172.6	4,740.0	4,949.5	8,833.0	7,488.3	22,335.0	22,610.4
Feeder calves	1,000 head		6,866.5		3,340.9		5,054.6		15,262.0
Beef (cull cows)	1,000 m.t.		600.2		301.9		419.3		1,321.4
Beef (≥ 1 year)	1,000 m.t.		1,992.6		0		0		1,992.6
Beef (≤ 1 year)	1,000 m.t.				0				0
Total beef	1,000 m.t.		2,592.8		301.9		419.3		3,314.0
Veal	1,000 m.t.		426.8		136.8		131.4		695.0
Pork	1,000 m.t.	1,344.0	1,624.1	528.0	411.0	3,575.0	2,407.9	5,447.0	4,443.0
Poultry	1,000 m.t.	680.0	791.6	532.0	455.9	514.0	475.4	1,726.0	1,722.9
Eggs	1,000 m.t.	621.0	850.5	480.0	416.1	1,225.0	997.4	2,326.0	2,264.0

[a] Actual and predicted food grain and feed grain production levels are not strictly comparable. No distinction is made between food grain produced for human consumption and for livestock consumption in the published data as was the case in this model.

Source (actual): [11].

Table 12-9. 1968 Transfer Levels: Total Grain

Importer / Exporter		France	Italy	Germany-Benelux	EFTA	Eastern Europe	Other Europe	Africa & Mid East	Other Asia
		(1,000 metric tons)							
France	Actual	22,423.6	322.8	3,230.2	1,561.1	418.2	552.0	1,843.9	768.0
	Model	24,954.1	364.1	3,656.3	1,845.5	1,104.9	927.6	966.6	414.3
Italy	Actual	2.5	14,033.7	13.3		0		242.4	
	Model	1,145.3	13,774.0	249.7		0		274.9	
Germany-Benelux	Actual	7.6	2.8	20,690.7	457.1	100.6		382.5	176.7
	Model	0	91.9	21,476.7	659.8	160.4		320.7	106.9
EFTA	Actual			653.2					
	Model			499.4					
United States	Actual	725.6	2,350.6	5,521.0					
	Model	820.9	1,708.6	2,217.1					
Canada	Actual	50.9	358.3	673.6					
	Model	111.7	179.2	626.4					
Latin America	Actual	165.4	2,961.2	1,145.5					
	Model	329.4	2,268.9	656.0					
Africa & Mid East	Actual	39.3		203.6					
	Model								
Australia, New Zealand, South Africa	Actual		440.9	292.5					
	Model		95.2	3,418.7					

Source: Tables 12–10 and 12–11.

Table 12-10. 1968 Transfer Levels: Food Grain

Exporter	Importer	France	Italy	Germany-Benelux	EFTA	Eastern Europe	Africa & Mid East	Other Asia
				(1,000 metric tons)				
France	Actual		179.8	1,097.0	612.4	418.2	1,843.9	768.0
	Model	5,195.9	268.9	2,407.8	690.6	1,104.9	966.8	414.3
Italy	Actual	0	8,155.4	11.8		0	242.4	
	Model	0		0		0	274.9	
Germany-Benelux	Actual	7.6	0	4,169.4	383.6	100.6	382.5	176.7
	Model	0	0		160.4	160.4	320.7	106.9
United States	Actual	345.3	213.7	1,041.9				
	Model	167.6	89.6	469.7				
Canada	Actual	50.9	358.3	673.6				
	Model	111.7	179.2	626.4				
Latin America	Actual	46.0	437.9	59.8				
	Model	111.7	268.9	156.6				
Africa & Mid East	Actual	0						
	Model	0						

Source (actual): [11], [21].

Table 12–11. 1968 Transfer Levels: Feed Grain

Exporter	Importer	France	Italy	Germany-Benelux	EFTA	Other Europe
				(1,000 metric tons)		
France	Actual		143.0	2,133.2	948.7	552.0
	Model	19,758.2	95.2	1,248.5	1,159.4	927.6
Italy	Actual	2.6		1.5		
	Model	1,145.3	5,618.6	249.7		
Germany-Benelux	Actual	0	2.8		73.5	
	Model	0	91.9	17,307.3	538.1	
EFTA	Actual			653.2		
	Model			499.4		
United States	Actual	380.3	2,136.9	4,479.1		
	Model	653.3	1,619.0	1,747.4		
Latin America	Actual	53.7	2,523.3	1,085.7		
	Model	217.7	2,000.0	499.4		
Africa & Mid East	Actual	39.3		203.6		
	Model	0		0		
Australia, New Zealand, South Africa	Actual		440.9	292.5		
	Model		95.2	3,418.7		

Source (actual): 11.

duction relative to actual production in France is also up—by over sixteen percent. This added French production is then shipped to Italy and Germany-Benelux.

As in the 1964 model the increased beef production in France requires substantially more feeder calves than are produced in France. About two-thirds of both Italian and German-Benelux feeder calves were shipped to France. Again since a large portion of France's demand for feeder calves is supplied via imports, this model predicts a milk surplus only a third as large as that actually existing in France in 1968. A self-sufficiency position, with no milk surpluses, is predicted for both Italy and Germany-Benelux. Since French beef production replaced Italian and German-Benelux production, their imports of feeder calves fell substantially.

France's increased meat production caused corresponding repercussions in the feed grain section of the model. The increased demand for feed grain in France is met by over a 2.6 million metric ton increase in production and over a 1.5 million metric ton increase in imports (two-thirds of which were from Italy). The corresponding decrease in demand for feed grain in Italy and Germany-Benelux lead to a drop in their imports. Italy's imports from both the United States and Latin America fell by over 500 thousand metric ton. Not only did Germany-Benelux's imports fall by over 500 thousand metric ton but the composition of the remaining imports changed. There were reductions in German-Benelux imports from the United States, France, and Latin America, while at the

Table 12-12. 1968 Transfer Levels: Beef and Veal

Exporter	Importer	France	Italy	Germany-Benelux	All Other Countries
		(1,000 metric tons)			
France	Beef and veal: actual	1,493.1	11.4	119.0	20.2
	Beef and veal: model	1,362.9	436.3	1,220.3	0
	beef: model	964.4	411.7	1,196.7	0
	veal: model	378.5	24.6	23.6	
Italy	Beef and veal: actual	0	589.6	0.4	0
	Beef and veal: model	0	438.7	0	0
	beef: model	0	301.9	0	0
	veal: model	0	136.8	0	
Germany-	Beef and veal: actual	15.1	62.6	1,619.2	8.9
Benelux	Beef and veal: model	0	9.8	541.0	0
	beef: model	0	9.8	409.6	0
	veal: model	0	0	131.4	
EFTA	Beef and veal: actual	2.6	50.9		
	Beef and veal: model	10.0	88.0		
	beef: model	10.0	88.0		
Eastern	Beef and veal: actual	4.5	45.7		
Europe	Beef and veal: model	0	58.6		
	beef: model	0	58.6		
Latin	Beef and veal: actual	8.5	40.9	63.5	
America	Beef and veal: model	10.0	107.5	32.8	
	beef: model	10.0	107.5	32.8	

Source (actual): [11], [21].

same time a significant increase in imports from Australia, New Zealand and South Africa.

The model also shows at least a twenty-five percent increase in German-Benelux imports of food grain. With two exceptions the transfer pattern for food grain is reasonable. Germany-Benelux imports food grain from France at the expense of the United States. The excess production of France is shipped to Germany-Benelux and Eastern Europe in the model rather than Africa and the Mid East and Germany-Benelux.

To summarize the grain sector, the 1968 model shows a shifting away from food grain and toward feed grain production in the EEC (especially in Germany-Benelux). As a result of this shift, their net imports of grain fell. A large portion of this drop in imports was at the expense of United States exports to Germany-Benelux and Italy. As in 1964, the model shows feed grain production in France and Germany-Benelux to be composed chiefly of denatured food grain.

Theil's Inequality Coefficient—the 1968 Model. If we rank the sections of this model as to their relative goodness of fit (see Table 12-1) the poultry transfer section would have the best fit. Falling into a second category come the total grain transfer, the production, the total model, pork transfer, and

Table 12–13. 1968 Transfer Levels: Feeder Calves, Pork, Eggs, Poultry

Exporter		France	Italy	Germany-Benelux
Feeder calves (1,000 head)				
France	Actual		569.5	248.8
	Model	6,820.1	46.4	0
Italy	Actual	0		0
	Model	2,089.0	1,251.9	0
Germany-Benelux	Actual	40.6	370.9	
	Model	3,456.3	46.4	1,551.9
EFTA	Actual		464.4	930.6
	Model		123.6	237.4
Eastern Europe	Actual	0	1,472.2	460.2
	Model	0	77.3	36.5
Pork (1,000 metric tons)				
France	Actual	1,338.7	1.8	1.4
	Model	1,159.7	44.9	419.5
Italy	Actual	0	528.0	0
	Model	0	411.0	0
Germany-Benelux	Actual	105.1	24.4	3,443.0
	Model	48.3	29.1	2,330.5
Eggs (1,000 metric tons)				
France	Actual	613.4	1.9	3.6
	Model	602.9	70.0	177.6
Italy	Actual	0	479.6	0
	Model	0	416.1	0
Germany-Benelux	Actual	12.7	3.1	1,195.8
	Model	6.1	4.9	986.4
Poultry (1,000 metric tons)				
France	Actual	662.0	0	10.0
	Model	624.0	82.1	85.6
Italy	Actual	0	529.4	2.1
	Model	0	455.9	0
Germany-Benelux	Actual	1.2	1.1	498.0
	Model	0	0	475.4

Source (actual): [11], [21].

total transfer activities. Next come the egg, beef and veal and feed grain transfer activities. A final grouping consists of the food grain and feeder calves transfer activities.

The ranking is again consistent with the sections where the major deviations occur between the 1968 predicted and the 1968 actual results—the transfer of beef and the resulting effects on grain and feeder calves. The inequality coefficient shows that the 1968 model is better than the 1964 model (0.18 to

0.29). At the same time, however, the coefficients for the separate sections of the model tend to be larger. This is in large part due to the fact that Theil's inequality coefficient measures relative error. The 1968 model does as good a job as the 1964 model does in predicting the major activities. However, the error on the minor activities in 1968 tended to be larger than in 1964. This caused the coefficients to increase somewhat in size.

The Sign Test—the 1968 Model. Again the hypothesis that the distribution of the predicted quantities equaled the distribution of the actual quantities was tested for the sections of the 1968 model by sign tests. This hypothesis was accepted at the 0.05 level for all parts of the model (Table 12-1).

Regression—the 1968 Model. The hypothesis that the intercept equaled zero was accepted for all groupings of activities except feed grain transfer on the basis of a t-test at the 0.05 significance level. With the same type of test the hypothesis that the slopes of the regression equation equaled one was accepted for the production, the food grain transfer and the poultry transfer activities. This hypothesis was rejected for the other activity divisions. Since the slope coefficients (with the exception of total grain transfer) are all less than one, this implies that the 1968 predictions tend to underestimate actual activity levels.[9]

Rejection of the hypothesis that the slopes of the regression equations equal one is not inconsistent with the results of the sign test. It does, however, emphasize some of the shortcomings of the sign test. The sign test is only concerned with whether you overestimate or underestimate. It is not concerned with the size of either the absolute error or the relative error—just the sign of the error. The 1968 model did not predict the large valued transfer activities with as much accuracy as did the 1964 model. More often than not it tended to underestimate these values. This caused the slope of a regression equation to be less without affecting appreciably the number of overestimations and underestimations.

TEST CONCLUSIONS

One objective of this research was, using only easily available input data, to develop a simple model that was able to simulate the grain-livestock economy of the EEC. Given this objective it seems reasonable to conclude that this model is a good first approximation. While it may be possible to further improve the model's goodness of fit, it could only be done by expanding the size and complexity of the model and/or by utilizing better, more detailed input data. This takes us further away from our objective, especially since some of the data required by a better model are not presently available.

The differences between actual and predicted values can be accounted for by any of a combination of three factors. The first hinges on the characteristics of a linear model. Activities enter a linear model one at a time. For example, consider restriction twelve. Without this minimum historical percent transferred over any given route, only one purchase or sale activity would enter the model. This restriction allows some of the linear properties of the model to be overcome. It is this type of problem that causes so little feed grain to be produced in France and Germany-Benelux. It is more profitable to produce food grain for feed purposes than feed grain. The linear model also does not allow for diminishing returns on the production activities (or transfer activities for that matter). With sufficiently detailed data concerning the shape of the production function (and therefore the total revenue curve), step functions could be included for all activities.

 Second, differences between actual and predicted values are also a function of the accuracy and availability of the input data in the model. Whenever two alternative activities are good substitutes, errors in the data (be it in the objective function or in the coefficients of the restrictions) can cause activities to enter at different rates and times. Data for intercountry models tend to be inadequate and incomplete. This coupled with the necessity for comparable data for all countries causes the collection of even minimum input data to be a problem of some magnitude. For this model improved transport costs and forage and grain conversion factors for livestock should improve the predictions. This is particularly true for transportation costs within Europe. The lack of comparable data will also account for the feeder calves transfer section of the model performing so poorly. The data are not comparable. The predicted values are in terms of feeder calves while the actual values are in terms of live cattle. To the extent that live cattle transfers are not feeder calves, comparison between actual and predicted values are not completely valid.

 A final reason for the models divergence from reality lies in the theoretical structure or framework of the model. If the framework of the model does not accurately represent the structure of the economy you are trying to simulate, the model will not predict reality. This final reason, coupled with the lack of data, is probably the major reason why the 1964 model differed from reality. This model predicted a shifting of livestock production to the area which generates the greatest EEC revenue—France. This shift is based on four relative factors alone: product prices, land availability, feed conversions and transport costs. The model does not consider the importance, cost and availability of other factors of production. Even if France is the best producer, livestock production may not shift from Italy and Germany-Benelux. Whether production shifts or not depends upon the alternatives of the other factors of production. If livestock production is their best alternative, then this may offset the reasons for shifting. Livestock production would then stay in Italy and Germany-Benelux. Even if this phenomenon of shifting livestock production is occurring, the model cannot adequately account for the inertia of the real world. Time is only superficially a component of the model. This same type of reasoning could also explain why the model shows food grain being utilized as feed grain.

A final reason for concluding that this model is, at least, a good first approximation of reality is a normative reason. The major deviations this model shows from reality are all in the direction that economic theory would tell us to expect them to be. If this optimizing model does in any sense represent how an efficient economy should operate, and if the EEC will over time move from a less efficient to a more efficient position; the errors in this model will decrease in importance over time. Therefore, as better, more accurate data are introduced into this model, not only will the model move closer to simulating the real world, but the real world will move closer to what the model says it should be doing.

SHORT RUN PREDICTIONS—1970

This section presents the results of predictions for 1970. Since the MSU-USDA study made projections to 1970, this same period was used for prediction here. The MSU-USDA study presented price projections for some commodities in terms of a range of prices; therefore, this study also presents predictions based on this same range of prices.

The results for the 1970 predictions are presented in Tables 12–14 to 12–16. These tables give the results for both the low price, 1970(L), and the high price, 1970(H), projections. As the only differences in the two sets or predictions lie in the beef transfer activities, the 1970(L) and 1970(H) are reported together for the other sections of the two models.

For veal, pork, eggs and poultry the model restricted production to a 100 percent self-sufficiency level. No exportable surpluses were allowed the Community for these products. Therefore, the production levels for these commodities are restricted to that level necessary to meet internal demand. Both models show Germany-Benelux essentially self-sufficient in poultry with a few imports from France. On the other hand twenty percent of the Italian poultry consumed comes from France. About twenty percent of both the eggs and the veal consumed in Italy and Germany-Benelux originates in France. France also supplies twenty percent of Germany-Benelux's and thirteen percent of Italy's demand for pork. Italy and France import some pork from Germany-Benelux as well.

Beef production levels are the same in both the 1970(L) and 1970(H) models. In both cases France produces over three-fourths of the beef produced in the EEC. With the low beef price projections, France supplies Germany-Benelux with over seventy percent of the beef they consume. France finds it more profitable to export beef to Germany-Benelux in the 1970(L) model than to consume it domestically. After supplying Germany-Benelux they must import beef to meet their domestic demand. The 1970(L) model shows France importing beef from Italy, however, this is in reality transhipped beef from Latin America.

Table 12-14. 1970(L) and 1970(H) Production Levels

Commodity	Units	France	Italy	Germany-Benelux	European Economic Community
Total grain	1,000 m.t.	31,507.1	15,307.8	21,143.9	67,958.8
Food grain	1,000 m.t.	6,856.0	8,297.2	8,081.1	23,234.3
Denatured food grain	1,000 m.t.	22,651.1	0	8,591.8	31,242.9
Total food grain	1,000 m.t.	29,507.1	8,297.2	16,672.9	54,477.2
Feed grain	1,000 m.t.	2,000.0	7,010.6	4,471.0	13,481.6
Total feed grain equivalent	1,000 m.t.	26,022.3	7,674.4	13,709.3	47,406.0
Beef and veal	1,000 m.t.	3,039.0	433.0	645.6	4,117.6
Milk-beef-feeder-calves	1,000 head	10,112.5	4,983.4	8,989.9	24,085.8
Feeder calves	1,000 head	6,826.0	3,363.8	6,068.1	16,257.9
Beef (cull cows)	1,000 m.t.	596.6	299.0	512.4	1,408.0
Beef (≥ 1 year)	1,000 m.t.	1,888.5	0	1.0	1,889.5
Beef (< 1 year)	1,000 m.t.		0		0
Total beef	1,000 m.t.	2,485.2	299.0	513.4	3,297.6
Veal	1,000 m.t.	553.8	134.0	132.2	820.0
Pork	1,000 m.t.	1,980.7	403.8	2,445.2	4,829.7
Poultry	1,000 m.t.	866.7	416.8	711.5	1,995.0
Eggs	1,000 m.t.	1,046.6	505.6	1,081.8	2,634.0

Table 12-15. 1970(L) and 1970(H) Transfer Levels: Grain

(1,000 metric tons)

Exporter	Importer	France	Italy	Germany-Benelux	EFTA	Eastern Europe	Other Europe	Africa & Mid East	Other Asia
France	Total grain	25,418.0	262.2	2,099.7	1,575.3	411.4	780.7	685.6	274.2
	Food grain	3,276.2	164.1	399.1	274.2	411.4		685.6	274.2
	Feed grain	22,141.8	98.1	1,700.6	1,301.1		780.7		
Italy	Total grain	1,682.3	13,293.5	0		0		331.9	
	Food grain	0	7,301.5	0		0		331.9	
	Feed grain	1,682.3	5,992.0	0					
Germany-Benelux	Total grain	0	92.9	19,942.0	379.5	80.8		484.9	161.6
	Food grain	0	0	6,464.9	242.4	80.8		484.9	161.6
	Feed grain	0	92.9	13,479.3	137.1				
EFTA	Total grain			10,334.6					
	Feed grain			10,334.6					
United States	Total grain	977.2	1,833.0	2,462.6					
	Food grain	232.7	164.1	478.8					
	Feed grain	744.6	1,668.9	1,983.8					
Canada	Total grain	58.2	246.1	558.5					
	Food grain	58.2	246.1	558.5					
Latin America	Total grain	2,499.1	2,093.2	616.8					
	Food grain	2,250.9	328.2	79.8					
	Feed grain	248.2	1,765.0	567.0					
Africa & Mid East	Total grain	0		0					
	Food grain	0							
	Feed grain	0							
Australia, New Zealand, South Africa	Total grain		196.3	283.5					
	Feed grain		196.3	283.5					

Table 12-16. 1970(L) and 1970(H) Transfer Levels: Feeder Calves, Beef, Veal, Pork, Eggs, Poultry

Exporter	*Importer*	*France*	*Italy*	*Germany-Benelux*	*All Other Countries*
Feeder calves (1,000 head)					
France	1970(L)	6,780.5	45.4	0	
Italy	and	2,182.7	1,181.1	0	
Germany-Benelux	1970(H)	4,490.6	90.8	1,486.7	
EFTA	are the		121.1	227.5	
Eastern Europe	same	0	75.7	35.0	
Beef and veal (1,000 metric tons)					
France	1970(L)	1,609.5	44.1	1,385.4	0
	1970(H)	1,754.2	518.9	765.9	0
Italy	1970(L)	144.7	288.3	0	0
	1970(H)	0	433.0	0	0
Germany-Benelux	1970(L)	12.9	63.6	469.1	0
	1970(H)	12.9	63.6	569.1	0
EFTA	1970(L)	0	74.2		
	1970(H)	0	74.2		
Eastern Europe	1970(L)	0	63.5		
	1970(H)	0	63.5		
Latin America	1970(L)	12.9	693.7	36.5	
	1970(H)	12.9	74.2	656.0	
Beef (1,000 metric tons)					
France	1970(L)	1,122.3	10.6	1,352.3	0
	1970(H)	1,267.0	485.4	732.8	0
Italy	1970(L)	144.7	154.3	0	0
	1970(H)	0	299.0	0	0
Germany-Benelux	1970(L)	12.9	63.6	436.9	0
	1970(H)	12.9	63.6	436.9	0
EFTA	1970(L)	0	74.2		
	1970(H)	0	74.2		
Eastern Europe	1970(L)	0	63.5		
	1970(H)	0	63.5		
Latin America	1970(L)	12.9	693.7	36.5	
	1970(H)	12.9	74.2	656.0	
Veal (1,000 metric tons)					
France	1970(L)	487.2	33.5	33.1	
Italy	and	0	134.0	0	
Germany-Benelux	1970(H)	0	0	132.2	
	are the same				

Table 12–16 continued

Exporter	Importer	France	Italy	Germany-Benelux	All Other Countries
Pork (1,000 metric tons)					
France	1970(L)	1,333.9	65.6	581.2	
Italy	and	0	403.8	0	
Germany-Benelux	1970(H) are the same	85.1	35.3	2,324.8	
Eggs (1,000 metric tons)					
France	1970(L)	659.3	120.1	267.2	
Italy	and	0	505.0	0	
Germany-Benelux	1970(H) are the same	6.7	6.3	1,068.8	
Poultry (1,000 metric tons)					
France	1970(L)	748.0	104.2	14.5	
Italy	and	0	416.8	0	
Germany-Benelux	1970(H) are the same	0	0	711.5	

This beef is shipped through Italy because of the lower variable import levy into Italy relative to that into France. This model also shows that over fifty percent of the beef consumed in Italy comes from Latin America, with another twenty percent from EFTA, Germany-Benelux, Eastern Europe and France.

Under the high beef price predictions France supplies domestic consumers first, then Italian and finally German-Benelux consumers. Thus France does not import beef from Latin America in the 1970(H) model. Since France does supply Italy, Italian imports from Latin America drop drastically relative to the 1970(L) model. After supplying Italy, France's remaining excess production is shipped to Germany-Benelux. This, however, along with German-Benelux production, is not sufficient to meet their consumption needs. The remaining German-Benelux demand is met through Latin American imports. The exports of Latin America are the same for the 1970(L) and the 1970(H) model. The different beef prices just cause a rerouting of Latin American and French beef exports.

In as much as both models show France producing over three-fourths of the beef and only a little over forty percent of the feeder calves produced in the EEC, France must import feeders. The main movement of feeder calves is from Germany-Benelux and Italy to France with them supplying thirty-three percent and sixteen percent respectively of the French demand. To do this required Germany-Benelux to ship over seventy percent and Italy over sixty percent of their feeder calf production to France. Since beef production in Italy and Germany-Benelux fell, the demand for feeder calves in these two countries fell. Thus imports of feeder calves from Eastern Europe and EFTA fell substantially from their 1968 levels.

While France imports a substantial number of feeder calves, it only imports a little over ten percent of the feed grain used for livestock. It does import some feed grain from Italy (which it hadn't been doing in the past), the U.S. and Latin America. Germany-Benelux on the other hand produces somewhat less than half its needs. A third of its demand is supplied by imports from EFTA, with the rest coming from the U.S., France, Latin America and Australia, New Zealand, South Africa. To the extent that EFTA cannot supply the indicated amounts of feed grain, feed grains transfers will be shifted to first Australia, New Zealand, South Africa, then in order Latin America, the U.S., Africa and the Mid East.

With the exception of EFTA, the 1970 model shows external EEC feed grain trade down from the 1968 levels. The model shows U.S. exports of feed grain down from actual 1968 levels by over a third. Exports to France are up by 95.8 percent but down to Italy by 21.9 percent and to Germany-Benelux by 55.7 percent. Since EFTA and Australia, New Zealand, South Africa would, in all likelihood, not be able to supply Germany-Benelux with that amount of feed grain indicated by the model, United States exports to Germany-Benelux and, therefore, the EEC would be larger than indicated. If the exports of EFTA and Australia, New Zealand, South Africa were at a level equivalent to three-fourths of their total feed grain exports in 1968, then U.S. feed grain exports to the EEC would increase about five percent rather than fall by a third. Under this assumption, U.S. exports to Germany-Benelux would be up by about nine percent.

The 1970 model shows that the EEC is a net importer of food grain. The exports of food grain would primarily be soft wheat, while the imports would be hard wheat. Compared to the 1968 trade levels France has moved from a net exporter of 4,469.5 thousand metric ton to a net importer of 333.2 thousand metric ton of food grain. It reached this position by substantial reduction in its exports to Germany-Benelux, EFTA, Africa and the Mid East and a major increase in imports from Latin America. Italy remained a net importer in the 1970 model; however, due to decreases in the level of imports from North America from the 1968 level, their net import position fell from 935.3 thousand metric ton to 570.6 thousand metric ton. The significant drop in U.S. food grain exports to Germany-Benelux caused them to move from a net import position of 1,833.1 thousand metric ton to one of 546.5 thousand metric ton.

Relative to 1968, this model shows the United States losing 45.3 percent of their EEC food grain market. Their exports to all three regions fell with the greatest decline being in the Germany-Benelux market.

The EEC was a net importer of grain in 1968. Not only does the model predict them to be a net importer in 1970 but it predicts that their net grain imports should rise by 87.2 percent. This increased demand for grain is met through an increase in grain imports (42.0 percent) and a decrease in grain exports (20.6 percent). According to the model, however, the U.S. position in the EEC total grain market deteriorates. In 1968 the U.S. exported 8,597.2 thousand metric ton of grain to the EEC. This model shows exports of 5,272.8 thousand metric ton, a drop of 35.2 percent. Even allowing for the above postulated shift from EFTA exports of feed grain to U.S. exports to Germany-Benelux, the total grain exports of the U.S. to the EEC will fall about five percent from their 1968 levels. The only place where the U.S. increases its exports is to France. This is because the increased feed grain exports off-set the decrease in food grain exports.

Projected total grain production was down two percent from the 1968 levels. As was the case with the two post-dictions, the model shows total feed grain to be composed primarily of denatured food grain for both France and Germany-Benelux. The main reason for the decreased production in the EEC involves a decline in the crop land available for grain production.

CONCLUSIONS

The intent of this study was to develop a predictive model for EEC grain-livestock trade. Within the rather severe limitations imposed, the results show that this model does show some predictive ability. As important as this model's ability to predict, and possibly more so, is its' facility to highlight areas where we lack knowledge of the system. This model provides insight into the two areas which normally cause predictions to be in error—the quality of the input data and the underlying structure of the model.

During the process of collecting input data for this model certain quality gaps were found. Very little effort has been directed toward the understanding of the European transportation system. Not only are no detailed transportation cost data available, but also little has been done concerning methods, routes, capacities and relative costs of the different transportation methods for grain-livestock products. The same is true for data on feed-livestock conversion. Not much of the input-output type data is available for alternative production methods, particularly for forage utilization. Another area, involving both data quality and model structure, that may cause inaccurate predictions concerns the appropriate decision making criteria. A revenue maximizing criteria may not be the best. However, even if a cost minimizing or a profit maximizing objective function provides a better predictive structure, no detailed cost of production data are available for grain-livestock products.

Relaxing some of the structural restrictions of the model, while increasing the complexity, also gives some indication of being able to improve the model's predictability. By relaxing the self-sufficiency restrictions for pork, veal, eggs, and poultry additional real options become available to producers. Another option is expansion along product lines. The grain-livestock sector is not independent of dairy products and, to the extent that dairy policy changes over time, predictions for the grain-livestock sector based on a constant dairy policy will be inaccurate. Disaggregation of the products included in the model may also improve predictability. To the extent that food grain isn't wheat, feed grain isn't corn, corn isn't barley, and French beef isn't the same as Italian beef, excessive aggregation may introduce more errors than it eliminates. It is also obvious that the model does not include the right criteria for determining how much food grain will be denatured. If we knew more about denaturing policy, the structure of the model could be changed to improve it's ability to predict.

The model may also be expanded by internalizing some of the countries that are now represented only by purchase and sale activities. To the extent that countries are internalized, this puts restrictions on the maximum amounts of a product that can be sold to or purchased from them (sales by demand and purchases by productive capacity). The first step here should be to include the U.K., Ireland, and Denmark so that the model would represent the new expanded EEC. Due to the importance of this market to North America it might be of interest to internalize the U.S. and Canada. Ultimately it would be possible to develop a world trade model where all regions are included through production and transfer activities rather than purchase and sale activities.

The model assumes production to be a function of one factor of production—land (two for livestock-land and grain). With more information the production functions could be expanded to include other factors of production.

To the extent that the economy that we are trying to simulate is not linear, predictions from a linear model will not be accurate. Additional predictive accuracy may be gained by moving away from the simplest linear model. This could be accomplished by expanding certain activities through the use of step functions. The most promising candidates here would be the production functions and the transportation functions. Or alternatively this spatial equilibrium model could be reformulated in a quadratic programming framework.

NOTES

1. This joint product is a milk cow that produces three separate products; milk, feeder calves and cull cow beef; over her productive life.
2. $E_i^k = 0$ for $k \neq 2$.
3. $M_i^3 = D_i^{4'}$.
4. G may be negative if the grain-livestock sector of the EEC contributes a net revenue to the European Agricultural Guidance and Guarantee Fund.
5. This model differs from a transportation type model in that it is not a closed system. It would be, however, if all countries were specified in the same manner as the EEC countries.
6. When $i = j$, $\%_{ij}^k$ represents the amount of domestic consumption that is satisfied via domestic production.

7. $\%_{ij}^{k} = \dfrac{X_{ij}^{k}}{D_{j}^{k}}$ or $\%_{ij}^{k} = \dfrac{X_{ij}^{k}}{S_{i}^{k}}$

8. That is $P_i = \beta_0 + \beta_1 a_i$ with $\beta_0 = 0$ and $\beta_1 = 1$.

9. The negative sign on the feeder calves transfer activities can be explained by the Italy-France and Germany-Benelux-France transfers. The divergence between actual and predicted is so great for these two activities that they completely dominate the regression coefficients; resulting in an equation with a negative slope.

REFERENCES

1. Bates, Thomas H. and Andrew Schmitz. "A Spatial Equilibrium Analysis of the World Sugar Economy." Giannini Foundation Monograph Number 23, California Agricultural Experiment Station, University of California, Berkeley, California, May 1969.

2. Bawden, D. Lee. "A Spatial Equilibrium Model of International Trade." Paper presented at annual meeting of Econometric Society, New York, N.Y., December 30, 1965.

3. ———. "A Spatial Price Equilibrium Model of International Trade." *Journal of Farm Economics* 48 (November 1966): 862–74.

4. ———. James G. Kendrick, Carmen O. Nohre and Howard C. Williams. "A Model for Agricultural Trade Analysis." June 17, 1968. (Mimeographed).

5. Bjarnason, Harold Frederick. "An Economic Analysis of 1980 International Trade in Feed Grains." Unpublished Ph.D. dissertation, University of Wisconsin, Madison, Wisconsin, 1967.

6. Dean, Gerald W. and Norman R. Collins. "World Trade in Fresh Oranges: An Analysis of the Effects of European Economic Community Tariff Policies." Giannini Foundation Monograph Number 18, California Agricultural Experiment Station, University of California, Berkeley, California, January 1967.

7. Epp, Donald J. "Changes in Regional Grain and Livestock Prices Under the European Economic Community Policies." Research Report No. 4, Institute of International Agriculture, Michigan State University, East Lansing, Michigan.

8. Fox, Roger William. "Some Possible Production and Trade Effects of the EEC's Common Agricultural Policy for Grains." Unpublished Ph.D. dissertation, Michigan State University, East Lansing, Michigan, 1965.

9. Kost, William Elvidge. "Trade Flows in the Grain-Livestock Economy of the European Economic Community." Unpublished Ph.D. dissertation, Michigan State University, East Lansing, Michigan, 1971.

10. Mangum, Fred A., Jr. "The Grain-Livestock Economy of Italy With Projections to 1970 and 1975." Research Report No. 2, Institute of International Agriculture, Michigan State University, East Lansing, Michigan.

11. Organization for Economic Co-Operation and Development. "Agricultural Statistics: 1955–1968." Paris, 1969.
12. Petit, Michel J. and Jean-Baptiste Viallon. "The Grain-Livestock Economy of France With Projections to 1970 and 1975." Research Report No. 3, Institute of International Agriculture, Michigan State University, East Lansing, Michigan.
13. Rojko, Anthony S., Francis S. Urban and James J. Naive. "World Demand Prospects For Grain In 1980, With Emphasis on Trade By The Less Developed Countries." Foreign Agricultural Economic Report No. 75. Economic Research Service, United States Department of Agriculture, Washington, D.C.: Government Printing Office, December 1971.
14. Rossmiller, George E. "The Grain-Livestock Economy of West Germany With Projections to 1970 and 1975." Research Report No. 1, Institute of International Agriculture, Michigan State University, East Lansing, Michigan.
15. Samuelson, Paul A. "Spatial Price Equilibrium and Linear Programming." *American Economic Review,* 42 (June 1952): 283–303.
16. Sorenson, Vernon L. and Dale E. Hathaway. "The Grain-Livestock Economy and Trade Patterns of the European Economy Community With Projections to 1970 and 1975." Research Report No. 5, Institute of International Agriculture, Michigan State University, East Lansing, Michigan.
17. Takayama, T. and G.G. Judge. "An Intertemporal Price Equilibrium Model." *Journal of Farm Economics* 46 (May 1964): 477–84.
18. ———. "Equilibrium Among Spatially Separated Markets: A Reformulation." *Econometrica* 32 (October 1964): 510–24.
19. ———. "Spatial Equilibrium and Quadratic Programming." *Journal of Farm Economics* 46 (February 1964): 67–93.
20. Theil, H. Economic Forecasts and Policy. Amsterdam: North-Holland Publishing Company, 1961.
21. United Nations, Statistical Office of the United Nations, Department of Economic and Social Affairs. "Commodity Trade Statistics." Statistical Papers, Series D, various issues.
22. United States Tariff Commission. "Domestic and Foreign Government Programs and Policies Affecting U.S. Agricultural Trade." Report on Investigation No. 332–59 Under Section 332 of the Tariff Act of 1930, as amended, TC Publication 613, Washington, D.C.: October 1973.

Chapter Thirteen

Conclusions: Commodity Modeling in Perspective

Having examined some commodity models at first hand, let us now review how the developments contained therein as well as other recent advances can help to improve model construction and use. Improvements are first suggested within the context of the modeling process itself: specification, estimation, validation, simulation, and policy analysis. Next we reconsider the methodologies presented in Chapter 1, emphasizing possibilities for combining them with other modeling and programming techniques. Policy analysis is then taken up more fully by focusing on modeling applications which would be most useful to conduct. In the conclusions, the problems and deficiencies of modeling are summarized, so as to suggest directions for future research.

THE MODELING PROCESS

Specification

Many commodity models have been limited in that they reflect an oversimplified market structure; however, we are now seeing a number of notable advances. These include the portrayal of noncompetitive structures (see Chapters 4, 12), specification as a set of differential or difference equations which illustrate market dynamics (see Chapters 6, 7, 8, 9), and various programming formulations which would optimize commodity transfers over time or space (see Chapter 12). Because of the gap existing between the complexities of commodity markets and the simplified nature of typical model structures, any improvement in the modeling process should begin with model specification. For example, one might want to include quadratic or other nonlinear relationships into a model structure as well as to experiment with disequilibrium forms of models. To perform the latter would undoubtedly involve considering commodity models in the form of differential equation systems (see Chapters 6, 7); this would help not only in describing commodity decision making as a continuous process but also in introducing appropriate expectational phenomena.

Estimation

In general, estimation of commodity models has required the use of methods less advanced than those applied to macroeconomic models. Ordinary least squares or an appropriate distributed lag technique has sufficed in most cases, depending on the nature of the data and the assumptions made. Where typical problems of short time series or the equivalent lack of degrees of freedom have appeared together with simultaneity, the two-stage principal component method of Kloek and Mennes [31] has been brought into play, as has the method of decomposing a model into several subsystems. Possibilities now exist, however, of using full information maximum likelihood methods where practical. For example, Chow and Fair [11] report on an estimation procedure to be used with simultaneous equation systems which include autocorrelated disturbances. Goldfield and Quandt [23] suggest possibilities for estimation of nonlinear systems. Wymer's [51, 52] SIMUL and RESIMUL programs can be used to estimate differential equation systems. And the recently developed TROLL computer program [21] can both estimate and simulate commodity models of a fairly complex nature (see Chapter 3).

Though these developments satisfy a number of requirements of commodity model builders, other estimation needs relate to the problem of incorporating prior information obtained from sources outside the basic sample employed for system estimation. Zellner [53] has demonstrated how initial beliefs represented by prior probabilities can be combined with information in data by means of Bayes theorem to yield posterior probabilities relating to parameters or hypotheses of interest. An application of this method to commodity problems is found in the work of Dreze [18], who has devised a Bayesian limited-information estimating procedure and has applied it to reduce some of the vagaries surrounding the estimation of commodity demand and supply elasticities.

There are other ways of introducing prior information. Mixed estimation methods known for some time can be helpful. Here I refer to the need to incorporate into a model the exact value of a parameter, to establish an exact relationship between two or more parameters, to introduce an unbiased estimate of a parameter, or to utilize information regarding the range of values of some parameters. Durbin's generalized least squares [19] or Theil and Goldberger's mixed linear estimation method [48] can be applied to introduce this information. There are also the methods of Byron [10] and of Court [13], which incorporate the constraints of economic theory in estimating the demand equations for a group of commodities, so as to provide suitable direct- and cross-price elasticities.

Validation

Commodity models also have not been validated with the same rigorous tests that macroeconomic models undergo, although certain exceptions exist [27, 41]. Perhaps this is the result of a greater need to effectively discriminate among models describing the same national economy. Where commodity models are concerned, the procedure most typically followed up to now has been to determine the internal consistency of a commodity model based on the properties of its final form (see Chapter 8) and/or to apply certain parametric and nonparametric tests to its *ex-post* and *ex-ante* predictions, i.e., typically those described in Labys [35]. One possibility for improving the validation of commodity models in the future would be to adopt Howrey's [26] approach which features three distinct validation stages: determination of model consistency, comparison of model outcomes with those of other models, and evaluation of the model from the point of view of its effectiveness in decision making.

Simulation

Naylor's policy simulation approach [40, 50] has been applied extensively as a means of assessing the welfare impact of commodity policies. Here the target or dependent variables entering the welfare function of the policy maker are determined by conducting successive simulations based on a set of exogenous variables or instruments, which reflect alternative policies that he can control. One possibility for improving simulation analysis of commodity models which Naylor [40] suggests is to conduct the simulation as a problem in experimental design. The object is to learn more about the model being investigated by examining the surface generated by the endogenous variables in response to changes in levels of the instruments or factors.

These experiments can be organized in several ways. The most well known of these is data analysis, consisting of regression analysis and analysis of variance. The latter can be in the form of F-tests, multiple ranking, spectral analysis, or multiple comparisons (see Chapter 4). Exploratory experiments where the relationships between the instruments or factors can be found include full and fractional factorial analysis, rotatable designs, and response surface designs. The design experiments which have proven most popular thus far have been randomizations. Including stochastic disturbances in commodity simulation experiments can help to evaluate policies where climate influences production (see Chapters 4, 7, 8, 9) or else to validate a model where its cyclical or stability properties are of interest. See, for example, studies by Howrey and Witherell [27] as well as by Naylor, et al. [41]

Policy Analysis and Control

Although optimal control theory is closely tied to simulation analysis, we consider it separately because of its considerable potential for improving the application of commodity models. The varied mathematical approaches suggested by Athans and Kendrick [6] point up the many opportunities for conducting commodity control experiments. Economists would begin with the "certainty equivalence principle," which can be incorporated with concepts of dynamic programming to solve problems classified under linear-quadratic-stochastic feedback control. Or they might consider the maximum principle of

Pontryagin. This makes optimal control solutions possible for problems of planning optimal growth, where nonlinear dynamics and nonquadratic criteria are involved. Other approaches as developed by control engineers include the Kalman-Bucy filter and other state and parameter estimation schemes. Finally, there is adaptive control theory, whereby initial uncertainties about the parameters or functions within a system are reduced or eliminated as it moves forward in time.

One policy area that fits naturally into the control theory framework pertains to commodity stabilization schemes. Since these schemes involve operating an export norm and/or buffer stock mechanism where supply and demand tend to fluctuate stochastically, one can apply the approach of stochastic feedback control as illustrated in the Kim, Goreux and Kendrick study of the cocoa market (see Chapter 9). One should see also the study of Rausser and Freebairn [43], who have analyzed the optimal import quota for beef using adaptive control techniques such as sequential stochastic, sequential adaptive covariance, and M-measurement ahead feedback controls.

MODELING METHODOLOGIES

Individual Methodologies

The following methodologies are generally applicable to commodity modeling: econometric market [35], industry process [1], spatial equilibrium [47] including reactive programming [28], industrial dynamics [39], systems simulation [24], world trade flow [44], recursive programming [14], input-output [32], linear programming [25], network flow [16], and multistage transfer [8]. Among these, only the first five have been featured in the modeling studies presented here. World trade flow models would have to be operated on a multicommodity or disaggregated trade basis, requiring a large and complex model structure. Recursive programming models center upon industrial and agricultural development, and, as such can barely be termed commodity models in a full market sense. The remaining methodologies are somewhat specialized for commodity applications; only time will tell whether they can be employed more fruitfully in this area. Since each of these methodologies and their potential contribution has already been described in Chapter 1, we concentrate here on the potential of combining them with other modeling and programming techniques.

Combined Methodologies

Econometric – Biological/Technological Models are just beginning to receive attention for those commodities whose behavior is highly interrelated with biological or technological systems. These models would integrate a micro-econometric market structure with a set of mathematical equations or programming models describing biological or technological relationships. Improvements in modeling most likely to take place relate to the supply side. A marine production system could be introduced, where maximum sustainable yields are described using a logistic decreasing returns function which combines factors of logistic growth of the biomass of, say, fish with a relationship describing decreasing returns from effort. The Bell et al. model is one of the more advanced models of this type (see Chapter 10 as well as Bell's [9] study of the U.S. lobster industry).

An industrial production system could be incorporated where the relationship between commodity inputs and product outputs is described using a linear program, cost minimization being assumed. The Adams and Griffin model is a good example of this approach (see Chapter 2).

An energy production system could be modeled such as that involving oil or gas wells where geological, engineering, and production factors must be interrelated. Some work in this direction has been reported by Avramides and Cross [7]. Also to be included in a system of this type might be relationships linking costs of pollution and of environmental quality as well as of energy conservation.

Agricultural production systems also would lend themselves to this approach. Animal productions systems could include relationships describing breeding, nutrition, feed, and disease control. As for crop production, probabilistic functions can be introduced which represent the likelihood of variations in climatic conditions.

Commodity Oriented Development Models represent the first of two possibilities to improve model structures by linking commodity models with country models (see [34]). These models would interrelate a macroeconometric planning model for a developing country with several world commodity models. This would provide certain advantages for planning in countries which are typically small but highly specialized in the export of a small number of primary commodities. Such export specialization is revealed not only in the very high proportions of the country's major exports in the total export bill but also in their large contribution to foreign exchange and domestic product. Since foreign exchange earnings as well as tax revenues greatly influence a country's capability for self financed development, it would be valuable to determine to what degree any changed allocation of resources among commodities would influence these and other performance outputs.

The methodological incentive for a combined model structure arises from the premise that the magnitude of exports of one or more commodities may be sufficient to influence world price and equilibrium conditions. Thus, the impact of any changes in domestic investment strategy can be measured only by linking these exports to one or more commodity models reflecting world market conditions. This advances the typical development growth model beyond its dubious assumption that exports grow exogenously. One proposed model [34] uses Malaysia as an example with rubber, palm oil, timber, and tin being the commodity models of interest.

Commodity Link Models.   The second possibility for combining country and commodity models is to integrate one or several commodity models with country or area models for the major consuming and producing countries. This idea was originally suggested by Klein [30], who saw this integration as necessary for improving the explanation of world trade patterns by the Project LINK model. In brief, the economic relationships between the developed and developing countries depend largely on the quantities and prices of commodities in world trade. Exports of commodities from developing countries depend on the income and activity variables of the importing countries. In turn, income and industrial activity in the latter depend on the regular availability of these commodities. Price formation then depends on the world imbalances between supply and demand. Since this process is intrinsically tied to the transmission of business cycles from developed to developing countries, it would be important to incorporate commodity effects into any comprehensive world trade model.

Adams [2] has made the first attempt to introduce a commodity model into the LINK model by his adapting the copper model constructed by Fisher, Coouner and Baily (see Chapter 3). Here recognition is given to demand and supply as cross-national phenomena, with emphasis placed on the relations between economic activity and demand, the impact of commodity prices on imports and exports, and the impact of production and earned income on the producing economy. It is probable that other such modeling efforts will soon be made in LINK, petroleum being the next likely candidate.

Corporate Commodity Models represent an improvement yet to come. Many firms already utilize projections of national economic and financial conditions to operate models describing their own product markets, cash flows, costs, and profitability. Further information as to the actual structure of several of these models can be reviewed in Naylor [40]. Adams [1] would extend this approach using a modeling framework which integrates related parts of national models and industry or commodity models with a model of a single firm within that industry. One major use of the model would be to answer "what if" questions, including the impact on the firm of changes in corporate policies such as investment strategies, changes in the related commodity or product markets, changes in national variables such as interest rates, or episodic events such as the petroleum crisis.

An existing approach which could be adapted to include commodity models is that of Eckstein and McLagan [20]; a computer time sharing model is employed that links national and corporate information interactively so as to produce long term forecasts of important corporate variables such as sales, profitability and cash flows, given changes in factors such as those mentioned. To this must be added information and a modeling structure related to the commodities of interest. In linking these with management objectives, Arthur [5] has already indicated some of the corporate effects of commodity purchasing and inventory strategies as well as of commodity futures strategies. Two publicized corporate models which could easily be expanded in this direction include the sales model of the Goodyear Tire and Rubber Co. [20] and the fertilizer business network simulation model of the Agricultural Chemicals Group of the W.R. Grace and Co.[15]

MODELING APPLICATIONS

Applications of commodity models resemble those of econometric models in general: explaining market behavior or reconstructing history; searching for optimal policy decisions related, for example, to growth, stabilization and market organization; and forecasting and planning. Up to now, commodity studies have been concerned with policy problems relating to agriculture, trade, industry, price forecasting, location and distribution, commodity agreements and stabilization, and regulatory proceedings. These are likely to expand in a number of ways.

A first consideration involves the structuring of models to deal with multicommodity phenomena, principally because of the need to decipher the complex nature of complementarities and substitutabilities among commodities. A multicommodity model is also a convenient approach for obtaining aggregate and individual forecasts for a group of highly interrelated commodities. Examples of this can be found in the present study. Myers and Havlicek show how substitution occurs between meats at the retail level as well as between market levels or channels (see Chapter 5), and Haidacher, Kite and Matthews work with demand substitution among a number of food commodities in their decision-planning model (see Chapter 10).

One would also like to determine the influence of financial and speculative factors on commodity markets. Most recently, there have been several modest attempts in this direction. Here, I refer to studies by Ridler and Yandle [42], by Dominguez [17], by Lovesay [38], and by Labys [36] examining the commodity impacts of inflation and/or of devaluation and changes in exchange rates. Speculation and hedging effects, having also received only limited empirical study [37], will be researched at greater lengths in the future. Not only must the U.S. deal with policy questions regarding the regulation of its international futures exchanges, but the U.K. may also conduct such an investigation before too long.

Cyclical analysis and problems of stabilization should also be examined. There is a need to study the transmission of commodity cycles between countries as suggested by Adams [1] in applying his "Commodity LINK" model. Also the analysis of commodity stabilization schemes (see Chapters 8, 9) could expand very rapidly, should the U.N. actively pursue its recently proposed "Program of Action" [49]; this would call for the stabilization of commodity export earnings for developing countries through organizing buffer stock schemes for a number of key commodities.

Current relative scarcities in the world will make natural resource commodities an important subject of modeling. As part of its study on exploitation of the "sea bed," UNCTAD has begun building models for cobalt [3], manganese [46], and nickel [4]. Energy, now a major resource consideration, has already been the subject of some 94 modeling studies, as works by Limaye [33, 55] reveal. Also pointing in this direction, Searl [45] reviews a number of energy models both constructed and in progress. And *Energy Policy* has compiled a study [22] which not only examines the state of the art of energy modeling, but also describes objectives and techniques for future modeling research.

A final possible area of application to be explored relates to the role that commodities will play in the future international economic order. In particular, recent crises have underscored the necessity of considering commodity modeling from a global viewpoint. Models should examine not only world balances, deficits and surpluses of strategic commodities, but also the possibilities of accumulating buffer or security stockpiles. Here, studying the distribution of commodities between the northern and southern hemispheres or between the developed and the developing countries would be highly useful. Commodities mentioned in this regard are foodstuffs such as wheat, rice and soybeans as well as fertilizers and fuels, e.g. see Blakeslee, et. al.[54].

CONCLUSION

Our survey of commodity modeling reflects an overall optimistic if not sanguine attitude towards present developments. Perhaps this arises from the recent growth in commodity models which, as Figure 13-1 shows, has been exponential. But let us not forget that there are a number of serious problems which remain to be dealt with.

Among the methodological problems, we must bring our models closer to reality. Too often neglected is institutional information, which might be included in the modeling process, at least in some simple form of dummy variable construction. Previously mentioned has been the need to introduce non-linear relationships to help predict sharp upturns and downturns in a market. There are also those general problems related to econometric modeling such as constructing models which might be applicable to both short run and long run phenomena. Finally, the difficulty of rapid structural change in commodity markets can result in the inaccuracy of certain model coefficients over time. One should vary these coefficients continuously, perhaps by making them a subject of time or by adjusting them using methods of feedback control theory.

Less directly related to methodology is the problem that many of the models built are only of academic interest, having passed few of the tests that determine the inherent validity and usefulness of a model. If one wishes to construct large and more complex models (those with many equations and mathe-

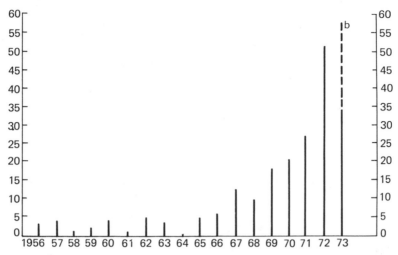

a Based on a tabulation of the models appearing in the Appendix.
b Tabulation incomplete for 1973.

Figure 13-1. Yearly Publication of Commodity Models.[a]

matical intricacies), one must provide a structure which will facilitate interaction between the model and the decision maker (see Chapter 10). Otherwise it
makes sense to work with smaller, more elementary models which the decision
maker can readily understand. Similarly, the Appendix shows that, for certain
commodities, a number of models already exist. Rather than going immediately
to more sophisticated designs, one should perhaps carry out a comparative study
of the available models, and then select the structure or components of the best
models for further work. We should also remember that even the most elaborate
models need judgmental observation when used for forecasting.

A recurring problem continues to be the poor quality of some of the
data used. Some particular commodity difficulties include the lack of country
and world balance sheets where the differences between demand and supply
could be fairly accurately identified as the change in inventories, but also the
failure to disaggregate inventory data according to producer/consumer/specula-
tive holdings or some other meaningful breakdown. Agricultural data is often
published according to a crop-year format, and without supporting monthly
figures it is difficult to relate such data to national income or financial statistics
reported on a calendar-year basis. Many countries also do not compile commodity
data with the care that other data receive. It is thus essential to avoid modeling
beyond the limits of our data.

In conclusion, we need to prove to decision makers the validity and
worth of commodity models in helping them reduce uncertainty and in improv-

ing their ability to forecast outcomes. Validation can be improved upon not only by using some of the methods mentioned to monitor the performance of models over longer periods but also by determining their effectiveness in decision making. Sensitivity analysis can indicate which parts of a model are more reliable, as well as which of the data represent limiting constraints. If we can only move a small way to solving these and related problems, the future should witness an increase in the quality, performance, and fruitful application of commodity models.

REFERENCES

1. Adams, F.G. "From Econometric Models of the Nation to Models of Industries and Firms." *Wharton Quarterly Business Review* Spring (1973).
2. Adams, F.G. "The Integration of World Primary Commodity Markets into Project Link: The Example of Copper." Paper prepared for the annual meeting of Project Link, Stockholm, September 3–8, 1973.
3. Adams, F.G. "Exploitation of the Mineral Resources of the Sea-Bed Beyond National Jurisdiction: Issues of International Commodity Policy— Case Study of Cobalt." UNCTAD TD/B/449/Add.1, Geneva, June 1973.
4. Adams, F.G. "The Impact of Nickel Production from the Ocean Floor: An Econometric Appraisal." Prepared for the Commodities Division, UNCTAD, Geneva, 1974.
5. Arthur, H.B. *Commodity Futures As a Business Management Tool.* Boston: Harvard University Graduate School of Business Administration, 1971.
6. Athans, M. and D. Kendrick. "Control Theory and Economics: A Survey, Forecast, and Speculations." Department of Economics, University of Texas at Austin, October 1973.
7. Avramides, A. and J.S. Cross. "NPC Analysis of Oil and Gas Supply." In *Energy Modeling,* M.F. Searl (Ed.), Working Paper EN–1, Resources for the Future, Inc., Washington, D.C., 1973.
8. Bell, Jr., D. *Models of Commodity Transfer.* Giannini Foundation Monograph No. 20, Berkeley, 1967.
9. Bell, F.W. "Technological Externalities and Common-Property Resources: An Empirical Study of the U.S. Northern Lobster Fishery." *Journal of Political Economy* 81 (1973): 148–58.
10. Byron, R.P. "The Restricted Aitken Estimation of Sets of Demand Relations." *Econometrica* 38 (1970): 816–30.
11. Chow, G.C., and R.C. Fair. *Maximum Likelihood Estimation of Linear Equation Systems with Autoregressive Residuals.* Res. Mem. No. 118, Econometric Research Program, Princeton University, 1971.
12. Cochrane, D. and G.H. Orcutt, "Application of Least Squares Regression to

Relationships Containing Autocorrelated Error Terms." *Journal of the American Statistical Association* 44 (1949): 32–61.

13. Court, R.H. "Utility Maximizations and the Demand for New Zealand Meats." *Econometrica* 35 (1967): 424–46.

14. Day, R.H. and W.K. Tabb. "A Dynamic, Microeconomic Model of the U.S. Coal Mining Industry." SSRI Research Paper, University of Wisconsin, 1972.

15. Dean, S., Forsaith, R. and G. Hvidsten. "A Business Network Simulation System: An On-line Corporate Modeling Technique." Agricultural Chemicals Group, W.R. Grace and Co., New York, 1970.

16. Debanné, J.G. "A Systems Approach for Oil and Gas Policy Analysis in North America." *Proceedings of the Eighth World Petroleum Congress.* Moscow, 1971.

17. Dominguez, J.R. *Devaluation and Futures Markets.* Lexington, Mass.: Heath Lexington Books, 1972.

18. Dreze, J.H. "Bayesian Limited Information Analysis of the Simultaneous Equation Model." CORE discussion paper No. 7111, Center for Operations Research and Econometrics, Catholic University of Louvain, 1971.

19. Durbin, J. "A Note on Regression When There Is Extraneous Information About One of the Regressors." *Journal of the American Statistical Association* 48 (1953): 799–808.

20. Eckstein, O. and D.L. McLagan. "National Economic Models Help Business to Focus on the Future." *Computer Decisions,* October 1971.

21. Eisner, M. *A Researcher's Overview of the TROLL/1 System.* Department of Economics, Massachusetts Institute of Technology, 1971.

22. *Energy Modeling.* A special *Energy Policy* publication. London: IPC Science and Technology Press, Ltd., 1974.

23. Goldfeld, S.M. and R.E. Quandt. *Nonlinear Methods in Econometrics.* Amsterdam: North-Holland Publishing Co., 1972.

24. Haidacher, R.C., Haynes, R., Culver, D. and J.L. Matthews. "A Planning-Decision Model for Surplus Commodity Removal Programs." Mimeographed. Economic Research Service, U.S. Department of Agriculture Washington, D.C., 1973.

25. Hoffman, K.C. "A Unified Framework for Energy System Planning." Mimeographed. Department of Applied Science, Brookhaven National Laboratory, Upton, N.Y., 1973.

26. Howrey, E.P. "Selection and Evaluation of Econometric Models" in *Computer Simulation Versus Analytical Solutions for Business and Economic Models.* Gothenburg: Graduate School of Business Administration, 1972.

27. Howrey, P. and W.H. Witherell. "Stochastic Properties of A Model of the International Wool Market." Econometric Program Research Memorandum No. 101, Princeton University, 1968.

28. King, R.A. and Foo-Shiung Ho. "Reactive Programming: A Market Simulat-

ing Spatial Equilibrium Algorithm." Economics Special Report, Department of Economics, North Carolina State University at Raleigh, 1965.

29. Klein, L.R. "Estimation of Interdependent Systems in Macroeconometrics." *Econometrica* 37 (1969): 171–92.

30. Klein, L.R. "Some Notes on the Introduction of Commodity Models into Project LINK." Mimeographed. LINK Working Paper, 1971.

31. Kloek, T. and L.B.M. Mennes. "Simultaneous Equation Estimation Based on Principal Components of Predetermined Variables." *Econometrica* 28 (1960): 45–61.

32. Liebeskind, D. "Forecasting Industrial Chemical Prices Within a Planning Framework Using Disaggregation of Input-Output Tables." Unpublished Ph.D. dissertation, New York University, 1972.

33. Limaye, D.R., Ciliano, R., and J.R. Sharko. *Quantitative Energy Studies and Models.* Council on Environmental Quality, Executive Office of the President, Washington, 1973.

34. Labys, W.C. and Weaver, T.F. "Towards a Commodity Oriented Development Model." SEADAG Paper, Seminar on Directions in Rural Development Planning, New York, July 9–11, 1973.

35. Labys, W.C. *Dynamic Commodity Models: Specification, Estimation and Simulation.* Lexington, Mass.: Heath Lexington Books, 1973.

36. Labys, W.C. "A Taxonomy of Commodity Models and Their Policy Applications." Prepared for the International Seminar on the Implications of Inflation in Industrial Countries and of Fluctuations in the Exchange Rates of Major International Currencies for the Primary Exports of Developing Countries. Oxford University, October 2–4, 1973.

37. Labys, W.C. and C.W.J. Granger. *Speculation, Hedging and Commodity Price Forecasts.* Lexington, Mass.: Heath Lexington Books, 1970.

38. Lovesay, G. "Forecasting Inflation Effects on Prices of Primary Products." IBRD Working Paper, Washington, D.C., 1973.

39. Meadows, D.L. *Dynamics of Commodity Production Cycles.* Cambridge: Wright-Allen Press, Inc., 1970.

40. Naylor, T.H. *Computer Simulation Experiments with Models of Economic Systems.* New York: John Wiley and Sons, Inc., 1971.

41. Naylor, T.H., Wallace, W., and W. Sasser. "A Computer Simulation Model of the Textile Industry." *Journal of the American Statistical Association* 62 (1967): 1338–64.

42. Ridler, D., and C.A. Yandle. "A Simplified Method for Analyzing the Effects of Exchange Rate Changes on Exports of a Primary Commodity." *IMF Staff Papers* (1972): 559–78.

43. Rausser, G.C. and J.W. Freebairn. "Approximate Adaptive Control Solutions to U.S. Beef Trade Policy." *Annals of Economic and Social Measurement* 3 (1974): 177–203.

44. Rhomberg, R.R. "Possible Approaches to a Model of World Trade and Payments." *IMF Staff Papers* 17 (1970): 1–28.

45. Searl, Jr., M.F. (Ed.) *Energy Modeling.* Working Paper EN-1, Resources for the Future, Inc., Washington, D.C., 1973.

46. Shaw, J. "An Econometric Model of the Manganese Ore Industry." UNCTAD TD/B/483/Add.1, Geneva, April 1974.
47. Takayama, T. and G.G. Judge. *Spatial and Temporal Price and Equilibrium Models.* Amsterdam: North-Holland Publishing Co., 1971.
48. Theil, H. and A.S. Goldberger. "On Pure and Mixed Statistical Estimation in Economics." *International Economic Review* 2 (1960): 65–78.
49. United Nations. "Program of Action." In *Study of the Problems of Raw Materials and Development,* UN/A/9556 (Part II), New York, May 1974.
50. Vernon, J., Rives, N. and T.J. Naylor. "An Econometric Model of the Tobacco Industry." *Review of Economics and Statistics* 51 (May 1969): 149-157.
51. Wymer, C.R. "SIMUL, RESIMUL, Computer Program Manuals." Mimeographed. London School of Economics and Political Science, 1974.
52. Wymer, C.R. "Econometric Estimation of Stochastic Differential Equation Systems." *Econometrica* 40 (1972): 565–78.
53. Zellner, A. *Bayesian Inference in Econometrics.* New York: John Wiley and Sons, Inc., 1971.

Published since this book went to press

54. Blakeslee, L.L., Heady, E.O., and C.F. Framingham. *World Food Production, Demand and Trade.* Ames: Iowa State University Press, 1973.
55. Limaye, D.R. *Energy Policy Evaluation.* Lexington, Mass.: Heath Lexington Books, 1974.

Appendix
Bibliography of Commodity Models*

ALUMINUM

1. Rasche, R.H. "Forecasts and Simulations with an Econometric Model of the Aluminum Market." Special Report, Wharton Economic Forecasting Associates, Philadelphia, 1970.
2. Schlager, K.J. "A Systems Analysis of the Copper and Aluminum Industries: An Industrial Dynamics Study." Unpublished M.S. thesis, Massachusetts Institute of Technology, 1961.

APPLES

3. Brandow, G.E. "A Statistical Analysis of Apple Supply and Demand." *Penn State Agricultural Economic and Rural Sociology Report 2*, University Park, Pa., 1956.
4. Baritelle, J.L. "Supply Response and Marketing Strategies for the Washington Apple Industry." Unpublished Ph.D. dissertation, Washington State University, 1973.

ASPARAGUS

5. Grossman, E.C. "National and State Level Econometric Models of the U.S. Asparagus Industry, 1948–1969." Unpublished Ph.D. dissertation, Rutgers University, 1973.
6. Matthews, J.L., "Price Determination and Supply Adjustments in the United States and California Asparagus Economies." Unpublished Ph.D. dissertation, University of California, Berkeley, 1966.

*Items included refer principally to commodity models which describe demand as well as supply aspects of market equilibrium and price determination. Econometric studies of demand or supply *per se* are too numerous to list. One possible source of such listings is the bibliography in W.C. Labys, *Dynamic Commodity Models: Specification, Estimation, and Simulation*, Heath Lexington Books, Lexington, Mass. 1973.

BANANAS

7. Guise, J.W.B. and W. Aggrey Mensah. "An Evaluation of Policy Alternatives Facing Australian Banana Producers." in G. Judge and T. Takayama (eds.), *Studies in Economic Planning Over Time and Space.* Amsterdam: North Holland Pub. Co., 1973.

BRUSSELS SPROUTS

8. French, B.C. and M. Matsumoto. *An Analysis of Price and Supply Relationships in the U.S. Brussels Sprouts Industry.* Giannini Foundation Research Report No. 308, California Agricultural Experiment Station, Berkeley, 1970.

BEEF

9. Brodnax, Jr., H.D. "The Effects of Various Tenure and Tax Revenue Management Strategies on Organization of Beef Cattle Ranches in the Gulf Coast Area of Central Florida." Unpublished Ph.D. dissertation, University of Florida, 1972.

10. Chafin, D.G. "Economic Analysis of Futuristic Beef Cattle and Forage Production Systems." Unpublished Ph.D. dissertation, Ohio State University, 1973.

11. Freebairn, J.W. "Some Adaptive Control Models for the Analysis of Economic Policy: U.S. Beef Trade Policy." Unpublished Ph.D. dissertation, University of California at Davis, 1972.

12. Hunt, R.D. "The Contrasted Effects of Quota, Autarky, and Free Trade Policies on U.S. Beef Production and Prices." Unpublished Ph.D. dissertation, University of Minnesota, 1972.

13. Kulshreshtha, S.N. and Wilson, A.G. "An Open Econometric Model of the Canadian Beef Cattle Sector." *American Journal of Agricultural Economics* 54 (February 1972): 84–91.

14. Langemeier, L. and Thompson, R.G. "Demand, Supply, Price Relationships for the Beef Sector, Post W.W. II Period." *Journal of Farm Economics* (February 1967): 169–83.

15. Manetsch, T.J., Hayenga, M.L. and A.R. Halter. "A Simulation Model of the Nigerian Beef Industry." Mimeographed, Michigan State University, East Lansing, 1968.

16. McGarry, M.J. "The World Beef Industry." Unpublished Ph.D. dissertation, University of Wisconsin, 1968.

17. McGrann, J.M. "Microeconomic Analysis of Opportunities for Increasing Beef Production: The Pampean Area, Argentina." Unpublished Ph.D. dissertation, Texas A & M University, 1973.

18. Sohn, H.K. "A Spatial Equilibrium Model of the Beef Industry in the U.S." Unpublished Ph.D. dissertation, University of Hawaii, 1970.

19. Unger, Samuel G. "Simultaneous Equations Systems Estimation: An Application to the Cattle-Beef Sector." Unpublished Ph.D. dissertation, Michigan State University, 1966.

See Also *Livestock, Meat.*

BROILERS

20. Lee, T.C., and Seaver, S.V. *A Positive Spatial Equilibrium Model of Broiler Markets: A Simultaneous Equation Approach.* Storrs Agricultural Experiment Station Bulletin No. 417, University of Connecticut, Storrs, 1972.
21. Fisher, M. "A Sector Model—The Poultry Industry of the U.S." *Econometrica* 26 (1958): 37–66.
22. Meadows, D.L. *Dynamics of Commodity Production Cycles.* Cambridge, Mass.: Wright-Allen Press, 1970.

CHEMICALS

23. Liebeskind, D. "Forecasting Industrial Chemical Prices Within a Planning Framework Using Disaggregation of Input-Output Tables." Unpublished Ph.D. dissertation, New York University, 1972.

COAL

24. Tabb, W. "A Recursive Programming Model of Resource Allocation and Technological Change in the U.S. Bituminous Coal Industry." Unpublished Ph.D. dissertation, University of Wisconsin, 1968.

COBALT

25. Burrows, James C. *Cobalt: An Industry Analysis.* Lexington, Mass.: Heath Lexington Books, 1971.

COCOA

26. Chong, K. "A Simulation Policy Analysis of the Western Nigeria Cocoa Industry." Unpublished Ph.D. dissertation, Michigan State University, 1973.
27. Goreux, Louis M. "Price Stabilization Policies in World Markets for Primary Commodities: An Application to Cocoa." Mimeographed. International Bank for Reconstruction and Development, January 1972.
28. Kofi, Tetteh A. "International Commodity Agreements and Export Earnings: Simulation of the 1968 Draft International Cocoa Agreement." *Food Research Institute Studies* 11 (1972).
29. Mathis, Kary. *An Economic Simulation Model of the Cocoa Industry of the*

Dominican Republic. International Programs Info. Rep. No. 69–2, Department of Agricultural Economics and Sociology, Texas A & M University, 1969.

30. Melo, F.H. "An Analysis of the World Cocoa Economy in 1980." Unpublished Ph.D. dissertation, North Carolina State University, Raleigh, 1973.

31. Weymar, F. Helmut. *The Dynamics of the World Cocoa Market.* Cambridge, Mass.: The M.I.T. Press, 1968.

COCONUTS

32. Labys, W.C. *An Econometric Model of the International Lauric Oils Market: Considerations for Policy Analysis.* UNCTAD/CD/Misc. 43/Rev.1, UNCTAD, Geneva, 1971. See also the description of this model in *Dynamic Commodity Models: Specification, Estimation and Simulation.* Lexington, Mass.: Heath Lexington Books, 1973.

33. Librero, Aida R. "The International Demand for Philippine Coconut Products: An Aggregate Analysis." *The Philippine Economic Journal* 10 (1971): 1–22.

COFFEE

34. Bacha, E.L. "An Econometric Model for the World Coffee Market: The Impact of Brazilian Price Policy." Unpublished Ph.D. dissertation, Yale University, 1968.

35. Epps, Mary Lee S. "A Computer Simulation Model of the World Coffee Economy." Unpublished Ph.D. dissertation, Duke University, 1970.

36. Wickens, M., Greenfield, J., and Marshall, G. *A World Coffee Model.* CCP: 71/W.P.4, Food and Agricultural Organization of the United Nations, Rome, 1971.

COPPER

37. Ballmer, R.W. "Copper Market Fluctuations: An Industrial Dynamics Study." Unpublished M.S. thesis, Massachusetts Institute of Technology, 1960.

38. Behrman, Jere R. "Forecasting Properties and Prototype Simulation of a Model of the Copper Market." Special Report, Wharton Economic Forecasting Associates, Philadelphia, 1972.

39. Ertek, Tumay. "World Demand for Copper, 1948–63: An Econometric Study." Unpublished Ph.D. dissertation, University of Wisconsin, 1967.

40. Fisher, F.M., Cootner, P.H., and Baily, M. "An Econometric Model of the World Copper Industry." *Bell Journal of Economics and Management Science* 3 (Autumn 1972): 568–609.

41. Khanna, I. "Forecasting the Price of Copper." *Business Economist* 4 (Spring 1972).

42. Mahalingsivam, Rasiah. "Market for Canadian Refined Copper: An Econometric Study." Unpublished Ph.D. dissertation, University of Toronto, 1969.

COTTON

43. Hakim, O.A. "The Effects of the U.S. Cotton Policy on the World Market for Extra-Long Staple Cotton." Unpublished Ph.D. dissertation, University of Arizona, 1972.
44. Kolbe, H., and Timm, H. *Die Bestimmungsfaktoren der Preisentwicklung auf dem Weltmarkt für Baumwoole: Eine Okonometrische Modellanalyse.* NR 4, HWWA Institut für Wirtschaftsforschung, Hamburg, July 1971.

DAIRY

45. Kottke, M. "Allocation of Milk Through Space and Time in a Competitively Mixed Dairy Industry" in G. Judge and T. Takayama (eds.), *Studies in Economic Planning Over Time and Space.* Amsterdam: North Holland Pub. Co., 1973.
46. Louwes, S.L., Boot, J.C.G., and S. Wage. "A Quadratic Programming Approach to the Problems of the Optimal Use of Milk in the Netherlands." *Journal of Farm Economics* 45 (1963): 309–17.
47. Rojko, A.S. *The Demand and Price Structure for Dairy Products.* Technical Bulletin No. 1168, United States Department of Agriculture, Washington, D.C., 1957.
48. Wilkinson, J.K. "Analysis of Retail Dairy Feed Markets and Buyer-Seller Procurement Practices in Selected Kentucky Counties." Unpublished Ph.D. dissertation, University of Kentucky, 1973.
49. Wilson, R.R., and Thompson, R.G. "Demand, Supply and Price Relationships for the Dairy Sector—Post W.W. II Period." *Journal of Farm Economics* 49 (May 1967): 360–371.

EGGS

50. Gerra, M.J. *The Demand, Supply and Price Structure for Eggs.* Technical Bulletin 1204, U.S. Department of Agriculture, Washington, D.C., 1959.
51. Hoffman, R.G., "Quarterly Egg Production Estimators." *Southern Journal of Agricultural Economics* (December 1970).
52. Judge, George, G. *A Spatial Equilibrium Model for Eggs,* Competitive Position of the Connecticut Poultry Industry, No. 7, Conn. Agricultural Experiment Station Bulletin No. 318, Storrs, 1956.
53. Roy, Sujit. "Econometric Models for Predicting Short-Run Egg Prices." Mimeographed, Pennsylvania State University, 1971.

ENERGY*

54. Baughman, M.L. "Dynamic Energy System Modeling: Inter-Fuel Competition." Unpublished Ph.D. dissertation, Massachusetts Institute of Technology, 1972.

55. Deam, R.J., et al. "World Energy Model: Description and Results," in *Energy Modeling.* London: IPC Science and Technology Press, Ltd., 1974.

56. Debanne, J.B. "A Pollution and Technology Sensitive Model for Energy Supply-Distribution Studies," in *Energy Modeling,* M.F. Searl, ed. Working Paper EN-1, Resources for the Future, Inc., Washington, D.C., 1973, pp. 374–409.

57. Hoffman, K.C. "The United States Energy System—A Unified Planning Framework." Unpublished Ph.D. dissertation, Polytechnic Institute of Brooklyn, 1972.

58. Hughes, B., M. Mesarovic, and E. Pestel. "Energy Models: Resources, Demand and Supply." Multilevel Regionalized World Modeling Project, Case Western Reserve University, Cleveland, March 1974.

59. Iliffe, C.E. "The Systems Approach in Economic Assessment of Nuclear Power," in *Energy Modeling.* London: IPC Science and Technology Press, Ltd., 1974.

60. Limaye, D.P. *Energy Policy Evaluation.* Lexington, Mass.: Heath Lexington Books, 1974.

61. Reardon, W.A. "An Input/Output Analysis of Energy Use Changes from 1947 to 1958 and 1958 to 1963." BATTELLE, Pacific Northwest Laboratories, 1972.

62. Rolph, E. and Lees, L. "California's Projected Electrical Demand and Supply." Environmental Quality Labs., California Institute of Technology, 1972.

63. Hudson, E.A. and D.W. Jorgenson, "U.S. Energy Policy and Economic Growth, 1974–2000." Disc. Paper No. 372, Harvard Institute of Economic Research, Cambridge, Mass., June 1974.

See also *Gas, Petroleum.*

FATS AND OILS

64. Armore, Sidney J. *The Demand and Price Structure for Food Fats and Oils.* Technical Bulletin No. 1068, Economic Research Service, U.S. Department of Agriculture, Washington, D.C., 1953.

65. Drake, A.E. and West, V.I. *Econometric Analysis of the Edible Fats and Oils Economy.* University of Illinois Agricultural Experiment Station Bulletin No. 695, Urbana, 1963.

*A listing and comparison of a number of energy models appears in Limaye, D.R., Ciliano, R., and Sharko, J.R., *Quantitative Energy Studies and Models,* Council on Environmental Quality, Executive Office of the President, Washington, 1973.

66. Labys, W.C. "An Econometric Model of Demand and Substitution Patterns in the U.S. Oils and Fats Market." Mimeographed, Graduate Institute of International Studies, Geneva, 1974.

67. Thiam, T.B. "The Palm Oil Industry of Malaysia." Unpublished Ph.D. dissertation, North Carolina State University, Raleigh, 1973.

See also *Lauric Oils; Soybeans*

FEEDGRAINS

68. Ahalt, J., and Egbert, A.C. "The Demand for Feed Concentrates: A Statistical Analysis." *Agricultural Economic Research* 17 (April 1965).

69. Berreyro, H. "An Analysis of the Supply of Grains in the Pergamino Region of Argentina: A Dynamic Approach." Unpublished Ph.D. dissertation, Texas A & M University, 1971.

70. Bjarnason, H.F. "An Economic Analysis of 1980 International Trade in Feed Grains." Unpublished Ph.D. dissertation, University of Wisconsin, 1967.

71. Chung, C.H. "Interregional and International Economic Analysis of the World Feed Grain Economy in 1980 with Emphasis of the U.S.N.C. Region." Unpublished Ph.D. dissertation, University of Wisconsin, 1972.

72. Foote, R.J., Klein, J.W. and Clough, M. *The Demand and Price Structure for Corn and Total Feed Concentrates.* Technical Bulletin 1061, Economic Research Service, United States Department of Agriculture, Washington, D.C., 1952.

73. Guedry, L.J. "An Application of a Multi Commodity Transportation Model to the U.S. Food Grain Economy" in G. Judge and T. Takayama (eds.), *Studies in Economic Planning Over Time and Space.* Amsterdam: North Holland Pub. Co., 1973.

74. King, G.A. *The Demand and Price Structure for By-Product Feeds.* Technical Bulletin 1183, U.S. Department of Agriculture, Washington, D.C., 1958.

75. Kite, R.C. "An Interregional Analysis of Livestock Use of Selected Food Ingredients." Unpublished Ph.D. dissertation, Purdue University, 1973.

76. Leath, M.N., and Blakley, L.V. *An Interregional Analysis of the U.S. Grain Marketing Industry, 1966–67."* Technical Bulletin No. 1444, Economic Research Service, United States Department of Agriculture, Washington, 1971.

77. Meinken, K.W. *The Demand and Price Structure of Oats, Barley and Soybean Grain.* Technical Bulletin No. 1080, United States Department of Agriculture, Washington, D.C., 1953.

78. Mielke, K.D. "The Demand for Animal Feed: An Econometric Analysis." Unpublished Ph.D. dissertation, University of Minnesota, 1973.

79. Moon, P.Y. "An Analysis of Foodgrain Markets in Korea." Unpublished Ph.D. dissertation, Oregon State University, 1973.

80. Roy, S.K. and Ireland, M.E., *An Analysis of the Structural Relations in the Grain Sorghum Market.* College of Agricultural Sciences Publication No. T–1–122, Department of Agricultural Economics at Texas Tech University, May 1974.

FERTILIZER

81. Bell, D.M., Henderson, D.R., and Perkins, G.R. *A Simulation Model of the Fertilizer Industry in the United States: with Special Emphasis on Fertilizer Distribution in Michigan.* Agricultural Economics Report No. 189, Department of Agricultural Economics at Michigan State University and Marketing Economics Division, Economic Research Service, U.S. Department of Agriculture, Washington, D.C., 1972.

FISH (MARINE RESOURCES)

82. Bell, F.W. et al. "The Future of the World's Fishery Resources: Forecasts of Demand, Supply and Prices to the Year 2000 with a Discussion of Implications for Public Policy." Mimeographed. National Marine Fisheries Service, Economic Research Laboratory, Washington, 1970.
83. Broderick, D.G. "An Industry Study: The Tuna Fishery." Unpublished Ph.D. dissertation, Columbia University, 1973.
84. Farrell, Joseph E., and Lampe, Harlan C. *The New England Fishing Industry: Functional Markets for Tinned Food Fish, I and II.* Agricultural Experiment Station Bulletins Nos. 379 and 380, University of Rhode Island, Kingston, 1965.
85. Ladipo, O.O. "General Systems Analysis and Simulation Approach: A Preliminary Application to Nigerian Fisheries." Unpublished Ph.D. dissertation, Michigan State University, 1973.
86. Segura, E.L. *An Econometric Study of the Fish Meal Industry.* FAO Fisheries Technical Paper No. 119, FIEF/T119(En), Food and Agriculture Organization of the United Nations, Rome, August 1973.

GAS (NATURAL)

87. Erikson, E.W., and Spann, R.M. "Supply Response in a Regulated Industry—the Case of Natural Gas." *Bell Journal of Economics and Management Science,* (Spring 1971).
88. Federal Power Commission. "Natural Gas Supply and Demand: 1971 to 1990." Staff Report No. 2, Bureau of Natural Gas, Federal Power Commission, Washington, D.C., 1972.
89. Khazzoom, Daniel J. "The FPC Staff's Econometric Model of Natural Gas Supply in the United States." *Bell Journal of Economics and Management Science* 2 (Spring 1971): 51–93.
90. MacAvoy, P.W. and R.S. Pindyck. "Alternative Regulatory Policies for

Dealing with the Natural Gas Shortage." *Bell Journal of Economics and Management Science* 3 (1972): 454–98.

91. Waverman, L. "National Policy and Natural Gas: The Costs of a Border." *Canadian Journal of Economics* 5 (1972): 331–48.

GOLD

92. Michalopoulos, C.S., and Van Tassel, R.C. "The Commercial Demand for Gold." *Western Economic Journal* (1971).

HIDES

93. Cohen, Kalmen. *A Computer Model of the Shoe, Leather and Hide Sequence.* Englewood Cliffs, N.J.: Prentice-Hall, 1960.

94. Singh, B. "An Econometric Study of Raw Materials in International Trade— A Case Study of Hides and Skins." Unpublished Ph.D. dissertation, University of Pennsylvania, 1971.

HOGS

95. Elliott, D.P. "Effects of the Enlarged EEC on the Danish Pigmeat Export Industries." Unpublished Ph.D. dissertation, University of Hawaii, 1973.

96. Haas, J.T. "An Economic Analysis of the Effects of Optimizing Hog Shipment Patterns and Market Structure on the Efficiency of a Country Hog Marketing System." Unpublished Ph.D. dissertation, University of Maryland, 1972.

97. Harlow, Arthur A. *Factors Affecting the Price and Supply of Hogs.* Technical Bulletin No. 1068, Economic Research Service, U.S. Department of Agriculture, Washington, D.C., 1962.

98. Harlow, Arthur A. "A Recursive Model of the Hog Industry." *Agricultural Economic Research* 14 (1962).

99. Leuthold, Raymond M. "An Analysis of Daily Fluctuations in the Hog Economy." *American Journal of Agricultural Economics* 5 (November 1969): 849–65.

100. Meadows, D.L. *Dynamics of Commodity Production Cycles.* Cambridge, Mass., Wright-Allen Press, 1970.

101. Naill, R.F. and D. Mass. "Dynamic Modeling as a Tool for Managerial Planning: A Case Study of the U.S. Hog Industry." Mimeographed, Thayer School of Engineering, Dartmouth College, Hanover, 1973.

102. Strom, J.L. "Simulation of a Swine Breeding Herd." Unpublished Ph.D. dissertation, Purdue University, 1973.

103. Zellner, Jr., R.E. "A Simultaneous Equation Analysis of Selected Terminal Hog Markets." Unpublished Ph.D. dissertation, University of Mississippi, 1971.

See also *Livestock; Meat.*

IRON ORE

104. Margueron, C. "A Quantitative Analysis of the Supply-Demand Patterns in Iron Ore: The Future Possibilities of Brazil." Unpublished Ph.D. dissertation, Columbia University, 1972.

JUTE

105. Khan, A.S. "An Economic Analysis of 1980 International Trade in Jute with Special Reference to Pakistan." Unpublished Ph.D. dissertation, University of Wisconsin, 1972.

LAURIC OILS (see *Coconuts*)

LIVESTOCK

106. Crom, R.J., and Maki, W.R. "A Dynamic Model of a Simulated Livestock-Meat Economy." *Agricultural Economic Research* 17 (1965).
107. Egbert, A.C., and Reutlinger, S. "A Dynamic Model of the Livestock-Feed Sector." *Journal of Farm Economics* 47 (December 1965): 1288–1305.
108. Filippello, N.A. "A Dynamic Econometric Investigation of the Japanese Livestock Economy." Unpublished Ph.D. dissertation, University of Missouri, Columbia, December 1967.
109. Foote, R.J. "A Four-Equation Model of the Feed Livestock Economy and its Endogenous Mechanism." *Journal of Farm Economics* 35 (1953): 44–61.
110. Fox, Karl A. "A Spatial Equilibrium Model of the Livestock-Feed Economy in the United States." *Econometrica* 21 (1953): 547–66.
111. Hayenga, M.L., and Hacklander, D. "Monthly Supply-Demand Relationships for Fed Cattle and Hogs." *American Journal of Agricultural Economics* 52 (August 1970): 535–44.
112. Hildreth, C., and Jarrett, F.J. *A Statistical Study of Livestock Production and Marketing.* New York: John Wiley and Sons, 1955.
113. Judge, G.G., Havlicek, J., and R.L. Rizek. "A Spatial Analysis of the U.S. Livestock Economy," in G. Judge and T. Takayama (eds.), *Studies in Economic Planning Over Time and Space.* Amsterdam: North Holland Pub. Co., 1973.
114. Kost, W.E. "Trade Flows in the Grain Livestock Economy of the EEC." Unpublished Ph.D. dissertation, Michigan State University, 1971.
115. Nores, Gustavo, A. "Structure of the Argentine Beef Cattle Economy: A Short Run Model, 1960–1970." Unpublished Ph.D. dissertation, Purdue University, 1972.
116. Maki, W.R. "Forecasting Livestock Prices and Supply with an Econometric Model." *Journal of Farm Economics* 45 (1963): 1670–74.
117. Meadows, D.L. *Dynamics of Commodity Production Cycles.* Cambridge, Mass.: Wright-Allen Press, 1970.

118. Myers, L.H. and J. Havlicek, Jr. "Monthly Price Structure of the U.S. Livestock Meat Sector." Mimeographed. Purdue University, Lafayette, 1973.
119. Rahn, A.P. "A Quarterly Simulation Model of the Livestock and Poultry Subsectors of Use in Outlook and Price Analysis." Unpublished Ph.D. dissertation, Iowa State University, 1973.
120. Sasaki, K. "Spatial Equilibrium Analysis of Livestock Products in Eastern Japan," in G. Judge and T. Takayama (eds.), *Studies in Economic Planning Over Time and Space*. Amsterdam: North Holland Pub. Co., 1973.
See also *Beef; Feedgrains; Hogs; Meat.*

LUMBER

121. Adams, F. Gerard, and Blackwell, J. "An Econometric Model of the U.S. Forest Products Industry." Discussion Paper No. 207, Department of Economics, University of Pennsylvania, Philadelphia, 1971.
122. Gregory, R.B. "Estimating Wood Consumption with Particular Reference to the Effects of Increased Wood Availability." *Forest Science* 12 (March 1966).
123. McKillop, W.L.M. "Supply and Demand for Forest Products—An Econometric Study." *Hilgardia* 38 (March 1967): 1–132.
124. Robinson, V.L. "An Econometric Analysis of the Softwood Lumber Market, 1947–67." Unpublished Ph.D. dissertation, University of Georgia, 1972.
125. Row, C. "Probabilities of Financial Returns from Southern Pine Timber Growing." Unpublished Ph.D. dissertation, Tulane University, 1973.
126. Thevenon, M.J. "An Economic Analysis of Pulp, Paper, and Board Exports from the Pacific N.W." Unpublished Ph.D. dissertation, Oregon State University, 1972.

MACHINERY

127. Beck, F.V. "An Econometric Model of International Trade in Machinery and Equipment." Unpublished Ph.D. dissertation, University of Maryland, 1969.

MANGANESE

128. Shaw, J. "An Econometric Model of the Manganese Ore Industry." U.N. Conference on Trade and Development, TD/B/483/Add.1, Geneva, April 1974.

MEAT

129. Bergstrom, A.R. "An Econometric Study of Supply and Demand for New Zealand Exports." *Econometrica* 12 (1955): 258–76.

130. Chetwin, J.A. "A Model of the United Kingdom Wholesale Meat Market." Mimeographed, Lincoln College, New Zealand, 1965.
131. Crom, R. *A Dynamic Price-Output Model of the Beef and Pork Sectors.* Technical Bulletin No. 1526, Economic Research Service, U.S. Department of Agriculture, Washington, D.C., 1970.
132. Duewer, L.A., and Maki, W.R. "A Study of the Meat Products Industry through Systems Analysis and Simulation of Decision Units." *Agricultural Economics Research* 18 (1966): 79–83.
133. Elam, T.E. "A Model of the Monthly Structure of the U.S. Beef-Pork Economy." Unpublished Ph.D. dissertation, University of Tennessee, 1973.
134. Faure, H. "Etude Econométrique de la Demande de Viande." *Annal du Credoc* (1967): 3–26.
135. Fuller, W.A., and Ladd, G.W. "A Dynamic Quarterly Model of the Beef and Pork Economy." *Journal of Farm Economics* 43 (1961): 797–812.
136. Graham, J.D. "A Multiperiod Cash Management Analysis of Problems Facing a Commercial Meat Packing Firm." Unpublished Ph.D. dissertation, Purdue University, 1973.
137. Haimerl, J. *A Blockrecursive Structural Model of the Cattle, Beef and Veal Market in West Germany.* Sonderhelt 41, Agrarwirtschaft, A.S. Verlag, Hannover, 1970.
138. Kettunen, L. "Demand and Supply of Pork and Beef in Finland." Publication No. 11, Agricultural Economics Research Institute, Helsinki, 1968.
139. Myers, L.H., Havlicek, J., and Henderson, P.L. *Short Term Price Structure of the Hog-Pork Sector of the U.S.* Purdue University Agricultural Experiment Station Bulletin No. 855, Lafayette, Indiana, 1970.
140. Saleh, H. "An Econometric Analysis of the Demand for Animal Protein in Iran." Unpublished Ph.D. dissertation, Cornell University, 1973.
141. Trierweiler, J.E. and J.B. Hassler. *Orderly Production and Marketing in the Beef-Pork Sector.* Research Bulletin 240, University of Nebraska Agricultural Experiment Station, Lincoln, November 1970.
142. Wallace, T.D., and Judge, G.G. *Econometric Analysis of the Beef and Pork Sectors of the Economy.* Oklahoma State University Technical Bulletin T.75, Stillwater, Oklahoma, 1959.
143. Yandle, Christopher A. "A Model of the New Zealand Domestic Market for Meat." Technical Paper No. 7, Agricultural Economics Research Unit, Lincoln College, Canterbury, New Zealand, 1969.
See also *Beef; Hogs; Livestock.*

MULTICOMMODITY

144. Alm, H., and Duloy, J., and Gulbrandsen, O. "Agricultural Prices and the World Food Economy." Institute for Economics and Statistics, University of Uppsala, March 1969.
145. Blakeslee, L.L., Heady, E.O., and C.F. Framingham. *World Food Production, Demand, and Trade.* Ames: Iowa State University Press, 1973.

146. Egbert, Alvin C. "An Aggregate Model of Agriculture, Empirical Estimates and Some Policy Implications." *American Journal of Agricultural Economics* 51 (February 1969): 71–86.

147. Evans, M.K. "An Agricultural Submodel for the U.S. Economy," in *Essays in Industrial Economics—Vol. II.* L.R. Klein, Ed. Philadelphia: Wharton School of Finance and Commerce, 1969.

148. Haidacher, R.C., et al. "A Planning-Decision Model for Surplus Commodity Removal Programs." *Agricultural Economics Research* 26 (January 1974) No.1.

149. McFarquhar, A.M., Mitter, S., and Evans, G. "A Computable Model for Projecting U.K. Food and Agriculture," in A.M. McFarquhar, *Europe's Food and Agriculture.* A Comparison of Models for Projecting Food Consumption and Agricultural Production in Western European Countries to 1972 and 1975, Amsterdam: North-Holland Publishing Co., 1971.

150. Roy, D.E. "An Econometric Simulation Model of U.S. Agriculture with Commodity Submodels." Unpublished Ph.D. dissertation, Iowa State University, 1972.

151. Wang, Kung Lee, and Kokat, R.G. *An Inter-Industry Structure of the U.S. Mining Industries.* Information Circular 8338 Bureau of Mines, U.S. Department of the Interior, Washington, D.C., 1967.

NEWSPRINT

152. Gillion, C. *Newspapers and the Demand for Newsprint.* Research Paper No. 2, Economic Contract Unit, New Zealand Institute of Economic Research, Wellington, 1969.

NICKEL

153. Adams, F.G. "The Impact of Nickel Production from the Ocean Floor: An Econometric Appraisal." Prepared by the Economics Research Unit, University of Pennsylvania for the United Nations Conference on Trade and Development, Geneva, March 1974.

OLIVE OIL

154. Al-Zand, Osama A. "Olive Oil Trade and Trade Policies in the Mediterranean Region." Unpublished Ph.D. dissertation, University of Minnesota, St. Paul, 1968.

ONIONS

155. Suits, Daniel B., and Koizuni, S. "The Dynamics of the Onion Market." *Journal of Farm Economics* 38 (1956): 475–84.

ORANGES (FROZEN CONCENTRATED ORANGE JUICE)

156. Dean, G.W., and Collins, N.R. *World Trade in Fresh Oranges: An Analysis of the Effect of EEC Tariff Policies.* Giannini Foundation Monograph No. 18, California Agricultural Experiment Station, Berkeley, January 1967.
157. Matthews, J.L., Womack, A.W. and Huang, B.W., "The U.S. Orange Economy: Demand and Supply Prospects 1973/74 to 1984/85." *Fruit Situation* 190 (February 1974): 39–52.
158. Powe, E.E. "A Model for Evaluating Alternative Policy Decisions for the Florida Orange Subsector of the Food Industry." *American Economist* 16 (Fall 1973).
159. Raulerson, Richard C., and Langham, M.R. "Evaluating Supply Control Policies for Frozen Concentrated Orange Juice with an Industrial Dynamics Model." *American Journal of Agricultural Economics* 52 (1970): 197–208.
160. Rausser, Gordon C. "A Dynamic Model of the California-Arizona Orange Industry." Unpublished Ph.D. dissertation, University of California, Davis, 1971.
161. Zusman, P., Melamed, A. and I. Katzir. "A Spatial Analysis of the EEC Trade Policies in the Market for Winter Oranges." in G. Judge and T. Takayama (eds.), *Studies in Economic Planning Over Time and Space.* Amsterdam: North Holland Pub. Co., 1973.

PEANUTS

162. Jellema, B.M. "Analysis of the World Market for Groundnuts and Groundnut Products." Unpublished Ph.D. dissertation, North Carolina State University, Raleigh 1972.
163. Mehta, V. "India's Position in the World Peanut and Peanut Oil Markets." Unpublished Ph.D. dissertation, North Carolina State University, Raleigh, 1972.
164. Song, Inbum. "Demand Characteristics for Peanuts and the Impact of a Direct Price Support Program on Farm Income, Government Cost and Peanut Consumption." Unpublished Ph.D. dissertation, Oklahoma State University, 1970.

PETROLEUM

165. Adams, F.G., and Griffin, James M. "An Econometric-Linear Programing Model of the U.S. Petroleum Industry." *Journal of the American Statistical Association* 67 (Sept. 1972): 542–51.
166. Hughes, B., M. Mesarovic, and E. Pestel. "World Oil: Model Description and Scenario Assessment." Multilevel Regionalized World Modeling Project, Case Western Reserve University, Cleveland, April 1974.
167. Mitchell, A. "The Demand for Texas Refined Petroleum Products: A Study

in Econometrics." Unpublished Ph.D. dissertation, University of
Texas, Austin, 1972.

PHARMACEUTICALS

168. Tsurumi, H., and Tsurumi, Y. "An Oligopolistic Model of a Japanese
Pharmaceutical Company." Discussion Paper No. 22, Institute for
Economic Research, Queens Universitv. Kingston, Ontario, 1970.

PHOSPHATE

169. Hee, O. *A Statistical Analysis of the U.S. Demand for Phosphate Rock,
Potash, and Nitrogen.* Information Circular 8418, Bureau of Mines,
U.S. Department of the Interior, Washington, D.C., 1969.

PORK BELLIES

170. Foote, R.J., Craven, A., and Williams, J. "Pork Bellies: Quarterly 3-Equation
Models Designed to Predict Cash Prices." Mimeographed. Texas
Tech. University, 1971.

POTATOES

171. Armbruster, W.V. Garoian, J.L., and Yonde, J.G. *Simulation of Farm Bargaining Policies in the Western Late Potato System.* Oregon State
Agricultural Experiment Station, Technical Bulletin No. 119,
Corvallis, 1972.
172. Hee, O. *Demand and Price Analysis for Potatoes.* Technical Bulletin No.
1380, Economic Research Service, U.S. Department of Agriculture,
Washington, D.C., 1967.
173. Kristianslund, I. "Analysis of Intraseasonal Potato Price Movements."
Unpublished Ph.D. dissertation, Michigan State University, 1972.
174. Zusman, P. "Econometric Analysis of the Market for California Early
Potatoes." *Hilgardia* 33 (December 1962): 539–668.

RICE

175. Boonma, C. "Modeling Rice and Corn Markets in Thailand." Unpublished
Ph.D. dissertation, University of Illinois at Urbana-Champaign, 1972.
176. Holder, Jr., S., Shaw, D.L., and Snyder, J.C. *A Systems Model of the U.S.
Rice Industry.* Technical Bulletin No. 1453, Economic Research
Service, U.S. Department of Agriculture, Washington, D.C., 1970.
177. Nasol, R.L. "Demand Analysis for Rice in the Philippines." *Journal of
Agricultural Economics and Development* 2 (1971): 1–13.
178. Pandey, V.K., and T. Takayama. "Temporal Equilibrium of Rice and Wheat
in India." in G. Judge and T. Takayama (eds.), *Studies in Economic*

Planning Over Time and Space. Amsterdam: North Holland Pub.
Co., 1973.

RUBBER

179. Behrman, J.R. "Econometric Model Simulations of the World Rubber
Market." in *Essays in Industrial Economics*—Vol. III, L.R. Klein, Ed.
Philadelphia: Wharton School of Finance and Commerce, 1971.
180. Cheong, T. "An Econometric Model of the Malayan Rubber Industry."
Unpublished Ph.D. dissertation, London School of Economics and
Political Science, 1972.
181. Horowitz, I. "An Econometric Analysis of Supply and Demand in the
Synthetic Rubber Industry." *International Economic Review* 4
(September 1963).
182. Kolbe, H., and Timm, H. *Die Bestimmungsfaktoren der Preisentwicklung
auf dem Weltmarkt für Naturkautschuk: Eine Okonometrische
Modellanalyse.* NR 10, HWWA-Institut für Wirtschaftsforschung,
Hamburg, June 1972.
183. Noor, M.H. "The Malaysian Smallholder Rubber Sector: Implications of
Ethrel Stimulation and the New Processing Technology." Unpub-
lished Ph.D. dissertation, Michigan State University, 1972.
184. Teken, I.B. "Supply of and Demand for Indonesian Rubber." Unpublished
Ph.D. dissertation, Purdue University, 1971.

SHRIMP

185. Doll, J.P. "An Econometric Analysis of Shrimp Ex-Vessel Prices, 1950–
1968." *American Journal of Agricultural Economics* 54 (August
1972): 431–40.
186. Gillespie, E.C., Hite, J.S., and Lytle, J.S. *An Econometric Analysis of the
U.S. Shrimp Industry.* South Carolina Agriculture Experiment
Station Bulletin No. 2, Clemson, 1969.
187. Hooker, P.J. "Systems Analysis of U.S. Management Strategies in the Gulf
of Mexico Shrimp Industry." Unpublished Ph.D. dissertation,
University of Florida, 1972.
188. Timmer, C.P. "A Projection Model of the U.S. Shrimp Market." *Stanford
Food Research Institute Studies* 8 (1968): 243–56.

SILVER

189. Burrows, J.C., Hughes, W., and Vallette, J. *An Econometric Analysis of the
Silver Industry.* Charles Rivers Associates, Cambridge, Mass., 1972.

SOYBEANS (OIL, MEAL)

190. Free, Joe W. *The Future of the South in the Soybean Processing Industry,
1970–1975.* Bulletin No. 168, Southern Cooperative Series, Tennessee
Valley Authority, November 1971

191. Houck, J.P., and Mann, J.S. *An Analysis of Domestic and Foreign Demand for U.S. Soybeans and Soybean Proucts.* Technical Bulletin No. 265, University of Minnesota Agricultural Experiment Station, 1968.

192. Houck, J.P., Ryan, M.E., and Subotnik, A. *Soybeans and Their Products: Markets, Models and Policy.* Minneapolis: University of Minnesota Press, 1972.

193. Leunis, J.V. and R.J. Vandenborre. "An Interregional Analysis of the U.S. Soybean Industry," in G. Judge and T. Takayama (eds.), *Studies in Economic Planning Over Time and Space.* Amsterdam: North Holland Pub. Co., 1973.

194. Matthews, J.L., Womack, A.W., and Hoffman, R.G. "Formulation of Market Forecasts for the U.S. Soybean Economy with an Econometric Model." *Fats and Oils Situation* 260 (Nov. 1971): 26–31.

195. Vandenborre, R.J. *Economic Analysis of Relationships in the International Vegetable Oil and Meal Sector.* Agricultural Economics Experiment Station Bulletin No. 106, University of Illinois. Urbana-Champaign, 1970.

STEEL

196. Beeck, J.G. "An Econometric Model of Steel Prices in the EEC." Mimeographed. Central Planning Bureau, The Hague, 1972.

197. Friden, L. "Instability of World Trade in Steel: A Study of Price and Quantity Fluctuations, 1953–1968." Mimeographed. Institute for International Economic Studies, Stockholm, Sweden, 1969.

198. Higgins, C.I. "An Econometric Description of the U.S. Steel Industry," in *Essays in Industrial Economics– Vol. II,* L.R. Klein, Ed. Philadelphia: Wharton School of Finance and Commerce, 1969.

199. Labys, W.C. "Simulation of a Basing Point System." Unpublished M.B.A. thesis, Graduate School of Business, Duquesne University, 1962.

200. Mo, W.Y., and K.L. Wang. A Quantitative Economic Analysis and Long-Run Projections of the Demand for Steel Mill Products. Information Circular 8451, Bureau of Mines, U.S. Department of the Interior, Washington, D.C., 1970.

201. Nelson, J.P. "An Interregional Recursive Programming Model of the U.S. Iron and Steel Industry: 1947–67." Unpublished Ph.D. dissertation, University of Wisconsin, 1970.

202. Tsao, C.S. and R.H. Day. "A Process Analysis Model of the U.S. Steel Industry." *Management Science* 17 (1971): 588–608.

203. Watanabe, T., and Konishita, S. "An Econometric Study of the Japanese Steel Industry." Discussion Paper No. 155, Harvard Institute of Economic Research, Cambridge, 1970.

SUGAR

204. Bates, H., and Schmitz, A. *A Spatial Equilibrium Analysis of the World Sugar Economy.* Giannini Foundation Monograph No. 23, California Agricultural Experiment Station, Berkeley, May 1969.

205. Flores, A.S. "Spatial Equilibrium Analysis of the U.S. Sugar Industry Under Alternative Policy Measures." Unpublished Ph.D. dissertation, University of Hawaii, 1972.

206. Niles, J.A. "Analysis of Systems of Coordinating Agricultural Production and Processing Operations with Special Reference to Beet Sugar Scheduling." Unpublished Ph.D. dissertation, University of California at Davis, 1972.

207. Tewes, T. "Sugar: A Short-Term Forecasting Model for the World Market, with a Forecast of the World Market Price for Sugar in 1972–1973." *The Business Economist* 4 (Summer 1972): 89–97.

208. Wymer, C.R. "Estimation of Continuous Time Models with an Application to the World Sugar Market." Mimeographed. London School of Economics and Political Science, 1973.

SULFUR

209. Hee, O. "Industrial Demand for Sulfur and Alternative Inputs." Mimeographed. Bureau of Mines, U.S. Department of the Interior, Washington, D.C., February 1972.

TEA

210. Murti, V.N. "An Econometric Study of the World Tea Economy 1948–1961." Unpublished Ph.D. dissertation, University of Pennsylvania, 1961.

211. UNCTAD. "The Effect of Supply Change on Short-Term Movements in Tea Prices." UNCTAD/CD/Misc.47, Geneva, 1972.

TEXTILES

212. den Hartog, H., and Fraenkel, M. "An Econometric Model of the Textile and Clothing Industries in the Netherlands." Mimeographed. Central Planning Bureau, The Hague, 1972.

213. Miller, R.L. *A Short Term Econometric Model of Textile Industries.* Discussion Paper No. 188, Institute for Economic Research, University of Washington, Seattle, 1971.

214. Naylor, T.H., Wallace, W.H., and Sasser, W.E. "A Computer Simulation Model of the Textile Industry." *Journal of the American Statistical Association* 62 (1967): 1338–64.

215. Tierney, D.F. "The Interaction of the Apparel and Textile Industries with the National Economy: An Econometric Analysis." Unpublished Ph.D. dissertation, Temple University, 1972.

See also *Cotton; Wool.*

TIN

216. Desai, M. "An Econometric Model of the World Tin Economy, 1948–1961." *Econometrica* 34 (Jan. 1966): 105–34.

TOBACCO

217. Mann, J.S., "A Dynamic Model of the U.S. Tobacco Economy," *Agricultural Economics Research,* Vol. 25, No. 3 (July 1973): 81–92.
218. Vernon, J., Rives, N., and Naylor, T.H. "An Econometric Model of the Tobacco Industry." *Review of Economics and Statistics* 51 (May 1969): 149–57.

TOMATOES

219. Lee, W.B. "The Competitive Nonlinear Spatial Equilibrium Analysis: An Empirical Study of the U.S. Tomato Industry." Mimeographed. Bloomsburg State College, Bloomsburg, Pa. 1973.

TUNG OIL

220. Matthews, J.L., and Womack, A.W. "An Economic Appraisal of the U.S. Tung Oil Economy." *Southern Journal of Agricultural Economics* (December 1970): 161–68.

TUNGSTEN

221. Burrows, J.C. *Tungsten: An Industry Analysis.* Lexington, Mass.: Heath Lexington Books, 1971.

TURKEYS

222. Bawden, D. Lee., Carter, H.O., and Dean, G.W. "Interregional Competition in the United States Turkey Industry." *Hilgardia* 37 (June 1966): 1–95.

VEGETABLES

223. Shuffett, M.D. *The Demand and Price Structure for Selected Vegetables.* Technical Bulletin No. 1105, United States Department of Agriculture, Washington, D.C., 1954.
224. Tramel, T. and Seale, Jr., A.D. "Reactive Programming of Supply and Demand Relations—Application to Fresh Vegetables." *Journal of Farm Economics* 41 (December 1959): 1012–22.

WATERMELON

225. Suits, D. "An Econometric Analysis of the Watermelon Market." *Journal of Farm Economics* 37 (1955): 237–51.

WHEAT

226. Ahn, C.Y., and I. Singh. "The Future of Agriculture in South Brazil: Some Policy Projections with a Dynamic Model of the Wheat Region, Rio Grande De Sol (1972–85)." Mimeographed. Department of Agricultural Economics and Rural Sociology, Ohio State University, Columbus, 1973.

227. Barr, T.N., "Demand and Price Relationships for the U.S. Wheat Economy." *Wheat Situation* 226 (November 1973): 15–25.

228. Hoffman, R.G., "Wheat-Regional Supply Analysis." *Wheat Situation* 225 (August 1973): 15–24.

229. Hoyt, R.C. "A Dynamic Econometric Model of the Milling and Banking Industries." Unpublished Ph.D. dissertation, University of Minnesota, 1972.

230. Meinken, R.W. *The Demand and Price Structure for Wheat.* Technical Bulletin No. 1136, U.S. Department of Agriculture, Washington, D.C., 1955.

231. Mo, Y. *An Econometric Analysis of the Dynamics of the United States Wheat Sector.* Technical Bulletin No. 1395, U.S. Department of Agriculture, Washington, D.C., 1968.

232. Chai, J.C. "An Econometric Analysis of the Demand and Price Structure of Wheat for Food by Classes in the U.S." Unpublished Ph.D. dissertation, University of Minnesota, 1967.

233. Schmitz, A. "An Economic Analysis of the World Wheat Economy in 1980." Unpublished Ph.D. Thesis, University of Wisconsin, 1968.

234. Vannerson, F.L. "An Econometric Analysis of the Postwar U.S. Wheat Market." Unpublished Ph.D. Thesis, University of Wisconsin, 1963.

WINE

235. Biondollilo, A.L. "Social Cost of Production Instability in the Grape Wine Industry: Argentina." Unpublished Ph.D. dissertation, University of Minnesota, 1972.

236. Labys, W.C. "Preliminary Results of an Econometric Model of the International Wine Market." Mimeographed. Graduate Institute of International Studies, Geneva, 1973.

WOOL

237. Duane, P. *Analysis of Wool Price Fluctuations: An Economic Analysis of Price Formation in a Raw Materials Market.* Wool Economic Research Report No. 23, Australian Government Publishing Service, Canberra, 1973.

238. Durbin, S.I. "A Sample Wool Marketing Simulation Model." Unpublished M.Sc. thesis, Massey University, New Zealand, 1969.

239. Emmery, M. *The Price Elasticity of Demand for Wool in the U.K.* Wool
      Economic Research Report No. 11, Bureau of Agricultural Econom-
      ics, Canberra, Australia, 1967.
240. McKenzie, C.J. "Quarterly Models of Price Formation in the Raw Wool
      Market." Unpublished M.Sc., thesis, Lincoln College, Canterbury,
      New Zealand, 1966.
241. Witherell, William H. *Dynamics of the International Wool Market: An
      Econometric Analysis.* Research Memorandum No. 91, Princeton
      University, Econometric Research Program, 1967.

Index

About the Editor

Walter C. Labys is Visiting Professor at the Graduate Institute of International Studies in Geneva where he teaches econometrics, quantitative methods, and micro-economic theory. His modeling interests include the construction of national and international commodity models and their application in market forecasting, policy evaluation, stabilization, and economic development. Other interests include the analysis of commodity resource problems and the role played by speculation and hedging in commodity price formation. The commodities studied include the oils and fats group, wines, cocoa, steel, and copper.

Practical extensions of his work have taken a variety of directions. Serving as a consultant to UNCTAD, he has built a model of the international lauric oils market and has applied the model to the analysis of policy problems in this area. Efforts in investigating commodity problems in developing countries have involved participation with the Southeast Asia Development Advisory Group, the Economic Development Institute of the World Bank, and the Development Academy of the Philippines. He is also editor of a series of commodity modeling books forthcoming from the Ballinger Publishing Co. Former research and consulting activities have included forecasting, gaming, growth, and urban economics with firms such as Unilever, New England Life, Westinghouse, and Abt Associates. He was a member of the Department of Economics at the University of Rhode Island during 1971-72 and the University of Nottingham during 1966-68.

Dr. Labys completed his Ph.D. in Economics at the University of Nottingham in 1968. A recipient of several academic awards, he earned a M.A. in Economics from Harvard University, an M.B.A. in Economics and Operations Research from Duquesne University, and a B.S. in Electrical Engineering from

Carnegie-Mellon University. He is the author of *Speculation, Hedging and Commodity Price Forecasts* with Clive Granger (1970) as well as of *Dynamic Commodity Models: Specification, Estimation and Simulation* (1973), both published by Heath Lexington Books. His memberships include the Econometric Society and the American Economic Association.